Ignacio

IGNACIO

The Diary of a Maya Indian of Guatemala

Translated and edited by
JAMES D. SEXTON

upp

University of Pennsylvania Press
Philadelphia

Copyright © 1992 by James D. Sexton

Library of Congress Cataloging-in-Publication Data
Bizarro Ujpán, Ignacio.
    Ignacio : the diary of a Maya Indian of Guatemala / translated and
edited by James D. Sexton.
        p. cm.
    Includes bibliographical references and index.
    ISBN 0-8122-3113-9. — ISBN 0-8122-1361-0 (pbk.)
    1. Bizarro Ujpán, Ignacio.   2. Tzutuhil Indians—Biography.
3. Tzutuhil Indians—Social conditions.   4. Tzutuhil Indians—
Religion and mythology.   5. Guatemala—Social conditions.
I. Sexton, James D.   II. Title.
F1465.2.T9B589   1991
972.81′004974—dc20   91-29765
                                                        CIP

Contents

Acknowledgments

I SHOULD LIKE TO EXPRESS MY APPRECIATION to Ignacio and the people of Guatemala, who have welcomed me as a guest in their country during my visits over the past two decades. Also, I should like to thank my research assistants, Mimi Hugh, Gwenn Gallenstein, Lisa Leap, Rose Marie Havel, and David Ortiz, and my wife, Marilyn, for aid in helping me translate and edit specific sections of this manuscript. Two Guatemalans (whose names I shall not reveal), currently living in northern Arizona, kindly gave special assistance in translating a number of Guatemalan expressions. My appreciation goes to numerous students who have read *Son of Tecún Umán* and *Campesino* and given me invaluable feedback. Throughout this project, the Committee for Organized Research at Northern Arizona University, chaired by Henry Hooper, has generously supplied financial support during the summers, including a field trip to Guatemala in the summer of 1987 and a sabbatical leave to Guatemala in the fall of 1988. I also greatly appreciate a grant from the American Philosophical Society which covered travel and living expenses during my sabbatical research in the fall of 1988, and I should like to thank Robert Harman, Michael Olien, and Frances Berdan for agreeing to serve as referees for this grant. Earl Backman, dean of the College of Social and Behavioral Sciences at NAU, has supported my research proposals and has kindly provided a new office computer when it was needed the most, and I appreciate his support. Gary Buckley has graciously discussed portions of this book with me. My late brother, Mel, and late brother-in-law, J.B. Brooks, gave me more academic inspiration than they will ever know. In peace may they rest. Norman Schwartz, Michael Olien, and Anne Manning carefully read the entire manuscript and made numerous useful suggestions. My first Spanish teacher, Elaine Avila Jamison, encouraged me to pursue the language. Finally, special thanks go to my wife, Marilyn, and my son, Randy, for their ability to cope while I'm doing field research in Guatemala and while I'm at my home or office computer in Flagstaff.

Introduction

As the 1980s closed, the electronic and printed media coverage of Central America focused on guerrillas battling the Salvadoran Army in the streets of San Salvador, the U.S. invasion of Panamá to oust Manuel Noriega, and the defeat of Daniel Ortega by Violeta Barrios de Chamorro in the 1990 presidential election of Nicaragua. While these are noteworthy events, little or no attention has been given to the relatively low-keyed but persistent civil disturbances in Guatemala and the severe economic crisis that had been developing there.[1]

This volume covers the story of a Guatemalan Indian, Ignacio Bizarro Ujpán, and that of his town and country, from 13 May 1983 to 9 August 1987, a period of four years which saw declining civil instability but increased military surveillance. There was a return to civilian governance both locally and nationally, but the Guatemalan army still holds the real power and civil disturbances continue, albeit on a lower level of intensity than during the peak years from 1979 to 1983.

Addressed to anyone interested in Guatemala and Central America, the book is a sequel to Campesino, which covered the period from 5 February 1977 to 13 May 1983, six years of unparalleled violence. Campesino in turn is a sequel to Son of Tecún Umán, which included both an autobiography from Ignacio's birth in 1941 to July 1972 and a diary covering August 1972 to 4 February 1977, a period of five years, ending a year after the 4 February 1976 earthquake and its numerous aftershocks. A summary of the first two volumes can be found in the appendix. Thus, Ignacio completes a trilogy of books, spaced almost equally apart, covering three periods in a person's life and three junctures of dynamic social history in Guatemala. Nothing else in the literature about Central America is comparable.

The new episodes in Ignacio include information not found in the first two volumes or anywhere else, such as cultural information on ancient Tzutuhil Maya customs and beliefs that persist to the present date, the spirit world, naguales (spirit and animal forms of humans, especially of witches), shamanism, dreams and their interpretation, curing, destiny, celebrations, cofradías (religious brotherhoods), proverbs, and local and national conflict. The new episodes also cover the aftermath of the most intense cycle of insurgency and counterinsurgency in Guatemala's history.

Thirty-two years after Columbus landed in the New World, the Spaniards conquered Guatemala along with Mexico and the rest of Central America. They introduced a new culture to the Indians and set in motion cultural conflicts that have persisted until the present. Ignacio's diary chronicles the latest of these conflicts. It has some parallels to an earlier colonial text titled The Annals of the Cakchiquels *(or the* Memorial de Sololá), *the last entry of which is dated 1601 (Recinos and Goetz 1953). The* Memorial, *written by Indians in Sololá (a town close to San José and often mentioned by Ignacio), became in its latter sections a community annal (or diary) describing the Spanish conquest, violence, and hardship. "There is a sad, eerie continuity between the last pages of the* Memorial *and those of Ignacio's diary," notes Schwartz (1984). "Everything has changed for the Indians of Sololá and San José and nothing has changed. One could begin a course on Guatemala with* Memorial *and conclude it with Ignacio's diary."*

Ignacio's life story is the only one available on the Tzutuhil Maya, members of an ethnic group considered by some to be an endangered subculture because of their relatively small numbers. While major themes of poverty and, to a lesser extent, political violence continue in Ignacio, *new dominant themes emerge in the present volume. These include religious beliefs and practices threatened by outside interests such as reformed Catholicism and Protestantism; the impact of a new secondary school that Ignacio plays a key role in establishing; intracultural and intercultural conflict in the form of rivalry between the people of San José and San Martín (both predominantly Tzutuhil Mayas) and in the display of ambivalence, if not hostility, by both toward Ladinos in general; an attempt to return to democratization at both the national and local level after three decades of military presidents and five years of mayors appointed by military governors; problems associated with the civil defense patrols and military control of the countryside; and concern with holding accountable the offenders against human rights.*

Although there is an extensive list of anthropological publications on Central America, especially Guatemala, life histories for this major cultural area are almost totally neglected. Only two other book-length treatments are in print. The first is on the life of Abel Pat, translated and edited by Norman Schwartz (1977) with an insightful cultural analysis. Abel is a Ladino milpero (small-scale farmer) who resides in the lowlands of Petén in the town of San Andrés (a pseudonym). The second is on the life of Rigoberta Menchú, edited by Elisabeth Burgos-Debray (1984). Unlike Ignacio, a middle-aged man with a wife and eight children, Rigoberta is a young, unmarried, exiled Quiché Maya woman, a former revolutionary.

Rigoberta's story is intense and fascinating, but Ignacio's is the more culturally comprehensive of the two highland life histories. As Schwartz (1984)

comments, "One has to go to the Mexicanists studies to find anything comparable—the works of Oscar Lewis [1959, 1961, 1964]." In addition, Ignacio's account is
the more balanced. As Preuss (1986) notes, Ignacio's perspective is unmarred by the
infiltration of leftist or rightist views.

Viewing Central America from the eyes of a peasant who lives there (an
insider's perspective) helps us better understand the complex problems of the region
in terms other than just a simplistic, East/West dichotomy. Ignacio's words
enlighten us as to the nature of social, personal, economic, medical, and religious
matters as well as political issues relating to the great masses of Latin America's
poor. His unique perspective from the bottom up as a person occupying a position in
two worlds—indigenous and Ladino—makes him uniquely qualified to describe
life in rural Guatemala.

The main strength of this approach is that it provides a personal, first person
portrayal of life, customs, and events in a different setting from our own. "It is this
humanistic quality, this individualized touch with reality that makes life histories
such a powerful medium, a medium where the words of one person often are more
persuasive and forceful than unlimited, often faceless, statistical data" (Logan
1987:155).

When I began this project in 1972 during my third season in Guatemala, I
asked Ignacio, who had been a research assistant on a large project studying
modernization and development in fourteen towns, to keep a diary about what
was happening in his life, including his work, his social and religious activities, his
family, and even his dreams. My intent was to accomplish a diachronic, holistic
description of contemporary Tzutuhil Maya life in a relatively undeveloped town
from the eyes of a person who was living it. From the start the episodes that resulted
were varied and rich in ethnographic detail and included noteworthy events in
other towns surrounding Lake Atitlán and in Guatemala in general. My role
has been to translate and edit his handwritten and typed pages and taped
accounts from Spanish into a free translation of readable English, staying as close
to his own words as possible.[2] I have only deleted repetitious information, so the
text represents largely what Ignacio chose to include. In eight later trips (since my
first three) to Guatemala, I have asked him to amplify certain events that he had
only touched on in his first drafts. In each instance I have included in italics the
questions that I used to solicit more detail, so that the reader can readily discern
what kind of information Ignacio volunteered and how much of the material I
solicited from my own perspective. I have added notes on my own observations and
additional research when necessary to explain events further. I also have provided
introductions and appendices that place the story in its local, national, and
international context.

Like other descendants of the classic Maya, who make up over half of the eight million people of Guatemala, Ignacio has been profoundly influenced by the culture of both the ancient Maya and the conquering Spaniards. In a sense, all those who continue to participate in a Maya Indian way of life are children of Tecún Umán, the Quiché warrior prince who resisted the Spaniards. But, as Salovesh (1986) points out, the Spaniards did conquer the Maya, and so in another sense the Indians are also fictive sons of Pedro de Alvarado, who killed Tecún Umán in hand-to-hand combat. Unlike most other inhabitants of the shores of Lake Atitlán, Bizarro Ujpán bridges the worlds of the Indian and the Ladino (a person claiming Hispanic ancestry and culture)—his native tongue is Tzutuhil Maya and he and his townspeople are more Maya than Spanish, but unlike many of his peers, he speaks Spanish fluently and has served as a labor contractor for large cotton farms on the southern coast that are owned and managed by Ladinos. Also, he has served in the Guatemalan army (from 1961 to 1962) has been active in both local and national politics, and has worked as a research assistant on a large project studying modernization and development in highland Guatemala. Still he is mainly a campesino, working in his fields to support his family, and his daily social participation is mostly with other Indians in his town of San José (a pseudonym).

As Salovesh (1986) points out, perhaps Bizarro Ujpán is best viewed as a cultural broker, an intermediary who makes it possible for local Indians and Ladino outsiders to communicate with each other. With his knowledge of Spanish and experience dealing with anthropologists and other outsiders, Ignacio has learned what things an outsider is likely to question or be interested in reading, and he has learned to report matters that an inexperienced chronicler would see as too ordinary to be worth mentioning. Ignacio's sense of what to record is fruitful expressly because he lives between two worlds rather than in just one or the other. Looking at Indians from the viewpoint of an outsider and at Ladinos from the point of view of an Indian, he takes the reader deep inside both cultures. As a participant in both the indigenous and Ladino worlds, he is able to document beliefs and behavior to which an anthropologist would have limited access even if he or she lived in San José the year around. His alternation in viewpoints shows us, outsiders to both his worlds, much that we would not discover without his assistance (Salovesh 1986). By coming to a better understanding of his two worlds—Indian and Ladino—we come to a better understanding of ourselves and our own world.

Diary (1983–1987)

Accused in the Military Detachment of the Navy: A Repression

7 to 8 March 1983

I was accused in the military detachment of the navy; I don't know exactly when.[3] What I know is that during the night of 7 March they called me to the office of the military commissioner, telling me that I had to present myself to the military detachment in San Luis for an urgent matter. When I returned from the office, I had to look for the *jefe* [chief, head, boss] of the commissioners to accompany me. But then later, I decided to go without him. Instead, I asked a friend, Miguel, "Come with me, amigo. I might die. You need to witness what might happen and advise my family."

"Very well," he told me, "I will accompany you."

But always I was with doubt because I didn't know why they had called me. I felt somewhat nervous and a little afraid.

Tuesday, the eighth, dawned, and I went to San Martín to catch the launch, but beforehand my family was worried because the situation was delicate. When I arrived in San Luis, we went to eat breakfast. I drank a beer, and I went to the detachment, which is about four kilometers from the town. When I arrived, I had to wait until they were ready to receive me. In doing this, I met ten *Martineros* [people of San Martín]. I didn't know what they were doing, but there had been a lot of kidnappings and violence in their town. We had to wait for the *Martineros* to leave.

Then they received me in the office of the army. "Come in, what do you want?" the captain said.

"My captain, I have received your order to present myself here."

"Fine, come in," he told me. "What is your order?"

"Look, I don't have an order. I just came to present myself because you have called me to come."

"Have you served in the military?"

"Sí." And then I showed him my name on my certification of service.

"What problems do you have with the *jefe* of the military commissioners?"

"No problem."

"Ah, very well," he told me. "Are you part of the civil defense patrol of San José?"

"Yes, indeed," I told him.

"Ah, fine, and you have taken your turns?"

"Of course, I have," I told him.

"How can you prove that?" he asked me.

Well, I had brought a notebook with the dates that showed I had taken turns and the notes taken of the incidents in which we had encountered persons, cars, and all of this, and I showed this to the officers. "Look, I have taken turns; these are my notes."

"Ah, very good," he told, "come forth, let's talk. I was told that you did not take turns."

"Who told you that?" I asked.

"The *jefe* of the military commissioners came to tell me that you are a capricious person, that you don't want to guard your pueblo."

"On the contrary," I told him. "I'm a person who likes to guard his town because we are honorable workers," I told him. "The commissioner became angry at me because he asked for a quetzal from each of us—we are more that 400 persons, which would be Q400. And this is an arrears for us poor people. Just because I was the one who said that it was better not to give him a quetzal, he accused me here," I told the captain.

"Ah, fine," the captain said, "but that's not what he told me. He told me that you were capricious, you don't want to take a turn, you don't want to take your turn guarding the town, you don't want to collaborate."

"I know that I have collaborated. I have my dates."

For sure I didn't know that the *jefe* of the military commissioners had accused me of anything until the captain told me. But the reason is that he once asked me for money. I told him that I didn't have any money to give away and that if he wanted money he needed to work because only the blind should be given money since they were unable to work. This was what made the military commissioner angry. He accused me of disobedience and nonfulfillment of service of the civil patrol.

Why did he want money?

He wanted a lot of money from all the civil defense patrol. Earlier, he said it wasn't much, just 25 centavos from each member of the patrol to buy some patches to put on the arm that say PAC [Patrullo de autodefensa civil]. This was money for a typical, simple strip of cloth that cost 25 centavos. Then, as we are many, he collected a lot of money [for the patches].

Then this commissioner met another woman, who had a *mantel* [cloth] that was blue, a little finer than the yellow ones that we were already wearing on our arms. And he commissioned more cloth, finer yet, from her, and it cost a quetzal.

Why do you think he wanted to buy new cloth from her?

He wanted to give her this business so that he would become her lover.

And then I told him, "Please, I'm not giving more money. Why do you want an insignia that says PAC? We lose time in the patrols and the meetings, and you even ask for a quetzal. I don't believe this is just. A quetzal will serve for a pound of corn for our children. There are people much poorer than we," I told the commissioner. And this was the only fault that I committed—that I didn't accept. And the other muchachos followed me and didn't want to give him money. And then he became angry that I was the first to tell him that I was not going to give him money. I had two quetzales in my *bolsa* [bag, purse]. "Here I have two quetzales in the *bolsa*, but I don't want to give one to you," I told him, "because I know that this is an exploitation of the people." And that's the way it was. And he told me neither good nor bad. But later I received a call from the military detachment in San Luis in which the telegram told me to present myself at 10:00 a.m. in the military detachment.

By the grace of God, I had remembered on this day to carry my notebook of events where I had been putting down the dates and the events each time I take my turn in the civil defense patrol. When the captain saw that everything had been fulfilled, he said nothing bad to me. It was at this point I learned that the commissioner had accused me.

"Very well," the captain told me, "you have been in the army?"

"Yes, indeed," I told him, "I have lent my services and my obligations. With everything, I know how to respect the civil and military authority. For me, there is no problem with respect because respect is a security for the citizen."

"Very well," he told me. "Look," he said, "please come here. Let's talk the two of us."

"That's fine." Then Miguel stayed to one side.

"Look," he told me, "you know the attitude of the commissioners?"

"No," I told him, "I know them, but their attitudes I don't know."

"I don't know, but I was told that they are raping women," he replied.

"Maybe," I told him. "I don't know. I can't say anything about that."

"Look, please, we'll pay something for friends," he told me.

"What is it about?" I told him.

"You can be a person collaborating with me. You can gather all the information on the demeanor of the commissioners, and each time something happens, please come and inform me," he told me.

I didn't say no.

"Well, if there is cause, then I will come, but if not, then I will not come. What would I come for, to lie? I can't tell lies," I told him. "If there are things that are serious, then I will come and tell you. Otherwise, no."

"But let's do something. You don't have any fault. I only want to say that you can be my friend. You can come and give information about what happens in your town. I'm not telling you to come and accuse guerrillas, but the attitudes of the commissioners because I know that they are acting very bad. You can be a very confidential person of mine. Tell me when there are abuses."

"It's fine," I told him in order to not incommode him, because I know that the military are a bit *bravos* [irritable]. I told him, "It's fine." But from there, I did not go to him, not one time more.

Who was the jefe *of the military commissioners?*

It was Fernando Timoteo.

At 4:00 p.m. I arrived home. My family was very happy. I didn't go again to the detachment with the information they asked of me because I do not want to be involved in such things.

The *jefe* of the commissioners saw that there was nothing against myself. One night when he was drinking he said, "I accused you unjustly."

"Don't be ashamed," I told him. "I'm not one of those slanderous men. I like to be sincere and not hypocritical. Good-bye."

Domingo Arturo Coché Disappears
3 May 1983

Domingo Arturo Coché, a member of the cooperative, was working in the Aduana Central [Central Customs]. They say that he was kidnapped in the month of January, 1982, for having contact with the left. He is the brother of María Luisa Coché, who was killed in August 1981. [See *Campesino*: 254–58.] His body has not appeared.

Does anyone know what happened to him?

He could be dead or in Cuba. He was renting a house in Guatemala City. They said he had left for San José, but he never arrived. His brother, who also worked in customs, said he had been sent to jail three times for opening foreign packages. But he paid off the *jefe* to keep his job. His brother thought that might have been why he disappeared. No one knows for sure.

Octavio Tuc, Shaman
3 May 1983

Octavio Tuc was born in Santo Tomás Chichicastenango in the month of July, 1915. As a child, he went to live on the Horizonte *finca* [farm], on the frontier (border) with Mexico. Later he lived on the La Abundancia *finca*. Also he was on the Colima *finca*. His stay on the three *fincas* was for 14 years.

When Octavo was 22 years old, he came to live in the Tzarayá *aldea* [village], in the jurisdiction of San José la Laguna. He had lived a year in this village when he began to work at the things of the world, while he was working in this town as a helper of others. He told me about the things [for divining] (crystals, jade, obsidian in the form of volcanoes, people, and animals that represent gods) that he had picked up in Cojox, Xetuy, and Xebitz. After finding these objects, he began to dream strange things.

He says that sick people presented themselves to him in a dream, and he cured them with *zacates* [grasses, herbs]. Also, the dream revealed that there was a need to learn the names of the days. That was when Tuc began to investigate the names of the 20 days, each representing a god.

That is how it was when Tuc went with another shaman as his student. Tuc learned a little about the names of the days, and also he had to do *costumbres* [customs, rituals] in different places so that the *dueños* [owners, masters, gods] of the world would hand over to him *el poder* [the power, or ability]. With everything he had learned in the first year, he began to perform his first *costumbre*, and looked for the day, Ajau [God] Kjánel, because he says that his mother had said when he was a small boy that the day on which he was born was Ajau Kjánel, the most complete (full) day. Thus it was when El Mundo [God of the World (Earth)] gave him the power to conduct *costumbres* and to cure the sick.

In his sleep, when they gave him the name of the *zacate* that serves to cure each kind of sickness, they also imparted the names of the gods of the days and whether a sick person was going to be cured or not. If the *dueño* [owner] (god) of the day says to the shaman that the patient is going to die, then the shaman is not going to do a *costumbre* because it will do no good. But if the patient is going to live, the shaman begins to make *costumbres*, depending on the day that the patient was born.

During the 44 years that he had been working as a shaman, he saved about 200 persons by means of the *costumbres* that he did to the gods of the earth. But he says that also a lot of those people that he treated have died. I asked him why these sick people died, and he told me that the illness was stronger and also that the kin of the sick persons didn't comply to perform the necessary *costumbres* and that the patients didn't take the medicine he gave them. Also, he told me that when a patient was about to arrive for treatment, the things that served to divine (jade, transparent stones, and volcanic rock of different shapes) moved suddenly from the spot he had kept them, indicating there would be a sickness.

But it happened that Octavio Tuc quit being a shaman in the month of September of last year (1982). He says that the military commissioners of the *aldea* arrived at his house and took the things of *suerte* [luck] to divine and cure, including a small [image of] Maximón.[4] They took them to the municipality of San José as evidence for a trial held later for Señor Octavio, together with his wife and one of his daughters. The commissioners claimed that Octavio Tuc was making *costumbres* for the guerrillas to combat the army. This was when Octavio was put in jail. His wife and he were sentenced to 60 days, and all his things were seized and put in the municipality. After the sentence, they didn't give them back to him. They remain confiscated in the municipality.

After Octavio served his sentence, the commissioners made him take part in the activities of the Evangelical church. Fearing that they would otherwise kill him, he had to convert to the Evangelical church, Tabernáculo. He has been in this religion for six months. Still, I asked him if he were able to get again the things of the Santo Mundo [Sacred World]. He told me no, because the luck of a person once and for all is lost, and one is unable to grasp it again. But he indeed told me that he could never forget the names of the days and that he always dreams about them and likes to perform *costumbres* for himself about them.

Explain the dreams.

He dreamed twice when he was a Protestant that he would like to do more *costumbres*. Then he left the Protestants.

This Pertains to My Situation
May to June 1983

Also, my family suffers a lot of the same things others are suffering. Because of the situation in Guatemala, it is more difficult to get the basic grains and other foods for human beings to consume daily. The prices are high. Well, I planted corn and beans last year, but owing to the scarcity of rain, the harvest did not turn out well for me. Since there are a lot of us in the family, we ran out of corn at the end of April. We are using 10 to 12 pounds of corn daily; and there are other expenses. These expenses oblige me because I have six children and I have the responsibility for my grandmother and my uncle, José. I take care of my grandmother because she is very old and my uncle because he is mute. I'm giving them what they need. I'm suffering this crisis, and moreover the expenses for my work in the field. I'm working very hard because I can't pay *mozos* [helpers] for the work. It's true that *mozos* earn very little, but considering everything, money is very scarce. Also, I'm losing time in the business of the cooperative. At times I have a commission for two or three days. It's true they give me travel money and food, but I lose the days. Nevertheless, I'm making the effort because it is a commitment to the community. I'm unable to say no because I'm ashamed, and moreover I have sworn that I have to do my duty to comply with the needs that confront the cooperative. For these reasons I'm bearing these *cargos* [offices, burdens]. My companions, on the board of directors, only send me on the commissions because the statutes say that the president is the legal representative of a cooperative. This is the reason they don't want the assignments. Some of them don't want to lose their days [of work] because the situation is very critical.

This was the case during the month of May and June when I went several times to Chimaltenango to negotiate fertilizer for all the members of the cooperative. The Federación de Cooperativas Agrícolas y Mercadeo "Quetzal" (FECOMERQ) [Federation of Agricultural and Trade Cooperatives "Quetzal"] agreed to grant us 300,000 pounds of fertilizer on credit to be paid the month of November of this year. Altogether the federation gave us 600,000, but we bought 300,000. That is to say we paid for 300,000 and got 300,000 on credit. We paid Q3,660; the debt in this federation is Q4,820. I'm responsible for this credit until the debt is paid. When the fertilizer is transported to this cooperative, the credit is given to the associates to be paid in November and December of this same year under contract and with the authorization of the *comisión de vigilancia* [committee of control] if the member really has crops to pay for this credit. We went to the municipal secretary and he told us that each contract costs Q2 to draft. But I thought that Q2 was a lot. Instead, I could make the contracts for 50 centavos each; it's easier for them to pay 50 centavos. And, by the grace of God, I had the typewriter. Thus, I helped them. In all, I did 85 contracts, which stay in the possession of the cooperative until the members pay for the *quintales* [hundred-pound units] of fertilizer that they owe. This is why I say that I lose much time. What I do in the cooperative is beneficial for many, but it's taking part of my time. But always, I'm struggling.

In the month of June, the committee of control authorized me 1,000 pounds of fertilizer on credit to fertilize my cultivations. They also gave 1,000 pounds to my wife, Josefa. In all, we got 2,000 pounds of fertilizer that we are going to pay for in the month of November or December. We also have a contract. It's true that I also am responsible for credit in the federation, but I'm not able to abuse what is said in the statutes.

Ex-Commissioners
21 to 22 June 1983

The problems with ex-commissioners of San Martín continue. During the first days of the month of June, they were transferred to the jail in Sololá from the jail in Quezaltenango. One piece of news says that they will have to spend time in all the jails of all the 22 departments of the country.

Their families and friends fought a lot for their liberty, but it was all futile. Also, Señor Juan Mendoza Ovalle struggled a lot, but he was unable to do anything. The kin of these men are now unhappy with this señor because they had given him a lot of money. They even gave him a piece of land as payment for his work, but he has been unable to free them. This man, instead of working for the prisoners, took money to go many times to Guatemala [City] and told the families that the prisoners weren't going to spend much time in jail. But this Señor Mendoza, more than anything else, was negotiating work for his son in the national police.

This version is true because his son makes little as an agent of the national police in Guatemala. I don't know why the kin of the imprisoned confide in this man [Mendoza]. Now that the families of the imprisoned don't have any more money, everything is finished. Señor Mendoza is abandoning them.

Jailed with the ex-commissioners is a son-in-law of Mendoza. When these men were given the authority to be commissioners, they looked for women to have as their concubines. In the case of Mendoza's son-in-law, he has a *Martinera* wife, but when he was commissioned, he chose Juanito Mendoza's daughter, Berta Mendoza Sumoza, for his second woman. She now lives in the house of the imprisoned ex-commissioner, Raúl Barrera. In another house lives her real husband of matrimony. In total, the imprisoned ex-commissioners have two to three women, and two of them have acquired concubines of San José la Laguna. Now, I've said that one is the daughter of Juan Mendoza, but the other is Marta Juana Ujpán Sánchez, who is my sister by my father. We, however, don't talk as brother and sister, just as *Joseños* [people of San José].

The 21st of June, we went to Sololá to check on the dentures for my wife. That was when she had the opportunity to chat with the wife of one of the prisoners, who told her that very soon they would be transferred to other jails. The woman said that they had been in the jails of the departments of El Quiché, Quezaltenango, Huehuetenango, and now Sololá. Already the relatives had exhausted their money trying to get them out of jail. More than anything else, they now just go to visit them.

In the afternoon of this same day, the wife said that two *policía judicial* [judicial police] arrived in San Martín la Laguna to investigate the case of each prisoner to see whether it's true that they have two to three wives and if their houses and office are well furnished. They went to the house of each prisoner and chatted with the women. But the woman of the prisoner, Lucas Chac (Bolaños), realized that those who were talking to her were police. She had not been getting along with her husband from the time he fell prisoner. Moreover, she didn't visit him in jail because she didn't like the disgraces that he had committed [including] threatening to disappear [kidnap, kill, and hide the body of] her father, Miguel Flores, if he didn't give him Q400. The poor father-in-law had to raise Q400 to give to his son-in-law to save his own life. From that point Lucas's woman lost confidence in her own husband. She thanked God when he was jailed. In this afternoon when the police came to her house, she told them the misdeeds that her husband had committed when he was a commissioner.

On Wednesday, 22 June, about 8:00 a.m., without [anyone] suspecting anything, suddenly a launch arrived in San Martín la Laguna. News traveled to San José that the ex-commissioners had returned. Then the judge of the court of first instance came to get the judge of San José to go investigate the case of the jailed. Only then did we find out that the prisoners weren't free.

The news says that the prisoners asked for a new investigation in the place where the acts had been committed. To fulfill the law the judicial authorities brought back two of the prisoners, José Méndez Puac and Raúl Barrera, the ones who kidnapped the municipal commissioner, Santiago García Ajacac, in his own commissary. The *alguaciles* [municipal police, aides, and runners] and guards had recognized the kidnappers, but at the same time they said that they didn't advise anyone. Thus was the kidnapping of the municipal commissary, and the best identified [culprits] were José Méndez Puac and Raúl Barrera.

At the request of the father of the kidnapped, Señor Eduardo García Méndez, they all went to the commissary where the kidnapping had taken place to carry out the new proceedings (inquiry). That is to say, they measured the height of the commissary and the distance to the tribunal, and they examined the witnesses who saw the kidnapping. The *alguaciles* and municipal guards said to the face of the prisoners that it was true that the ex-military commissioners had kidnapped the commissary. The municipal *alcalde*[5] [mayor] was asked why he didn't investigate the kidnapping of the commissary, since he was a member of the municipality. He answered that he also was threatened by an unidentified group; for that reason it was all negative.

The authorities came only to investigate the kidnapping. In conducting the inquiry, they called many people to ask them when they had lost money and when they had been caused much damage. All these people said that it's true that they had given large sums of money, even to the point of selling their land to raise the money. When the inquiry was completed, the authorities got the prisoners out of jail, handcuffed them, and took them to their houses to search their possessions.

In the house of José Méndez Puac they found sheets of paper of subversion. With these papers the ex-commissioners had threatened the people, saying that they had something to do with the left, but the ex-commissioners themselves earlier had distributed these papers. All of these papers were taken to the courthouse in Sololá.

After searching José's house, the two prisoners and the superior authorities went to the house of Raúl Barrera. There they didn't find anything. After searching these two houses again, they took the ex-commissioners toward the municipality. At 2:00 in the afternoon of the same day, they took them in the same boat back to the prison of Sololá. The saddest thing is that they didn't allow them to eat lunch.

When they went to the shore of the lake, they shackled the pair. That is to say, they handcuffed the hand of one to the hand of the other. All of this caused grief to some of the townspeople, but it made the majority of them happy. One version says that these men will be saved from the firing squad but that they will have to stay in jail for a long time. However, the townspeople are not happy with the penalty of prison. The accusers insist on capital punishment. Nevertheless, what the sentence will be is uncertain. Also, it is unknown whether the authorities are going to bring the other prisoners for new inquiries, or just these two.

A Trip to Panajachel, Wife's Dentures, and Ex-Commissioners
28 to 29 June 1983

In the month of June, my situation worsened. My wife was suffering with her teeth, and we needed money to pay the dentist for the setting of false teeth. When we got the dentures, we owed Q35. When the fiesta of the town of 24 June arrived, as always, it was customary to buy things to eat and wear. We bought nothing. But not just my family was in this predicament; the majority of us live very poorly. And there are those poorer than we are, who have to work on the main day of the fiesta to earn their daily keep.

I didn't work on the principal day of the fiesta because previously I had worked three days, continuously making bread for the people who have little money, but I was like a *mozo*—they gave me the materials needed. Also, my son José worked three days and three nights. We earned Q35 and we made some bread to sell, but we sold little because the people did not have money. But this was the case with all the bakers, since we observed bakers from other towns that came to sell bread during the fiesta. They sold little. What helped me was that I made bread for others and therefore earned a little. The bread that we made to sell after the fiesta, we sold. But after the fiesta I was again broke because the little that I had earned I used to hire workers to have the milpa cleaned [weeded]. Moreover, the children always want money. But earlier I had mailed a letter in which I asked a person, Señor Sexton, for Q200, asking God to have this friend help me in the situation in which I find myself.

I'm writing the truth. On 28 June I left to work for a place called Xichal to clean milpa. In the afternoon when I returned from the work, my wife told me that they came to call me to the post office. After washing my hands I went to the post office, and they gave me an envelope where I signed the *libro de conocimiento* [book of acknowledgment]. When I arrived in the house, I opened the envelope and found the check of two hundred dollars[6] and felt the glory of God. I told my wife that we had been helped by our friend, James D. Sexton. Only then did I feel relieved. Then I told my wife, Josefa, that tomorrow I would go to the bank in Panajachel to cash the check.

When I arrived in Panajachel, I waited until they opened the bank, and without any problem they cashed the check because now the manager knows me. I'm friends with him. After cashing the check I went to the beach to see if there was a boat leaving for San Martín since it was the day of that town's fiesta. Always there are tourists or sports launches that go to other towns.

But when I arrived at the shore of the lake, the launches had already left, including the one going to San Luis. I thought about making the return trip via Los Encuentros and then going by foot from Santa Elena [to San José]. I sat down on the Bermuda grass. Suddenly, I saw some *Martineros*. When they asked me where I was going, I told them to San Martín. They said if I wanted I could go with them. I thanked them, and we boarded a canoe with a motor. As we chatted, I asked them where they had been, and they told me that they had gone to Sololá to visit the prisoners (ex-commissioners). Included among the *Martineros* was a woman by the name of Helma Cojox, the wife of the *ex-jefe* of the commissioners, José Méndez Puac. I asked her if it were possible that the prisoners would be set free. The woman told me that Juan Mendoza had been involved in trying to release them, but he could do nothing. That's all that the woman told me. She didn't give more details. Also, I didn't want to bother her because she was feeling sad for her husband. I talked about other things with the muchachos who came in the same boat. They told me they had gone to leave food for the detained because it was the day of the titular fiesta of their town.

At 11:00 in the morning, when we arrived in San Martín, my wife and kids were waiting for me. The day before, they had made a promise to go visit the image of San Pedro Apóstol and attend the mass, but when we arrived all the religious activities had ended. My wife had carried tortillas from home. We ate lunch in front of the church. After eating, we waited a little for José, who had walked to the soccer field. At 3:00 p.m. we arrived home, giving thanks to God. From there we paid the debts that we had pending with the money that my friend had sent.

Not until then was I able to clean the milpa. By the grace of God, I received this help. I have planted 20 *cuerdas* [1 *cuerda* = 0.178 acre] of milpa, 15 on rented land. I only have 5 that are my own—all of it is cleaned and fertilized. Also I'm making an extra effort. I have sown 10 *cuerdas* of chickpeas on rented land. I still haven't done the second cleaning, but God willing, I will do it. Times are difficult and hard—everything is expensive. There are days when my family and I scarcely eat. In reality, I'm working, but I'm not getting money because we still haven't seen the harvest. Not until November and December will we realize whether we are going to profit. Thanks to Mother Nature, there is now plenty of rain, and the crops are growing well. This year there has only been about 15 days without rain—last year there was more than two months. It's for this reason we're suffering—partly because of the weather and secondly because of the rulers of the country who have raised the prices of things.

Instituto Básico, *the New Primary School, and a False Accusation*
June 1983

Education in this town is very backward. This is because of the local authorities; that is to say, because the mayor just looks for problems with the teachers of the national school system. In the past few months, the director of the school and the rest of the teachers planned to establish, or take steps to acquire, an *instituto básico* [secondary school similar to a junior high school] for the *Joseños* who want to continue their studies. The director and teachers assembled the parents of graduates of the sixth grade. The parents said they were ready to pay a small fee for the mentioned education. Also, they solicited the support of the mayor to require that the municipality enact a fee of Q25 a month to help the people with education. But what the mayor said was that the municipality lacked the funds and was unable to give the quantity mentioned. Then the people and the teachers were not able to do anything. Also, the mayor said that if the teachers continued this promotion of taking steps to get an *instituto básico*, the municipality would ask for the dismissal of the teachers. There was a faction of the people with the mayor. There is, however, a minority of the people who want to continue with the establishment of this institute. Because the municipality, or, better said, the mayor, certainly doesn't realize that education is needed by the townspeople, he is a mayor wallowing in black ignorance.

Is this the same school building as the new primary school?

This is the new school with the names of the other Central American countries on the door. It is used as a primary school from 7:30 to 12:30.

From 1:30 to 6:30, it is used as a secondary school, or the *instituto básico*, which borrows the building.

Before the coup d'état in 1981, the town had organized a collective to buy some real estate to build a new primary school since the number of students was growing greatly and the new primary school building could be used as a secondary school at night. The president was Benjamín Letona, who gave the town materials, such as cement, *láminas* [pieces of sheet metal for roofing], lumber, and money to pay the construction workers. The people, moreover, provided labor. But when the coup took place, the work was not yet finished and lacked materials. The new government that took over then didn't provide the materials to finish the construction of the work. That's why, at this point, the windows have no glass. Because of the extreme need, the committee of the new school allowed the children to use the new school anyway. When the mayor found out that the new school already had children, he ordered the *alguaciles* and guards to evict them. The poor children were receiving classes on the porch of the assembly hall and other groups in the parochial assembly hall.

Thus, the children of the people were suffering a lot. Then the committee asked that the ministry allow the occupation of the school. It was then that in the month of March of this year (1983) the school was inaugurated. Not until then did the children occupy the classrooms. They sat on the floor because the new school lacked desks and places to write.

Was this the official inauguration?

No, this was really the first occupation. The official inauguration wasn't until January of 1984.

Through the steps of the committee, they obtained 250 desks for the new school. We, parents, only gave a quetzal for the transportation. The mayor wasn't in accord with the committee for the construction of the school, and he claimed that the committee had stolen some lumber that served for the formation of the work. But it is not true. The wood they took was for another part, for other work. The mayor informed the *jefe* of the military detachment of San Luis [wanting] to punish them, but sincerely the committee worked well. When the *jefe* of the detachment found that the committee didn't owe anyone, everything was resolved. The mayor, Andrés, hated the committee because when he solicited these things, he was unable to get anything. That is the reason for the complete rancor of the *alcalde*. When the committee tried, it was indeed able to get something for the students. Seeing that the mayor was not in agreement with the committee, it abandoned its work. It was then that the people became aware that everyone of the members of the committee had lost 45 days (day's wage) for the benefit of the town.

The school was still without windows. That is when the teachers decided to look for funds to cover the cost of windows. First, they solicited used clothing from Cáritas of Guatemala [an aid organization of the Catholic church]. Then the teachers asked the priest, Rutio Estrada, of the parish of San Martín. After they had asked him, Cáritas responded that it would get the used clothing for the teachers of San José. The teachers also mobilized to raise money for the transport of the parcels of clothing. The clothing came addressed to the priest to inform him that they had responded as asked.

We're not going to say anything bad when something is good. The priest sent the parcels of clothing to the school of San José at low prices for the poor, the children as well as adults. I went myself to buy three pairs of trousers, each costing 75 centavos—a very favorable price for us poor people. I also bought two shirts at Q1 each. I chatted with the teachers, asking what the money would be for. The director told me that they are planning to buy glass to cover the windows when they have a good sum of money. I was very appreciative of the idea that they had because it was very important.

When the mayor and the military commissioner realized that the teachers were selling used clothing, they imposed much oppression. The teachers had to stop. Then they returned the clothing to the priest in San Martín. The authorities passed false information, saying that the clothing the teachers were selling was the clothing of guerrillas killed in combat. This frightened the people so that they would not continue buying the clothing and made them too scared to communicate with the teachers. Then the mayor heard the testimony of the priest on behalf of the teachers. On Sunday when the priest came to celebrate mass in the church, he announced publicly that the mayor and the military commissioner were bearing false witness against the teachers because the clothing the teachers were selling was a gift from foreign countries. He said that the teachers were selling it to obtain a little money to buy glass for the windows. When the mayor and the commissioner heard him, they became enemies of the priest for having criticized the civil and military authority. The rest of the clothing was sold in San Martín.

The Life of a Principal
1983

I don't know whether it is possible to include in *Campesino*[7] these data that were taken in 1982. One of my first cousins by the name of Fidel Bizarro Quic and I got the idea to begin a cultural magazine for the town. But due to lack of financial resources we have not been able to publish the magazine. Perhaps someday we will be able to publish one. What we need is a camera to take photographs of the *principales* [town elders]. What we have been thinking about is to produce the magazine with photos and captions and stories, including their ages, from where they got their surnames, their hardships, their feelings of those [past] times, and also their years of free service.

Here is a sample taken on 7 November 1982 of the *principal*, Antonio Ramos Cholotío. His heritage is Patzún, Chimaltenango; his parents were Abraham Bizarro Cholotío and Juana Ramos. He says that Abraham and Juana were born in San José, but the parents of Abraham and Juana were from Patzún, Chimaltenango. It's very strange that the surnames of their parents were different from their own surnames. Abraham's father had the surname Batz and Juana's father Potz. It is not known why they put Bizarro Cholotío for the surname of their first son who was born in San José. Antonio's family was the first family with the first surname, Ramos, in the Moján canton.

Antonio says that when he realized that there was good business on the southern coast, he went often to Mazatenango, Retalhuleu, Tiquisate, and San Felipe to sell merchandise, but he says that two days on the road were needed to reach the mentioned towns. Also, he told me that he sold [things] in Santo Tomás la Unión, Chocola. With his strength, he made it in one day with 150 pounds of cargo on his back. On the return trip, he carried back bananas. He spent four days carrying the cargo on his back each week. He says that in those days, the money that circulated was the peso, real, *tostón* [coin valued at one-half peso], and *cuartillo* [coin valued at one quarter of a real].[8]

Antonio spent five years as an *alguacil* and five years as a *mayordomo* [low ranking officer of a *cofradía*], three years in the *cofradía* of Santo Domingo Guzmán, and two years in the *cofradía* of San Juan Bautista. He also spent 15 months as the municipal syndic, 16 months as the head of the municipality, and a year as the head of the *cofradía* of San Juan.

He served in the barracks of Sololá for 15 months, rising to the rank of corporal in the infantry. That was when a soldier earned Q3 a month. According to him, earlier there were no military commissioners in the towns. The first military commissioner, Señor Gregorio Pérez, was named by the governor of Sololá, but Antonio didn't elaborate about him. During that time, Antonio served two years in the volunteer company. When Gregorio quit as military commissioner, Abraham Gómez Chavajay replaced him. When Abraham left, Antonio Ramos Cholotío replaced him. He held the post for 15 years without pay.

When Antonio was in the volunteer company, he had to march to Guatemala [City] to celebrate the day of the national army. When they left San José, they traveled by canoe to Panajachel and from Panajachel on foot to Patzún, where they slept for the first night. The following day they walked from Patzún to Chimaltenango where they slept the second night. On the third day, they hiked from Chimaltenango to Guatemala (the capital). There was already a road, but they had no money to pay for a ride. When they marched, they carried tortillas from their houses. Each one had to carry enough food for five days. They heated their tortillas, made their coffee, and cooked their *chirmol* [sauce of chili and ground corn]. After the march, they were given an allowance of Q3 per person for the return trip to San José. Only then were they able to buy some refreshments. Also, with this money they paid for their return trip on a bus, Transportes Orellana, the only line then running from Panajachel to Guatemala and back.

In 1948, he was the *alcalde* of the town without a salary. For a year, he was *fiscal* [person in charge of the local Catholic church where there is no resident priest]. When he was the municipal *alcalde*, the office of *intendente* [term that in 1935 had replaced *alcalde* to designate the political chief of a municipality] was eliminated. Antonio was municipal *alcalde* at the same time he was tutor of the Dance of the Conquest..[9] Also, he was a dancer in the position of Tecún Umán. He says that earlier the *intendentes*, when it was about time to begin the office, bought a canoe to serve the community to communicate with the towns of Panajachel, San Luis, and others surrounding the lake. Antonio Ramos, when he left the tribunal, bought a big canoe of 10 *varas* [27.5 feet], which was the last canoe in the history of this place. From that point, the buying of canoes for service of the community was terminated. Earlier, his father had a canoe to rent, which was the only one found on the shore of the lake. When he was much older, he could not buy one.

Weren't there any canoes to buy?

No, his father had owned a canoe that would hold 20 *quintales* and ten persons. After the canoe wore out, his father wasn't able to buy a new one because he was too old. When Antonio was mayor, he commissioned a canoe for the community that would hold 40 *quintales* and 20 persons— about 10 *varas* long. So for a time the community had two canoes to use to go to sell things in Sololá and for other transporting needs.

During his public life, he participated four times in the Dance of the Conquest, three times fulfilling the position of Tecún Umán. He didn't want to because he didn't have any money, but it was obligatory. He had to comply. Also, he had to do it once for his father.

In all, Antonio served unpaid, without receiving a single centavo, for 31 years and 5 months. For 15 months, while in the regular army, he only received a salary of Q3 monthly. Altogether, he served 32 years and 10 months.

Civil Defense Patrols of Santa Elena and Other Towns
20 July 1983

In nearly all the departments of the west, *patrullas de autodefensa civil* are organized. The obligation of these patrols is to see that no guerrillas enter the towns. If, on occasion, the patrols encounter guerrillas, they must sound the alarm so that the people will confront them and run them out with sticks, stones, machetes, and even shotguns but shotguns of very short range. In the highlands like Huehuetenango, Quiché, and parts of North Cobán and Salamá, things have happened, but always many of the members of the patrols have died. However, in these parts in the southwest of Sololá, no one has died.

When the civil self-defense patrols were organized, the national army had more courage because it knew that in the towns there was then more control so that the guerrillas couldn't enter and carry out operations. Each group of patrolmen takes a 24-hour shift. Turns are taken according to how many groups the population has. For example, San José has 18 turns; that is to say, 18 groups, so each group takes a turn every 18 days. In San Martín there are 30 groups, successively taking turns according to the number of inhabitants. This is how it is in all the towns.

It happens that this is an obligation. Anyone not wanting to join the organization is sent to jail and given three days of hard work. After the three days, they make him join the organization anyway. There are towns in which the commissioners are crueler—they send people to jail if they are only five minutes late to take their turn. It's natural to be late because the poor people come from work and have to eat before taking their turn at 6:00 in the evening. It's a loss of time because the patrol sits down at the entrances and exits of the town, and each group is composed of 15 to 18 members daily. A day's wage is lost, and the people, being poor, need to earn their daily sustenance for their family. This organization is causing a crisis in the small towns. In the big towns like San Luis, there are more than 100 persons taking turns with pleasure. Also, in Samayac, there are 100 persons taking turns daily.[10]

They say that at the end of July, in Santa Elena, it was time for a group to take its turn, but it was missing a *compañero* [companion]. Then they sent a runner to call him to present himself for his turn. The hombre was found under the influence of alcohol. He presented himself in the headquarters and asked to be excused because he was drinking. Then the *jefe* of the patrol walked up without paying attention to what the man was saying, and with the fist of his hand landed a tremendous punch to the temporal bone of the man's skull. The man fell to the floor dead. They tried desperately to resuscitate him, but it was all useless. The same companions went to advise the justice of the peace. Then they carried the cadaver of the man to Sololá for the legal, medical autopsy. When they opened the head, they found damage to the brain. With the medical report, the six patrolmen actually were imprisoned in the penal farm of Quezaltenango.

Only one was, in fact, responsible, but five of them went to jail for complicity in the act. It is unknown how many years they are going to remain in jail. This story is true because, when I took my turn on 12 August, the *jefe* warned us of what had happened and gave us orders from headquarters to take care when a companion is sick or drunk not to accept him in the service, lest we suffer the same consequences.

In the same town of Santa Elena, it happened that in the *aldeas* and the cantons the *patrullas* are also organized. Those of the patrol of the Mocha canton of the said pueblo, similarly decided to take money from a *ganadero* [cattle dealer]. The señor is named Teodoro Yotz. One night some men arrived at his house with their faces covered with ski masks. When they entered the *sitio* [homesite], they asked for Señor Teodoro. When he got up, they asked him to give them Q600. If he refused, they said they would kidnap him and he would not return home again. They say that the señor answered that, at the moment, he did not have the money to give them. He did, however, say that he had some bulls that he had not sold yet, and he asked them whether they would like to have them. The men answered that they didn't want animals; what they needed most was money because they were guerrillas. Then they told the man that they would give him a period of 15 days to get the money and that they would return to collect it. If he did not have the money within that time, he would be executed. That saddened Señor Yotz, and he struggled to raise the money. However, he could raise only Q300.

The day came when the men were going to arrive to collect the money they had asked for. Señor Teodoro called his sons to stay with him during the night because he felt afraid since he didn't have the Q600. At 11:00 at night, the same men arrived again with covered faces. When they asked for the Q600, Teodoro told them that he only had Q300. They agreed to accept the Q300. After receiving the money, they warned Teodoro not to tell anyone or he would pay with his life. Then they left. Teodoro's sons realized that the robbers were of the same canton. Without doubt, they recognized the voice of the one who received the money. When the robbers left the house, Teodoro and his sons went to tell the military detachment, which was about three kilometers away. Then the soldiers came running, some in back, others in front with the señores [his sons]. When they arrived in the place where they maintain the patrolmen, no one was there. In the darkness, they saw the fire of a cigarette. Little by little, the soldiers drew nearer without the culprits realizing it. When they were already surrounded, the *jefe* approached them and saw them dividing the money. He made them stop with their hands up. The men wanted to run, but as they were well surrounded by soldiers, none could escape. They were captured. The soldiers, realizing that the culprits were of the same canton, took them to jail.

The patrolmen said that they were doing it because of need, that they didn't have a salary or anything with which to support their families and that they were losing a lot of time. It was then realized that the civil defense patrols were committing serious crimes. These unfortunate patrolmen of the Mocha canton of Santa Elena are in jail. There are 16 in the group, and all of them are imprisoned. This warning also came in the headquarters of the military commissioners in this municipality so that the patrols would take more care not to fall into crime.

The same thing is happening in Chichicastenango. The *patrulla de autodefensa civil* was accused before the new chief of state, Brigadier General Oscar Humberto Mejía Víctores, of being responsible for 17 kidnappings and assassinations. The news on the radio says that the *patrulleros* [patrolmen] took these 17 persons out of their homes, tortured them, and gave them death in the *oratorio* (small church) of the same canton of Chichicastenango. This is true because the bulletin that the chief of state sent was read on Radio Nuevo Mundo on their news program called *El Radio Periódico el Independiente* [The Independent Newspaper Radio] in September of the present month.

Reflections on Murdered Priests
27 July 1983

It's true that priests have died in these latest times because they share their love with any person and say good things about humanity and spiritual life. They are persecuted mostly for this. Well, not all of them. There are also cowardly priests who don't proclaim the truth. These are the ones who aren't persecuted. But the Bible says: "Blessed are those who work for peace because they shall be known as the children of God, and blessed are those who are persecuted for the sake of good because theirs is the Kingdom of Heaven." Moreover, it says, "Blessed are those who for my sake are cursed, persecuted, and have false accusations brought against them. Rejoice and display your happiness because the reward you will receive in Heaven will be great for you. Know well that the prophets that went before you were treated the same way." This is what those who are now being persecuted are doing—even losing their lives.

Well, these things are causing much sadness in the Catholic community. I remember the case of Padre Juan Smith, who was assassinated in San Luis in the last days of the month of July in 1982. It left much sadness in the village of San Luis, as well as in all the neighboring villages. Father Juan died physically, but he lives in history. Now in this town of San Luis there is a new institute with the name Juan Smith. The inscription on the institute says: JUAN SMITH "XWAAN" TZUTUHIL INSTITUTE. "XWAAN" is Tzutuhil. In Spanish it means Juan. Why did the people say XWAAN?

Because when he was alive, it pleased him the most when they said his name in the Tzutuhil language. So, the people mostly called him "Xwaan," including when he came here to San José during the fiestas. He did not want them to call him "Father." He liked "Xwaan" more, which now lives forever.

The same thing was done with Father Fray Agusto Ramírez Monasterio in Antigua, Guatemala. The violence continues in our Guatemala, resulting in great sorrow in the Catholic church for the death of the Spanish priest, Padre Fray Agusto Monasterio, of the Franciscan congregation in the parish of Antigua, Guatemala, where they held religious services. The news on Radio Nuevo Mundo and, in fact, on almost all the broadcasting stations of the country, gave news of the assassination. Heavily armed, unknown men took him out of the convent where he was living and away in a car. The assassins were very protected men because they kidnapped the priest of Antigua and gave him death at an eastern exit at a bridge called the Bridge of Incense. The priest had been missing since Monday, the 7th. The body of the priest was found only Wednesday, 9 November. All broadcasting stations lamented the assassination of the priest.

On Radio Nuevo Mundo, the reporters interviewed a priest in a church in Antigua, Guatemala. The grieving priest declared all that had happened with Father Monasterio. He said that in the month of November last year (1982), Father Agusto Monasterio was captured by members of the national army (*soldados Kaibiles*) [special forces similar to U.S. Green Berets]. They tied him up with straps (lassos) for eight hours. From that date (November 1982), Father Fray Agusto Monasterio was paralyzed in the left arm. From then on Señor Monasterio suffered great pain in his body because of the binding during the eight hours of torture. Although part of his body was disabled, he indeed was fulfilling his obligation as a priest.

One version says that the death of the priest, Monasterio, was just for collaborating. A guerrilla entered in the convent of his town looking for amnesty from the government. The priest took the repentant guerrilla to the authorities for his pardon because the government had decreed amnesty (pardon or reconciliation) with the fatherland. The communiqué of the government says that the guerrillas who want to be given amnesty can enter the barracks, detachments, tribunals, churches, and other institutions. No doubt, for that reason the guerrilla came into the church of Antigua, Guatemala. Then the noble priest said that Monasterio went to get the authorities for this man. Days later, they killed the priest just for the simple deed of accompanying a guerrilla. Another version says that the authorities thought that the priest was also one of the subversives and for that reason killed him.

The Spanish priest was buried inside the Church of Brother Pedro of Antigua, Guatemala. There was much sorrow in all Guatemala, and the same in my town.

Strange Things That Only Now Are Coming to Light

7 August 1983

In the month of June, precisely on the 23rd before the main fiesta of the town, a woman named Alejandra and her husband named Marcos, children of religious families, who have been living in matrimony for some years, had their third child. But the woman suffered a lot to give birth to the baby. The midwife, Viriginia [Ramos] Hernández, from San Martín, seeing that the woman was in danger, went to call the municipal *alcalde* to inform him that the woman was going to die.

Minutes after the *alcalde* arrived at the home of the woman, the woman gave birth to an infant. They say that minutes after birth, the infant stood up and wanted to run outside. What a very strange case—a newborn gets up and wants to run outside! The *alcalde* and the midwife were frightened and killed this baby by suffocating it. They did not let it go running about. They killed it! The parents, midwife, and *alcalde* said that the baby had been born dead to avoid the judicial investigations. The townspeople were only interested in the fiesta. These things always come to light, however, but only now is the news known. The parents and those who witnessed this birth say that the devil incarnated was born. They thought so because a baby at birth is unable to stand up, much less run. The people say that the devil, or a demon, wanted to go around in a human body. For me, it was a pity that they killed it. It could have been something important. Perhaps it came to announce good and bad things. They should have let it live. Many say, however, that it was best that the baby was killed. They didn't want it in this world.

The 7th of August of this year (1983) we had to sponsor a wedding both in civil court and in the church. We did it modestly, but we had to accept since they were depending on us. After mass, the parents of the girl invited us for lunch. Everything went well and without alcohol. The parents of the girl are Feliciano Yojcom and Juana Pérez, and the parents of the boy are Manuel Bizarro Temó and Isabel Bizarro. We are *compadres* [ritual co-parents], as an indication of respect. Then one day, my *compadre*, Feliciano, helped me clean chickpeas for a day and told me about the birth that had occurred on 23 June. He says that they knew of it because they are *mozos* of the father of the baby.

Fiesta of Santa Ana and My Birthday
12 to 13 August 1983

The fiesta of Santa Ana la Laguna is the grandest day for the inhabitants of this town, but because of poverty, this 12 August about 40 persons left in a *cuadrilla* [crew]. For sure, I didn't ask them which *finca* they went to, but I saw with my own eyes that they left for the southern coast because on this day we were planting chickpeas near the road. These poor people left for the coast when it was the main day of the fiesta. It is because they didn't have anything with which to buy corn, and they couldn't hold out a day longer.

On this day, 12 of us were planting chickpeas near Chonco Road, which goes to Santa Ana. In the afternoon, some friends who had gone to see the fiesta passed by sadder than in previous years. These friends gave me apples and peaches.

On 13 August, my birthday, there wasn't any money to celebrate. But I was content with my family. For lunch we ate herbs and tortillas, giving thanks to God for having lived another year. I worked on this day—there was no rest for me.

During the month of August, I worked very hard in the fields and in the bakery, but I ran out of money and was unable to buy flour and other things. For lack of money, it has been 20 days since I have made bread. I don't know when I will be able to make it again, perhaps in November. I'm scarcely able to have daily food because I'm doing work for myself and am not able to work for others because I would have to abandon my own work.

The Ex-Commissioners Continued
10 June to end of August 1983

I'm continuing the issue of the ex-commissioners of San Martín la Laguna, who continue serving their punishment in various jails in the country. They spent some months in prison in Sololá. Well, the defender for them was Señor Juan Mendoza Ovalle, who promised their families that he would do something for their liberty. According to the information of Señora Rolanda García, wife of the ex-commissioner Jaime Quen Pop, who came here to my house to consult about her problems that had happened, Juan Mendoza promised the women that he would get the ex-commissioners out of jail. She said that each time he traveled to Guatemala, they gave him Q40 to Q50, just for food and travel. Moreover, for his trouble they had to pay him fees. Also, each time he returned from Guatemala, he said that they would be free in just a few days. This went on for many months. It happened that, at the beginning of the month of June, the said Mendoza arrived anew at the families of the imprisoned to ask them if they wanted their husbands to be set free in this month. Well, to this the wives said yes. They were very happy because in the month of June is the fiesta of the town. Undoubtedly, they would spend the fiesta with their spouses. She said that Juan Mendoza said that each wife had to give him Q110 to pay the lawyer and to pay the expenses for travel and food for their husbands when they got out of jail. Thus, the poor women were motivated to get the money that he asked of them. Some of them borrowed the money while others sold their *sitios*. Señora Rolanda told me that she sold a piece of coffee land, but at a low price, because the people are almost enemies to the families of the ex-commissioners and don't want to pay the going price for the land. Thus, this is what they did.

When they had raised the money, they gave it to the "lawyer" Mendoza. She said that one of the women wasn't able to obtain the money and that Señor Mendoza told her to sell her land in order to put down the necessary money. The poor woman gave up her land so that Mendoza would have the money, but it was all a lie. Rolanda told me that on 10 June 1983, he received Q880 for the freedom of those imprisoned, and the poor women were hoping that their husbands were going to arrive to spend the fiesta, San Pedro Apóstol, together with them on 29 June.

The day of the fiesta came, and the prisoners were still in jail. Rolanda said that the women then asked Mendoza when their spouses were leaving jail. Señnor Mendoza said not until the middle of July. That's when the poor women of the prisoners were demoralized. They asked for their money back, but he said that he had left it with a lawyer as a deposit. When 15 July arrived, the women again asked him if their husbands would get out of jail, but he said he wasn't going to Sololá to find out. Then they asked him to which lawyer he had given the money, but he wouldn't tell them the name. Finally, the women got Mendoza to go to Sololá with them to investigate the case of the prisoners. When they arrived at the park in Sololá, he left them and he went to the police station to get documentation stating that, in a recent incident, Señor Juan Mendoza had been assaulted by delinquents that took the quantity of Q880 in this city. This man got this information because in Sololá his son is a member of the police force. When he returned from the police department, he told the women that it was a lie that he had deposited the money with the lawyer—the money was robbed by thieves who nearly killed him, and he showed the women the paper that advised the police of the robbery of the money. Then he told the women not to think any more about the money because it had been stolen and that if they wanted a sure solution, they needed to raise more money because what they had given him had been lost. Then the women went to tell their husbands that they could do nothing because Señor Mendoza stole the money.

What the hombre claimed was a lie because he celebrated the Fiesta of San José well. Without doubt, he enjoyed the fiesta with the money of the *Martineros*. Then Señora Rolanda asked me to go with her to get Mendoza to pay back the money. I told her that it would be better for her to go with a lawyer to file a suit against this man to make him pay back the money. I told her no because I didn't want any black arbitration; I only gave her the idea to sue the thief. In the beginning of August, all of the women went to the *juzgado de primera instancia* [court of first instance] of Sololá. They found a lawyer and presented an *escrito* [a writ] stating that the mentioned Mendoza had to appear in court. He had to leave a paper as a contract to cancel the debt in the month of January, 1983, for the quantity of Q880. He confessed that he had spent the money because of much necessity. He was nearly jailed.

Rolanda told me what had happened to this man in the courthouse because she was very appreciative for the idea that I had given her. I didn't want to go to Sololá for the reason that I didn't wish to remain the enemy of Mendoza, but it's certain that he had received more money previously. I don't know how much time these men will spend in jail. Fifteen days ago they were transferred to the Cantel penal farm in Quezaltenango, but already they were saved from execution because now the case is in *tribunal comunal* [common court, ordinary court] and not the *fuero especial* [special law court] as before. Yet, the people don't want these men to be freed. They continue with the accusations. And they say that there are 30 more persons implicated in the same crime and possibly that these 30 persons will have to be interrogated by the judicial authorities.

Ten days ago a group of men came in a car. When they arrived in town, they stopped near the soccer field and went to get a companion of the ex-commissioners. They took away this man at 5:00 a.m., when he was still sleeping. His wife said that when the captors entered the house, they got him up, put him on his feet, handcuffed him, and took him to who knows where. To this date, it's a mystery. It's unknown if he's in jail. What is known is that he was an accomplice to the kidnappings and assassinations that were committed in this town. The news has spread that they have to get the rest of them, but no one knows when.

Reflections on the Situation in Guatemala
End of August 1983

Who knows now about the situation in Guatemala? The people were very happy with the coup of March 1982 [by Efraín Ríos Montt that overthrew Romeo Lucas García] because the war had threatened them a lot. But little by little it crumbled. It's believed that the guerrillas didn't cause anything more to change than the decrees that president Ríos Montt enacted. When he had been well into serving his term, he said on the *teleprensa* [television news] that the price of things had to come down to help the poor who had scarce resources and that the campesinos and workers had to earn a just salary. Well, in November the price of sugar went down, with a *quintal* [one hundred pounds] worth Q11. Thus, the prices of all the products were lowered. All Guatemala was very content because they said that the new president was going to improve the country. Well, corn cost Q10 per *quintal*, but this was due to the dryness of the time. It happened that in the month of January, there was another change in prices. That is to say, when the year began, sugar cost already Q18 per *quintal*—an increase of Q7 per *quintal*. And so went the prices of other products, almost all of them increased. The people were alarmed. They could not petition to lower the prices because the president put the country *en suspenso de garantías* [in a state of suspended constitutional rights]. He said that no one could impede what he ordered. Thus, the people had to conform.

The most serious thing was that the salary of the workers was lowered to Q1.50. Moreover, the work on the *fincas* remained suspended because the same government now didn't give credit to the *finqueros* [farm owners and administrators]. It was thus when the salaries hit rock-bottom. Furthermore, one could not find work, and the prices were high—it was nearly a calamity in all Guatemala. Even now the only ones who live well are those who have good jobs with the government. Also the military live happily, but the majority do not.

March was another month in which the price of products rose yet higher. But the saddest thing Ríos Montt did was to decree for many months a state of suspension of rights. For that reason the people could say nothing. Moreover, he closed the borders to El Salvador and other Central American countries, prohibiting the export of vegetables. Take onions as an example. We *Joseños* plant a lot of them, and in May and June when they are scarce in neighboring countries, our product sells at more or less a good price. But from last year until this year onions were cheap because they did not let them go past the border.

It's thus that many people owe the banks and the transporters and many now don't sow the said crop. The most fatal thing is that there is no work for the men. The cultivations of the poor folks are priced very low. A day's work of the *jornalero* [day laborer] in these parts is worth only 75 centavos, but corn actually is 15 to 18 centavos a pound. The families that have many children, at times, only eat twice a day because they cannot scrape up the money to buy the sacred corn. Many suffer in these parts.

When the political leaders speak about what the government is doing with the poor, many wind up jailed and persecuted for speaking the truth. In the month of June, President Ríos Montt was told by his secret agents that there would be a coup on the 29th of the same month (June 1983) to overthrow him. Because of fear, he put the country under a state of alarm,[11] prohibiting all kinds of meetings, even in the churches of different beliefs from his own, and including in the cooperatives. But they were lies. There wasn't going to be another coup. It was the same suffering, what he was doing to the people of Guatemala.

In the month of July of 1983, when the country was in a state of alarm, the same president Ríos Montt decreed to implement the *impuesto del valor agredado*, *IVA* [value-added tax]. Together with private universities, the University of San Carlos protested a lot. Journalists and other groups asked the president to repeal the tax because it would hurt the poor the most, but as the country was in a state of alarm, the president declared that the people would abide by his order and say nothing.

On the first of August 1983, they initiated the value-added tax. That is to say, each person, when he buys something, has to pay ten centavos for each quetzal (ten percent). Let's suppose that a person made a purchase at some store for Q100. In the store, he has to pay Q10 for the state, and thus it happens with all the products. Although they say that the tax will not affect a person, the truth is that it is affecting the people who don't have resources, mainly us poor folks who don't have salaries. Everything is high in price, such as clothing, shoes, food, and daily consumer goods.

Eight days later, 8 August 1983, Ríos Montt thought about what he had done to the people of Guatemala. His minister of defense, Brigadier General Oscar Mejía Víctores, took power and became chief of state, although they said it was another coup. The people of Guatemala know that this is a lie to confuse them because the same people say that the new *jefe* is better than the one who left. But it's not true. The people know better—that they only changed faces, not ideology. The new *jefe* of state said that there was going to be a possible change of the value-added tax, but later he forgot. That is when the people of Guatemala realized the magic of the self-appointed rulers of Guatemala.

Cutting Off Ears in Chicacao, Suchitepéquez, and Military Commissioners
September 1983

The news says that guerrillas captured two members of a patrol during the night when they were taking their turn. They took them outside the town, but they didn't kill them. They only punished them by cutting off both of their ears. When they were found the following day, they were taken to the hospital. They are still alive, but they don't hear because they don't have ears to collect the sounds of words. It is strange but true that in this town there are two men without ears.

No one knows what's happening with the military commissioners of these towns. In San Martín they chose a commissioner, Gaspar Yotz Ajcac, because they thought him to be an honorable man from a good family. It's not known why he turned out to be bad. Less than one year after having filled his position, he looked for a woman to be his concubine. He totally abandoned his wife of matrimony and his four children. Now he lives with the woman of the ex-commissioner, Lucas Chac Bolaños, who is actually imprisoned in jail.

The same thing happened with a commissioner of San José. At the beginning of this year the chief of the commissioners changed. José Carlos Pinto left, and Fernando Timoteo Ramos Castro took over. But in a few months, he had problems with his wife. On the fourth of this month, they separated. The woman of this man is a member of the cooperative. She said that she separated from her husband because he has two concubines; moreover, he doesn't work. Who knows how he can obtain money? This was the problem, and for that reason they separated.

Crisis in Church and Town Continues
18 to 25 September 1983

We inhabitants of these towns are in crisis. So are the churches. The Catholic Church of this town now is unable to cover its expenses. It's unable to pay for the electricity and other expenditures such as the sacrifice of the mass. The directors handed out envelopes to the houses, soliciting financial help, but the people are unable to give because there is hardly any money. The church depends on the faithful, and when times are good we always help with alms to cover expenses.

What is the sacrifice of the mass?

A person works to make an offering to God. Actually, the mass is a sacrifice! The payment to the priest is the sacrifice; now Q10 is an offering of respect, not an obligation.

Until September I was doing everything. During the month of June, I was aware of everything going on in Catholic Action. Five hundred envelopes were handed out to the men and 500 to the women, asking for financial help. In total, 1,000 were distributed. The catechists carried these envelopes to each house. They thought the help that they asked for would cover the expenses of the titular fiesta of the town on 24 June. But the señor president of Catholic Action, Samuel Luciano Tuc García, informed me that, of the 1,000 envelopes, only 140 were deposited in the church with minimal offerings so that the fiesta scarcely was celebrated, unlike in previous years. This they told me 18 September when the church called me for a meeting with the *principales*, catechists, and *cofradías*. They told me that they needed my help for the reception of Monseñor Benando Gálvez, Auxiliary Bishop of Sololá, who was visiting San José for the first time. The men of Catholic Action realize that I have a diploma of *promotor social* [social promoter], and for that reason they called me to see if I would collaborate with the church. Well, when I arrived in the parochial *salón* [anteroom, lounge, sitting room], the president of Catholic Action had opened the meeting to talk about what to do for the reception for Señor Gálvez. The *principales* and the catechists said that all the Catholics should be called so that each one could give a contribution to cover the expenses of the reception of Monseñor Gálvez. Others said to make an obligatory contribution. I just analyzed the opinions of each group. In conclusion, I told them that the people could not be obliged to make contributions because it is certain that they are having difficult times. For the reception of Monseñor Gálvez, it would be better to organize a provisional committee for six days, which would go from house to house, trying to appeal to the conscience of the Catholic people to give voluntarily their financial help for the reception of the bishop.

Then the *principales* supported the motion that I presented, and the decision to organize a committee was made. But it happened that when they chose the persons to make up the committee, they placed their confidence in me to be president. I didn't deny them. It's true that I don't attend the church much, but the señores of the church wanted to see my attitude, whether I'm an obedient person. This is what I thought because in the meeting some very religious persons arrived. In contrast, they did not give them their confidence. Señor Santiago García Cholotío was selected as vice-president, but he did not want to serve in this capacity because he already was president of Catholic Action and he did not want an inferior position. That is to say, this man wanted a higher position and didn't want to be ordered what to do by another person. Then I told him that the members of this committee are servants, not bosses. Moreover, I told him in front of the *principales* that it would be better to let Señor Santiago be president and me be vice-president. For me it was no problem; it would be just for six days. Then the *principales* and Catholic Action stood firm, and at the same time I told the president to announce in church that tomorrow the committee will arrive at the homes to ask for help for the reception of Monseñor Gálvez. At the same time they gave us notebooks and pencils.

This meeting lasted three hours. Following it, the members of the committee met alone to stipulate the hour when they would go to the houses.

At 4:00 p.m., Monday, we left to go to the houses of the Catholic people in town. With soft, very serene words of encouragement, we spoke to the people, making them understand the need of the church. During the five days, Monday to Friday, we succeeded in collecting Q154.45.

It is true that during these six days we worked very hard. On Saturday, the 24th, we had to fill in the potholes in the road and make adornments in the streets of the town. We bought a dozen *bombas* [bombs, fireworks shot from mortars] for Q24. We paid Q20 for a sacrifice [offering, mass] and for other expenses. In all, we spent Q138.21. An amount of Q16.24 remained in the treasury.

The procession of Monseñor Benando Gálvez was very joyful from the gate to the cemetery to the church, with the streets covered with carpets of colored sawdust.[12] Well, the truth is that Monseñor Gálvez was very appreciative of his reception by the people. After celebrating mass, Monseñor was served a snack (cake) that had been prepared for him and his mother, who lives in Panajachel. Monseñor Gálvez bought a basket of bread and gave it to all the children, fulfilling what the Bible says, "Let the children come to me because theirs is the Kingdom of Heaven."

This afternoon was very solemn. Monseñor appeared very moved and without any other interest. He didn't want any money or anything else. His visit was purely to stimulate Christianity. He gave me a word of appreciation. In this event, I performed another service to my town. I have demonstrated that indeed I'm able to collaborate.

On the 25th, Sunday, 1983, after the church service, I asked the president to have all the *principales*, *cofradías*, and the people present go to the *salón* in order for me to give them a report. All went to the parochial *salón* where I let them see the money collected, all the expenses met, and what we had in the treasury of Catholic Action, the remainder of Q16.24. Moreover, we included the Q1.39 donated after the reception. When everything was explained, they asked me to continue more in the future with religion, saying that having observed my good behavior, if I wanted, they would give me a diploma of catechism. I told them I did not want to be a catechist and direct a religious group because I did not have time, that I have many obligations with the cooperative and other social obligations and with my family. For this reason I said no. But I told them that, in whatever case of collaboration, indeed with much pleasure I will help them because that is one of my obligations as a social promoter.

More Problems with the School and Teachers
28 to 29 September 1983

For the first time in history, I acted bad against the teachers, but this was for the benefit of the future of the people of San José la Laguna. During the four days from 28 to 29 September of this year, 1983, at the level of competition of the first through sixth grade in sector 15 of the towns of San Benito, San Jorge, Tzancuil, San Martín, and San José, the teachers organized the first mini-Olympics at the school level. Well, they organized many sporting events such as a marathon, swimming, races, basketball, soccer, high jump, and regular jump [high jump of lower levels]. In these towns the *Martineros* predominate. There are more teachers in our town that are *Martineros*. This is also true in San Jorge, San Benito and Tzancuil, and, most of all, in San Martín. In these events, all the teachers were in favor of their own town. They didn't practice "professional ethics." The obligation of teachers should be to look after the town where they work and not the town where they were born, but not for these teachers—nothing of the sort.

I was very interested in watching these games because many of the inhabitants of my town say that the teachers are bad. However, I have not much believed them because, when I chat with the teachers they always tell me good things. During these events, I was like an observer. At times I was protesting the poor behavior of these teachers.

The greatest fault they committed was to allow only the town of San Martín to make any points. That is to say, they believe that only this town has good students and they say that they are the best students of all the towns. This is a lie. The other towns have just as many good students as San Martín, but it is a pity that the teachers don't support them. The children of San José want the same thing, but it's our misfortune to have to protest the errors of the teachers. At the end of the games, they deceived the people of

San José. First, they did the marathon of 5,000 meters with girls and boys. In the final lap, when the teachers saw that San José was going to win, they ordered the *Joseños* to continue running, allowing a *Martinero* student to come out champion. They made the *Joseño* student run six laps; that is, he ran 6 kilometers. The authorities and I realized it. I had to protest that they take more care with the children and not deceive them, but the teachers told me it was a school matter and they did not have to talk to the residents. I replied that indeed we have the right to speak for the children of San José and that we are not talking bad only to overprotect the children but because the children of San José were told to run six kilometers and those of San Martín only five. Thus, one could say that they really had a lot of interest in the children of San Martín winning, and, as the teachers are *Martineros*, they did not have compassion for the children of San José or of the other towns.

The same thing happened with swimming. When there were no residents observing, they took advantage. They sent only the *Martinero* students to swim for competition, not the participation of the rest of the towns. In the results, the *Martineros* came out the winners. Indeed, I asked for the participation of the students, but the teachers told me that I didn't have anything to do with the students in this event and that I should talk to the mayor. But they had no respect for him either.

When we watched the soccer game between San Martín and San José, the students of San José showed their strength, making three goals to their one. When the teachers saw that the students of San Martín had lost, they wanted to repeat the soccer match. The people said no, but couldn't make their case with the teachers, owing to the fact that they are *Martineros*. When we, the people, realized that the teachers were exploiting the children of San José a lot, we united. When the second game was repeated between San José and San Martín, the majority of the people were at the field protesting and encouraging the *Joseño* students. Well, a day before, I presented to the coordinator of the 1983 mini-Olympics a petition for a neutral umpire who would not be from San Martín. We had signed the document with the president of the municipal sports committee. Having to look for a neutral umpire offended the teachers. They had to select a teacher from San Diego la Laguna.

The same thing happened in the second soccer match. The team of San José came out winners. In first place was San José, second was San Jorge, and third was San Martín. The same thing happened with the basketball match: San José in first place, San Martín second, and San Benito and

Tzancuil third. The two towns San Benito and Tzancuil were in last place, owing to the teachers not being concerned with their students.

These events ended 1 October, with the 1983 mini-Olympics closing its games. At two in the afternoon, they commenced to hand out the certificates to the winners and to the soccer scorers. My son José Juan was the leader of the goal scorers. They gave a certificate to him and also to my daughter, María, as champion of basketball. My son Ramón Antonio, who participated in category C, also won a certificate. Just the goal makers get a certificate; the winning team gets a trophy. But the people did not like something when they handed out the trophies. Although San José was in first place in soccer and basketball, when they gave the prizes, the team of San José did not get anything. Only the teams of San Martín got the prizes, leaving the champions deceived. I say this because San José showed the town of San Martín its spirit in soccer, but there was nothing in the way of prizes for them. The people were waiting for them to award the champion teams. Only the teachers of the school of San Martín are at fault. The other teachers of the other towns hardly could do anything because the *Martinero* teachers are greater in number than those coming from other towns. The *Martinero* teachers just received the prizes and left. The only teachers remaining were the ones that were not from San Martín, along with the children not from San Martín.

Then I went to the board of directors to talk with the director to find out why they gave prizes only to the *Martineros* and nothing to the *Joseños*. This is when the director told me that those who made the mistakes were the ones who gave out the prizes. Almost all the prizes were carried to San Martín, but were they the champions?

We had problems with the director, Angel Ajcac Yocom. When some residents saw that I was going to the board of directors, they followed me to find out what would happen. When the residents drew near, they intended to beat the director, but things were calmed.

After we had left the director, we went to the tribunal to consult with the mayor about what had happened. Then they called the director, and he said the same things. Although we demonstrated our total repudiation of these teachers of San Martín, we didn't include the three from Totonicapán because we knew that these three could do nothing against so many *Martineros*. The town drew up a memorandum to the ministry about what had happened. The memorandum was drawn up in the municipal tribunal, asking the government for new teachers and no more *Martinero* teachers because of their behavior in the town. More than 200 residents signed, asking the transfer of the *Martinero* teachers.

When the teachers saw that a memorandum was drawn up against them, they thought they would make out by going to the national army in San Martín. A day later they went moaning, complaining that they were innocent of what they had done. The captain was in San Martín, and for that reason the *Martineros* could easily communicate with him. When he heard that the people had drawn up a memorandum against the teachers, he sent a writ of summons to the mayor that he was to appear in the headquarters in San Martín. It was in San Martín where they oppressed the mayor. They told him he had to have compassion with the teachers, if the people had drawn up a memorandum against them, and that the mayor should take into account these considerations in order that the army take into account the protection of the mayor. Well the mayor respected what they told him, and then he didn't certify the papers for the governor.

But we appealed to the secretary. He sent memorandums to the señor governor concerning all that had happened because the superior might believe that we are sowing thorny problems between the teachers and the residents and because we don't want the teachers to behave poorly against the town since our children have the same worth as those of other towns. When the señor governor realized the situation, he conferred with the supervisor and other functionaries of the department. They sent word to the mayor that they would arrive on 13 October 1983 to investigate the matter. Then the mayor sent me a summons for the tribunal, telling me to be present for this day of the investigation. But it was a pity that I had a meeting in Guatemala [City] to attend in the chamber of commerce pertaining to the cooperative.

So I was at the meeting on 12 October, which did not end until 7:00 p.m. Thus, I had to remain in Guatemala [City]. I left from the capital at 5:00 in the morning on the 13th. I arrived via the southern coast in San Luis at 10:00 in the morning, constantly thinking about the meeting with the governor and the others. By God's grace, when I arrived in San Luis, a boat was leaving for San Martín, and we arrived there at 11:00 a.m.

I had just left the launch and had taken the road for my town when I met a car. The people in the car told me that in a few minutes the governor would arrive. I indeed ran because I was very interested in participating in the meeting.

When I arrived home, the house was closed. I just left my *bolsa* and went to the municipality. Near the municipality some women told me that the residents needed me. I told them not to worry that I was going to the municipality, and the women returned with me.

When I arrived in front of the municipality, the people were happy to see me because they knew that I was fighting for the welfare of the town. I arrived suffering from the heat and asked permission to enter the tribunal where they were meeting. The señores allowed me to enter, and they made the governor see all that the teachers had done. The supervisor was on the side of the teachers. In conclusion, the governor said to ask the people whether they were against the teachers. He gave us a moment of time. Then I got the idea that nothing would be helped by requesting the dismissal of the teachers. We asked the departmental supervisor for the establishment of an *instituto básico* that the people need so much because already there are a number of residents that have completed primary school. The supervisor and the governor promised to establish the institute that we asked for.

We asked for these things before they had opened the public meeting in the tribunal before the municipality. I know that teachers want to help the town in this way because much earlier we had chatted with them. We even had gone to the houses of the people to take a census of those who wanted a school, and we succeeded in making a list of 22 persons. But that was last year, when we didn't have problems with the teachers. Now that we were having difficulties, I wanted to win their confidence. Thus it was that, when we left the tribunal, the residents were waiting for us to find out what solution we had found for the problems. In the open session, I told the people that we should forget the problems that had happened and that it was better to find a solution in which the *Martinero* teachers would continue working but collaborate in offering the second level of teaching to our children because it is certain that we don't have money to send them to other towns to study.

But there was the matter that the mayor was not in agreement with giving the quota of money according to the law. All the municipalities are obligated to provide for the education of their people and pay each year Q200 for the maintenance of the establishment. For that reason the mayor didn't want the institute to function. However, realizing that the majority of the people were in favor of a secondary school, in this meeting the mayor was obliged to contribute to the community. The governor said the same thing, and then the teachers promised in front of the people to work during 1984.

Many of us were very pleased because a problem was converted to a joy. This would not have been accomplished, however, if we had not protested. Thanks to God, the *Martineros* thought badly for our children, but everything went badly for them instead because, in return for not losing their jobs, they promised to work honorably with the people of San José.

These persons swore before the people and before the superior authorities of Sololá, and, at the same time, a memorandum was drawn up and signed by the governor, the supervisor, the captain of the national army, and the local authorities. Also, the teachers agreed to sign the act. They will only receive the amount of Q100 monthly. That is to say, each student will give Q5 each month. But this Q100 is for all the teachers that teach the basic courses. The regulation of the ministry says that after three years they will be paid by the state. In addition, the residents also promised to enroll their children next year for secondary study.

The Situation Continues to Get Worse and My Aged Grandmother Is Dying
8 November 1983

In the highlands the situation is getting worse. The terror between the right and left continues. But the misfortune is that the guerrillas just use ambushes and have caused the deaths of innocent people. Also, members of the right capture innocent people, saying that they are guerrillas.

On 8 November, the news said that the guerrillas were near Santa Bárbara, at the hamlet of Quineo, where they met the civil defense patrol of that hamlet. The unofficial news circulated that the guerrillas asked the members of the civil defense patrol who it was that had ordered them to patrol. They answered that it was the military commissioner. Then the evil men went looking for the commissioner, and when they found him, they killed him with firearms. They told the people not to take any more turns in the patrols because the civil defense patrols don't have the capacity to confront guerrilla warfare.

When the authorities found out about the death of the commissioner, they sent advice to the military zone. A platoon of soldiers left to finish the guerrillas, but when the soldiers approached the scene of the crime, they were told that a platoon was not capable of standing up to them because there were more than 200 subversives. The soldiers retreated, thinking that they would for sure lose their lives. It's true because they passed in our town but very sober.

The subversives are threatening. We are terrified because last week they were only four kilometers from town in a place called Apazote. For sure they have not come into town, but they are in the area. It is noted that they are strong because they are not afraid of the army. We realize that the people of these towns are not obliged to the guerrillas because they are dedicated to their work. What we don't understand is from whence they came, to what town they belong, or to what town they will go.

The guerrillas caused a lot of damage this Sunday, 20 November, between San Diego la Laguna and San Luis, according to exact information that circulated through these towns. At 6:00 a.m., the guerrillas captured a bus of the Rebuli line. When they evicted the passengers, two of them did not want to leave the bus, so they left it wounded with bullets. The bad men did not allow the passengers to take down their suitcases from the rack, which they doused with gasoline and set afire. The traveling bags were consumed by the flames together with the bus.

It's not known who went to advise the military detachment of San Luis. The soldiers went to investigate the scene of the crime. Before they arrived where it had happened, they were ambushed by the guerrillas. Soldiers died and many were wounded, including a military commissioner of San Luis. The ambush was at 8:00 in the morning, according to the radio and the *Prensa* [*Libre*, a national newspaper], but they did not give the number of deaths. Some *Joseños*, however, observed when the dead and wounded arrived in Panajachel. They said that there was an auxiliary boat of the Selta (express) line. They saw seven dead and 18 wounded. They radioed from San Luis to Military Zone Number 14 of Sololá what had happened to the soldiers. Then Staff Colonel Luis Alfonso Rebuli, Commander of the Military Zone of Sololá, went in a car with a chauffeur and a *guarda espalda (de seguridad)* [security bodyguard] to the place where it had happened. Before reaching the location where the soldiers lay dead, the colonel also was ambushed. They put Claymore mines on the road so that when the car passed over one, it detonated and killed the colonel. On this day the exploding bombs were heard. Undoubtedly, it was Colonel Luis Alfonso Rebuli, brother of the owner, Rodolfo Rebuli, of the bus that burned. These things scared us because the news said that the same evil men are in the village of Pachichaj of San José, writing notices on the walls saying that they are responsible for the victory. They entered the *tienda* [small store, shop] of José de León Tuc, where they drank sodas and ate bread but paid for it. After eating, they asked permission to make signs of subversion. This man told them no because his house was a *tienda* and not to be used for bad things. When they heard this, they tied him up and then began to write subversive inscriptions anyway. Well, this village is 12 kilometers from our town. Moreover, it is nearer the mountains. At present they almost never enter our town, but suddenly it could be more critical.

For more than two months, my granny has not walked—she is bedridden, awaiting death. Some days she is close to death, others she recovers and wants to live. But her age does not help. Aging itself is not useful, only the children and grandchildren of the aged suffer. We are experiencing such a situation with my granny.

We are suffering a lot because we are afraid to leave her alone in the house since she may fall out of her bed. To take care of her, we have to sleep on the floor. On days when her condition is critical, it is difficult to change her clothing. What astonishes us is that she eats three times a day, and she complains when we are late serving her food. Since we have a big family, my wife, Josefa, needs a lot of time to prepare the food. But my granny wants her breakfast at six in the morning, and the children complain to us.

Since my grandmother lives closest to us, we are the ones who have to take care of her well. She has two other children, but they have moved away. When her sons come to visit, we argue a lot because my granny complains that we don't give her food on time. At times my wife gets very angry and argues a lot with me. What I tell her is to have more patience, because we don't know how our lives may turn out. Only then does my wife calm down.

My wife has good reason to be mad because my grandma has a lot of grandchildren, but of all the grandchildren, only I, along with my wife, am taking care of her. I cannot make the rest of the grandchildren be conscientious.

Taking care of my mother's mother takes a lot of effort. Many tell us not to give her food and abandon her at night so that the *dueño* of death can come and take her spirit. They say that because of us, the spirits of the dead don't come since the spirits of the living are stronger than the spirits of the dead. Others tell us that we need to take more care with the old ones, to give her food and things to eat, and especially not to leave her alone because evil will enter and she will be able to die. They also say that we should take care of her as a gift from God because not all persons live such a long time.

It's hard to understand these things. Different people say different things. During the night when we are taking care of granny, we have heard many voices of women, but suddenly they disappear. One night, we heard a voice that was talking in the patio of the house, but the voice we heard was that of my grandma. She was walking on the patio with her cane. I wanted to open the door to see whether someone else was walking on the patio, but those with me would not let me do so. The truth is I wanted to see if some ghost was walking. I did not feel afraid. What I wanted to do was to see in order to believe whether there was some ghost, but it was impossible because they would not let me leave.

My mother had a dream four days ago. She said that she dreamed of a señora who had died more than forty years ago. The woman was named Bizarro, and this woman didn't have a son during her life. The señora talked to my mother, and in the dream she told her that it would be better to abandon the patient, Isabel, because now it is time that she go where the dead are. She told her also that Isabel is not going to die because we are giving her food, that it's better not to give her food, and that if we continue giving her food she's not going to die. Indeed, someone else in the family may die because she has a very strong *nagual* [spirit]. Before she dies, first someone in the family who lives in the *sitio* must die. Now we are worried.

Also, my wife was dreaming. She said that in her dream she was chatting with the grandparents of her father, but the grandparents of her father have been dead for years. In her dream, she was talking to dead persons. She said that they told her that Señora Isabel will not die for some time and that she should take special care because the day when my granny was born was the day of Ajpub [one of the 20 Day Lords]. What astonishes us is that the two dead ones told my wife to take care because Señora Isabel was born on the day of Ajpub. Her *nagual* is stronger. She does not want to die before someone else dies, and it's possible that two or three persons have to die. We worried about the dream, but, God willing, we have to bear these things.

My health is a little better, but I'm spending money for my recuperation. Before I liked some cigarettes, but because of my health I am unable to smoke or drink. I suffer headaches, and, moreover, high blood pressure. Since quitting smoking and drinking, I feel better. At times, both my head aches and my heart aches, but with a little rest, I feel better. Always I am taking medicine. At times, I do not want to chat with the people who look to me for various things about the cooperative, but I am fulfilling my obligations, doing what is possible.

The Problems in San Martín Continue and a Kidnapping
20 November 1983

The mayor who took over during the time of Ríos Montt is called Juan Sicay, but they say that he was an accomplice of the ex-commissioners who are imprisoned. They are guilty of kidnappings and crimes that they committed in this town. Then the people united to ask the governor to change the mayor. Finally, the governor respected their request and named Señor Ignacio Robles to occupy the tribunal. When everything was ready for him to receive his office, another group organized in opposition to him. They collected names on another petition outlining their disagreement. Then the departmental government named Haroldo Puzul, who also was not received for the tribunal. Now the *Martineros* have a serious problem—they do not have a mayor. For the administration of justice and judicial matters it is the mayor of San José who is responsible for the office of the mayor of San Martín. The tribunal of San Martín is in the office of the mayor of San José. They say that it is the first time in the history of the two towns that this has happened. They also say that in San Martín there are better men, but it's not true because now, in actuality, we are seeing that for whatever matter or claim, they have to come here to San José for the mayor to carry out justice. It's a very strange story.

During the last week, three *Martineros* were kidnapped. It's unknown where they are. Two they kidnapped in town, and the third they kidnapped in Guatemala City. His name is Haroldo Méndez Xico, an avocado merchant. He appeared 6 days later. It was just to put fear into him so that he would not speak so loud against the government again. He buys avocados by the thousands and sells them in Guatemala [City]. But the avocado business is at rock bottom, and the news says that Haroldo made a statement on the radio, Nuevo Mundo. He said that he had spent four days with his bundles of avocados, and he still had not sold them. Already he had nothing with which to buy tortillas. He explained on the radio what was happening with the government. It was not allowing agricultural products to be exported to the other countries of Central America. Also, he said that before the coup, business was much better than it is now. This was Haroldo's crime. He went back to where he had his bundles of avocados, and later some men arrived and kidnapped him. In these times, one has to take care when expressing his thoughts. They say that there is freedom of expression, but in this country there is no freedom of expression. When they give us free expression, we suffer insults. In order to speak, one must think first about what one is going to say.

Have the other two Martineros *appeared?*

No, they haven't appeared, but Haroldo appeared days later. I was able to talk to him. He was with his bundles of avocadoes when some men arrived and took him away in a car. He told me he didn't suffer anything. He wasn't maltreated; he was not hit. He only was hidden for 6 days.

Another missing man is Juan Yocom Tepaz, who was mayor. He spent much time in the army as a cook, and now he is retired from the army. But who knows who kidnapped him. Until now, he hasn't appeared. It is unknown if it was the right or the left. I had conversations with a friend who told me that in the United States there are two refugees from San Martín but of the last name García. But two of the lost are named Ixtamer. Maybe they thought, so that they would not be found, they would change their names. Perhaps they are refugees, but until now, not one of these three men has appeared. This ex-mayor, he was named by General Ríos Montt when the mayorship was integrated. Who knows what discourses caused him to resign and leave the vice-mayor in power. The people of San Martín say that he was an accomplice of the ex-commissioners' violence. No one knows where he is now, whether he is alive or dead.

My Cousin and Half-Brother Are Beaten by Police
20 to 25 November 1983

At times, we ourselves want bad things. On 20 November my half-brother, Gerardo, went with a cousin named Igor to Huehuetenango to buy used clothing to sell to the tourists in Panajachel. Igor carried the quantity of Q800, but Gerardo didn't have any money. He thought he would do business with Igor's money. When they left for Huehuetenango, I resented their not having told me of the trip. I also wanted to go with them for this business. But as they did not inform me, they went and I stayed.

When in the afternoon on Wednesday, the 23rd, telegrams arrived from the two men saying that they were imprisoned in Quezaltenango, no one knew why. At 2:00 in the morning four residents left for Quezaltenango to see what the two had done to get themselves in jail. Igor and Gerardo didn't return until the morning of the 25th. Then I went to chat with Igor to find out what had happened to cause them to be thrown into jail. When I arrived at his house, he was resting in his bed and was very sick because of the blows and the wounds that they had given him. We chatted and he told me what had happened. He said that they went to Huehuetenango to buy the clothing, but there had not been much to buy. They just found a little. They left with most of their money. Already night had fallen in Quezaltenango, and when they got out of the car, they went to look for an inn. Just before arriving at the inn, they met some policemen dressed in civilian dress. The cops took each of them to a dark spot. They asked Igor if he had any money. "No," he said. Then they hit him and took him where they had taken Gerardo. They asked them whether they were guerrillas, and they said no. Then they separated them again until they found the money. Igor had fastened the money on his waist with a handkerchief, and for that reason they did not easily find it. When they found it, they gave him a quick blow with an object that they carried. When he felt the blow, he already was injured. Then they told them that they had been taken as subversives, but the truth is that these men aren't bad.

How much money did the police take from them?

The police took Q700 from them. They had only spent Q100 on the used clothing. Moreover, of the Q700, they took Q500 as a fine.

When I found out about these things, I realized that I too would have suffered had I gone with them. It is true that I had wanted to go with them, but if I had, I would have suffered the same misfortune. For that reason I say that at times we ourselves desire bad things, however unintentionally.

The Oldest Shaman in San Martín Dies
25 November 1983

Eight days ago the oldest shaman in San Martín died. His name is Santiago Cojox Senior. Many are sad because he lived a long time in San Martín, performing *costumbres* for the adults and children who were sick. He was very famous because it's true that he cured a lot of people with natural medicines (herbs) and invoked a lot of the gods of the earth. May your soul be with God, Don Santiago Cojox, and may your body rest in peace! It's a pity that a son Santiago Cojox, Junior, and a grandson Antonio Cojox, of this man are imprisoned, and, at present, no one knows in which jail they are. Don Santiago still had resistance, but he became serious when his son and grandson were jailed. Since their imprisonment, it was impossible to chat with Santiago because the people were very suspicious of anyone talking to him. For that reason it wasn't possible to communicate much. But such is life!

Problems of Soccer in San Martín la Laguna
Sunday, 4 December 1983

It happens that they are competing for the championship of the department of Sololá. Last Sunday, representatives of Santa Elena came to San Martín la Laguna for a soccer meeting, but the news said that the umpire of the meeting was from San Martín. When he saw that the *Martineros* were unable to do anything to conquer the muchachos of Santa Elena, the umpire marked a goal in favor of his town. But truly, there was no goal. Then the boys of Santa Elena protested to the umpire. The *Martineros* didn't like the fact that the team protested, and the public went on to the field to throw out those of Santa Elena with sticks and stones. Many ended up wounded. I was aware of this because they passed through the street toward Santa Ana.

In our town, they had left a car because the road is very steep. For that reason we saw the muchachos of Santa Elena beaten and injured. In these times, one is witnessing a lot of savagery. Already they have lost the respect of their ancestors. The old folks say that in San Martín there used to be men of much respect, but not now. What's most distressing is that among the bad *Martineros*, many are students of different professions.

The Case of My Granny
8 December 1983

For a month, my granny has been in bed and unable to walk. Her illness is due to old age. She speaks, eats, sees, and thinks well. She doesn't suffer with her lungs, doesn't take medicine, and is living only on food. Every minute she entrusts herself to God, and in her prayers she gives in to dying. What she says is that God is not happy with her because he has not heard her prayers and that if God had heard her prayers he would receive her for death. What she has told us is that it's unnecessary to take care of her at night. We are sleeping in our house. When she had fallen from her bed, we spent some nights sleeping on the floor to take care of her in her house because we thought that she could fall from her bed again. Seeing that we were suffering to sleep on the floor, she told us to sleep in our own bed in our own house. So we did. Now she is alone, but she told us she is not afraid nor does she fear death. She doesn't drink liquids other than hot coffee and sugar. For her, tortillas are better than bread. Not all food hurts her.

After each meal, she chats with us, instructing us to train and train our children, not to be mean to them so that they won't get bad ideas because parents should be good examples for their children to behave well. She does the same to the children, telling them, "Respect and obey your parents. Respect and obey the people in the streets. Don't steal things." These are the recommendations of my granny, Isabel.

She tells us that she was born on 25 November of 1879. She was named Isabel because she was born on the day of Santa Isabel. It's true because it says so on her *cédula* [national identification card]. She tells us that eight days after giving birth to her, her mother died; she had breast-fed for only 8 days. Her father was called Bonifacio Soto, and her mother was named Juana Toc. The one who took care of her when she was a baby was her grandmother, Rosaria Soto, a midwife who got her a little milk from the breasts of women in their houses.

Also, she tells us that when she was a child, there had been a lot of sickness, cholera morbus, but she says it was not called cholera then. For the people it was an illness from God. In Tzutuhil it was called *Ruk'ak Tiox*; that is to say, sacred fever of the saints. She says that two to three persons died daily—men, women, and children. That was when San José was depopulated. In all the homes there were deaths, and the only one to bury the dead was Santiago Ujpán. He dug each grave only a *vara* [linear measure, 32 to 33 inches] deep for each body. For children, one tomb was used for two to three dead persons. The deceased were not given coffins. When a person died, he was wrapped in a *petate* [palm-mat of *tul*, or lake plant]. Señor Santiago Ujpán had to carry the load of the dead across his back with a *mecapal* [porter's strap] to the cemetery. He ate well. The chickens were not sick, and when he returned from burying the dead he ate one or two of them because many homes didn't have any owners. So he got the animals. That was when Señor Santiago Ujpán realized the value of eating chickens. He also earned some pesos because sick people were dying quickly and the survivors paid him in either money or chickens. Within two to three days a sick person died.

My granny was sick, but she only had a high temperature. However, close kin of her family died. Very few people remained in the town, and those that stayed, little by little, went to the coast to work on the *fincas*. Later a few returned. But some families stayed as tenants on the farms of Suchitepéquez. That was when those "very clever" persons began to sell their land into the hands of the rich of San Martín but at a very low price. She says that they let go of land for *arrobas* [25 pound measures] of corn.

My granny is very advanced in age and now is unable to walk, but she does not ache anywhere. We treat her as an invalid. As I have said, we had been sleeping nights in her house, but we had been taking turns. At times my mother has slept with her. What is strange is that one time, when my mother was in the house of her mother, my mother was about to go to sleep at 10:00 in the night of 1 November. When she was arranging her bed clothes on the floor, suddenly three women arrived. She clearly heard the footsteps as they came through the door of the house. They began talking.

"What's the invalid doing?"

"That old woman is crying in her bed. In a few days she will come with us," the other said.

"Later we'll come for her," responded the first one.

"Let's go to the house of Isabel Bizarro Flores (granny's niece) to see if we can take one of her daughters." The voices could not take Isabel Soto because she wasn't ready to die.

My mother said that she didn't see the women; she only heard their footsteps and voices. Suddenly, their voices faded away. At this instance my granny was asleep. My mother was greatly frightened because she thought the women were *dueñas* of death. About an hour later, my mother recuperated and went to wake us up to tell us what she had heard. She didn't see anyone because the door was closed.

Incredible but true, in three days a child of Isabel Bizarro Flores, a daughter named Juana, died. What my mother heard the voices say turned out to be true, "Let's go to the house of Isabel to see if we can take a daughter." It's a fact that in three days Isabel Bizarro's daughter died—very strange for us.

We are thinking a lot about these things. Perhaps we are mistaken, but what we think is that they are evil (malicious) spirits that come and capture the spirit they find.

It's certain that a spirit of the dead sometimes appears with the ghost two days before the fiesta of the dead that is celebrated on 2 November. A boy by the name of Abraham, son of Juana Vásquez, clearly saw an old man walking in the *sitio* about 6:00 in the afternoon, passing in front of the house and going to the other side. Abraham went to tell his mother, but when she went with him, they didn't see anything. They looked for the old man, but it was impossible to find him.

When the family gathered and talked about what Abraham had seen, they concluded that he had seen the ghost of the deceased Vicente García Pérez, because, when the children of Vicente Pérez asked Abraham what kind of clothing the old man was wearing, Abraham said he was wearing white trousers, *caites* [typical (Indian-style) sandals], a red *sute* [cotton headcloth], and a black wool jacket. This is the same clothing that Vicente always wore. That is the reason for the belief that the dead sometimes appear only to the children because they are innocent of sin. What is most unusual is that the child identified the form of the man and the clothing he was wearing even though the child is scarcely nine years old and Señor Vicente has been dead for 14 years. It's very strange!

Changes in Customs
1 January 1984

Today certain changes in customs have taken place. Before, at 8:00 p.m., the new *alguaciles* and guards, one by one, were brought from their houses by those who were leaving by means of the flute and drum. They were posted in order of the importance of their offices on the porch of the municipality with their new, white clubs. By 11:00 at night, all those leaving and those assuming their offices were united. They embraced and together entered the tribunal in order for the mayor to give them the oath of the office. Then both those entering and those leaving would accompany the mayor and go to the church at midnight. When those whose terms had expired left the church, they were already free. Then they would return to the municipality where they had the right to drink their drinks and dance among themselves as an expression of farewell. The arrival of women was never permitted. When they got drunk, because of the drinks, they formed their groups and went home, being very careful, as they had been for fifteen to twenty years, to show respect for the new *alguaciles* and not lose anyone in the streets. But little by little, this demonstration of respect has fallen by the wayside, especially this year.

There wasn't any marimba. They changed the form of bringing the *alguaciles*. The commissaries, guards, and *alguaciles* met in a private house. At 11 p.m., they presented themselves in the municipality to take possession of their offices. It seems that they are copying the custom of San Martín. They are forgetting the customs of our ancestors, but what can one do? The *principales* were bothered, but they were unable to do anything. They wanted to do the customs as before. There is a saying, "*No hay mal que dure cien años, ni enfermo que los resista* [There's no ailment that lasts a hundred years nor a sick person who endures it; that is, either the sick person dies or gets well, either way there will be a change]."

The *patrulla de autodefensa civil* always guards the town to find out what is happening and to insure that strange hombres don't enter. But since this was a holiday, all the *patrulleros* drank their *tragos* [drinks] until they got drunk. They didn't realize that today at 4:00 in the morning a military ambulance passed through the town coming from Huehuetenango, carrying the body of a soldier originally from San Martín la Laguna. The information says that five soldiers died in an armed confrontation with the subversion. The encounter was on 30 December in Huehuetenango. It resulted in five dead soldiers, all from towns around Lake Atitlán—one from San Martín la Laguna, one from San Luis, one from Panajachel, one from Godínez, and the last from San Diego la Laguna. The cadaver of the *Martinero* they buried in the cemetery of the town at 3:00 p.m. There was much sadness in the town.

On this date, we of the cooperative had a game of soccer with the team, Quetzal, of the same locality. We lost by one goal—7 to 6. It was very curious because my companions certainly have not played soccer for a long time. For about eight years I had dropped soccer, but indeed we still can play a little. The people were most curious, especially the children, because a lot of them had not seen us play soccer. We played very peacefully, without a fuss or insult.

Earlier in Son of Tecún Umán *you said that when you were in the army you played goalie but that you also made a lot of goals. Isn't it difficult for a goalie to make goals?*

Yes, but I also played other positions in which I could make goals.

Pregnant Woman Gives Birth in a Cuadrilla *on the Coast*
2 to 5 January 1984

Earlier I had talked to Antonio Castro and José about a trip to the southern coast to take a *cuadrilla* to pick cotton. Antonio secured the contracts. He just asked me to teach him how to do this work because there were other contractors more able than he. Not to appear egotistical, I agreed, but I told him I would only do it for a few months because I don't have time to take crews to the coast.

During the night that dawned 2 January, I took my turn in the *patrulla de autodefensa civil*. After completing our turns, we drank chocolate and ate bread.

On this day, my friend Antonio came to tell me that he only had Q100. I only had Q130, and my friend José gave us a loan of Q50. So we only had Q280 for the *cuadrilla*.

During the day, I went two times to San Martín to look for a truck. Indeed, I found it, but the owner told me that he could only take the *cuadrilla* to Santa Lucía Cotzumalguapa because on this same day he had to go to carry a cargo of bundles of avocadoes to the capital.

In the afternoon, we gathered a number of workers to pick cotton. A lot of people wanted to work, but since we had little money to give the workers in advance, we weren't able to take many.

On 3 January I got up at 5:00 in the morning and went to San Martín to fetch the transport. Antonio went in one truck to Tzancuil, and I stayed with the other in San José.

We left town at 9:00 a.m. for Santa Lucía Cotz. There we ate lunch. After lunch, we hired a bus, loaded the luggage, and went to the *finca* where we arrived at 3:00 p.m. We were very happy. But the *jefes* were very bad and mistreated us with harsh words.

At 5:00 p.m., the truck with Antonio arrived. Then we went to the Lauseles *finca*, where we left the people in the shed. I had to walk 6 kilometers on foot to tell the administrator. Indeed, this Señor received us with good conditions. But during the night, because of much poverty, more than 500 workers arrived.

We got up at 4:00 a.m. and began to make the list and check the money. Then we went to the office to give them the list. There were a lot of problems with the work because there were too many workers for the amount of cotton to be picked.

In the afternoon of this same day, we went for the first time through the village of Santa Odilia, municipality of Nueva Concepción, to get to know it. We had to take a launch to get to the other side.

At 12:00 midnight, I was very sleepy, but I heard them awake my companion José. He returned at 2:00 a.m. to tell me what had happened. A female miller had begun labor, undoubtedly because of the jarring of the truck over the bad roads. We had been unaware that anyone in the crew was pregnant. We had scarcely spent a day working; there were no midwives.

Because there were many people in the sheds, they went inside the cotton plant (there was no other place to go) where the baby was born at 12:30 a.m., assisted by a man named Luciano Palmer and José. The baby appeared to be normal, but it must have been injured in the ride to the *finca*. It died. The woman, who had separated from her husband, had come to work with her father, a field boss of the crew. Her father went to advise the *finca* of the baby's burial. My friends and I gave them a little money. I just gave Q4.00 to help the señora. Poverty caused the death of this baby, and, also, because we did not realize her condition. It would have been better not to have taken her to the coast. I felt a sadness. I thought it better to quit this kind of work.

I didn't see when or where they buried this baby because we left the farm at 6:00 a.m. We arrived home at 1:30 p.m. I was resting a little when my señora told me that she was very sad because her mother was very seriously ill; she didn't know whether she would live or die. She said that today they again took her to the hospital in Sololá, but the sickness the woman is suffering from is alcoholism.

Día de Reyes (Epiphany, 12th Day): Spirit of Dead Returns
6 January 1984

The *cofrades* [members of the *cofradías*] and catechists passed by, accompanying the image of Jesús and visiting in the houses. We were somewhat happy but constantly thinking about my wife's mother, who had returned from the hospital.

A very unusual thing happened. The news ran throughout the entire town that two days ago the children of Gilberto Tuc saw Señor Santiago García Cruz inside their house, but this señor has been dead for five months. The boys say that they saw Señor Santiago putting on his shoes near the bed, and suddenly he disappeared. They fell to the floor, shouting and trembling. The parents of these children were in the church in a spiritual retreat. A neighbor lady went to call the parents, and only then did the children talk and tell them what they had seen. They say that it's certain that in this house there was a pair of shoes that belonged to the deceased Santiago García Cruz. When he died, he left a lot of clothing and shoes, which were given to relatives, which is why Gilberto Tuc had the shoes.

There was a lot of talk about this event. They say that the spirit of the fallen was not able to enter heaven because when he was in this [present] life he was very mean to the people and he was egotistical. Others say that one should not give away things of the dead because they get angry. Others say the spirit of the dead should be helped with prayers so that it will not continue appearing to the living. My thought is that Señor Santiago used the shoes a lot and they were his, and the children knew they were his. Without doubt, they saw the ghost of the deceased because the Bible says that always the ghosts of the dead appear.

There is communication among the ill. When my grandmother was unconscious because of her illness, lying in her bed about 11:00 a.m., she suddenly began to talk. A voice came to her saying, "Buenas tardes, *comadre* [woman friend]," and my granny answered with the same words. When she opened her eyes, she was shouting for us to bring a chair to her *comadre* so that she could sit with her, but there was no one there. On this same day and at the same hour, we met the husband of my mother-in-law, who was in the hospital at the time, and he told us that the patient had remembered her *comadre*. But more clearly it was 11:00 a.m. when my grandmother remembered her *comadre* (my mother-in-law). Also, at the same time my mother-in-law in the hospital had remembered my granny. I don't know if this is clear because this was like a communication in spirit because my grandmother was in San José la Laguna and my mother-in-law was in the hospital in Sololá. It's true that the spirit wanders when one is sick.

At 7:00 p.m. the whole town gathered to hear the speech of the national army. They said this speech was important for the working people and that they are looking for peace in this town. Also, if there are guerrillas in this town, they should be apprehended before they place the town in danger. However, we have observed that in the town there are no guerrillas. All the *Joseños* live poorly, but never are they guerrillas. It's true that we have faults, but they are common ones.

On 8 January, I was fast asleep when about 12:30 a.m. I suddenly woke up when I heard the door of the big house, where we have the bread counter, open two times. I clearly heard that someone was inside. I thought about going to see, but I changed my mind because I thought it might be some evil thieves. I didn't leave the house in which I was sleeping, but it bothered me. I didn't get up until 4:30, when it dawned 9 January. When I opened the door, everything was in order; nothing was lost. Perhaps some spirit entered the house.

Constructing New Latrines for the New School
8 January 1984

On this day, the children made the bread. I just helped them with part of the work. All day I worked for the cooperative, putting in order 84 contracts for associates obtaining fertilizer on credit.

As president of the board, I presented before all the associates the problem of the children in the new school and the suffering of the neighbors. When they built the new school, those in charge of the work didn't think it was important. They dug a latrine only two meters deep. With so many children, it filled up, and foul odors penetrated inside the classrooms and the houses of the unfortunate neighbors that were near the school.

The school has windows, but since the government didn't finish the work, no glass was put in the windows. When the sun is hot and the wind blows a lot, the bad odors enter the classrooms. I smelled them myself when I twice visited the children in the sixth grade. I talked with some neighbors who said that the smells, which penetrate the *ranchos* [rustic houses], are horrible and abominable. When they consulted with the mayor, he told them they had to bear it and if they insisted with their complaints, they would soon be consigned to a military detachment. This was the solution the major offered to the inhabitants.

It was thus when the teachers called me to witness how the students were suffering. I told the teachers that first I was going to tell all the associates because they too had children in the school. Thus in the afternoon of this day I met all the members of the cooperative to get their approval to dig new pits for the latrine of the children. Most of them approved, and I told them that on Thursday, 12 January, we would begin digging the pits because the children and the neighbors have been suffering since the year of 1982.

Each associate had to lend a hand to dig the pits and to give money for the construction of the house over the latrine.[13] Not all of the associates gave money, but a portion of each associate's loan was held out in the quantity of Q4 for the buying of cement, lime, wire, a little *lámina*, and money for a mason. The adobe we made ourselves. We didn't finish this task until the month of March. Both the children and those who lived nearby were very content and appreciative, although some associates were bothered by the work. For this job, the cooperative received a diploma of honor, awarded by the committee of control and the committee of education. With all the days' wages and money, it only cost Q600.

Harvesting Corn in Tzarayá
9 January 1984

I got up at 5:00 a.m. and arranged my nets and other things. Ramoncito, Ignacito, and I ate breakfast and then we went near Tzarayá to harvest corn. In the afternoon, we went to the village of Tzarayá to buy bread and eggs. For the night, we ate bread and coffee. We slept in the milpa. We made a big fire because the cold was immense. We were tired because the place where we planted corn is sloping. One has to have patience to extract the corn. We made a *champa* [little hut with a roof] of corn stalks and slept in the field to guard the corn from thieves.

At 6:00 a.m. we got up, made coffee, cooked eggs, warmed *tamalitos* [little tamales], and ate. For lunch we had fresh fish, a lot of tortillas, and coffee. With four beasts, we transported the corn. I paid Q27 for the animals and *mozos*. This does not include the expense of food or my wages. Indeed, we earned a bit with the harvest of corn. We arrived at 5:30 p.m., and I bathed with hot water. I didn't eat dinner because I felt sick to my stomach.

A Drowning and Accusation of Murder: A Sad Case of a Young Man
10 to 11 January 1984

They say that at 2:00 in the afternoon of 10 January Martín Ixtamer Vásquez, a sixth grade student, drowned. This boy was the son of the most prominent fisherman, Alejandro Ixtamer. The deceased was also a professional fisherman, but no one knows why he fell out of his canoe. He did not shout when he fell, and his companions were unaware of it. A brother named Juan Ixtamer was fishing in another canoe, but he had not noticed either. The brother saw that the canoe was drifting. When he caught up to his brother's canoe, he saw his brother in the brightness of the sun, but deep in the bottom of the lake. He went to advise his parents, but they didn't believe him because they are all experts at handling canoes and fishing. Then many people of San José and San Martín went to try to find the cadaver, but it was impossible.

In this same afternoon they took to jail Sr. José Coché. They say that this señor is an enemy of the young drowned man and by the accusation of his father, they jailed him. There's a lot of sadness in the town. There's also a division among the people (two groups). One group was in favor of the deceased, and the other group was for the señor that they put in jail because he is an honorable man and worker. It isn't known exactly why he's suspected.

Since an early hour today, 11 January, all fishermen of San José and San Martín, military commissioners, and other collaborators were on the lake looking for the body. At 9:00 a.m. the body was found at a depth of 11 meters. It was taken out by some boys of San Martín. The cadaver was put in a *salón*. The authorities directed that the dead person be taken to Sololá for an autopsy, according to law.

To collaborate, we went to San Martín to look for a truck to carry the deceased. Señor Emilio Dardón agreed to make the trip for Q100. We brought the truck, but when we arrived in San José, the parents and a good group of *Joseños* asked the justice of peace to bury the body without informing the authorities in Sololá. We were very appreciative. We just paid the señor Q10, and the truck returned to San Martín. We went to open the grave. None of the *mayordomos* was there. All of them had gone to the coast.

The burial of Martín took place at 5:00 p.m. A young, good friend of everyone, who was very religious, was lost. The municipality had prepared an inauguration of the new school, but now it was not done because of the death of the young Martín Ixtamer.

Inauguration of the Instituto Básico
12 January 1984

In 1981 and 1982, we had dealt with the teachers and the mayor to try to establish an *instituto básico* that the town still didn't have. For two years I went with the teachers to look for a number of 20 students, minimum, required to establish it. It's a pity that the municipality didn't help us, and all was lost. Although the teachers from San Martín had agreed to give the classes and the municipality had agreed to pay the Q200 fee in accordance with the law, it was completely impossible because many parents didn't help us to get the 20 students needed to obtain authorization from the ministry of education. Lamentably, the parents told us that they didn't have money to pay the Q5 monthly fee for their children to study. Thus it remained. No one could do anything.

Since a number of parents had weakened and it would be a lot of work for the teachers, the latter, in the beginning of January, didn't want to fulfill their obligations in establishing the institute. The fifth of January was the ultimatum that the teachers and the supervisor gave us to get the minimum number of students for the founding. If we didn't have the required number by the end of the night, on the sixth day there would not be the opportunity of creating the said institute. Unfortunately, many of the parents who had children that already had graduated from the sixth grade had gone to the coast to pick cotton. Only four of the parents accompanied me to complete the required number of 20. It took us until 11:00 p.m. to finally get the number and draft the official communiqué to send to the supervisor for his approval and to set a date for an inauguration. Only three teachers helped make the document. They were the teachers from Totonicapán, not from San Martín. Also, the mayor stayed until this hour. We had to collect the money for travel for two of the teachers to take the papers to Guatemala [City].

On 10 January they had told us for sure there would be an inauguration of the new *instituto básico* on Wednesday, the 11th, but owing to our not being organized and the death of Ixtamer Vásquez, it wasn't. It's true that there had been a committee, but five members of this committee had been on the coast. But by the grace of God, my friends, Francisco, Bernardo, Roberto, and José didn't abandon me. We struggled a lot. They helped me organize the inauguration.

Thus was the inauguration of the new school, *Instituto Básico por Cooperativa "Joseña"*.[14] The date was 12 January 1984. In the afternoon of this day, there were five hours of a marimba sponsored by the municipality to enliven the acts and to announce to the citizenry that there is something new in town. We, the friends and parents of the students, prepared a refreshment. I myself gave large pastries to the representatives the government. The dinner was in the house of our friend Alfelfo Ujpán García.

In the act of inauguration, they gave me a part in the activities. The teachers and supervisors introduced me because of the fight I have made for this new institute. I said words to inspire the youngsters—that all should rise to the occasion and not one be left behind. There was much happiness, but some were bothered—they think that I have a personal interest, but my intention was for the community. Francisco and Bernardo behaved a little bad toward me only because they were unable to do these things. I think that if they are intelligent, both they and I will be able to do something for our town. One day I'm going to arrange for them to make a contribution so that the people will thank them too. Also, some students do not care about what we are doing because they are studying in distant towns.

What did you say at the inauguration?

I only wanted to be grateful for all the effort to accomplish what we had done. In the first place, I said:

> Señor Municipal Mayor, Señor Secretary, good evening. I want to thank you, in the name of my town, San José, for all the struggle and effort in one form or another in helping us, the parents, to acquire the founding of this basic institute.

Señor Supervisor of middle education from the center of San Luis, I want to thank you for the gesture of going to Guatemala [City] for the foundation of this new *instituto* here in this town of San José. It's the first time in the history that we will see our sons and daughters study middle education.

Also, I want to thank the teachers who will impart their classes in this *instituto*, for the collaboration they will offer our children is worth much more because they will not yet receive a salary on behalf of the state. I know that they will collaborate for one or two years until the government authorizes a salary for them. Señores Teachers, forgive us for the small payment that the parents will give to you. It's the salary of Q5 for each child for each month. At the same time I want to exhort that we are here to help you with anything that our children need and to see what we can do so that our *instituto* will not be cancelled by the government. Then, I also said to the parents:

Señores Parents, I want to thank each one of you for your effort. We have traveled many times to San Luis, and also we have had problems with the teachers. But thanks to God, that from a pain, He gave us a joy. I know when it was initiated it was a problem from the beginning with the teachers in the town. But thanks to the understanding of the teachers and of us parents, we have taken advantage of founding today an *instituto básico*. I urge each parent to send his or her children so that they can study because a good deed must be taken from an opportunity. Now we have here the establishment, or *instituto*, but if we do not send our children, what will we gain? If we want to have a change for the people in the future, we need to send our children so that they study. And I want to encourage all that have children in the fourth, fifth, or sixth grades to send them to school, especially those that have children who will graduate this year from the sixth grade. Enroll your sons and daughters in the *instituto* so that each day they will be obtaining new knowledge. Thank you very much for your attention.

My name is in the document of inauguration for collaborating. The document is in the municipality and a copy in the institute.

Visit of Bishop Benando Gálvez
28 January 1984

Since September I have been collaborating with the Catholic Church for the reception of the bishop of Sololá. At 10:00 a.m. the religious groups began to decorate the streets with carpets of natural and artificial flowers. We committee members just coordinated the efforts, and we met to adorn the front (atrium) of the church and collect the donations for the mass.

By 2:00 p.m. the streets were decorated. With everything completely ready, we organized the people in two files, one of women and one of men in order to show more respect. I gave a speech to the congregation, exhorting, "Forget envy, hatred, and discrimination. Follow the advice of Jesucristo who said, 'Peace I give you, peace I offer you.' May the peace of the Lord be with each one of us."

The bishop arrived at 4:00 p.m. and celebrated a solemn mass. There were a large number of people confirmed. Everything was over at 6:30 p.m. We spent only Q39.50 on flowers and Q25 on the mass. Eighty-two quetzales and thirty-five centavos were left over from the donations so we gave it to the treasurer of Catholic Action. The committee paid for the *bombas*. Everything turned out well, and not a single centavo was lost.

Soliciting Books for the Institute
29 January 1984

On this day, we had a very amazing trip to Santa Bárbara to speak to a religious person of Spanish origin named Ignacio. The reason that we went was to solicit some books for the library of the institute.

Francisco, Bernardo, José, and I left San José at 9:00 a.m. We talked with Brother Ignacio. By the grace of God, he gave us hope that we could get books. He gave us a lot of addresses of bookstores where one can ask for books. This señor gave us 24 pencils as a gift for each student. It was very pleasant. When we returned, we had to eat lunch in Santa Ana. We arrived in town at 3:30 p.m.

On Terrorism and Fincas
31 January to 2 February 1984

This was an unforgettable day. I went to the southern coast where I had contracted work crews to say good-bye to my friends, the *jefes* of the *finca*, and cancel my name as a contractor. I will go no more to the coast. In these times, there are many terrorists just going around persecuting working people. The terrorists have killed many contractors, saying they are doing it because the contractors continue taking crews to the *fincas*. They say that when the contractors have quit taking *cuadrillas* to the *fincas*, the terrorists will become the owners. Also, they say that when *cuadrillas* are no longer brought to the farms, the terrorists will leave. Moreover, I realized that with these jobs on the farms, the poor person is never able to find a better life because the millionaire continues hoarding more and more millions of quetzales while the poor remain each day with very bad wages, eating, dressing, and sleeping poorly. They say there is a law of minimum wage of Q3.20 a day, but what happens with the *finqueros* is that they pay Q3.25 for a *tarea* [job] that the poor person takes three days to complete. Then it's true to say that the poor continue to be exploited by the big millionaires.

Another thing that the terrorists say is that they are in favor of the poor, but these are lies—they look out for their own interests. They have killed honorable people to rob their money, and in this case they are not in favor of the poor. Between these two groups, there is no understanding. The rich kill the poor with heavy work, and the terrorists kill honorable people. For that reason it's worth saying that these two groups have no understanding. That is when I decided to quit working on the coast. I felt that continuing to take *cuadrillas* to the farms is very dangerous for the workers and also very dangerous for me.

On 1 February I left the coast at 4:00 a.m., arriving in San Luis at 10:00 a.m. There we ate in the market. When we arrived at the shore of the lake, there had been many military personnel. There were about 300 soldiers that had been searching for guerrillas around San Luis. The owners of the launches were obligated to take the soldiers to Panajachel. That is why the passengers were abandoned in San Luis. The owner had to conform. The boats carried the military toward Panajachel.

I was able to go on the launch as a helper since the owner of the launch wanted us to give him some company. Since our boat wasn't very large, only 43 boarded. Thus we went to Panajachel. For me it was very pleasant, but for the owner of the launch, it was very distressing because they didn't pay him for the trip. They did, however, give him fuel. When we returned, a strong wind caught us, and we nearly sank. At 3:00 p.m., I arrived in San José.

Can you explain your reasons more for quitting contracting?

For many years I worked on the coast. My wife and I suffered a lot working on the farms. We worked as *jornaleros* on the Caoba, Pacaja, and San José del Carmen farms. Also, I planted milpa at Memoria, Las Flores, and Chipo. I suffered a lot during the years that I was working—eating poorly, eating tortillas and *tamalones* [large tamales that may last 8 to 12 days], drinking dirty water from the rivers, and sleeping under the trees.

When Andrés Bizarro and I began to make contracts, we worked honorably. We paid our helpers, legally conforming to the amount they worked. At times we drank *tragos* because the work of the contractor is very complicated. Working with people is very delicate—the people have different customs, different ideas, and different habits. When you combine these three things, the contractor has to accept these conditions. The contractor has to look for a mechanism to find a solution for the person. It's the same thing for the worker as for the *jefes* of the *fincas*. A contractor needs to be a conscientious and respectful person because he also works with women of different habits who make love for money and who drink and gossip. Many contractors fail just because they lose the respect of the other workers.

At times I helped on the Caoba, Pacaja, and San Juan las Bordas farms. I worked just as a peon in Santa Canderia, Totonicapán, Esquipulitas, and La Molta. But more than the others, I worked on Pangola, Pangolita, Los Alamos, San Marcos Niza, and El Carmen.

I worked as a contractor for ten to eleven years. It's certain that it's a kind of work with much suffering because at times there are good *jefes* and at times bad ones. Also, the worker has problems in the field because the work is very bad. The worker talks to the contractor for a solution to labor problems. Then the contractor consults with the field boss, then the administrator, and then the supervisor of labor. If these *jefes* have some compassion, they consider raising the price of the load. Then the contractor returns to the workers to tell them whether the price has been raised. If the *jefes* are bad, the contractor cannot find relief for his people. It's true that there are bad *jefes*. In all the time that I was working as a contractor, I only met a few administrators who understood the needs of the poor people well: Marcos Ponce (one year in Pangolita and a year in Tolimán); Gerardo Fuentes and his son-in-law, Pedro (one year in Niza and El Carmen); and Juan Jorge Ramos Corzo, a Spaniard on the Alamo farm (just for one year). A contractor could talk with them. The rest were stupid.

I quit the work on the farms most of all because of the violence—the terrorists persecute the contractors. They don't want the contractors to take *cuadrillas* to the farms; they don't want anyone to work with the *finqueros*. And when the *fincas* are abandoned, the terrorists say that they are going to distribute the land to the poor. Who knows?

The people who worked with me when I was a contractor now are working for themselves. Some work for others, but now they hardly go to the *fincas*. They used the money well that they earned in the *cuadrillas* and bought themselves some *cuerdas* of land. They planted coffee, and they are now harvesting it. They also built their little houses. It's true that they don't live well, but for the most part, they have a place to stay.

I did the same. I built my two little houses and bought some *cuerdas* of land. By the grace of God, I get along well with the *Joseños, Martineros, San Beniteños* [people of San Benito], and the people from Tzancuil.

On the Pangolita *finca*, the guerrillas were looking for me to kill me. It was the same on the Los Alamos *finca*. Many times they tried to kill me, but with the help of God, I was free of these bad people. I slept in one house one night and changed the house where I slept for the next night. I did this to make money, entering on one side and leaving by another. I had a lot of problems because the money with which I worked belonged to others. Of the people who lent me the money to advance to the *cuadrillas*, one, Rudy Rivera, has already died. The others are Miguel Tuc Ixtamer, Elena Ixtamer, and Alfonso García. Sometimes the cooperative lent me money.

With the help of God and my efforts, I paid everyone. I don't owe any of them, although Lucas, the transporter, asked me if he could lend me money. Now I tell him, "No, I have ended my life on the coast."

Earlier in a letter to me you said that you thought the finqueros *were oppressing the poor. Do you remember what you said?*

No more on the coast for me. I understand a lot of things. The *finqueros* are very much oppressing the indigenous people. They put a very heavy work load. At times the poor person works 10 to 12 hours to earn a daily wage.

That was the way it was when they formed the group of subversion. Now the subversives oppress the *finqueros*. Many have died. The guerrillas have reasons because they always are helping the poor people against the repression of the *finqueros*, who would be treating the people much worse without the guerrillas. There's just one thing—I don't like the use of arms!

Sometimes the people would say, "Ignacio, go look for work on the coast!"

And I would say, "No, I don't want to," because I was a little afraid. But they would oblige me, and out of my own necessity I would go out because I needed the money. The poor women with their babies suffered a lot in the trucks. The roads are bad. In reality the situation in our country is very delicate. Now we contractors don't have problems with the army. The army helps us because we are working people. The ones who chase us are the guerrillas because they don't want us to take people to the *fincas*. They want to eliminate the *finqueros* and keep their lands. Because of that, the guerrillas searched a lot for us. For that reason I was a little afraid to risk my life with those people. I had to abandon my work on the coast.

During the night of this same day (1 February), I met with the rest of the parents of the students of the *instituto básico* to organize a committee of friends of the institute. We met in the house of Señor Donaldo Ramos Asturias. Everyone talked about the necessity to organize the committee. Also, *profesor* [teacher] Fausto de Dios Flores met with us. But for me, it was not good. It's certain that I am in agreement with enlivening the organization of the committee, but what happened is that my *compañeros* saw that I have an interest in the institute and named me president of the committee. The truth is that with all my other obligations I was unable. Knowing that Señor Martín Yojcom García is eager to hold some office, I recommended him as president. But the committee chose him as vice-president and me president.

On 2 February at 8:00 p.m., the committee members and the señores met in the municipality to legalize the committee. Donaldo Ramos and I spoke, but the señor mayor didn't understand us until we told him in Tzutuhil the reason for our going to the municipality. Not until then did he understand and ask if we wanted to legalize the committee. Everyone answered yes. Those present felt good, but I didn't because it's just another obligation. The señores of the municipality said that we were going to wait until next Monday night at 8:00 to endorse the act in the presence of the municipality and then later to legalize the committee in the presence of the departmental government of Sololá. Also, the mayor and the military commissioner said they would become advisors to the committee being formed.

Godparents, Guerrillas, and School
3 to 5 February 1984

In the afternoon, my wife and I went to San Martín to buy a small pair of trousers and a shirt for a baby, who is going to be baptized on Sunday. It's the custom that each godparent has to give a little gift for his godchild as a token of being godparents.

In San Martín, they are talking about another Rebuli bus that was burned during the day. This act was committed in Santa Alicia where the road divides for the coast and Godínez. Also, the information says that they killed a famous assistant of the military commissioners, Eduardo Portillo.

Those unfamiliar with the process of education have done some bad things. In the same new school building where the children of primary school are receiving classes, other children are receiving classes of *básico*. Students in *básico* do not begin their classes until 2:00 p.m. and do not finish until 7:00 at night. Instead of supporting the students, the mayor of our town turned off the electricity, saying that using the electricity caused more expenses for the municipality. I don't believe one hour of electricity is much of a daily expense. Since the students were without electricity, we had to go to the mayor to tell him to turn it back on, and he promised that he would do so soon.

On 4 February we began to make bread at 6:00 p.m. and continued until 1:00 a.m., 5 February. As the day broke, we were giving thanks to God, and we went to the church for the mass. After mass, the baby, Wilson Gregorio Bizarro Pichijay, was baptized. His parents are Diego Bizarro and Faena Cuc. The father of this baby belongs to the Central American [Protestant] Church, but he baptized his little boy in the Catholic Church. After the baptism, they invited us to their house to eat lunch together. I bought a little beer and some shots of *aguardiente* [firewater, sugar cane rum], which cost Q7.20. When lunch was finished, we went home. We were happy.

Also, today was the anniversary of the group, Alcoholics Anonymous, Camino de la Felicidad [Path of Happiness]. These friends invited me to celebrate with them, but I wasn't able to because of the baptism. A mass was celebrated for the members of Alcoholics Anonymous. With them was a North American priest named Samuel. The priest is indeed worthy because he knows how to give good advice in the mass.

Soldiers Visit
6 February 1984

All day I worked making bread until 5:00 p.m. As we had arranged yesterday, today was supposed to be the day of legalizing the committee, Friends of the Institute. But I don't know why the mayor is not sincere. Again they told us that we would not draw up the *acta* [memorandum of action, official document] until Wednesday.

On this day, a lot of soldiers came into the whole town. But by the grace of God, nothing happened. They say that the soldiers are very bad, but here one is seeing that neither the soldiers nor the residents are bothering anyone. Both extremes are behaving well (civilians and military).

On this day, there are two students less in the institute. Already they are not continuing with classes. No one knows why.

How many soldier were there, and what were they doing?

About 100 to 125. They went to the mountains just to patrol them to see if there were guerrillas.

Legalizing the Committee for the Instituto Básico
8 February 1984

On this day an *acta* was drawn up before the municipality to legalize the committee, Friends of the Institute. It was nice, but who knows if what was said is going to be done? On Friday there will be a trip to Sololá to legalize the committee with the departmental government. After drawing up the *acta*, we ate bread with coffee.

Husbands Who Don't Appreciate Their Wives
10 February 1984

We have bad husbands who don't know how to appreciate their wives. It happened in the case of Señora Susana Ixtamer Sumoza, who belongs to the Central American Church. Her husband is Jaime Vásquez. Señora Susana had a baby 11 days ago, and the señora became sick. The parents of this woman called the doctor for a cure who said that it would be better to send her to the hospital because the sickness was very serious. But the ungrateful husband didn't want to send her to the hospital, saying it was better if she died so that he would be able to have another woman. It's certain that the woman died and left the baby.

Can you explain a little more about the husband who mistreated his wife?

Yes, it was a case that always occurs in the indigenous family, doesn't it? Sometimes we are too irresponsible, like what occurred with this marriage, right? The poor woman suffered much. She would go out to gather wood and to work in the field. The husband would also work. But, what happened was that the husband was very sorry. He would dress up a lot, buying good clothes and good shoes, but he would not buy food for his woman. That's why the woman fell very ill with the first son that she had. Then, she recuperated. When another little boy was born, she fell ill again. Since the woman was giving birth every two years and had a third child, a girl, she did not recuperate because she was suffering severe malnutrition. The doctor told them to take her to the hospital in Sololá to buy her medicine to put serum [IV fluid] in her blood. The ungrateful husband, however, didn't want to cure his wife, and he didn't take her. She died. Then the baby girl was given away to some relatives. Now she is big. The husband still lives, but he has another woman. There is always, though, the law of life. He's a little *jodido* [screwed up]. He's suffering now. That young man, or man, I should say because he's now about 30 years old, every little bit gets sick. Since his wife died, he has come back three times from the hospital in Sololá. Maybe it's the law of compensation because he mistreated his wife.

Trip to Sololá to Legalize the Committee
14 February 1984

We went to Sololá to legalize the committee in the presence of the departmental government. For the honorariums, they charged us Q12. They told us in the future they would give us credentials but for the authorization of the committee we had to agree to raise an amount of Q10,000 for the purchase of the property for the construction of a separate building for the *instituto básico*. But who knows when or in how many years?

Will Q10,000 buy both the property and the building?

The *sitio* alone will cost Q10,000. The building will cost at least Q25,000.

My Friend Francisco Refuses to Collaborate as a Secret Military Commissioner

19 February 1984

It was very nice for the first time in the history of the town. The students of the *instituto básico* left toward Santa Bárbara to take part in a sports event of basketball and soccer with the students of that town. The students of San José came out winners; more precisely, the boys won and the girls lost.

On this same date, we went to the soccer field to amuse ourselves a little. While doing this, my friend Francisco told me that he was called by the military commissioner to be included as a collaborator of a secret investigation of different organizations to see whether the people say bad things about the army or against the military government. This friend told me to take more care in the meetings of the cooperative because it's certain that in San José there are three men who are collaborating as secret agents. Francisco told me that he didn't want to do it because he was afraid.

On this date, a lot soldiers of a mobile detachment arrived and occupied the building of the old municipality. Always we are living in fear.

What were they doing?

They were looking for guerrillas. Two hundred soldiers were in the field.

Bookkeeper of FEDECCON Assassinated

20 February 1984

David and I left San José for Guatemala [City] to make an inquiry in the Federación Guatemalteca de Cooperativas de Consumo [FEDECCON, Guatemalan Federation of Cooperatives of Consumption]. They say that the cooperative has bad (late) credit. They sent us a telegram to pay soon, but we are ignorant of the reason because our cooperative does not have any outstanding debt. Thanks to God, when we arrived at the federation, we asked about an inquiry. When the director looked in the loan book, he didn't find any pending debts of the cooperative. The doubt is with the cooperative of San Luis. He told us that things were in a mess since the bookkeeper, Amparo Graciela (a woman) was captured and assassinated. The same agent told us the bloody act was investigated by agents of the United States. They say it was done by groups of the right. When this errand was finished, we took the bus to Santa Ana, arriving home on the same day.

Selling Bread in San Jorge
25 February 1984

After finishing baking, we took Q75 worth of French bread and sweet bread to San Jorge for a private reception of a female indigenous teacher of that town who had earned her diploma for teaching. It was very nice.

School Commission and Registering Citizens to Vote
1 March 1984

They named me for a commission to San Luis to leave a petition with the supervisor of teachers. The reason for the petition was to ask the supervisor to name an Indian teacher, Isabel Ixtamer, director of the *instituto básico*. She was the only one who thinks a little better than the others for the good of the institute. But when I arrived in San Luis, the supervisor had gone to Guatemala [City]. I was only able to see the señor secretary. This was a little funny. A teacher had elaborated in the petition, but hadn't put down the place of origin nor the date. When we realized this, the secretary became a little annoyed.

On this date there was an order from the departmental government in Sololá that everyone must be registered on the electoral roll in order to really find out how many citizens there are in each town. They said that the enrollment will serve greatly to avoid fraud in future presidential elections and that the frauds began in the time of Colonel Arana.

Also, here they are registering all those of the town and the villages. They are causing fear because they are saying those who are not registered will be taken as subversives for disobeying orders.

History of the Assembly of God Church
4 March 1984

On this date, Señora Rosanda Temó, wife of the deceased Agustín Sumoza Bizarro, died. Tito Paredes and I interviewed this family in the year of 1972. I can't remember whether in 1971 Señor Sexton and I also interviewed this family. There is a good story about these two dead persons. My granny talked about when earlier Esteban Morán, Héctor Có Mirón, Agustín Sumoza, and his wife Rosanda Temó had struggled a lot to establish the Central American Church in this town of San José la Laguna. Who would know what problems they would have in the Central American Church? Don Agustín and Doña Rosanda themselves gave a house for the congregation *Pentecostés de América*. That was the name of a new church. They tried to establish it in San José, but they didn't attract anyone so it was not founded. That was in 1958, 1959, and 1960. Later, they rejoined the Central American Church. Still later they changed again because they thought about renting a house with Señor Pablo Temó. There they formed the congregation of the Assembly of God. Don Agustín and Doña Rosanda always had it in their heads that they were old folks but were setting an example by fighting for the welfare of a lot of others. With the help of the church of San Martín and San Jorge, they succeeded in getting a pastor and establishing the legal capacity of the church of the Assembly of God. With the help of the mission of the Assembly of God of the North Americans, who gave them money to buy the *sitio* and contributed their labor, they were able to construct the Liorio de los Valles Church of God.

I remember in 1975 and 1976 Don Agustín Sumoza and Doña Rosanda Temó worked very hard for the construction of the church. Don Agustín carried stones and worked as a mason's assistant, and Doña Rosanda transported stone and sand for the same work. Now, mercifully, they are resting. I went to the burial of the deceased Rosanda, but I didn't go to the burial of Don Agustín because I had gone to the coast.

Stuccoing the House
7 March 1984

We bought lime and cement. We are thinking about stuccoing a little of the house. We don't have the money to plaster all of it, and for that reason we will do just the inside to avoid scorpions.[15] The mason is Señor Ignacio Sánchez Hernández. We will pay him Q2.50 a day, and we are going to be his helpers.

On this date, we said our good-byes to the teacher, Bruno, who is going to work in the capital city. I invited him for a dinner, but he didn't come. Other friends, however, indeed came.

Buying Land, María's Birthday,
and an Order for Literacy
8 to 11 March 1984

I bought a small piece of land, one-half *cuerda*, with the money that my great friend James D. Sexton sent me.

This is the 15th birthday of my daughter María. My señora fixed tamales, and that is what we ate at noon for lunch, poorly but contentedly.

On this same date, the supervisor of San Luis came to give the order that everyone who is illiterate will have to learn to read and write. In the afternoon, the teachers had a meeting with the supervisor in which they named the new director of the *instituto básico*. Thanks to the understanding of the supervisor, they named *profesora* Isabel Ixtamer as director. In the middle of the afternoon, we ate dinner with the director and other teachers and friends, very happily.

For three days, I have been sad because when we went to pick coffee in Chimucuní I lost my wristwatch. I searched for it, but couldn't find it. Not until Monday, the 11th, did José find it. When he returned, he gave me the watch. Only then did I feel happy, and I promised José that I would give him a shirt as a reward.

The Mayor, Problems with San Martín, and Strangers in Town
16 to 20 March 1984

We have problems with the mayor, Andrés Bizarro, according to some news that is circulating through the whole town. It says that the mayor already has made a compromise with San Martín la Laguna to give them another headwater of a small river. This is the source of a river where one can make a tank and place pipes. The mayor took a bribe and promised the *Martineros* that they will receive another river. The mayor is only looking out for his own interest without giving any importance to the growth of the town. San José also needs more water because we are many and are lacking water. At times we spend two or three days without water in the homes. [The statutes of the cooperative say that the tribunal must help solve problems of the town, and the water was one]. This was the reason that Ignacio Cuéllar and I went to the office of the mayor to tell him that he will suffer the consequences from the residents, that he has no cause to do things behind the backs of the people, that he is only a de facto mayor who was not elected by the people, and that so as not to have serious things happen in the town, to suspend this project with the *Martineros*. He became angry with us. According to extrajudicial news, the mayor already had received Q1,000 as a bribe. Upset, he told us that we aren't God's children because we don't want to help our neighboring town.

On 20 March the situation was very delicate. In town was a group of strangers. Who knows if they are of the right or the left? They were in the street close to my house. I was very scared. I thought that perhaps they were going to break into my house. I just thought about God inside the house. Finally, they continued on the road to San Martín.

Trip to Hospital, Controversial Loan from USAID, and Terrorism
21 to 23 March 1984

I was working half the day making bread. Later at 4:35 p.m. we left in a friend's car to take Ignacio Arnaldo, who was very sick with his thumb, to Panajachel. On the road from San Luis to Godínez, three times we nearly ran into barrancas because the ground was covered with rain water and fog. By the grace of God, we arrived in Panajachel.

When we arrived, we first went to the volunteer firemen. But they said to take him to the hospital in Sololá. Our friend left us at the emergency room, and then we returned to Panajachel to the Santa Marta Inn to spend the night because it was very cold in Sololá.

On this same date the cooperative of consumption, Flor de Café, legally changed its name to Flor Joseña. All of the other associates drank and went to have lunch in Chuitinamit. There was a fiesta.

Why did you change the name?

"Coffee" in the name implied that it was an agricultural cooperative, but the cooperative is only of consumption and thus the name change.

We got up at 6:00 in the morning on Thursday, 22 March. We had coffee with Antonio Cholotío Canajay and then went by car to Santa Cruz del Quiché where we ate in a *comedor* [small restaurant]. But this trip had no value. We made it because the coordinator had told us that a meeting was to be at 1:00 in the afternoon about a gift for the highland cooperatives for sowing just corn, beans, and potatoes and not other cultivations. When they gave us the statement, it said that the Instituto Nacional de Cooperativas [INACOP, National Institute of Cooperatives] received a donation from USAID of five million quetzales for the departments that are very affected by subversion. All the associates of the cooperative and I thought that this was good for the indigenous peoples.

I always had the preoccupation to know how the work is done on the project, and I asked the manager, "When is it possible for the cooperatives to receive the money?"

"Possibly in two years," the *jefe* told me.

"Why the meeting now and the project not until two years?" I replied. "Is the money already in Guatemala or is it still in the United States?"

He told me that the money is already in Guatemala, that they had already used about a Q1 million for the payment of the chiefs and technicians, that they were spending another million for the *jefes* of INACOP, and that the loan for the cooperative would not be until 1986.

"Why is it like that? Why do you waste the money if that money is not the *jefes'* nor the technicians'? Rather it is for the project of planting potatoes, corn, and beans.

"We don't know," the manager told me, "We are just paid. The ones who dispose of the loan are the *jefes*, so be patient. Right now we are going to sign an act so that all of you will be in agreement to receive the loan. But I think within two years you will receive it," said the señor.

At this meeting I made three protests about what I didn't like. I'm the only one who didn't sign the act because first they said that they are already spending part of the money for the *jefes* and the technicians, and for the crops nothing would be spent until two years from now. The document says that it is for the help of the affected departments! But this is a lie because they are not going to do anything for two years and what are the people going to eat? We need it this year. It would be better to give this money to the people, who can't last this year to sow corn in 1984. The politics of the technicians and the *jefes* are that they are taking a lot of time to carry out the project. While they earn a lot of money, the cooperatives are in need; that is to say, the cooperatives aren't important. I didn't sign this act. I was the only one who protested there. The majority wanted to sign because they thought that they were going to be given money. Maybe they finished it. This is our situation for the moment.

Was this a loan?

No. It's a donation, or better yet a gift, for the poorer people. Lamentably, the *jefes* are the ones who consumed it.

The gift was intended for the cooperatives?

It was for the cooperatives of the towns most affected by the violence.

Why did the jefes *want the people to sign the act?*

The *jefes* and the technicians are spending it. They wanted the act signed because it would look good to USAID. But until now, and we are in the year of 1987, that money has never been seen.[16] Maybe they finished it. This is our situation for the moment.

When we were in Santa Cruz del Quiché we heard on the radio, Fabulosa of Guatemala, that in the jurisdiction of Chicacao, Suchitepéquez there was a confrontation between the military and the terrorists. The news said that 10 soldiers and an official of the national army died. There was much fear, but there was no news as to whether a terrorist died, perhaps not. When the radio reported the news, the people went home afraid. By afternoon a person already was unable to walk around; also the businesses closed. Then we went to stay in an inn.

On 23 March we left the inn and took a bus to Los Encuentros and then to Sololá, where we ate breakfast. There I certified a letter for Dr. Sexton. Then I went down to the hospital to see how Ignacio Arnaldo was, and he told me that he had to wait some days for an operation on his thumb. When I arrived home, I felt very sick with an ache in my chest. I was unable to move my neck.

I woke up sick still with an ache in my chest (rheumatism), but out of great necessity, I had to work with the youngsters, always with much fear because the situation is more critical than before since they say that the villages of San José have many guerrillas due to the mountains. By the grace of God, they have not come into the town. Still it troubles us at times because we always have to work.

Guerrillas and Military Clash
25 to 27 March 1984

Bad news arrived from Chicacao which says that many soldiers (more than 30) and innocent people died. This Sunday there wasn't a market in Chicacao. There was much repression. Merchants were forced to close their shops inside the market and were taken to the mountains to look for the subversives. Another piece of news says that, when the people went to look for the guerrillas in the mountains and at the foot of the volcano, the guerrillas went to the plains of the coast where it was quieter. Airplanes of the Guatemalan air force were bombing the high mountains, but the subversives were in the flat lowlands of the coast. All the people in the lands of Chicacao were under the repression of both groups.

The poor soldiers are suffering a lot because of the subversion. During the afternoon of this day, 27 March 1984, a big boat came to let off about 200 soldiers. Then they went to the villages where there are a lot of mountains. But in the night the military commissioners met to inspect the town because, when the soldiers went to the villages, the guerrillas were two kilometers from the town in a place called Pachul, a place where they grow a lot of vegetables. Some campesinos saw these bad men.

On this same day, on the mid-day news of radio, Nuevo Mundo, a spokesman of the army gave information about Nebaj, El Quiché. Members of the army were attacked, and two specialists [teachers] and four soldiers died. There was a lot of fear.

Why were teachers killed?

Unemployed teachers go to the towns to educate the people in propaganda.

Church Problems
1 April 1984

Also, in the churches there are a lot of problems. The priest Rutio Estrada abandoned the parish of San Martín. They say that he had more problems with the Protestants and that the Protestants speak badly about the Catholic Church, but it's generally known that the Protestants speak badly about the Catholic Church. So it's not really understood why the father left the church. He had scheduled a mass for this day in the towns. They were waiting for him, but no one appeared. It's certain what a proverb says: "*Los Justos pagan por pecadores* [the righteous pay for the sinners]."

Army Tracks Guerrillas on Coast and Gives Out Old Weapons in San José
3 to 4 April 1984

On this day my friend Rudy from Santo Tomás la Unión told me that it's very dangerous on the coast because the army is fiercely attacking the guerrillas. He also told me that many planes and helicopters are bombing the mountains of the southern coast and that 2,000 men were forced to search for the subversives, tracking them. They went to the mountains of Quezaltenango, but they didn't find anyone. Rudy said they spent three days in the mountains.

Also, on this day, there was a public announcement that tomorrow there will be a meeting with the army for some news.

It was the birthday of my youngster Erasmo Ignacio, but it wasn't celebrated for lack of money. For lunch we ate herbs and very hot tortillas. This boy is 10 years old. It's true that there's no money to celebrate, but that's life.

At 3:00 p.m. the military arrived and gave out 15 weapons, 7.62 rifles of the oldest vintage, which were the same that were used when I was in the army although these were not mausers. They said that these arms will serve to protect the entrance of the town from the subversives. The rifles are going to be used by the *patrullas de autodefensa civil*. The captain gave good advice to people in the use of the firearms because they are dangerous. He also recommended not participating or collaborating with the guerrillas.

What did the captain tell the people?

He said:

If here among you there are guerrillas, or if in this town there are guerrillas, we are giving this message so that they repent and don't continue in the mountains, so they don't continue persecuting the army. Everyone work with good intent. You are the ones who live in these towns, and we are the ones who take care of you. But what we ask of the people of San José is that there be no guerrillas among you because one, two, or three guerrillas that are in the town can bring to ruin the whole town.

These were the messages that they told us. Then, we also asked ourselves, who among us is a guerrilla? There isn't any because we know ourselves well. There are few people in all in the town, and everyone knows what job each person has. What was said was that there are guerrillas, but I know that in San José there are no guerrillas. Nevertheless, they came here to give that message. In addition, they said:

> Everyone should work honestly and earn money. We don't want false accusations in the army. We don't want to occur again what occurred in the time of General Lucas. Many lost their families, parents, or their children; many were killed possibly by the army. But that was not the fault of the army. Instead, it was fault of the persons who went to accuse particular people. Honest people were killed sometimes only because they had given someone money on a loan and the person to whom they lent the money didn't want to pay them back. Then the borrowers accused the lenders of being guerrillas. Other people had certain problems with women or had problems with property. And then came another person to accuse them, to say that the person was a guerrilla although it was not true. The army, previously, did not take measures to find out, but now we are finding out. Now a person will not be killed for fun. Nor are we going to lose lives even though we are taking care of the lives of the indigenous people. We only want you to collaborate with us. If you hear in which mountain there are guerrillas, tell us, and we will go find them, without the necessity of your going to the mountains. We will be in charge of finding the guerrillas.

These were the words that they said this evening. The military commissioners were very happy because they received their arms, but a majority of people are not in agreement to their having arms because a weapon only serves to cause death and perhaps there will be more innocent ones.

Rationing Food on the Coast to Keep it from Guerrillas
11 April 1984

There is news that life is very hard on the coast of Chicacao and San Antonio Suchitepéquez. The selling of corn, beans (things for daily sustenance), and other goods is completely prohibited. They say that a person can buy only one day's supply for one person, no more. They are doing this where food is sold to the subversives. Everyone is counted in the houses, and they will sell only what is needed for the number in the family. All the way to San Luis the people are controlled because they say that there they are taking provisions to the mountains. But who knows if this is true?

Getting a Loan
13 April 1984

I went to Sololá to the Banco Nacional de Desarrollo Agrícola [BANDESA, National Bank of Agricultural Development] where they gave me a loan to buy fertilizer. The plan of work is to plant onions and corn. The contract is for Q1,100, but they are going to give it to me in four pay periods, depending on the crop. For me it was favorable. This time they gave me Q550.

Injuring Fingers
15 April 1984

At 5:00 in the morning my youngsters and I began to work making bread, but we ran out of the tin plates. Then I began to open some small jars, but this work is very delicate, and I injured three fingers on my hand. Because the times are very dry and hot and I bled a lot, my temperature went up. I drank a lot of liquid and pills, but it did me no good. I was sick for many days.

Establishing AA in Tzancuil
Thursday, 19 April 1984

On this day the muchachos of Alcoholics Anonymous called me, and I had to accept the invitation. We paid for a car to take us to Tzancuil[17] to organize a new branch of Alcoholics Anonymous. When we arrived, some residents were waiting for us. Then we began to share with them the meaning of Alcoholics Anonymous. Well, they were astonished about the program. The discussion ended at 2:00 p.m. We arranged that next Sunday we would return in the same car. We only paid Q12.

A Tragedy on Holy Friday
20 April 1984

For me this was a day of rest. I didn't work on Holy Friday; we were just remembering the death of our Lord Jesucristo. A lot of people were making carpets of sand and flowers in the streets to receive the procession of the crucified Jesús. Also, we intended to receive the procession. Then Ignacito went to the field to look for wild flowers to make a little decoration in the street. But for bad luck, Ignacito fell from a tree and broke his foot and, moreover, injured his head. He bled a lot. Finally, Ignacito went to bed, and indeed we made our carpet in the street. Ignacito was cured by a *curandero* [curer] of bones, Ricardo Tziac Sicay.

Can you explain a little about Ignacito and the bone curer?

Now, look, sometimes we don't believe in these things, but sometimes they work. In reality, this time when the child fell from a tree to cut flowers, he fell and broke his foot. Then, what we only did was to send for the bone curer because with us there is no doctor nor are there pharmacies. When the señor, Ricardo, arrived, he saw that the youngster's foot was broken. He took out one of his little bones that serves him a lot to cure bones and passed it over the area on the youngster that was broken. That's what he did on the first, second, and third days. On the fourth day, the youngster could walk better—not much better, but yes he had an improvement. This is all that the curer did. That's why sometimes we don't believe in these things, but sometimes they help a lot because it was seen clearly that this *curandero* of bones can cure.

Was this a toe?

No, it was a foot. This [showing me his foot].

Repression in San Luis
Holy Saturday, 21 April 1984

All day long we worked hard making bread. We thought we would sell it in the market in San Luis. They told us there was a big scarcity of bread in this town because of the subversion. The breadmakers had taken a beating. They were afraid to sell bread. The situation in San Luis is very serious; a lot of people are dying. But they say it isn't because of the subversion but for personal vengeance, envy, property, businesses, or women.

What is happening in San Luis?

It's the day of Holy Week, right. The news says that bread was very scarce because there was little since there had been a battle between the guerrillas and the army. It seems that many soldiers died there, but the number wasn't clear. The bakers were suspended by the soldiers. They no longer permitted bread to come from the coast and other places like Santa Ana because they thought that in San Luis the guerrillas would buy bread to take to the mountains. The soldiers said, "No, you are not going to pass to sell bread because in the market of San Luis the guerrillas are buying bread and if you sell bread to the guerrillas you are our enemies. So please don't go. It will need to be seen who is selling bread to the guerrillas." That's why the vendors didn't go to sell on these days of Holy Week and the sale of bread and other products such as corn and vegetables was very scare, because the soldiers believed that from San Luis the guerrillas would take corn with them to the mountains. But this, I don't know for sure because I didn't see it.

Did you sell bread in San Luis?

We sold it but not until Saturday. With us there is no problem selling bread. We just take the launch to San Martín. In San Martín there aren't soldiers so we can pass.

On Saturday?

Yes. But, those who come from the coast encounter many soldiers. And a lot of bread comes to San Martín from the coast.

My Wife Has a New Baby
22 April 1984

At 2:00 in the morning my wife, Josefa, woke me to tell me that she was having labor pains. Then I made a fire, heated water, made coffee, and left for San Martín to call the midwife, Virginia. Well, the señora didn't deny us, and she came with me at 3:20 in the morning. When we arrived home, my wife was waiting. At 3:50 a.m. a beautiful baby, Samuel Jesús, was born. This baby was born when the church was celebrating the early morning Resurrection of the Lord Jesús. For me it was a very beautiful day.

At 8:00 in the morning I had to leave my wife in bed, but only to help others. The muchachos of Alcoholics Anonymous and I had arranged to go again on Sunday to Tzancuil to help establish a branch there.

At 10:00 a.m. we arrived in Tzancuil, and the señores were waiting. The meeting was started, and 20 men and 2 women were accepted. Thus was founded the group that is called "Resurrection," because it was founded on the Sunday of the Resurrection. When we left, we had to go by car. We only had to pay 10 quetzales for the fare and everything. It's true that since 1979 I relapsed from Alcoholics Anonymous, but it's indeed certain that the program of Alcoholics Anonymous is a good thing for me. I'm not going to say that I'm good. At times I drink my *cervezas* [beers], but now with enlightenment; the same thing the muchachos wanted me to do when I was in Alcoholics Anonymous. They cared about me a lot, and they still do even though I'm not attending the program. They always want me to go with them when they have sharing sessions in other towns. I always respect and never neglect them.

A Loan and a Deal on New Land
24 April 1984

On this day I went to Sololá to get the fertilizer from BANDESA that they had granted me on credit. As I said earlier, the contract was for Q1,100, but with the condition that they are going to give it to me in three payments [instead of four]. The last remittance is not until the month of July. The plan that I had presented to the bank was for planting corn and onions, and for that reason they granted me the money. But the truth is that I'm not going to use all the money for sowing. I have made a deal with a *Martinero* named Roberto Hugo García Tziac Luis about a piece of land valued at Q1,200. Before paying him the value of the land, we made a contract. He drew me up a bill of sale certified by a notary, and I presented the bank the bill of sale. I left the bill of sale deposited as a guarantee for the bank, and they gave me the loan. With this money I paid the *Martinero*. But the cancelation of the cost of the land is not until the month of July when the bank finishes giving me the money, and then I will finish paying the *Martinero*.

My policy will be to work very hard to be able to pay the bank. Only in this way can I get the land, but I have faith that God will help me. To make it more clear, the money that the bank gave me I gave to the *Martinero* for the value of the land.

Can you explain a little more about the property?

I thought I would be able to pay the *Martinero* for the loan, but because the times are expensive, I could no longer pay him. I already had given him Q200, but he was very conscientious with me. We went to a lawyer who authorized the title for me. With the same title I solicited the loan from the bank. When the bank gave me the money, I paid the *Martinero* for the property. The *Martinero* did me a favor. He never refused. He never said, "You aren't going to pay for the property." Rather he gave me the title like that, like credit. Then I paid the bank back little by little. I owed the bank for one year.

Without the document stating that you owned the property, the bank would not give you a loan?

Yes, with the title where it says that I am the owner of the property, the bank had a guarantee for the loan, and it gave me the money.

A little clever [laughing].

Yes [laughing].

A Little About Religions: Charismatics
25 April 1984

Who knows where many things are coming from that are appearing in the religions? Members of the Catholic religion and the charismatic religion say that the religions are the same, but they are not good leaders. That is, in the Catholic religion, that which we know is the *Santa Misa* [Holy Mass], *Santo Rosario* [*misterio*, or the rosary] and the procession. But now in the Catholic Church, those who are called the renovators have appeared. Also, they are called charismatics. They belittle the veneration of the images and do not recite the rosary. They say different prayers. They say that they speak with the Holy Spirit, make miracles, and cure sicknesses. They meet in houses and say that they speak new languages. When they begin to pray, there are many speakers, as if they were drunk. After a while they return to normality and begin to say what they said when they were concentrating. Some say that they saw Jerusalem; others say they saw different celestial things. It seems like a lie, but who knows?

The priest of San Martín says the charismatics can't be believed, that they are different from the Catholics. For a good awareness the priest ordered that the Catholics meet for two or three days. There they gathered at the parochial *salón*. The directors didn't allow them to leave or eat much, only food without fat. If they insisted on eating prohibited things, they would be expelled from the *salón*. The strangest thing is that they ordered them not to eat meat or bread and to sleep at nights in the *salón* (lounge). For the men to have a good communion with God, they told them that they had to abandon their wives for some nights and only in this manner abstain from sex. If they acted in this way their sins would be forgiven. On the last night at midnight, they made a procession in front of the church. They did the same thing with the boys. They left their homes and were shut up two to three days in the parish *salón*. And they did the same thing with the young girls. There is doubt, however, because they took the boys and the girls out of their houses although they are not married and the directors said that the withdrawal is to avoid sex in order to obtain pardon for their sins.

Story of Two Evangelical Pastors
April to May 1984

In the month of April of the present year, the Evangelical pastor, Justo Ajcac Yocom, graduated, completing his studies in the City of Chimaltenango. This señor was a good friend because when I was working as a contractor, he was the driver of a truck owned by Delfino Cojox. We drank *cervesas* together. He became afraid to drive after he had an accident and had to pay for the repair of a wall of the house he hit with his truck in San Martín.

When he gave up being a truck driver, he already was a man with a family. Then he obtained a scholarship in a church of Chimaltenango where he completed his theological studies. The 10th of April they gave him the title of Evangelical pastor. There was a big fiesta in San Martín because the father of this man was an Evangelist (Protestant), and there was a lot of celebrating. Then Justo, who already was a pastor, because of the emotion, began to sip liquor without those of the church realizing it.

On Palm Sunday, 15 April, Justo rented a car and took a lot of people to San Jorge to celebrate worship. He was very content, always preaching but also always sipping his drinks. They say that when he returned from San Jorge, he headed for his house and told his father to have someone buy him a bottle (*octavo* [one-eighth liter]) because he felt a great need for alcohol. But his father resisted. Then Justo made his way to his bed where he died of alcoholic intoxication [poisoning]. When his father went to him, he was already lying there dead. Then the news circulated throughout these towns that an Evangelical pastor died of alcoholism. It was very strange because the pastors never drank alcohol. Many say that one should not play with the word of God because that is what happens when one wants to deceive others, but if he is not upright, he pays with his life.

The other pastor is named Ilodoro Arnaldo Tuc, also my friend and associate of the cooperative. I have talked many times with him. He told me that he was the active director of the Catholic Church for several years in the village of Patzilín. He always honored the saints of the church, but he told me that he was disgusted with the other directors of this village. That is why he went to the charismatic congregation .

He was that way for a number of years, but he finally abandoned the charismatic congregation and then went to the church of the Assembly of God. After that he moved again—to his own *sitio* where he constructed a church with money from the *jefes* and some of his own. Gradually he won over the people to abandon their Catholic religion and indeed gained a number of people, who believed that Ilodoro Arnaldo was the real thing, and followed him. When he saw that he had a good number of followers, he baptized them and told them that they had to give something weekly—like money, corn, beans, eggs, chickens, bread, and other things.

Thus was the pastor. He deceived the poor people. Indeed, they did what he asked because he said that the Bible obliged them to pay the tithe. Ilodoro Arnaldo was a man who had a lot of land and money, but he didn't accept what he had—he had to ask more of the poor people, bettering himself a lot. Well, when the people converted to the religion of the Assembly of God, he made them burn their images because in the Catholic families, they were accustomed to taking care of the image of a saint as a protector of the family. But the Protestants are enemies of these things. So when a family wanted to quit being Catholic, it had to give up its custom of looking after its images. Ilodoro Arnaldo, as pastor of the church, obliged the people not to look after them but to burn them once and for all. He knew that the new Protestants were afraid to burn the images. In front of his church, he began to burn a number of images, including San Miguel, San Juan, San Gaspar, San Lorenzo, and others. He chopped them up with an axe, threw gas on them, and made a fire in the presence of the rest of the Protestants. A son of his was the one who was helping him a lot to burn the images. Some of the owners of the images were bothered, others not. The pastor was very content at having burned so many images of the saints.

Don Ilodoro Arnaldo on 14 May went to Quezaltenango to buy things, and when he passed by the village of Tzarayá he was bitten by a dog that tore out a piece of skin on the calf of his leg. He made a complaint to the auxiliary mayor. On Tuesday, the 15th, they took the dog to the municipality to check if the animal had rabies, but Ilodoro Arnaldo sent word that the dog's owner be present Thursday, the 17th, to pay for the five days of work he lost trying to keep the wound from becoming infected. However, Ilodoro Arnaldo had such bad luck that he was struck by a bolt of lightning when he went to inspect his field of corn in a place called Paquisi. What was surprising is that it had not been raining when suddenly a flash from the sky fell and killed Ilodoro Arnaldo walking together with his two sons. One of his sons witnessed the fire that hit him and his brother, who also fell down, but the latter didn't die. Then the authorities were notified to get the cadaver. They say that the lightening burned his clothing, his hair, and almost his entire body. They didn't carry the body to Sololá, according to the law. They appealed to the mayor, the justice of peace, to leave him alone and be free to bury him in the village.

A lot of people talked about this event. The same Protestants say that it happened because the pastor had two women; others say because of his mistreating people of other religions; still others say for being greedy because he had land and still asked the people to give him things. But most condemn him for having burnt many images of the saints. Fifty percent say it happened for having burnt the image of San Miguel because San Miguel represents the Archangel of God, man of fire, rain, and air. It seems certain because the strangest thing is that there previously had been neither rain nor thunder from a tempest and because the Bible says that there are many things that we aren't able to see, that which is invisible.

Books for the Institute Arrive
12 May 1984

Today I received a portion of the books for the library of the *instituto básico* from my great friend Gregorio Bernardo Urbina Hernández, who earlier had come to visit and offered to send me some books. What he had told me was true because in the afternoon of this day, I received a box of books, giving thanks to God. Then I took it to the *instituto básico*.

A Girl of Patzilín Is Chosen Queen of the Titular Fiesta of San José
2 June 1984

On this day they closed the voting polls for the election of the queen for the titular fiesta of the 24th of San José. There had been four candidates, two of them members of the Bizarro family and one of them from the village of Patzilín. At 8:00 p.m., the two Bizarro candidates, who are first cousins, had gained in the number of votes, and the girl from Patzilín was very far behind. But frankly, the queens of the fiestas had recently been of the surname Bizarro. Then some friends and I chatted, and we also talked to some friends from Patzilín. We decided to help the candidate from Patzilín.

We asked for help from many friends, and we collected a little money for the campaign. This was how the candidate from the village of Patzilín named María Toc Soto won with 9,972 votes. We did these things to gain the participation of the village because it was the first time in the history of the town that the villagers took part in these events. After the elections, those of the village invited us to the municipality to share the moment with Pepsi and coffee. On the one hand, it was very nice, but on the other hand, the Bizarro families got mad at us for not collaborating with them. That's the way it is in this world.

What is her responsibility?

To represent the town, fiestas, etc., like the Queen of Guatemala.

Soliciting Money for the Catholic Church
3 to 12 June 1984

In the morning of this Sunday some Catholic Actionists called me to ask me to collect funds to buy an apparatus for the church. Well, as social promoter, I had to accept to coordinate it for a few days. On this day we installed a loudspeaker in front of the church and we called the Catholic people to contribute to the purchase for the church for their own benefit. In all, 310 women, 280 men, and 250 children contributed. All day long we worked very hard, without eating lunch until 6:00 in the evening. When we counted the money, there were Q675.71.

From 4 to 5 June I was very sick with a cold. I felt very cold. The same thing on the 7th and 8th of May. Not until the 10th did I feel better.

On 10 May I went with the señores of the Church to collect the funds. In total we collected Q1,676.38.

What were you raising money for?

An amplifier, 6 horns, and 3 microphones.

On 11 June 1984 Arden Sumoza, the president, Alberto Mogollón, Mario Ovalle, Diego José Ramos, members of Catholic Action, and I left for Guatemala [City], where we bought the apparatus, which cost Q1,438. Each one of us was given Q20 for travel and lodging; Q138.38 remained as funds of the church.

The following day we arrived back in town, which received us well. To us only went money for travel and food, no more. The receipt was in the name of the Catholic Church. Well, when I was sleeping in the inn, Río Jordan, I had a nervous shock and almost died. My companions were very worried about me. But already in the morning I felt well. Perhaps it was from having talked a lot to the people when we were collecting the money.

What happened? Did you have a heart attack?

For three to four minutes I couldn't breathe. I think it was a lung that failed to work, not a heart attack.

On 12 June 1984, after leaving the church, we had to go to a meeting with the military in front of the municipality. At the meeting recommendations were given not to collaborate with the subversives and if anyone were to see groups of subversives, they were to immediately give notice to the military commissioners of the town.

Refusing to Get Involved in Politics
14 June 1984

I refused to get involved in some politics. They called me to the municipality to oblige me to continue fighting for the official parties. With oppression they were asking me to name persons who are with the *oficialismo* [bureaucracy]. I told them that I'm not obliged to any parties and to quit bothering me. It made me very angry because the sun was hot and I was working very hard when they called me to the courthouse.

Seeing a Friend Who Helped Me in 1979
15 June 1984

I went to Sololá on an errand to the government on behalf of the *instituto básico*, but they told me to go to Guatemala [City] to the Ministry of Government. I was in Panajachel at the Banco Mercantil to cash a check that Don Jaime had sent me. It's a pity that it was impossible to send a letter to my good friend. I was thinking of writing a letter in Sololá, but I couldn't because of an invitation from my good friend Borneo Granados Gómez. I had to accept the invitation because he is also an important person. He had done me a favor in 1979.

Student Sweetheart of San José and Problems in the Catholic Church
16 June 1984

All day my youngsters and I were working very hard making bread. In the evening, the Student Sweetheart of the *Joseño* students was crowned. This was the first time that the Student Sweetheart was named by the students. There was a folkloric presentation. Earlier the students that were studying out of town talked to me about a presentation to initiate a town fiesta. I had to say yes.

This piece of folklore was very nice for some, I believe, but perhaps for others it wasn't. Couples came out wearing the dress of 75 years ago; other couples appeared in suits of 100 years ago. We got out *trajes* [typical clothing] that were actually mixed [old and new], and we showed how the women behaved some 80 years past compared to the behavior of the women today. The audience could see the different customs and aspects of earlier times. All the people were present in front of the municipality. Also, there were many people from other towns, even people from Quezaltenango came to watch.

The Student Sweetheart of San José was Señorita Berta Bizarro Tuc, accompanied by a young man, Eldon Temó Ramos. The founding of the town, its earlier inhabitants and their customs, marimba, *chirimía* [flute], shamans, and witches were recounted. This was done with the help of the book, *La Cruz de Nimajuyú* [Aguirre 1972], and with a little aid that we got from the *principales*. The masters of ceremonies were Dacio Temó Sumoza and Gerardo García Cojox, a university student. They spoke in Spanish, and I translated from Spanish to the Tzutuhil dialect.

The sweetheart's mother, Juana [Tuc] Chavajay, and another older woman of 50 years of age, Isabel Soto, dressed the younger woman and did her hair. Later there was a problem with these two women. They were accused by the directors of Catholic Action before the priest. These women occupy the office of catechist, and the fault was that they didn't ask permission of the president of Catholic Action. Immediately they were expelled from their offices without knowing the reason. We are witnesses that the two señoras did not commit sins. They neither danced nor drank. The only thing they did was to do the hair of the student. This is what was taken as a sin. But this was ignorance, or better said, envy because the whole act was very good for many. The expelled women were Juana [Tuc] Chavajay and Isabel Soto.

The Death of My Grandmother
21 June 1984

I am going to write about the death of my granny, who died of old age at 1:00 a.m., Thursday, 21 June 1984. My granny, Isabel Soto Toc, who was very old—104 years—was of the pure Tzutuhil race. She never spoke Spanish, but she had a lot of good customs and upbringing. Moreover, she never consulted with a doctor nor took a shot nor pills until she was 102 years old nor suffered from her sight or hearing. She had very strong lungs and hardy muscles. I say so for on 16 September, about seven years ago, my granny broke her hip when she slipped on a stone and fell in front of her house, as I have already written.

She spent months in bed, but she was cured, little by little, and she was able to walk again. About 14 years ago, she broke a knee when she was carrying wood for the roof of her house. Again she was cured. When she broke the first bone, her *compadre* named Juan Gómez, a *curandero* of bones, fixed it. The second time he wasn't able to make her better. She had three *curanderos*, but they couldn't heal her. Then we called a *curandero* of San Martín by the name of Ricardo Tziac. Indeed this person was able to cure her hip, even though her bones were already old.

Ultimately, she wasn't able to walk well because of her old age. First, she walked with one cane, and finally, she had to use two walking sticks, one in each hand. Last year she still went to visit her grandchildren and family. But in the month of October she fell on her bed, saying that her bones were unable to move, and she asked God to let her die, calling on her parents and acquaintances who had already died to take her to rest where they were.

However, she didn't die, but she indeed ate. What she asked for was meat, bread, tortillas, and other kinds of food. We were ready to see whether she would die. We slept on the floor to take care of her because she might fall from her bed. A little later, she began to get up, but she was unable to walk. Like a baby, she crawled to go out in the sun, resting on the patio of her house. Then she returned to her bed. She did this, however, for only about three months. Later, she was like a seriously ill patient—just staying in her bed. Still, she ate well, recognized us, and told us what she wanted. Mainly the liquid she asked for was coffee. A few times she asked for refreshments, but she only asked for hot things. We asked her where she hurt, and she told us that she did not ache, only her bones were unable to move much. We asked her if she had a stomachache, and she told us no. Later, she wasn't able to rise from her bed. My mother was the one who suffered the most with her, changing her clothing when she had her biological functions. She didn't have much clothing, and my mother was in charge of washing it. Sometimes my wife did it, and at other times, another granddaughter.

I, a man, was unable to do anything with her, just helping her with money and giving corn to my mother so that she could take care of my granny. When she grew worse, she told us that God had forgotten about her because when she was born, without doubt, God had forgotten her name since she felt that it was difficult to die. At times she told us that perhaps it was witchcraft that kept her from dying. She wanted to die, but death did not come. [Finally], when death was only a few days away, she began to talk about very strange things. She said she was talking to people that had been dead for 70 to 80 years. We were surprised at the names she mentioned. Indeed she ate well, although, frankly, we didn't want her to eat. But she asked us and said that if we did not give her food that we could expect punishment. Thus, we fed her.

Then for two days she didn't eat while I wasn't there. I went on an errand to Chimaltenango for the cooperative. I arrived on Tuesday in the afternoon and asked how my granny was. I was told that she was the same.

On Wednesday, when I finished working in the bakery, I went in to check on my granny. Already she was getting cold and in her last throes, without shouts or pain—a very calm agony, which one could see in her face. During the night, my mother and I decided that we should watch over her to see if she was going to die. But owing to my weariness, I told my mother and others that José would remain with them to look after her and that I would take my turn at midnight, later. Thus we settled it. I came home to my house while my son José took care of her, together with my mother and my stepfather.

At 7:00 p.m., José arrived to go to sleep. I asked him why he had left the patient. He told me that his other companions had gone to sleep and that they would get up again at midnight to see what was happening with grandmother. But my mother didn't realize when midnight came, and neither did I. Not until 1:00 a.m. did my mother come to awake me, but I was in a deep sleep. Finally, she awoke me, and we went to the house of the deceased.

When we opened the door, we found her already dead. Her heart had stopped. Well, we had to accept it, and I told them not to cry so as not to alarm the neighbors.

There are certain ancient customs, or beliefs, that until then I did not realize. They say that earlier when my grandmother was feeling well, she herself had looked for an old woman to put in charge of bathing and dressing her. Thus when she died, my stepfather went to wake up Señora Rosaria Cholotío, who was 80 years old. When she arrived, she told us to heat water and to boil flowers. Then we went to pick flowers in front of the church and we cooked them.

I also worked. When the water was hot and the flowers were cooked, we prepared the water inside a big *traste* [plastic tub]. The señora began to wash the body carefully. When she finished bathing her, they put on her clothing and put patches of cotton in her nose, mouth, and ears [instead of embalming]. When this was done, four old folks put her into a *caja* [box, coffin]. The one who worked hardest was Señora Rosaria. Then, seeing that everyone was working hard with the dead person, I bought them a bottle of liquor to calm their nerves.

The water with which they bathed the body they gave to me to take to throw out in the cemetery, which was a *secreto* [sacred or magical act]. I had to go. Two others went with me, and we carried the water to the cemetery with all the soap and the *traste*.[18] We returned with nothing.

There is the belief that the body should be bathed to present it to God without the blemish of sin. They say that if one does not wash the body, the spirit presents itself before God with the sins that it has committed in its corporal life. If a dead person appears in a state of sin, she or he will be delivered into the hands of evil, or the devil. The water is thrown out in the cemetery so that the sin will remain in the cemetery and there it will disappear. So the *secreto* is that the deceased present themselves to the other life clean, without the filthiness of this world. Moreover, the belief says that when a body is not cleaned, its spirit begins to bother those who remain in the *sitio* because the sin was not able to leave the spirit.

With the body of my grandmother, they put other very special things—her *trajes antiguos* [old clothing], a bowl and a glass for her food, her two walking sticks, her wedding clothing, her comb, and a utensil for water. They placed the old clothing with her to make her recognizable to others who have died earlier, for example, her parents, other relations, and her husband. Dressed in this old *traje*, she will appear and be received as they knew her. The reason for the glass and bowl is so that the deceased will receive spiritually the gifts they are offered on 2 November (when the Day of the Dead is celebrated), such as ears of corn, pumpkins, *atol* [a ritual drink of corn meal or of rice, wheat or corn flour, boiled and served hot], and *tragos*. They say with her same canes she will be able to walk as she had walked in this life. The wedding clothes will allow her to appear before her husband in the next life, if she had observed the custom not to remarry.

What kind of wedding clothes?

A new big white blouse that goes to the knees, to where the skirt falls. The big blouse is decorated with red figures of birds and the faces of the Mayas. The women also wear a ring if they have one. My grandmother did not have a ring.

These old beliefs they still retain. All of these things they did at three in the morning.

Do you believe these beliefs?

Well, yes, I believe them. What can I do? My parents believed them a lot, and I have to believe them because this is the way we were taught.

Also it is the custom when someone dies to advise the head of the *cofradía* of San Juan Bautista so that he can tell the other *cofrades* to dig the grave. Together with José, I went to do this.

When we went to tell them, we also went to the president of Catholic Action to ask him permission to ring the bells as a sign of sorrow in the town. I had promised my granny as a token of good-bye a *misa del cuerpo presente* [funeral mass with the body present], but it was a shame that the priest did not have time. At 3:00 in the afternoon, we carried the cadaver out of the house to the church for a good-bye. Since she was Catholic, many prayers were said. Then we took her to the cemetery. A good number of people were there, especially women. When the burial was finished, we went to the church at 5:00 in the afternoon where the priest celebrated a *misa del réquiem* [funeral mass without the body present]. More than a thousand persons attended. When it was over, I went home because my family already had gone ahead.

During the night, my mother, aunts, and uncles were drinking in my granny's house. They got drunk. My wife and I didn't drink. It was difficult to understand them. Because my grandmother had given me the piece of *sitio* where I have the bakery, a son of hers and her grandchildren felt bothered since she hadn't given anything to them. But I don't know why, perhaps because of their disobedience. To avoid problems and respect the spirit of my grandmother, I didn't stay with them any longer. Many times she told me to be patient when she died, and this I had to bear in mind. I had to show her more respect.

Can you explain these burial customs a little more?

When a sick person is in agony, the kin get flowers and put them to cook in a large bowl, to boil well. When the person dies, they carefully bathe her in water of flowers, very hot, on the head and the whole body. They apply soap as if it were still alive. The person who bathes the deceased has to be someone of a lot of respect. Some days beforehand, that is to say, when the sick person is still able to speak well, her family asks, "Who's the person who is going to bathe you when you die?" Then the sick person says the name of her or his *comadre* or *compadre*, or another person. What the sick person says has to be respected. After the deceased is bathed, the water, soap, and the whole bowl are taken to the cemetery to be put in a special place where these objects of the dead are put.

When the person dies, they put the two hands on the chest with a cross in the hand. The cross is made of dry flowers that were used in Holy Week, or leaves of branches of palm that they got in church on Palm Sunday. The hands on the chest as if they were praying indicates asking forgiveness from God. The cross in the hand signals that in this world she was a Christian. Bathing the deceased is so that she will appear clean of sins before God.

The Tzutuhiles bury a person with the face to the east to enjoy seeing the light of a new day. On the ninth day after the death, the kin apply lime; that is, they whitewash the house of the dead. If there isn't any lime, then they apply yellow mud on the walls, especially on the front of the house, so that the spirit of the dead will not recognize her house and frighten the survivors still living in it. Also on the ninth day a cross is carried to the cemetery, which indicates that the life of the deceased is over. The kin can carry on as before, except they can't dance or attend any fiestas for 20 days. Without a cross the spirit will scare (molest) those who are still living.

More Problems with the Church: Catechists Against *Marimba*
24 June 1984

The patronal fiesta for the town was almost peaceful, by the grace of God, but it was a little sad because of the absence of my grandmother. We, however, are all going to have to die.

In the morning, the people were very happy making, small talk in front of the church. There were two marimbas brightening things up. One marimba was sponsored by the committee and the other was quite voluntary. These events were certainly pleasant! But the oppression of the catechists was a lot. The committee had problems this year. As in all the previous years, it was the custom of a committee to organize the titular fiesta. It is this committee that is in charge of taking up collections to support the expenses. Thus, all the *Joseños* gave their voluntary contributions of three to five quetzales. And that's what the committee was doing—asking for voluntary contributions. But in the Catholic Church, it was very strict. They gave orders that no one give money for the marimba—saying to have a marimba is bad. They said that the money should only be for the church in order to get forgiveness of their sins. Because the people are very ignorant, they all believe what the church tells them.

Moreover, in this titular fiesta they gave orders that no one was to dance because dancing is a work of evil. During this fiesta, they put catechists at the entrance of the marimbas so that no Catholic would enter to dance, and he who passed to dance would be expelled from the church. I didn't go to see the marimba, but they say that no one danced except the people from other towns.

Continuing Traditions of the Principales
25 June 1984

In the morning I gave thanks to God for another day. We ate breakfast, and then we went to the soccer field for a meeting of the boys of the town with a team from the city. We bought ice cream and fruit for the children. When we returned, it was late and we passed by to see the marimba. It's customary in the town that on the second day of the fiesta the mayor invites all the *principales* for a lunch. After lunch they enter the *salón* to dance to the happy sounds, remembering times past, when they held offices. Thus they remember their joys and sorrows of an earlier time. The intention of my wife and me was to go to watch the *principales* dance.

When we entered, the *principales* were going to eat lunch. One of them invited me to go eat, but I didn't. The president of the committee also invited me to go with them for lunch, but I didn't want to go because I was a little ashamed since I was only wearing a T-shirt and a completely patched pair of trousers. While we were eating, we listened to the marimba.

After lunch, they began the happy sounds, and then the *principales* began to dance in file—very pleasantly. From this point there were two hours of songs only for the *principales*. To show respect, no one else was able to dance. When the *principales* dance, they also drink their *tragos*. In this afternoon when they were dancing, they called me to dance with them, but I was too self-conscious to dance. So I just remained in their presence. They appreciated me, and I them. I spent Q15 on some drinks. Although I was with them, I didn't drink because I wanted to respect them.

When they left the *salón*, they went to a cantina, and I went with them. Some were crying because they had lost their wives to death. Others were grieved that earlier they didn't have money—it was difficult to spend a year as a member of the *cofradía* or the municipality. Still others were sad that their parents had sold their land into the hands of the *Martineros* so now they didn't have land for their children. Yet others cried because the former governments were bad and caused a lot of grief for the indigenous people when they ordered them to go to work on the *fincas*. Some cried because they didn't have the opportunity to learn to read, write, and speak Spanish. We began with happiness, but for me it was sadder when they began to cry. I left all of this at 5:00 in the afternoon.

My Wife Has a Dream to Cure Sickness
28 June 1984

The baby that my wife had in April was born with problems of health. Both my wife and the baby are suffering from an allergy. We have tried to cure the illness, but we have not found the medicine. We went to the doctors in Sololá, and I spent the little money I had. I had to get a loan from the father of my wife for the cure, but all of it went for the expenses. There was nothing else we could do. Only God could help us.

It was thus when my wife was continually asking God for her health. Suddenly one night she had a dream. She says that in her dream a woman named Juana Vásquez appeared and asked her, "Why are you sad, for your illness? You have used all the medicine, and it has not worked well. But now, I tell you, come with me." And my wife went with her to the shore of the lake. When they arrived, Juana said, "Take off your clothing." Both of them took off their clothing, and Juana told my wife to follow her. They began to bathe in the lake. Then she told her, "This is your medicine. Continue it until the illness disappears." She says that they then got out of the lake and put on their clothing. Juana said, "Have faith in God. Your sickness will be cured only by bathing in this sacred lake. Do not forget God or my advice." Not until then, in this same place, did the señora disappear.

When my wife awoke, she told us what she had dreamed. It encouraged us. The sickness was the same. Then at ten in the morning, my wife went to bathe in the lake at Paraxabaj because it is this place where she was told in her dream to continue bathing for many days. It's certain that the illness disappeared and she stayed healthy. But this dream was very strange for us. My wife told us that each time she prayed she always asked God and the Virgen María for a cure until at last her prayers were answered. By means of a dream, she regained her health. My wife is unable to read and write Spanish, but indeed she has much faith in God, and she is very devoted to the Virgen María. The word of Jesucristo is true—your faith will heal you.

Voting for the National Congress
1 July 1984

This was a day when the voting for the representatives of the constituent assembly took place. All the people were controlled by the national police and the army. There was no pressure, however. They were just watching. There was an order to suspend the sale of liquor, and for breaking this order there would be a fine of Q500 and the revocation of one's license.

In San José everything was normal. But in San Martín they were very strict to the point of closing the shops and the people not being able to buy things to eat. This, however, was an oppression of the military commissioners. The *Martineros* came to San José to buy their basic necessities. Twenty persons were imprisoned for suspicion of having ingested alcohol, but in San José, by the grace of God, nothing happened. In this town the party Democracia Cristiana won.

Dark Events in the Pavón Prison Farm, and Carnal Practices Among the Young
4 July 1984

Today the news was given throughout all Guatemala of the black things that had happened in the Pavón Prison Farm. Those who were imprisoned for the crime of seizure and kidnapping of an industrialist had been tortured and had their throats cut. They were a second lieutenant of the army, a qualified accountant, and a teacher. They were tortured and killed in the penal center. According to the news, the experts say that those responsible are the *jefes*. They were paid by the industrialist. The three men were killed for money. Many guards were dismissed for not having been aware of what happened, but the news says that the guards are not guilty. Those responsible are the director and assistant director. They allegedly paid other prisoners to kill the three men. Now the law is held in low esteem. What has value is money! This bloody deed was witnessed by a *Joseño* who was a guard in the central prison of Guatemala. The name of the ex-guard is José Sandoval Coché. In Guatemala life is not respected.

There are a lot of problems with life, mainly with the young people. It happened that in the neighboring town there is a boy in love with two pretty señoritas. Both loved the boy, gave in to enjoying sex, and became pregnant. The boy was scarcely 17 years of age, and the girls hardly 14 years of age. Both girls had a baby. Only five days had passed since the birth of the first when the other was born. In a period of five days, the 17-year-old boy had two sons! This happened because we parents are not educating our sons at an early age. It is also our grandparents' fault because they never said that a baby is born because of the love of a man and woman. To them it is sinful to say why a baby is born. They believe it is wrong for a child to talk about adult things. When a child is born, our ancestors tell the children that some animal brought it in the night or that the Ladinos bring them and give them to their mothers. More for that reason, when a boy and girl have coitus, they do not know that in this manner a baby is conceived. Nowadays these old fashioned things are still heard and spoken.

Another equal case is that of a boy and a sweetheart who set out to get married. The parents of the boy performed the custom of asking for the woman of their son, giving food (turkey, chicken, bread) and money to the parents of the girl. Thus, they fulfilled the customs and got the woman. The two joined in matrimony.

Three days later the boy was called by the justice of the peace who told him that he had to take home another señorita for his woman. He was obligated by the parents of the other woman, who was scarcely 14 years of age, because she was already pregnant. If he didn't take her home, he would be prosecuted. Whether he wanted to or not, he had to take her home. He already had one woman there, and when they arrived, he had two in the same house. Without any other recourse, he had to say good-bye to the first woman who had been asked for by his parents, get a divorce from her, and stay with the woman who already was pregnant. It seems that there are a lot of problems with the youth.

New Custom: Virgen del Carmen
6 July 1984

Year after year there are customs that are ending and beginning. On this day there was a very new custom. They say that it's better than those of before. They celebrated the day of Virgen del Carmen. In the morning there had been prayer in the church and a procession in the main streets of the town. They say that the Virgen del Carmen is the intercessor before God for the good souls so that the souls of the deceased will not be lost in hell.

Qualified Accountant Clears Me of Mishandling Cooperative Funds
24 July to 5 August 1984

We were working with the qualified accountant to correct the accounts of the cooperative. There was an error on the financial statement, which says that money was lost by the ex-board of administration and that the error happened when I took office. We were conscientious and did not proceed against them before the authority. But we drew up an act and presented it to the technicians of INACOP.

It isn't known for sure whether this money was lost or whether it did not exist because of an error in the papers. In order to come out clean in the time that I presided over the cooperative, I had to hire an accountant who found the error. The mistake was in the years of 1980 to 1981 and part of 1982. When I accepted the office, there had been a shortage of Q5,000. But it is not certain because the shares of the associates only came to Q4,000. This was just because they didn't know how to keep the books. The accountant found an error during my administration of a shortage of Q170, but it was interest that the cooperative paid to the federation of Chimaltenango for a credit for fertilizer to the associates. The associates, however, didn't pay the interest to the cooperative. Thus, the money was missing, but the account of the share to the associates was completely verified and exact.

I became very tired of carrying the burden of office in the cooperative. A lot of them had doubts. They think that I had grabbed the money of the cooperative. This is not true; these are lies because frankly I did not manage the money. It's the treasurer who has the cash box and the money. Yet, I'm unable to say that the treasurer took money from the cash box. Because the doubts were unabated, the accountant was hired. On this day I thought that, if the assembly did not relieve me of the office, I would resign myself immediately.

On 5 August 1984 I met with the four directors of the cooperative and told them to call all of the associates for an extraordinary assembly. The secretary said that we should wait for another day in order to prepare a better kind of refreshment. But I told them, "I'm very tired and I don't want it anymore." Finally, they were convinced.

At 9:00 at night the associates arrived. I brought up my departure because it had been more than two years that I had held office and, according to the laws of the cooperative, the offices of the directors should be held for only two years. Votes were submitted for new officers. The president came out to be Benjamín Peña Cholotío and the treasurer Abraham Có Bizarro. They were sworn into office at the same time. We arranged to hand over the papers in 15 days so as to clarify the questions about the bookkeeping. Because the mistake had actually been made four years ago, it was in the time of the señores of the ex-board. Unfortunately, the associates did not consider for whom they voted. The big error is that the same persons that handed over (the powers) to me are again in office. They themselves had received me. I have no confidence in them. Because of these things, we drank a lot of *aguardiente*. The people didn't know how to be grateful. I lost a lot of time, to the point of abandoning my own work to do something good for the cooperative, but they doubted my character.

Reflections on Leadership in the Cooperative
6 to 25 August 1984

I got up tired and sleepless for having ingested *aguardiente*. I'm beginning to realize that working for my indigenous people costs a lot; they are not understanding and they don't know how the cooperative works. They think to be in a cooperative is only to expect money to be handed out as a gift. It's true that I played a part in the error through my struggle before the Asociación Nacional del Café [National Coffee Association] when I managed to get a quota of 900 *quintales* of coffee for the cooperative, but it's for certain that we didn't have the amount of coffee that we said we would have. We had to sell the quota to a señor of Santo Tomás la Unión by the name of Barto Castillo de Dios for the amount of Q32,000. The sale benefited 32 associates of the cooperative, but it also depended on the number of *quintales* of coffee each member would have at harvest. Some members had reported up to 500 pounds of *café pergamino* (second-class coffee). Those who had reported 40 to 50 *quintales* profited Q1,200, others Q700, such as we did with the lowest number pounds of coffee reported. Of this money we apportioned Q100 for each member [Q3,200] to purchase the *sitio* of the cooperative.

In March of the same year, we got Q4,000 as a readjustment of the quota, but this was not given to the associates because the cooperative had a lot of extraordinary expenses. This is what I did for many. But in the years of 1983 and 1984, there was no money because the Asociación Nacional del Café cancelled the *tarjetas* [quota cards].

Why?

Imagine, this happened in 1981 and 1982. The people went to be inscribed in the Asociación Nacional del Café, individuals and members of cooperatives, to tell the association, "I'm going to produce 50 *quintales*."

"I'm going to produce 30 *quintales*."

"I'm going to produce 25 *quintales*."

Then those in the association thought that this would actually happen. They gave the quota to these people according to the amount that they had reported they would produce. But what happened was that when the quota cards were given, most of the people didn't harvest the amount of coffee that was stated on their card when they brought their coffee. Then they allowed them to sell their quota cards to those who had coffee because there were many people who had coffee but didn't have a quota card and thus couldn't sell their coffee at a good price. What happened was that a lot of people who had a *tarjeta* did not have coffee. Thus, it was a deceit. There were people who reported they would have 40 *quintales* and only produced 20 or 15. Thus, it was a calamity for those who really had coffee. Then the associates thought that in all the years they would be able to do the same thing. But the Asociación Nacional del Café received a memorandum from those who had coffee. Thus, what the association did was to cancel the quota cards. Now in the years of 1983 and 1984, it was seen that the reality was that those who had coffee could sell it at a regular price. They didn't give the quotas to the person—it now was the product. Those who had the product could sell it at a regular price, and the rest weren't going to earn any money. Formerly, all the associates of the cooperative thought that they would be able to earn something with the national association. They thought it would always be this way and they could get the quota cards that they had gotten and that they could sell their coffee even when they didn't have enough quantity. They could sell it to a señor who had plenty of coffee and make some money. For that reason when the national association quit giving out the quota cards, these associates were really annoyed and offended. But this was the reality—a person who didn't have coffee didn't have cause to exact a quota. This was just what happened with respect to coffee.

This happened in San José?

In almost all the departments that produce coffee. In Suchitepéquez, Antigua, Santa Rosa, Sololá, San Benito, Huehuetenango, and Cobán.

Everything had changed, but the associates thought it was still the same. They thought I had taken advantage of the money from a quota, but this was because of their ignorance. Frankly, I received Q600 of the quota, but this came designated from the association and a person is not able to receive more than that which comes from commercial control. I suffered a lot, but thus it is very clear what the text of the Bible says that, "*Nadie es profeta in su mismo pueblo* [no one is a prophet in his own nation]." It is true that not all the associates acted poorly; there are scarcely five persons that had said untruthful things. But, as I said, the people of my town are very ignorant and *llevaderos* [going along with whatever comes along, tolerant].

On 6 August I went to take part of the documents to the señores of the board of administration. I didn't leave until 8:00 at night.

I got up sick from having ingested alcohol. I didn't go to work in Chuitinamit until the 8th. I did the same thing on the 9th.

I'm a bit sad today, 10 August. I don't have any money, and the corn has run out. Nearly everything is in crisis. But with the help of God, little by little, we are passing the days. It's certain that I have crops, but a person has to wait a little for them. I have planted 15 *cuerdas* of corn (milpa). I do have eight *cuerdas* of coffee, and two *cuerdas* of beans. Some of the cultivations that I have are on rented land. I had corn from the harvests of 1983 to 1984, but I sold some of it to pay the helpers for work.

From 11 to 13 August I was working in the field, preparing a new piece of land. The 13th was my birthday, but because I had no money and a lot of work to do, I was unable to rest a day. Not until night was my wife able to make a dinner, which we ate with friends of Catholic Action.

On 23 August I went to San Martín to ask a friend, Herberto Pantzay, for an advance of Q100, and I will give him coffee at harvest time. This friend told me to come on 30 August.

In the afternoon of 24 August they told me that tomorrow they would need me at the cooperative to assist the qualified accountant to see how the situation of the cooperative is. The financial status had deteriorated since the ex-board had made an error four years ago. I felt clean, and that was the reason we had hired a qualified accountant to check for greater accuracy.

It was my wife's birthday, 25 August 1984, but because of lack of money we did not celebrate. All day long I was in the cooperative with the members of the board of administration to execute an act regarding the state of the cooperative. There are criticisms that I had stolen money, expenses for me, but this is not true. They say that they are going to seize a piece of land that I had bought from a *Martinero*. I told these persons they were loco because the criticism makes no sense, with pleasure they offend, or better said, that they are offending themselves by saying things that are untrue. I think that mainly there is a disgruntled catechist among them. We did not quit working with the accountant until 11:00 at night. After working, the accountant called me to visit with him a little. I did what he wished, and he told me that everything is going well. I drank some beers with him, and we didn't leave until 1:00 in the morning.

I got up somewhat sleepless and a little bothered because of the beers that we drank last night. I didn't go to the cooperative until 11:00 a.m. I wrote a paper authorizing the accountant to reduce the debts of 182 associates that had contracted for more than they had received. If a person asked for 10 pounds of fertilizer but was only given 8 pounds, he shouldn't owe for 10.

At 4:00 p.m. the qualified accountant was happy when the account of the financial state came out. By the grace of God, the account came out exact. The accountant was counting the merchandise, credits for payments, arrears in payments, medicine, money in effect, and, moreover, the losses for operations. That which was remaining was Q20, and the qualified accountant gave the order that these Q20 be put into the cash box. Also he said it would be better to give this money to a poor person. At this moment I felt happiness, giving thanks to God, for having liberated me from the mouths of the people. It's true that I reproached the board of directors for having said unjust things and that I had given credit in the *tienda* of the cooperative, but all is accounted for. All of those who thought bad of me were ridiculed and many of the associates reflected about what they had said. What a pity! I have to have compassion for them for they are my fellow men. God will reward me, as a whole, this is certain and sure.

Blue and White Sports Club and Problems with the Catholic Church
28 to 29 August 1984

I was resting at home, meditating, and thinking of my great friend James D. Sexton. I have faith in God and our new work. I hope in our struggle we are able to endure for the third book. God will help us because he gives us the understanding.

I'm going to talk a little about the Blue and White Sports Club and the Catholic church. As one of the founders, I am a witness that when the Blue and White Sports Club was very organized, we agreed to celebrate our anniversary of 29 August, which is also the day of the beheading of San Juan Bautista. Thus we organized a big committee and looked for persons who would help us to put up a marimba. It's certain that before celebrating our first anniversary, the then *principal*, José Temó, celebrated mass on this day. But we began to celebrate very grandly, and there was a little activity. These were social nights. When the directors of the Catholic church saw that the 29th was the anniversary of the Blue and White Sports Club, they organized a procession of the image of San Juan Bautista and many religious acts, and it was then said that this was the day to celebrate the beheading of San Juan Bautista. Thus it was when the Blue and White team used the day to celebrate its anniversary. It was the day, 29 August, for the Catholic church to be directly in charge of celebrating the beheading of San Juan Bautista.

On this 29th of August, however, it was not celebrated. They say that the priest [Rutio, not the North American, José] didn't give permission and he did not want to celebrate mass in the church. It is clear that celebrating the Blue and White Sports Club on the day of San Juan's beheading is all finished. It only lasted 13 years. It is because the directors of the church think different things. Thus are the times, "*Los hombres tienen sus tiempos y el tiempo tiene sus hombres* [Men have their times, and time has its men]."

Thieves Reported in the Cooperative
2 to 12 September 1984

It's somewhat amusing that they say on 2 September that the cooperative was robbed. The directors say the thief broke into the *tienda* but that nothing was lost. For me it was funny because they say it was robbed but nothing was lost. Without doubt, the person in charge of the *tienda* did not leave it closed during the night.

On 12 September 1984, at 10:00 p.m., they say that the *tienda* of the cooperative was robbed again. Two thieves broke into the *tienda* and took sugar, bread and cigarettes, but no money. They say that the one in charge had left money in the *tienda* but that the thief had only rearranged it. It is somewhat comical.

Our Sons Are Runners for Independence Day
13 September 1984

My wife was working very hard, preparing food for our three sons who are leaving tomorrow to carry the torch for the celebration of national independence. My señora and I said that it's better that our sons take their food because we don't have money for them to buy it. The two who are in the institute left for Quezaltenango while Ramón, who is in primary school, went to Antigua, Guatemala. The children departed at 5:00 in the morning.

Students and Independence Day
14 to 15 September 1984

I was making bread for the teachers. I finished at 6:30 p.m. At 8:00 at night we met with my companions on the committee, Friends of the Institute, to wait for the students of the *instituto básico*. We bought chocolate and brought bread to give to them. Some companions remained in charge of these things while we hired a car to go meet them. It's an exciting event because this was happening for the first time in history.

We passed through San Jorge and continued on foot to the summit of San Jorge and Santa Ana. We saw a soccer team pass below San Benito, and then the students of San Jorge passed. When we asked them, they told us that they had not seen *Joseños*. This made us nervous because it was only a few minutes to midnight, the hour when they should have arrived. We thought that they were coming back by the route of San Luis instead. At midnight we arrived in San José, and there was no sign of them. Then we returned again to see if we would meet them. They did not appear until 2:00 a.m. but under much rain. They say that the setback was that the car was blocked by mud. All of the acts weren't finished until 4:00 a.m.

On 15 September 1984, I went to the municipality for an invitation that the mayor gave me. During the night, a teacher, Alfonso, insulted me by saying we were of no use because there had been no marimba. A little while later this teacher was quarreling with his wife. He hit her and went to jail.

Friend's Baby Hospitalized and Scared by a Spirit
18 September 1984

I accompanied Fernando Timoteo to Antigua, Guatemala, to see his baby who is in the hospital. I was short of money, but for being a loyal friend, I had to go. In San Luis a friend of mine who is a policeman lent me Q5 and a *compadre* helped me with a loan of Q3. It's true that I had the travel money, but the route to Antigua, Guatemala, I did not know very well.

At 12:00 we arrived in Escuintla and from there we took a bus. At 4:00 p.m. we arrived in Antigua. Fernando talked to the doctor, who told him that the baby will be operated on this week and that he needed more money. Poor Fernando doesn't have any money because he is very poor. At 5:00 p.m. we left Antigua for Guatemala [City]. We just paid for lodging for one room, one of us stayed in bed while the other slept on the floor. We only ate two times a day, but very lightly.

On 19 September we got up very early and went to the house of a friend to ask him for collaboration so that Fernando would be able to take the baby from the hospital. The doctors need Q400 for the cost of the operation. The baby has been suffering since birth, lacking a piece of its upper lip. But it's a pity that Fernando is unable to pay. Unfortunately, when we arrived at the house of Fernando's friend, he wasn't home. We went down to the terminal to look for a truck driver who would give us a ride. We didn't eat lunch until Chimaltenango, which we reached at 3:00 p.m. There was a lot of rain, and when we were almost to San Diego la Laguna, there had been a landslide of the road, which cost us a lot of time. Not until midnight did we arrive in San Martín.

On the path from San Martín to San José, we were frightened. At times I didn't believe in these things, but this time we were scared. Well since 1950, when I was nine years old, my grandfather, Ignacio Bizarro Ramos, was spooked in this same place when he went to San Martín at night. When he had to return, he didn't have the courage to pass by it again. I thought they were lies, but now I believe it.

What scared you?

Perhaps it was a spirit who shook the trees and earth. My grandmother and uncle had said this place was haunted.

I always passed by the area, many years back, when I was with the cooperative and when I was working on the coast. I always went by there at 1:00, 2:00, 3:00 in the morning to take the van in San Martín for my trips to Guatemala or to the coast. Never had I been terrified. I had heard some shouting, but far away. However, this time, yes, they frightened us a lot. Earlier I never believed it was true that the place was haunted.

In June of 1950, when my grandfather, Ignacio, had left at night to see the fiesta of San Martín, he had left with drinks affecting his head. When he got there, to that place that we call Pasiguán, he says that they started to move the stones and the trees, which frightened him a lot. He returned to the house and went to sleep. The next day, he told us what had happened in the night. Well, since I was a *patojo* [youngster], more or less I was nine years old, I didn't give it much importance until this time when we were going to Antigua, Guatemala. They scared us, and I was very frightened. I never believed what my grandfather had told me before, but this time I believed it very much because, indeed, in that place they scared us. They were very close to us when they started to move the stones and the trees. What scared us more was that we were not carrying a *linterna* [bottle of kerosene with a wick, homemade lantern] nor a flashlight—we were going in the darkness. And yes, we arrived at the house with much fright. These are the things that sometimes one doesn't believe yet sometimes come to pass.

Do you think it was an earthquake?

It's not an earthquake because when an earthquake happens it's heard clearly. It's very strange. However, to me, well, I wouldn't believe it if I was a little drunk, but this time, no, I was going with my senses good. The only unusual thing was that it happened at night. Well, more than anything, I think that maybe some spirits are around that place or someone had died there earlier and we didn't know about it. Or the place is haunted, as they say. But, I'm not real sure. What I'm sure of is that there in that place they frightened us very much. That's all.

Juanito Mendoza Threatens Me
20 September 1984

At 6:00 in the morning we went to work in Xesucut. At noon I arrived home to eat lunch. When I arrived, some teachers of San José and San Martín invited me to drink a beer. To respect them, I had to accept. We chatted a lot. I didn't realize it was getting late. The teachers left, and I remained talking to other friends. I was doing this when Juanito Mendoza and another person arrived. Then he told me that he needs my support to be in the tribunal again. He told me that he's the only hombre in the town and that there isn't a better person than he for the office. I told him, "Better than you, there are many. It's better that you go to others. You can forget about me because I don't lend myself to the corrupt."

Juanito became angry with me and offered to kill me. I told him that no one is able to take the life of another person, only God knows of our lives.

The World Is Confused:
Assassinations and Taxes
1 October 1984

The world is confused. Almost everywhere they say to respect human rights and the laws. Moreover, they say there is peace. But all of this is useless. It's only said, not done. There's only blood and killing by the assassins. Take the case that I heard on the radio stations and saw in the newspapers in all the country, the horrible discovery of ten tortured and assassinated bodies in the jurisdiction of Mazatenango. None of the bodies of the cadavers could be identified, each was buried as "XX." Lamentably, the authorities did nothing to investigate these horrible killings. Thus it is in my Guatemala.

On this same day, 1 October, it seems that each new day brings something wrong. That is to say, in my Guatemala, each day brings more suffering because of the corrupt. Each time there are more taxes. When Ríos Montt was in power, he established the *impuesto tributario* [tributary, an obligatory sales tax] that was 15% but had gone up to 20%. We have the same thing nowadays, and all the prices have gone up. Unfortunately, we poor people are the ones who suffer the consequences. The rich approve the government's raising taxes by 50% of the value of each product. If a person appeals, they say that it's the government that is raising taxes more and that they have to raise their prices in return. That is the response of the big merchants. When the newspapers write their commentaries and criticize the government for what it's doing to the poor people, the ministry of economics says that it isn't the government but the middlemen who raise the prices without the authorization of the government. For that reason it's not well understood what's happening, and I say that it's we poor people who suffer from these things the most.

Criticism of the Government Continues
2 to 5 October 1984

Criticism of the government continues. Newspapers, institutions, private societies, trade unions, and other organizations, through all the channels of communication, ask for the resignation of the three ministers of state—the minister of government, minister of finance, and minister of economics. The people are doing this because of the high cost of living. The poor people are unable to do anything because when the people demand something in favor of the Guatemalans, the first thing that happens is that those who lead, or say the leaders of each organization, are assassinated, machine-gunned, or kidnapped with their entire family. This has happened in many cases when a Guatemalan speaks for the good of the people. He simply is threatened by those who have arms.

In the time of Ríos Montt, General Guillermo Echeverría Vielman was discharged just for being on the side of the people when the value-added tax, IVA, was imposed. The general raised petitions to the government of Ríos Montt to lower the tax a little to help the poor people because it is very harmful to the campesinos who do not earn a salary. The answer that the government gave, however, was to discharge General Guillermo Echeverría Vielman. Now he and the civilian people are calling for a peaceful demonstration against the increase in the prices and more taxes. An official spokesperson of the government said that the ex-general, Echeverría Vielman, is a subversive for being outside the military and inciting the minds of the Guatemalans. But the truth is that Señor Vielman is not a subversive. He, indeed, has the true spirit of being Guatemalan and senses the poverty of many. But with the military government, there is no dialogue or understanding. All is a repression and massacre.

In the afternoon of this day I went to San Martín to get a loan of Q50, not for me but to help my friend Fernando Timoteo to get his baby from the hospital in Antigua, Guatemala. I feel very sorry for this friend for the situation that he is in, but I don't have much money and for that reason I had to get a loan, or better said, an advance to keep helping my friend a little. We sent letters to the Evangelical church of San Jorge, San Martín, and our town, asking help to get his baby out of the hospital, thinking that those who say they are Evangelists would help the father of the baby. The letters that we sent them have Biblical themes because Lord Jesús said to let the children who come to me go, for theirs is the Kingdom of Heaven, and He talked about the nobility of the sick in Capernaum. Unfortunately, those who say they are Evangelists do not have compassion. The answer that they gave Fernando Timoteo was that they would help him if he would accept being an Evangelist, and if not, they could not help him. But who knows which of the four churches, all of which answered the same way, Fernando may join? It's somewhat funny.

On this date, 5 October 1984, the lamentations in Guatemala continue. With this news, they say that members of the political parties were also assassinated. A señorita of 19 years of age was kidnapped in the capital city. The kidnappers communicated by telephone with the father of the señorita saying that they have her well guarded and under protection and there is no problem, only they need an amount of Q55,000. At the same time they sent a letter to the same person, asking for money. The news says that the kidnappers are members of a political party and that the money they are asking for is needed for the next presidential campaign. This is what the corrupt have come to!

I Resign from Being President of a Committee of the Instituto Básico
5 October 1984

On this date I gave up being president of the committee, Friends of the *Instituto Básico*. I did not attend two meetings with my companions, and then they looked for a person who would assume the presidency. With many thanks, they looked for another person for president because frankly I do not have time to be in meetings. Thanks to God, they helped me a lot. I have a lot of obligations with my family. I need to establish my own cooperative with my children to help them a little. When they told me that they had named a new president, I felt joy because it is certain that I do not have time to be losing. It was the vice-president, Martín Pantzay García, but I know that he has personal interests.

What personal reasons did he have?

He wanted to get scholarships for his children. He needed the office for a connection to get the scholarships.

On Religious Changes
19 October 1984

I'm going to speak a little about the religions in which many things are happening in these times. In the Catholic church, there is a lot of daily activity. The people in the church are saying they are obtaining forgiveness for their sins and when they die they will be presenting themselves clean before God. Well, that's all right, but there are about 10 persons who are directing and indeed are winning the majority of the people to receive Holy Communion daily. But also these 10 persons are the *jefes*, who think they are saints. They are the ones that determine if someone is committing infractions. If a person participates in a group, for instance, in a social night of cultural and folkloric events, these directors are saying that these are things of the devil. And if these persons belong to the church they will be told that already they don't have a place in the religion for having participated in things of the world.

These same directors, however, are showing Mexican motion pictures in the parochial assembly hall two times a week. Although these things are bad, they say that indeed a person has to accept them once and for all. For example, the movies are an obstacle for the young people, especially the inexperienced. Most of us Indians want to raise our consciousness, and when we watch something good or bad we are already pretending to do it because we are uneducated. Movies and television are fine for the people who have a lot of educational development because when they see a movie or television story they are able to analyze them well to determine what is good and bad. But for us Indians, everything is the same; we are unable to separate the good from the bad.

This is happening with the young people of my town. Well, they say that they regularly attend church and take religious classes. Yet, they are not being educated because during the months of July, August, and September it happened that the people were saying that four of the Daughters of María got pregnant and another one of them already had a baby. It's a great pity that these girls begin to have sex with the altar boys of the church, or that is to say, with members of the same Catholic youth. These things emerged practically within the same church.

Well, it's natural that each man ought to have his woman and each woman ought to have her man, according to the scriptures. But now the young are giving in to licentiousness because we parents allow them to go out at night to the movies. It's certain that there are dangerous movies that make it easy for the poorly educated young people to stumble. I am writing these things because those who direct the church are at times those who are the most culpable. They say they only want the good things, but it is they who show the bad films. The oddest thing is when the four Daughters of María became pregnant, the directors said that then they should get married so that they won't remain in fornication. But what is happening? These people do not want marriage, and they are in the courts. The good that the directors of the church say is that they do not have to see to anything regarding these youngsters. The names of the women are Concepción Juana, Caria, Juana, Ellia, and Diana; and the boys are Mario, Abraham, Ignacio, Manuel, and Genero. Who knows how it will turn out. They're in serious trouble.

Why are they going to court?

The man impregnates the woman and says he didn't. The woman says he did. So, they go to court.

In this town, the church that is showing its respect in everything and hardly mistreats anyone is the Central American church—perhaps because it does not have many members. Indeed, one can notice that it is better classified in the town. From one point of view, it is this church that has first place.

Well, now we are going to talk a little about the Assembly of God. They have a lot of problems. They judge one another among themselves, and they say they are the best. They pray with wordiness and shouts to be heard by God. I took an opportunity to ask a member of the church why they shout so much and roll about on the floor to pray to God. He told me that they shout a lot and roll about on the floor and bang themselves a lot so that God will pay attention to them. They say that they are only heard by God through the shouts and blows since God is disgusted to the point of indifference because of the many sins of humanity. For that reason they use force to get God to listen. But as a consequence of the shouts and the blows, three of the members of this church became mentally ill. Two are of the church of San José, and one is of the church of Santa Bárbara.

The person from Santa Bárbara is named Eduardo Democrático, who was a member of the Assembly of God. Because of a lot of shouting and many blows that he caused himself when he prayed to God, he is now in the hospital for the insane. The two of San José are still in town. Their being sent to the hospital is pending. They are a woman named Juana Hernández Toc and a man called Benito Ixtamer; both are loco. There is also a third person of the same church who is suffering symptoms of mental illness. Most of the people say that this is due to the shouts and the blows they inflict on themselves when they pray. Moreover, the directors do not suffer these things because they are well fed and better educated. But, as I said, for us Indians the bad they tell us seems good for lack of education and knowledge.

School Classes: My Children Fail Two Subjects
29 October 1984

This was when school in the *instituto básico* was closed. There were problems. My two children, José and María, each failed two subjects, but almost the majority of the students lost out. Only six passed—four boys and two girls. In primary school, all went well. Ramón Antonio, Erasmo Ignacio, and Susana Julia all did well.

What did they do?

They didn't attend their classes over. María and José recuperated in January. They took the exams twice.

Loans at Cáritas Require Property as Collateral
5 November 1984

I went to Guatemala [City] to settle a debt in Cáritas of Guatemala. Everything went well, by the grace of God. In the afternoon of this day we went to a project, "Los Mayas," for the development of Guatemala. This is a cultural and scientific association that talks about large loans. The smallest loan is Q25,000. But first a person has to register his property for the appropriation of the loan as a guarantee he will pay it back. But as I don't have much property, I was unable to get a big loan.

On the U.S. Elections 1984: Mondale
6 November 1984

I left Guatemala [City] for my town very short of money, but by the grace of God, a little content. In Sololá I bought *Prensa Libre*, which had a lot of commentary about the election of the president of the United States. It says that according to the forecast, Ronald Reagan will be reelected and meanwhile Mondale will obtain 47% of the votes of the North Americans. Also it says that Mondale is not interested in winning [doing anything about] the election because the next Thursday, a day after the voting, he has planned a trip with his family to celebrate his defeat. This is the way it is when there is understanding. He who wins, wins; and he who loses, loses. One always has to accept it. For certain I liked a lot the declarations of Señor Mondale, thanks to the intelligence that he has.

But I'm going to talk a little about politics in Guatemala. When they lose an election, they begin to think about bad intentions of killing the winner. Never do they accept that he won. The *Prensa* says that Señor Mondale knows that Ronald Reagan won, and he saluted him by telephone. How good that the loser congratulated his adversary by telephone! But in Guatemala they congratulate with bullets. For this reason I say that wickedness rules more than friendship in my Guatemala.

José, the Traveler, God of Luck
11 November 1984

The case of Señor Ángel Flores of San Martín la Laguna is incredible but true. The family of Jesús says that he left his house with the intent to work in Chutuj, 12 kilometers from San Martín. He began to work very happily when suddenly he saw a strange child dressed in white. The child began to talk to Señor Ángel but in a different language. Señor Ángel was frightened and did not answer a word. Suddenly, the child disappeared in the same place. It was then that Señor Ángel Flores became even more scared. He didn't eat lunch. He asked the youngster who had gone with him to work, but neither of them could see anything. When Ángel arrived home, he told his family everything that he had seen. Then he went to lie down in his bed, without pain or shouts, and died tranquilly yesterday, Saturday. The vision was on Friday, the 9th.

There were many versions by the people about what had happened. Some say it was an evil spirit. Others comment that he had seen the god of magic where he was working. Still others say he had seen his own spirit. When I asked a shaman, he told me that it is possible he had seen José, the traveler, the god of fortune. The shaman told me that there is such a José who goes through the hills and presents himself to people, but not to all. It is rare that a person is able to see the traveler, José, but the shaman says that when one succeeds in seeing the *dueño* of fortune, one should not be afraid. After talking, one should leave a gift for the *dueño*, and this gift (a scarf; book of luck, or book of magic that can be bought in Quezaltenango; or small animals). One needs to treat the traveler well. If he or she does so, a person may achieve an improvement, such as obtaining a lot of money. The shaman told me that a lot of people of Chichicastenango have money only because the traveler, José, had given them fortune. But I do not know if these things are true.

Fate and the Military Commissioner: Agustín Molina of San Luis
End of December 1984

There is a refrain that is always true: "*El que mal hace mal espera* [He who evil makes, evil awaits, or what goes around comes around]." I'm going to talk a little about the town of San Luis. In this beautiful town a lot of bad things happened because of the violence. Many people have been kidnapped, taken out of their houses, tortured, had their throats cut, and shot. Many of the Tzutuhil people have suffered in that town. Many are the dead and those who have not been seen. Who knows where they took the cadavers to toss out. But the *Sanluiseros* [people of San Luis] say the wave of violence is caused by the military commissioner, Agustín Molina. They say that he is the one who has accused the indigenous people of being guerrillas, saying many of those murdered were nothing. But they had been accused of being subversives just for very personal reasons—perhaps for a piece of land, or for some woman, or for some business. They say that if some person is envious of another person, they just go to tell the military commissioner that the person is a guerrilla. Then the commissioner goes to the *jefes*. Soon after, this person will be kidnapped.

Also, they say that Agustín Molina asked for a lot of things from the poor people, such as money. When the poor people weren't able to give them to him, the person disappeared and appeared—but as a cadaver! Thus it was when Agustín Molina was empowered to be the king of all of San Luis—what he said was what one had to do. He knew the people and knew where they lived. It was no problem to kidnap them. And what happened later?

All the women and children of the kidnapped shed their tears for the disappearance of their spouses. They asked the Creator for justice for Agustín Molina, and they indeed got it. A black sickness befell Agustín. His face and parts of his body rotted. They didn't admit him to the hospital, saying that the sickness could not be cured by the doctors. They went to a shaman, who told them that he could do nothing. They say that they didn't want him in his own town for all the evil he had done with the native people. Before they said that they wanted to kill him, but not now because they wanted to see him suffering.

Agustín was taken out of the town because the people didn't want him. He gave up the office of commissioner and came to live in San Martín la Laguna because his wife, daughter of Eduardo Cuc, is from San Martín. What happened when the *Martineros* realized that Agustín Molina was living in this town? All the townspeople assembled, called the father-in-law of Agustín, and told him they were giving Agustín 24 hours to get out of town, or the father-in-law would be kicked out by all the people too.

Agustín left that same day. His father-in-law had to pay for a launch, and they went to leave him at the Zuzubjá *finca* in the jurisdiction of San Martín la Laguna. When the *Martineros* realized that Agustín was living on this *finca*, his father-in-law, Eduardo, was summoned by the civil authority and obliged to remove Agustín from this *finca* too. The administrator, Calixto Cabrera, had to say yes. "Poor" Agustín was taken from this *finca* that same day.

The people of San Martín behaved in such a manner because they say that Agustín cruelly punished many *Martineros* when they were carried to the military detachment for false accusations. For this reason nobody wants him. He came here to San José. For some days he stayed in the house of Juanito Mendoza because they were in the same army barracks together. But those who saw him say that he only stayed two days because no one could stand the bad odor of his body. He stunk a lot and no one could get near the man. For that reason he had to leave San José. They say that his wife had the same illness. Who knows what had happened? Not even death wanted them.[19]

The Civil Defense Patrols in Santa Bárbara
January 1985

To protect themselves from the cold and the rain when they were controlling for subversion, the patrolmen of Santa Bárbara collectively built a *rancho* with a straw roof at the main exit of the town. Well, they were always taking turns. One afternoon about dark when the patrolmen were in the *rancho*, suddenly a group of subversives arrived and made them all go home. The patrolmen abandoned the *rancho*, and the subversives set it on fire.

Then the commissioners informed the military zone in Sololá about what had happened in the town. Since it was already night, it was difficult for the military to come by car. They decided to cross the lake in boats. From Panajachel left three launches, but only two reached the other side. There was a lot of wind, and they lost control of the last launch, which was carrying 10 soldiers and an official. When it reached the vicinity of Tzancuil, the launch lost its equilibrium because of a strong Xocomil[20] and capsized. Six soldiers drowned. Those who were saved lost all of their equipment in the lake. One of the surviving soldiers swam ashore, walked from Tzancuil to San José, where his sister was living, and asked for clothes and food. This soldier was a native of Santa Ana. What is not known is whether the bodies were found. What was known is that afterwards one could see many launches in these parts (around San Jorge and San Benito). Without doubt, these boats were looking for cadavers.

The Story of the Loom of Typical Weavings
February 1983 to 2 July 1985

In February of 1983, when my son José Juan was enrolled to study the sixth year of primary school, my wife and I thought that we were unable to educate our son because we didn't have money to pay for his studies. We thought that he was going to learn tailoring, but in our town there are a lot of tailors and much competition.

The days passed. Then, we thought of a weaving project, but without knowing the necessary steps. Some days later, my friend Santos Mendoza

Cruz of Totonicapán, a professional weaver of typical skirts, came to our house and told us he had a foot loom available to sell. I thought about what my wife and I had discussed earlier. Then I asked him how much he was going to ask for the loom. He told me Q100 and said that he himself would be in charge of teaching the profession to my son. I thanked him and gave him Q60. The same señor replied that he would be in charge of sending it to me in some transport. It was true that on 13 March the friend sent me the loom in the car of Joel Pérez. In the morning of 14 March, Señor Joel brought me the loom that he had transported in his car. This man charged me Q60 for the value of transportation. It is certain that for the first time I saw in the house a loom. It is of very heavy wood.

A week later, Señor Santos came to collect Q40, the remainder of the price of the loom. I paid him with pleasure. I arranged with him that within a week he would come and stay in San José to set up the material and start with the instruction of the occupation.

He didn't come until the month of May. Santos set up the loom inside the house. After setting up the loom, he asked me for Q50 for the value of the material (cotton and wool thread). He told me that we weren't going to buy a lot of material because it is just a beginning. I gave him the Q50, and he went for Salcaja to buy the material. When he returned, he pleated the material in the loom, and he told me that he needed a lot of material to be able to weave. I didn't know anything about the profession of weaving. I told him that gradually we're going to buy the material that we need. He warped the material with a borrowed warper. Then he told me that he was going to weave a *corte* [skirt] next week, and he left for Totonicapán, his home territory.

He came on 4 June in the afternoon. Then he worked for two days and returned again to Totonicapán. He told me that also he had a son who is a professional weaver, and it's he who is going to teach José the trade. I told him okay.

A week later his son named Raymundo came and told us it was he who would stay in San José and teach the work to my son but with the condition that I had to pay him Q200 in advance. He said that he was in great need. My wife and I did what we could. To allow our son to learn the work, we sold a little coffee and corn that we were saving for our own consumption. We only made Q100. Still we went to borrow Q100 from my wife's father to pay the Q200. Then we gave this money to Señor Santos Mendoza Cruz with much trust. He appeared to be highly educated so we didn't make a document [receipt] for the money. Eight days later Señor Santos came to say that his wife was seriously ill and that it was necessary for his son to go say good-bye to his mother before she died. And thus they went to Totonicapán, and they never returned. I thought for certain that his señora died because I did not have news of her. But one time when I went to Panajachel, I met the señora of Santos on the launch, going about her business of selling *cortes*. Then I asked her how she was spared from death. The señora answered that she has not been sick nor did she know that her husband had taken money from me in San José. At this point I discovered that Señor Santos is a swindler.

My family and I suffered, thinking about how to pay our debts. They spoke badly of me for giving money to a thief. I was very patient. I never thought of going to the authorities about these things because the times are very delicate, as much for him as for me. I paid the debt with my father-in-law when I received a check from the University of Arizona for a percentage [of the royalties] of the book, *Son of Tecún Umán*. I gave many thanks to God when I received this check, which helped me a lot.

Thus we remained with the loom still installed inside the house with the pleated material. From June to October, I did nothing. A lot of people asked me about the loom, and I told them my situation. Some encouraged me, and others told me to give up. I know those who told me to give up. They are content with my adversity. But I always asked the real God that one day I be able to install a small workshop, not for me, but for my children and that He bless my future.

In the month of November of the same year [1983], Señor Tácito Morales, also a professional weaver who lives in San Martín la Laguna, came to my house. Seeing the loom inside the house, he told me that he had a lot of desire to do something for this town and that he's going to teach our son to weave. This man encouraged me again, and I thought it was a sure thing. I asked how much it would cost me. He said Q150, with the condition that he would spend only six hours a week for three months, and if the boy did not learn, we would have to make another agreement. I said, yes, that I was in agreement to pay him this quantity of money in three payments, that is, Q50 a month. This señor wanted me to pay him in advance for the first month. On this day, I went to San Martín to get the Q50.

Then I went to the house of Pascual Soto, a dealer in avocadoes, as I had some avocado groves to offer him, but when I got to his house, this friend had left for a trip to the capital. We returned for San José, and then I went to the house of Abraham Méndez to offer the harvest of the orchards.

This man only paid me Q40. On the following day, I arrived at the house of Tácito and told him that I only had Q40. He told me that it was okay, and I gave him the money. It was thus when we arranged the contract. This señor told me that there is no problem and he was confident that he was going to teach my son. Very contently, I returned home.

The following day, this señor chatted with my son as if he were interviewing him to see if he wished to learn this occupation. The day after that they fastened the loom and arranged everything properly. The third day, they wove a little, but just that. He said that he had problems with his woman and that they were going to Cobán, Alta Verapaz. He did not return again, and this was more problems for us.

Well, I had thought I could afford to pay what Tácito had asked me and all would be well, but everything turned out to the contrary. José was studying in the sixth grade of primary school, hoping that one day he would be able to learn weaving. It's a pity, however, that there is much egotism and envy because they know that in this town there is no weaver of *cortes* and, for that reason the teachers do not want to teach this office. They just want the business for themselves. Thus we were. I was so annoyed I felt like burning the loom, but finally I realized the material had done me no harm.

Well, it is certain that there is a weaver in this town by the name of Benito Bizarro Cholotío. He graduated from the development project in the community of Chinalla, Huehuetenango. He has his loom in his house, and he is always working on very simple weavings such as tablecloths and *fajas* [sashes, belts], but we haven't seen him weave fine *cortes*. This man came to me to tell me that he can weave fine *cortes*, the only thing is that he doesn't have the money to buy wool. He needs money. He told me that he can teach this work to José. This was in the last days of December of 1983. I told him to wait a few days for me to get money. My hope was that I would harvest a little coffee and sell it. Then I would be able to buy more material, because it's true that I had a little thread and wool that I had bought earlier.

In the month of January of 1984, Benito told me that he was very interested in working with and teaching José. Well, I arranged that Benito go to Salcaja to buy the *labores de jaspe* [works or adornment of tie-dyed thread or yarn] and more wool to combine the colors. In the afternoon, I gave him Q125 so that on the following day he could go make the purchase. He went on the Santa Ana bus and returned the same day. In the afternoon, José went to Santa Ana to meet Benito. Indeed, he bought a reel to wind thread that cost Q20, *labores de jaspe* for Q50, and wool for Q10. His traveling expenses were Q10, and he told me that the Q30 that he didn't have he had left as an advance payment for *labores* with an acquaintance and that when he returned it would be just to get the *labores*. I told him that it was okay.

The following day, they began to arrange the material, which they did in two days. Then they began to weave. In 15 days, they finished a *corte* of 7 *varas*. Benito could hardly weave better than the student. Benito can weave belts and tablecloths, but not *cortes*. This man took part of the wool to his house and did not want to work anymore. He is a thief because he told me he had left Q30 in advance for *labores*, but it was a lie because he never went to get them. Then he would not talk to me anymore, acting as if he were an enemy.

I certainly "appreciated" him. I gave him his money and other things that I had. I do not want to be disgusted with anyone, but he behaved very poorly. For me and my wife it was another great loss. Our son wished to learn the art, but it's a pity I didn't know whether it would be his fortune or not—the teachers wanted a lot of money. But truly I had given them money that I had struggled hard and suffered to earn, and I couldn't do anymore because I didn't have it.

José enrolled for the first year of *básico* in the new Instituto Joseño, but the loom was set up inside the house. Each time I asked my son if he wished or not to learn how to weave, he told me that he did but sorrowfully because he himself was realizing what the people had done. We always had hope that some day we would find a good teacher. With faith in God, although He was tardy in responding, indeed, we hoped we would be able to do something for our children, which would also be beneficial for our town. If God would show the way for my son to learn perfectly the occupation of making good *cortes*, we would sell them at a very fair price to help my people because we are all poor and it takes a lot of effort to earn our money. I knew very well that people of Salcajá, Totonicapán, and Quezalte-nango come to sell *cortes* in these parts with elevated prices because here in this part of the southern zone there are no weavers of fine *cortes*.

Weaving is not easy. One has to go through many stages. I just console myself with the refrain, *"El que quiere celeste que le cuesta"* [He who wants grand things has to pay for them]. It's true that we have suffered a lot but it's a pity that we haven't mastered this art. But that's life. One has to have patience because it's difficult to do something.

Half a day José helped me work and the other half he was studying in the institute. When we weren't baking, we were working in the fields. For lack of money, I had not been able to send my son to Totonicapán. In that town, there are good weavers.

Thus it was from February to September [1984], seven months without doing anything. In the latter days of September, I talked with my friend, José Pérez Méndez, president of the Federación Guatemalteca de Cooperativas de Consumo, who is from Totonicapán. Seeing that the loom was still in the house, he asked me how my weaving business was doing. I told him all that we had suffered. In consolation he told me that as president of a federation he could get a scholarship in the *centro de formación de desarrollo de la comunidad* [training center for community development] in the department of weaving in Totonicapán.[21] He also told me that his inquiry wouldn't cost me a single centavo. To express our friendship, I told him, "Many thanks, José, for your good intentions for us." That night, we made a modest dinner, and this friend slept in the house.

The following day, he left for his town, Totonicapán. We agreed that I would receive an answer by telegram. The month of October passed, as did November and December [1984]. Not until January [1985] did I receive a telegram from Totonicapán. The message said: "Two scholarships obtained, Rabinal, Baja Verapaz, urge send me names and studies completed."

For me it was a joy. Then I went to the house of Eduardo Hernández to ask him if his son wanted to study weaving. He told me that his son had been studying in San Luis for the last three days as a gift from his grandparents. Then I went to the house of Santos Mendoza [not Mendoza Cruz] and asked him the same thing. When he asked his son, he answered yes. After talking with his family, we determined that his son for sure was going to Rabinal. I told Santos that tomorrow I was going to bring the certified papers of study. However, when I arrived [with them], Santos told me, "No, Rabinal is very distant and the times are very delicate."

Then I headed for the house of my friend Antonio Cholotío Canajay to offer him the scholarship. He told me that he had to discuss it well so that nothing would go wrong. Later, Antonio gave me all the documents of his son Fernando Igor Cholotío Morales.

Days later I went to Totonicapán to take the papers of the two boys. Way before I arrived in Totonicapán, I had to go on foot to the canton, Xantún. I waited a long time, but José did not arrive home. Then I went to Totonicapán, looking for the region of the FEDECCON. When I arrived there, they told me that José had gone to Xela [Quezaltenango]. I had to wait.

José arrived at 5:00 p.m. and received me in his office. We chatted a lot, and I gave him the documents of the two boys. Then we went walking to get acquainted with the city a little. We met another friend who was a cooperative member, and they decided to drink in a restaurant. I told them I didn't have the money to buy liquor. They told me not to worry. Well, I drank some drinks but very carefully because I knew that I was with a person very superior to me. I don't know whether José had already had been drinking, but he got drunk, and we took him to Xantún. When we arrived, José went to sleep. His wife gave me a separate room, and I slept.

The following day, I got up at 7:00 a.m. because it was very cold. They served me breakfast, and afterwards, while I was waiting for José, a friend named Ignacio Bartolo arrived, who is a social promoter. He said that he was working with the Indian community, but, like José, he had gotten up somewhat hung over. Ignacio Bartolo sent for some liquor. They continued drinking, and I wasn't able to leave the house. We chatted and chatted, and so went the time. I was worried about my return trip to San José.

By 11:30 a.m. José was good and drunk, and I left for Totonicapán. I took a bus to Cuatro Caminos where I boarded the bus, Rutas Morales, for Panajachel. At 5:00 p.m., I arrived home. My family was very worried because I was supposed to have returned the day before.

Five days after my return to San José, Señor Antonio Cholotío came to my house to tell me that his son had changed his mind and did not want to go to Rabinal, and, moreover, he was not very interested in weaving and that travel expenses would be a lot of money. But I had taken the papers of the boy to Totonicapán. Señor Canajay caused me a problem because I had to look for another boy to whom to give the scholarship.

Then I went to the house of Benjamín Peña to ask whether his son wanted to study weaving by means of the scholarship. He told me that he would talk to his family that night and give me an answer. The next day Benjamín came to me to tell me that his son Ignacio Antonio would go to Rabinal to study weaving. Then we signed a document of the socioeconomic study. The next day I went to Totonicapán to change the name of Fernando Igor to Ignacio Antonio and also the certificates of study.

Then, taking Ramoncito with me, I went to tell José what had happened and that it was not Fernando Igor who was going to Rabinal but Ignacio Antonio. Then José had to change the contracts. Indeed, all went well. Benjamín, the father of Ignacio Antonio, helped me with Q2 for travel expenses.

We returned on the same day. I didn't have enough money for all the fare home. We had to wait to get off the bus and go on foot from a place called Mesebal. We walked until the summit. We rode on a bus to Santa Ana for 50 centavos. From Santa Ana we went on foot to San José, pretty tired.

José Pérez and I agreed that he was going to send me another telegram to tell me the date when the two boys were to present themselves in the training center in Rabinal. Then on 5 February [1985] I received a telegram which said that José Juan Bizarro and Ignacio Antonio Peña Bonilla should present themselves at Rabinal no later than the 18th of the current month. When we received the telegram, we mobilized to look for things such as work clothing, dress clothing, pajamas, soccer shoes, tennis shoes, and other things that are required at the institution. We bought a little used and new clothing. Also, they asked us to get him a suitcase, but we didn't buy one because they are too expensive. We just made a box out of wood in the form of a suitcase.

Then on Saturday, 10 February, we invited some catechists and a group of guitarists of the same Catholic church for a prayer session. All went well, and after giving thanks to God, we served coffee and bread as a refreshment. Also, the parents of my wife came to instruct their grandson to conduct himself well, not to get drunk, and set a good example.

During the month of January, José Juan had worked very hard, half a day he had helped me in the bakery and the other half he had worked gathering ripe coffee as a laborer, earning 50 centavos a *quintal*.

Sunday dawned and we got up at 4:00 in the morning to leave for a trip from San José to Panajachel on the launch and from Panajachel to Guatemala [City] on the Rebuli [bus]. In Guatemala, Benjamín Peña, Ignacio Antonio, José, and I ate lunch and bought some things and then boarded the Rutas Salamatecas bus. At 7:00 at night, we arrived in Rabinal. A man took us to the training center, No. 7, where they received us very well and gave us the place to lodge. We slept very tranquilly, but beforehand, we went to buy tortillas and got acquainted with the marketplace. We ate for only 40 centavos each.

Monday, 18 February, dawned, and we went to eat breakfast in the marketplace. Then we went to the center. We didn't meet the director, but the secretary received the two boys and at the same time took information from the parents such as age and address. Benjamín and I spent a day in the center and slept there until 2:00 a.m. Then we got up and left Rabinal, arriving in the capital at 9:00 a.m. After eating breakfast we took the Rebuli bus to Panajachel. In Panajachel, I sent a certified letter to my great friend James D. Sexton, which I had written in Rabinal. I had thought about certifying it in Rabinal, but it was a pity that we arrived very late at the office.

Well, when we left the two boys, I gave my son only Q10. There wasn't any more money. I spent it on clothing, the transportation for a round trip, and other things. Altogether I spent Q200. The following day after having arrived home, I began to work very hard making bread with my two small sons because we had to send José Q10 to buy sweets and sundry items when they allowed him to leave Saturdays and Sundays.

Days later, he sent me a message that he only was receiving two days of classes, and later he sent me a letter telling me that they have to leave on Holy Week. Then I sent him Q10 certified for the cost of transportation to come home. José came on the 29th of March. During the week, he helped me make bread. He left again Tuesday, 9 April 1985.

He said that on the road there was a lot of searching, and, for that reason their suitcases were misplaced. But they didn't give it any importance. They met up with their luggage in Antigua, Guatemala, by the good deeds of some friends.

Can you explain this more?

There were two Rebuli buses being searched at a check point and the people got confused and changed buses but the suitcases were on the first bus they were on. Friends on the bus sent the suitcases to Guatemala [City] and the director sent them on to Rabinal.

On 15 April, I received a telegram from José which said, "Please don't send money. I will arrive end of the month." Answering by telegram, I asked him, "Indicate reason leaving, furlough or problems." On the third day, I received the answer saying, "I'm wasting time, center doesn't have instructor, two days class a week."

This telegram bothered me a lot. I left on 24 April for Rabinal, arriving on the same day in the afternoon. Then I talked to the director. I told him that my son sent a telegram in which he told me that he was withdrawing from the center for lack of a weaving instructor. The director told me that tomorrow (the next day) he would give me the details of the situation. I slept in the same center, chatting with José who told me that the director gave only two days of classes a week. On Monday and Tuesday the students were sleeping below the looms. On Wednesday and Thursday they were receiving classes. On Friday, Saturday, and Sunday, they were sleeping. He says that in the mornings they give them a little exercise and they cleaned up. We chatted with the other students who told me that all are very desperate, but their parents were far away. All of them were ready to leave the center.

Thursday, 12 April, dawned. We got up at 5:00 in the morning. The two boys began to arrange their suitcases. At 8:00 a.m., I asked the director for the withdrawal of the two boys from the said center, but the director didn't allow us to leave without indicating on record in the center the reason for withdrawing the two students.

At 8:00 a.m., we entered in the office of the director. Then I told his secretary to draw up an act. When it was finished, they read it, and we heard that the act was in favor of the director and the center. They said that the two boys were withdrawing because they wished to do so. After reading it, I asked that they incorporate two more points, and if they would, I would sign it. Finally, they told me yes. I put on record that the director has manipulated his office, that the students only have two days of classes during the week—Wednesday and Thursday—and that Monday, Tuesday, Friday, and Saturday, they only sleep below the looms. Also, I asked in the act that the superior authorities of the training center first take more than marginal interest in the teaching of the Indian people, that the monopoly in the center be eliminated, that each room of the center have its own instructor, and that a certified copy be sent to the president of the training center for community development, who resides in the capital city.

The secretary did all the things that I asked but very angrily. They told me that I had to pay for the meals of the two youngsters. I told them very well, "We are going to make the payments, but there will have to be a confirmation as to whether these two boys are withdrawing because they just wanted to or because the director isn't concerned that each classroom has its own teacher." Finally, we signed the act.

Together we left Rabinal at 2:00 in the morning on the Salamatecas line, arriving in the capital city at 3:00 p.m. We were walking a little to visit our baking instructor, Pedro Jesús Novales Padilla, in Zone 3, but when we arrived at his house, they told us that he was working in Santa Catarina Ixtahuacán, training new aspirants in baking. We chatted with his wife, who gave us coffee and bread. Then we headed for Zone 1, and slept in the Río Jordan Inn.

On 26 April, we left at 4:00 in the morning from the inn to take the bus to San Luis. We arrived home at 12:00 noon. We ate lunch and began to work in the bakery. It's true that we aren't making much money, but this is helping us somewhat, depending on the quantity that we work. At times we only make three or four quetzales.

This same afternoon José became very sad and depressed when we were baking bread. I asked him what was wrong, and he told me that he felt a lot of grief for the money we had lost and that inside the house we had a loom without benefiting from it. I told him, "Be more patient. God knows what He is going to do with us. God and we will struggle, and one day we will be free of these things; always have faith in God that soon He will provide us a good teacher." I said this to console him. Also, the people asked what was happening with the *cortes*, and I told them, "Within a little while, indeed, we will sell you *cortes*."

Then my wife and I decided that we should make a trip to Totonicapán to speak with Señor Santos Mendoza because he owes us more than Q200. We thought that perhaps this man would want to teach the work to José with the condition that our son would go to work for him without earning anything, just so that he could perfect the occupation. We arranged that we would give him his food, clothing, and necessary expenses, including his travel. Also, the young lad was ready to work for the person who was going to teach him this art. I always was struggling to make the sacred bread. Also, I was working a lot in the fields because I have a big family and I don't have any money. But by the grace of God, I succeeded in selling a little more and got together Q30. Then I arranged that my wife and I would go to Totonicapán.

The 8th of May we left San José and arrived at Cuatro Caminos, a place near Totonicapán, where we ate breakfast. Then we took the road to Paxtocá, the place where Señor Santos lives, more or less eight kilometers away. When we arrived at the house of the señor, they were suspicious of us, thinking that perhaps we were evil people. But this was not true. We were just trying to find a solution to our problem. Finally, Señor Santos received us inside his house and gave us soft drinks. We chatted a lot. Then we ate lunch. After lunch, we arranged for this señor to teach the work to our son. They told us they were going to provide a room where he would sleep on the condition that the boy would work for them. We would have to give him food and necessary expenses. That is to say, we were going to pay them for his food. We were finishing the arrangements when suddenly the news arrived that a family member of theirs had died. Then the conversation that we had was forgotten, and they went to the house of the deceased.

We remained inside the house where we were able to talk to a son-in-law of theirs by the name of Juan Domingo Toc Cojox. He told us a reality. He said that we would be sending our son for nothing. He said that Señor

Santos wasn't reliable, that he just fought with his wife, that he owed a lot of people money, and that he had other women in Guatemala City. The son-in-law told us all the details, and, indeed, we believed him because Santos owed us.

Then while Santos was visiting the family of the deceased, Juan Domingo invited us to his house and served us coffee. That is when this boy told us that he wanted to work in San José although he would have to leave his family. He spoke very sentimentally saying, "We still had work to be done, and we were killing ourselves. We shouldn't be egotistical in this world." Also, his wife told us that her husband could go to San José. Well, we said yes because our objective was to get a teacher of weaving.

[We agreed that] Juan Domingo would earn Q80 including travel for a round trip home two times a month. Also, we would give him food and a house to sleep in. But he told us that he needed Q20 in advance for family expenses as a commitment from us. Then we agreed that we would return again to Totonicapán on Monday the 13th and that they would meet us in Cuatro Caminos to give them Q20. His wife told us that he didn't have any money because it has been a few days since having finished the construction of a house. She said that he had sold all of his materials for weaving, and for that reason he needed to work. Moreover, she said it was going to be necessary to spend about Q200 for materials. We promised that we would return Monday without fail with the money. But frankly, we didn't leave money in his house for the purchase of the materials.

When we returned to the house of Señor Santos, it was already night. They gave us dinner and a bed to sleep on. But the truth is that I didn't sleep at all. I just thought about what I was going to do to get the money. The next day, Thursday, we left Paxtocá at 5:00 in the morning. By God's grace, we rode in a car to Cuatro Caminos, then in a bus to Los Encuentros and from Los Encuentros to Sololá where we ate breakfast but did nothing else because the launch to San José left at 3:00 in the afternoon. When we arrived home, we told the children what had happened in Totonicapán. But we were worried a lot because we didn't have the necessary money. I thought about getting a loan, but I couldn't. During this afternoon, I was meditating hard.

Friday, my wife and I thought we would sell a piece of land with coffee trees. The land belonged to my wife. Her father had given it to her as an inheritance. But I had planted the coffee grove. On this day, Friday, 10 May, I offered it to two persons who said that tomorrow they would tell me yes or no. Saturday, 11 May [1985], Señor Agustín María Toc came to my house to ask about the value of the land. I told him that because I needed the money, I would sell it for Q500, but this señor only offered me Q300. When a person needs to sell something, those who have money take advantage of him. Frankly, the land was worth more than Q500, but because of my commitments I had to sell cheap. This afternoon I didn't make the agreement, I just prayed to God for a solution to my problems.

Sunday dawned with a lot of worry. I had not obtained the money. At noon, Alberto Mogollón came and told me that he would give me Q400 for the land but within a period of 15 days. He said that right now, he could not make the deal. At 8:00 p.m. my wife and I went to the house of her father to get a loan. We were there when Agustín María came again. We didn't get the loan. Instead, what we did was close the deal. Finally, he paid me Q450 for the land but with the condition that he is only going to give me Q400 now and the remainder of Q50 in the month of November during the coffee harvest. We had to agree because it was true that we had a critical need. He gave us the Q400, and from that time they became the owners, but not until November will we give them the deed.

When we returned, we were a little consoled, and we slept a little contentedly. More or less I had the money for the trip.

On Monday, 13 May 1985, at 5:00 in the morning, we left from San José to Cuatro Caminos, but we arrived there late. There was a lot of delay on the road because there weren't any buses running. In Cuatro Caminos, Juan Domingo and his wife were waiting for us. They said that they were getting desperate because we had agreed that we would arrive at 9:00 in the morning, but when they saw us, they became content. Then we went to Salcajá to buy the materials. We thought about coming back the same day, but it was impossible. A lot of people were shopping in the stores, and we had to wait. We bought thread, wool, a reed [for the loom], rake, reel, and dye to dye the *labores de jaspe*. And we gave Q20 to the wife of Juan Domingo. After buying all that was needed, we ate lunch in a *comedor*. At 3:00 p.m. Juan Domingo said good-bye to his wife and we went on a Los Higueros bus to Panajachel.

We thought about sleeping in an inn, but they wanted Q3.50 per person, which was very expensive. Thus, we decided to sleep on the beach. We ate a very poor dinner, and instead of sleeping in the inn, we bought a *chamarra* [heavy wool blanket]. The wind was very strong, and my wife and I couldn't sleep.

On Monday, we arrived home. We did an accounting for the Q200; all that remained was Q20. Then we ate breakfast. About that time, Juan

Domingo and José began to prepare the loom again, which wasn't in our house but in the house of my deceased grandmother, Isabel. The teacher didn't want to prepare the loom in my house because a lot of people come inside and he didn't want his concentration interrupted. Out of necessity, we had to use the house of my grandmother. After loading the loom, the teacher told me that he was going to need another loom so that he could teach and work so that he will not lose time. I had to do what was possible. I bought the wood, which cost me Q75. The construction cost me Q75, but it took a long time to make it. The carpenter was working on it, and Juan Domingo and José worked on the weaving loom.

Well, I also had to buy a *madejador* [hank or skein maker] and an *urdidora* [warper], which cost Q50. They were made here in San José, and they almost took the rest of the Q400.

I continued working hard in the fields to obtain food for my family. All the basic foods have increased in price. But I had faith in God that, one day in the not too distant future, *cortes* would be woven in my town.

I have a lot of poverty. I also have problems because I want to establish something for my people of San José. I believe that it isn't just arrogance for me because I am aging, but it is that I will bequeath something in history. My two small sons, who are working hard almost like grown bakers, are making an effort. We don't pay a helper for all the bread that we make. We make it by ourselves, and when there is time, I work in the fields, cleaning my milpa, and at night make bread. But finally the body must rest. On 30 May, when I was very tired and suffering from lack of sleep, I went on a civil defense patrol and fell in a ravine. Now I have a knee that gives way. I have already been to two bone curers. What they told me is that I need rest, but owing to the work needed to feed my children, I am unable to rest. So, I am still working with the fractured knee.

We continued with the weaving, and on 7 June 1985 we sold three *cortes* in San Martín at very reasonable prices because we needed the money to buy more wool. We made Q105 for the three fine *cortes*, which are the first works. We sold them in the shop of Ignacio Tuc.

On the 12th, Juan Domingo went to his town to buy material, and he returned right on time. On this date we sold three *cortes*. We sold them by the *vara* to the children in the school for small *cortes*.

The new loom was installed and began functioning on 2 July 1985. At present José has made four fine *cortes*, but they have not sold. By the grace of God, José can weave well, and he is able to make *labores de jaspe*. This is very delicate work. I don't get involved with them because I am unable. Up until now, we have seven *cortes*, which we keep in the showcase, but we haven't sold them because the people have no money in these times. I have faith in God, however, that they will sell in the month of Christmas.

Thanks go to the good heart of Jaime Sexton, who sent me a check that I used for my outstanding debts. But there is hardly any material. The boy wants to work, but there is no money.

More on the Ex-Commissioners
28 February to 29 July 1985

The problems with the ex-commissioners of San Martín la Laguna continue. Already I have said many times that the former commissioners committed many crimes—raping women, swindling lots of people out of their money, and claiming that the people were involved in subversive things. In this manner they took advantage of a lot of people. But finally, the inhabitants of the town realized what was happening and went to the high authorities of the army to ask that the ex-commissioners be shot. The military authorities did nothing for the residents because they say that members of that institution [the army] are implicated in that violence.

When the ex-commissioners were jailed, the *Martineros* looked for formal accusers to continue the proceedings before the courts of justice. The ex-commissioners were unable to get out of jail. They searched a lot for help, even selling their land and *sitios* to pay for legal aid, but it was useless. They stayed in jail anyway. The formal accusers named by the town were Señores Ignacio Puzul Robles[22] and Eduardo García Méndez, who were well paid to work with the lawyers in Sololá and in Quezaltenango. The group in charge gave them the necessary money for travel, food, and the salaries of the lawyers and themselves. The news says that the whole town gave money, according to each person's ability. They did this for more than two years.

Also, the ex-commissioners looked for Juanito Mendoza to get them out of jail. But it was futile. What happened was that Juanito just gained land and money.

When the ex-commissioners were imprisoned, Gaspar Yotz Ajcac became *jefe* of a new group of commissioners. Later another problem emerged—the accusation that this group of commissioners only drank and that two of them left their wives and took concubines, which was almost the same as the situation before. This was when the people arose again, asking that this new group be replaced. The military authorities agreed to what the people had asked for, and they named Señor Mario Puzul Cojox as *jefe* of the military commissioners of San Martín la Laguna. Mario is a nephew of Ignacio Puzul.

Well the people were very peaceful for a short time—Ignacio Puzul was always occupied with the lawsuit against the jailed ex-commissioners and his nephew with headquarters. But the group that was imprisoned had left a companion in the town. The information says that the friends of the prisoners collaborated with the *jefe* of the *cuartel* [barracks] of Sololá, and the latter gave the former work as confidants to investigate what was happening in the town—whether all the *Martineros* are good or have business with the terrorists.

Thus were the two groups always divided. The majority was with the commissioner, Mario, and a minority with the ex-commissioner and his group, although also there were some who abstained, but they were few. So the violent group was always against the new commissioners, and there never was peace between them. Here are the names of the *Martineros* who acted as *confidenciales* [agents, spies of the army]—Abraham Có Bizarro, José Sicay, Antonio Cojox, José Bizarro Có, Santos Alvarado, and Lucio Quic. They had their collaborators, and they were involved more. The information says that this group arrived to accuse the commissioner, Mario Puzul, saying that he had relations with terrorists who go to his house. But that was a lie they made up to kill him. They say that they gained the confidence of a second lieutenant of the army and made a plan to kill Señor Ignacio Puzul and his nephew Mario. One day the hombre, Antonio Cojox, accompanied by others, pointed out the house of the *jefe* of the commissioners. But Antonio was captured by the patrolmen. The *jefe* of the commissioners, Mario, and his group drew up an act stating that if a kidnapping or act of violence happened in the town or to the commissioners, the people should rise up against Antonio. Antonio confirmed that he had gone to point out the house of the *jefe* of the commissioners but that he was obliged by his uncle, José Cojox García, and the group of the *confidenciales* and that he was a secret agent of the army. Antonio is the son of Santiago Cojox, Junior, a companion of the ex-commissioners who are in prison. There had always been anger between the two groups, but no one ever imagined what would happen.

Mario was a decent, educated man. He was an Evangelist of the Assembly of God. Also he was the director of an ensemble of string musicians. As gifts, he gave records and cassettes of very good hymns. Mario was a poor man. He was in the army as a soldier, and he worked in my *cuadrillas* on the southern coast. For that reason I knew him well. We were very good friends. His father died in an accident when he was carrying avocadoes to Guatemala [City]. For that reason he began to work as a child.

Ignacio Puzul continued the suit against the ex-commissioners. Eduardo García got tired and already was not paying any attention. Thus, only Ignacio represented the people before the tribunals of justice, asking for the condemnation of the ex-commissioners. But the courts did nothing to condemn them nor to free them.

The news says that Ignacio Puzul then went to Sololá on Tuesday, 26 February 1985, to check on the suit against the prisoners. One of the spies, Señor Matías Bizarro Có, went at the same time, following his steps. When Señor Ignacio Puzul returned from Sololá and was waiting for the hour of the launch to arrive for the trip to his town, they were secretly waiting for him. He was already on the launch, and it was about to head out to San Martín when Matías told Ignacio, "Ignacio, up there, they're looking for you. Some men need to talk to you for a moment. But hurry because these men have to travel!" Matías said it was an important matter and the men were waiting very near.

"Yes," Ignacio said, and he got off the launch and went to where they were waiting for him. The other passengers thought that he had been taken to the courthouse or to the military zone [station], and they did not pay it any mind. He was kidnapped in Panajachel, in a car without a license plate. Some people saw the unmarked car. He was taken alive in the car to San Martín where he was killed. He left the launch because he thought they had good news for him.

The car with Ignacio inside stayed at the soccer field. Another car went to town to get Mario. It is believed that one of the imprisoned ex-commissioners, Santiago Cojox, was with the assassins. But this is strange because he would have had to have been let out of jail in Quezaltenango to go with them. Some say they recognized him, his form and his walk, even though all their faces were covered when they went to capture Mario Puzul. However, no one saw him directly. The news says that Santiago was the one who contracted the assassins, but sincerely I can't confirm this because the information wasn't presented by someone who said, "I knew Chago [Santiago]," or "I talked to him." No, they only said that Chago Cojox was one who was accompanying the assassins when they were cutting the throats and cutting out the tongues of Ignacio Puzul and Mario outside the town.

Everything was quiet that afternoon without anyone realizing that their countrymen had been kidnapped. Moreover, what happened later was that the family of Ignacio Puzul was quiet. At midnight on Tuesday, some *desconocidos* [unknown men] arrived in a [yellow] pickup. They went to the house of Mario Puzul, *jefe* of the group. They broke into his house and took him by force of arms to the car. His wife says that he recognized the *jefe* of the group and said, "Buenas noches, my lieutenant," but the lieutenant didn't answer. Mario said good-bye to his wife and his brother, Francisco. The car left, and then the uproar began, ringing the bells and the people gathering. But there was nothing they were able to do.

The *patrulleros* went into action. Later they realized that there had been two cars, one that was waiting near the town. Both left in the direction of San Luis. The uproar of the people and the ringing of the bells was heard in San José until 3:00 a.m. The *patrulleros* of San José were on alert, but in this town nothing happened. My wife and I got up at 3:00 a.m. to butcher a pig, and for that reason we were aware that the *patrulleros* were quite ready, but without knowing what happened.

Not until 5:00 a.m. were we told Mario Puzul Cojox, *jefe* of the commissioner of San Martín, had been kidnapped and many people had gone to look for him. At 7:00 in the morning a car left taking coffee to San Luis, but it had only gone 5 or 6 kilometers to the place called Chicá, where on the side of the road they found the body of Mario Puzul together with the body of his uncle, Ignacio Puzul, the two cadavers together. The driver of the car did not go on but informed the authorities.

They went to get the dead ones and take them to Sololá for the medical autopsy. But an hour after the kidnapping all the people demanded that Antonio Cojox and his group be put in jail according to the memorandum drawn up earlier when this man had gone to point out the house of the commissioner. Antonio was imprisoned, and then they took his companions to jail. Day broke with 17 *Martineros* in jail implicated in the kidnapping and assassination of the two men. They confessed only that they had collaborated with the kidnapping, but they didn't know who the kidnappers were.

In the same afternoon, the bodies came back from Sololá. They were watched over in their houses. Thursday, 28 February 1985, was a day of anguish and much pain for the *Martineros*. On this day they buried the remains of Mario and Ignacio Puzul. There were many declarations condemning the bloody deed. At 11:00 a.m. the mourners entered the office of the commissioners. Then there were acclamations on behalf of the people.

They took the bodies, one to the Catholic Church and the other to the Protestant Church. Later they went to the general cemetery. To Mario, they gave a *panteón* [above-ground tomb] where they put his body. On 1 March, they took the 17 *Martineros* to jail in Sololá. The army took them in a truck as if they were animals.

On 2 March, they also took to Sololá the *alguaciles* and municipal guards to give statements to the court of the first instance about what had happened that night. They returned the following day. No one knows what they stated.

In the last days of the month of March, the 17 *Martineros* left the jail in Sololá acquitted, claiming they knew nothing about what had happened. The people were so enraged about their liberty that they wanted to throw them out of town, together with their entire families. But the information says that they had a lot from protection from the army. When these men got out of jail, they had a party. They rented a car and went to have a fiesta at Chuitinamit with much liquor. We knew this because they bought the liquor in San José since no one in San Martín would give them any.

When these men left jail, they asked for protection from the army. A military detachment was placed in the town so that the people would do nothing. This is when the people united to legalize a committee for the defense of the town. But the governor didn't allow its legalization. However, they established this committee illegally and named two *Martineros*, Francisco Có and Bartolomé, to continue the suit against the 17 *Martineros*. With a lawyer of the same town named Pelayo Eduardo Ixtamer, these two again raised criminal procedures.

The *Martineros* gave up the suit of the eight ex-commissioners that were imprisoned in Quezaltenango. On 25 June, the ex-commissioners, Ernesto Quit, Lucas Chac, Abraham Méndez, Raúl Barrera, Federico Yojcom Sicay, and Diego Tul got out of jail. However, Santiago Cojox and the *ex-jefe*, José Méndez Puac, remained in jail.

One version says that the assassins of Ignacio and Mario Puzul were contracted by the same ex-commissioners that were jailed because Ignacio Puzul was named by the people of San Martín to carry out the penal procedures against them. The ex-commissioners knew that they were going to face even a harsher sentence and for that reason contracted the assassins. The other version says that Santiago was seen, but I can't confirm this because I don't have the proof to say it is true.

On 23 or 24 June, 1985, information says that three spies of the army were kidnapped—Juan Sicay, José Bizarro Có, and Matías Bizarro Có.

They looked for them everywhere, but they did not learn of their where-abouts. I realized this because a telegram came to the justice of peace of this town. No one knew anything about them, nor did they show up dead. Perhaps, they have been given asylum in some country. Who knows? [They were still missing in October 1988.]

On 29 July 1985 came the order of the court of first instance to jail again the other 14 *Martineros*, excluding the three who disappeared. Until this date, they are imprisoned in Sololá. On 22 August, I chatted with the lawyer Pelayo Eduardo Ixtamer, and he told me about the suit of the 14 persons. They are there for kidnapping, and they will have to spend a lot of time in jail. But still the sentence has not been declared. Who knows how many years or perhaps months they will stay in jail?

Where is Santiago Cojox now?

Since the two main enemies [litigants] of the ex-commissioners died, they got out of jail except José Méndez Puac, their *ex jefe*. Santiago Cojox now is found renting a house near Quezaltenango. He is selling vegetables and sacks of *pita* [agave string]. He no longer wants to live in his pueblo. Well, one reason that he can't live in his town is that when he was jailed he sold the *sitio*, the house, and other properties. If he wanted to live in San Martín, he surely could live there because he has one brother who has lots of property, lots of *sitios*, and who is the owner of the launches that travel from San Martín to San Luis. They say, and I suppose it's true, that Santiago is very badly seen by the people, and his own conscience bothers him. That's why he doesn't want to live in San Martín, because he thinks that if he lives there, the relatives of the dead will take revenge. More for that, Santiago can't live in San Martín now, for all the wicked things that he has done.

And what happened to the rest of the ex-commissioners?

One, Ernesto Quit, works in Guatemala [City] in a metal works factory. He was placed by a relative of his in the job. His sister told me on 27 June 1987 that he makes Q300 a month. The other, who's called Lucas Chac (Bolaños), is mentally ill in San Martín. He's a relative of the throat-slit ex-commissioner, Ignacio Puzul. Who knows what happened? I don't know if it's a punishment of nature or if when he was jailed, he was thinking many things. But now it seems that he is loco. In January of 1987 he nearly killed his mother.

The others are living in San Martín, but, more than anything, their lives are like those of animals because almost all of people of the town don't want them. But, also, maybe they can't find a life in another place; that's why they are in the pueblo. They don't go out alone. When they go out to work, they have to be accompanied by a relative. Federico Yojcom Sicay, Raúl Barrera, and Diego Tul are the ones that are working in San Martín. Their *jefe*, José Méndez Puac, who was sentenced to seven years, is still in jail in the *granja* [prison farm] of the Centro Penal Cantel of Quezaltenango. According to his relatives, he will not be able to regain his liberty until the year 1990.

Why did the ex-commissioners get off so lightly?

The truth is that they didn't spend much time in jail for all the crimes that they had committed in the town. The legal proceedings were begun by Ignacio Puzul. If Ignacio Puzul and Mario had not died, I am sure that the ex-commissioners would still be in jail. But since they succeeded in killing Ignacio and Mario Puzul, they recovered their liberty. Well, the town could have named others in place of Ignacio Puzul to continue the process against the ex-commissioners, but it was not possible because the town lives under fear that the same thing that happened to Ignacio and Mario can happen to them. And it's because of this that now nobody wanted to continue the process against these ex-commissioners. That's how it was that they were able to get out of the jails.

What happened to Renato Tuc, who was a secretary when the ex-commissioners had power?

Well, Renato Tuc now lives in San Martín. He was in jail at the time of the death of Ignacio and Mario Puzul. José Cojox, brother of the ex-commissioner Santiago Cojox, was in jail too. But, they were lucky because they got out of jail. They were only there about seven or eight months. Renato Tuc was a man that always liked to swindle the people because he was a pettifogger, working in the tribunals as an interpreter for the people who had various legal problems. Well, I didn't see him, right, because one needs to be clear and frank. But, what we do know is that he always had liked being the pettifogger. They say he was the secretary of the ex-commissioners. He wrote the anonymous letters to threaten the people, and, like that, the people had to pay a certain amount of money to not be persecuted by the ex-commissioners. Others that couldn't pay had to pay with their lives, right. He was one who caused a lot of damage in San Martín. During the time that he was in jail, he was almost well off because, through the mafia, he had been able to educate his children. He educated all his children, men and women. Now he has a family only of teachers. It's that, when he was in jail, he hardly suffered because his children paid for the food in a *comedor*. He didn't eat jail food; instead, to him they gave good food. That's all in reference to Renato Tuc. Now he lives in San Martín, but he isn't very calm because he doesn't go out, nor can he walk. Instead, he is like an invalid because now the town doesn't want him and doesn't accept him as before.[23]

Military Commissioners Give Advice
10 August 1985

My youngsters and I worked at making bread. The teacher of weaving did not work for lack of material for the loom. He was with us making bread. There was a lot of advice on the part of the military commissioners, saying that by order of the *comandantes* [commanders], it was urgent that all the commissioners and patrolmen present themselves in the field to receive classes. I didn't go on this afternoon because I was very busy making bread. My work ended very late, and for that reason I didn't have time to go. The news said that 100 persons were absent, and those absent were given the punishment of carrying firewood for cooking the food of the military. To obey I had to carry a little firewood to the detachment.

During the night of this day, I took my turn in the civil defense patrol. It is certain that there is a very strict order. For a fault one is taken to jail. They say he who doesn't respect the order is considered a subversive. But the truth is that in this town there are no subversives.

Civil Defense Patrols
Sunday, 11 August 1985

All of us, about 400 persons, in the civil defense patrol presented ourselves at the soccer field. Then they organized us into groups, and the specialists of the zone began to give us classes about the responsibilities of patrolmen. They treated us as if we were in the military. These things sometimes are somewhat funny because we patrolmen are unable to do what the military wants us to do. They say that we have to finish off the terrorists, and the patrolmen say yes. Who knows if we are going to do it.

At 12:00 noon they allowed us to go eat lunch and gave us the order that at 2:00 p.m. each patrolman return with a machete. When we arrived at 2:00 in the afternoon, we formed groups and began to clean the field. When we finished cleaning it, they told us that each one had to write down the obligations of a patrolman and how to handle firearms. In the afternoon we wrote down a song and at the same time we sang it.

What were the words to this song?

It was the "Hymn of the Civil Defense Patrol." These are the words:

I am a victorious soldier
of the civil defense.
Always nearby as brother
of the valiant army,
Always nearby as brother
of the valiant army.

For my fatherland Guatemala,
my flag of Blue and White,
for my land, my ideals,
I will fight like a jaguar.
For my land, my ideals,
I will fight like a jaguar.

When night falls,
the sun sleeps in the mountains.

I am vigilant; God helps me
to protect my family.
I am vigilant; God helps me
to protect my family.

For my fatherland I swear
to defend it until death,
to reject the subversive
and help my countrymen;
to reject the subversive
and help my countrymen.

Already the day breaks.
With my hands I will work.
But my weapon always ready
to fight for Guatemala,
but my weapon always ready
to fight for Guatemala.

This is similar to the "Hymn of the Army of Guatemala," which has the following words:

I am a soldier, patriotic and brave
of the land of liberty;
Guatemala will be independent
because I swear to serve with loyalty.

If I promote the peace and the land
of progress in the daily labor,
I am also prepared in war
to fight and die for your honor.

Chorus
My flag is a beautiful banner
sea and sky between *mallas de tul*
[meshes, or nets, of a plant],[24]
that I support as son of Mars
always high, very clear of blue.

Glorious champions leave
in history their names of light
because for the well being of the homeland they
fight with feather (pen), sword, or cross.
Military, follow the example
with loyalty, energy and valor!
The barracks, the home, is the temple
where you have your altar of honor

Chorus
My flag is the beautiful banner,
sea and sky between *mallas de tul*,
that I support as son of Mars
always high, very clear of blue.

At 5:00 p.m. everyone retired. Meanwhile, the commander of the detachment called Enrique Santos Alvarado Pantzay, Fidel Bizarro Quic, Jorge Erasmo Hernández Toc, Ignacio Ramírez, Valerio Teodoro Ujpán, and myself. They took us to a separate place among the coffee groves where the people couldn't see us. Then the second lieutenant said, "You are disobedient and don't wish to take your turn standing guard or obey the commissioners." This was a lie of the commissioners.

Then I told the second lieutenant, "None of the commissioners has talked to me. It's true that I missed three of the last shifts but that was when my knee was bad because I fell in a ravine during a night when I was taking my turn. It's for that reason I missed the turns."

The second lieutenant replied, "Be more careful not to miss any more. He who misses a turn will be taken to the zone of Sololá." Then they told the others present to give the reasons that they had missed turns. Everything was okay. There was no punishment or mistreatment.

At the same moment I told the new military commissioner Roberto Zacarías, "Take more care not to be accusing the citizens before the detachments. You have a lot to be desired as commissioner. If a person fails at his obligations, he should be called in the office of the commissioners to investigate the reason for two or three times missed. If this person incurs the same faults or demerits, only then send him to the *jefes* of the detachment of the respective zone. Indeed I know a little about the duties of the commissioner. Please don't continue doing more of this to the people because there are some who don't know to appeal to the *jefes*, and they will be punished."

The commissioner Roberto Zacarías told me, "Forgive me because I don't have much knowledge about how to handle people." At the same time we remained friends. The commandant of the detachment said the next punishment for the faults will be to be taken to the zone of Sololá to carry water in small fruit jars to fill four big drums at a distance of 100 meters. It takes a person three or four months to do it, and he is only given food once a day.

Warnings by the Military Commissioners
12 to 17 August 1985

Half the day I was working in Xebitz, spreading fertilizer on the fields. We didn't eat lunch until we got home.

At 3:00 p.m. they gathered us at the soccer field to receive classes. During these classes, they told us that the mission of the military is to help the community and to do what it takes to demolish the terrorists. Moreover, they told us not to collaborate with the terrorists and that he who collaborates with these people will be punished or shot so that they won't involve the good people. They didn't let us leave these classes until 5:00 p.m.

It is my birthday, 13 August 1985, and I thanked God for having given me another year of life. In the morning we went to work in Xebitz to clear the milpa, working a half day because they told us that at 2:00 p.m. we had to be present at the soccer field. When we arrived, however, they told us that there weren't going to be any classes because the *jefes* had been replaced. We returned home.

On 14 August we went to work a half day, making bread. In the afternoon, again we had to return to the soccer field to receive classes from the military. On this day there were no *jefes*. They said that they were bad, but that is not true. The military officials who arrived on this day were very humane, and they didn't mistreat anyone. They said that no one is able to accuse another person of subversion or anything else. First they have to investigate the case of the person to be sure that he is collaborating with the subversives. The official said:

Many come to accuse another person just because they are envious about a business deal or a problem with a woman or a piece of land or perhaps one person has more money than another, and then the person is accused of being a subversive. This is what you must not do. In San José nothing should happen as it has in other towns.

All the patrolmen were grateful.

On 15 August 1985 we only worked a half day again because they told us that in the afternoon there would be classes again. However, because of heavy rain, we only received a half hour of class. Many were not in agreement with these things, but one has to obey. If one does not, it is expensive—one pays with one's life.

We didn't work on 16 August 1985. We lost this day. After lunch we went to a new soccer field at 3:00 p.m. We sang the hymn of the patrolman. Moreover, we received classes on how to handle and shoot the rifle, mauser 7.62. There was a lot of nervousness among the personnel of the patrolmen, especially those who had not had military service. At times it was very funny. Many were not happy with these orders, but we were unable to do anything about it.

On 17 August, Saturday, all of us patrolmen had to be present at the soccer field very early to form military squads. It is certain that when we arrived, they assigned us and took us, five in each group, to the place where one is able to shoot. Each person who had not been in the military shot three times. Those of us who had served in the military were separated out as reserves to take care of those who hadn't.

We were last. We were only given one shot each. Some didn't fire at all because we ran out of ammunition. I shot once. Not until noon did we finish.

When we finished all of these things, the military officials were grateful for the participation of all the patrolmen. But there is one thing. The patrolmen murmured about losing time because we are poor and aren't accustomed to losing it. The murmuring that the patrolmen did was in Tzutuhil, and the officials are Ladinos who don't understand the bad words that the Indians speak. When the officials asked what it was that they were saying, others said that they were happy and saluted the military. But these were lies. The people actually spoke badly of them.

What kinds of things were the patrolmen saying?

They said: son-of-a-bitch, mother-fucker, go to hell. But they said these words in Tzutuhil. So when the *jefes* asked what they were saying, the others answered, "They are very happy."

About how many patrolmen were there?

Four hundred. All the men of 18 to 55 years of age. Later, they gradually lowered the maximum age to 50 years.

A Corte *Sells*
18 August 1985

Giving thanks to God that on this day a fine *corte* was sold to Josefa García for Q75. It is true we have some *cortes*, but they have not sold, not until now, giving infinite thanks to the Creator. With this money I paid the teacher Juan Domingo Toc.

On 19 August, María had the luck to sell a *corte* for Q75 to a North American. This was a relief to solve the necessities of the house. With so little work for me, it was a blessing because the people are hardly thinking about buying things since the times are very expensive. These days we are working in Xebitz cleaning the milpa.

Political Life in Guatemala and in San José
25 August to 6 September 1985

Politics in Guatemala are very complicated, and it would be better if the people were not divided. Everyone running for office says that he is a good candidate and that he will get the country out of the crisis that it is in. Who knows? There are scarcely two independent parties, and the rest are more co-aligned. The parties that campaign alone are the strongest parties, the Democracia Cristiana Guatemalteca (DCG) and the Unión del Centro Nacional (UCN). The Democracia Cristiana Guatemalteca is supporting *licenciado* [lawyer, licensed, or graduate] Vinicio Cerezo Arévalo for president of the republic; the Unión del Centro Nacional (UCN), *licenciado* Jorge Carpio Nicolle; the Partido Democrático de Cooperación Nacional (PDCN) and Partido Revolucionario Guatemalteca (PRG), the engineer Jorge Serrano Elías; the party, Movimiento de Liberación Nacional (MLN), and Partido Institucional Democrático (PID), *licenciado* Mario Sandoval Alarcón; the party, Central Auténtico Nacionalista (CAN), *licenciado* Mario David García; and the Partido Socialista Democrático (PSD), *licenciado* Mario Solórzano Martínez. The Partido de Unificación Anticomunista (PUA), Movimiento Emergente de Concordia (MEC), Partido de Integración Nacional (PIN), Frente de Unidad Nacional (FUN), and Partido Social Cristiano [PSC] (Católico) are backing the *bachiller* [high school graduate] Leonel Sisniega Otero. There are two candidates of the Partido Nacionalista Renovador (PNR), *licenciado* Alejandro Maldonado Aguirre for president and Mauricio Quixtán, a Quiché Indian, for vicepresident.

It is certain that in the highlands there are four who are predominant—Vinicio Cerezo, Jorge Carpio Nicolle, Jorge Serrano Elías, and Mario Sandoval Alarcón. But some information says that in the East, *licenciado* Mario Sandoval is strongest because that is where the Liberación had success in the year of 1954 when Colonel Jacobo Arbenz Guzmán was overthrown. The information says that the cradle of the party, Movimiento de Liberación Nacional, is Chiquimula and Zacapa, where they still have strong support. It is certain that those in the East are anticommunists because nothing is heard there of terrorism or subversion.

The information from the other parties says that Mario Sandoval Alarcón receives help from 55 anticommunist countries for his political campaign. I don't know if this is true. Also, it says that Jorge Carpio Nicolle receives help from *licenciado* Donaldo Alvarez Ruiz, who is sending money from New York. When Jorge Carpio wins the election, Donaldo will return to Guatemala. It seems true because the UCN uses the same words and criticism in its propaganda. "Peace, Work, and Liberty" is the same slogan that the PID is using. Also, it says that the other parties are getting help from communist countries, but I don't believe so because they are not running a campaign backed by a lot of money. Everything they are doing is with poverty and struggle.

The first four parties mentioned above are carrying out a campaign of luxury. Jorge Carpio Nicolle was in town last week (30 August 1985) at 4:00 in the afternoon. He was giving out T-shirts with the emblem of his party.

He had a marimba and passed out a lot of liquor and other drinks, and moreover, provided lunch for a lot of people. One of the directors told me that he had given money to cover other expenses. They say that the Unión del Centro Nacional is a new party, but who knows?

Now Jorge Serrano Elías has a lot of money because during the time of the earthquake of the year 1976, when a lot of people died, he was president of the national reconstruction, which received a lot of help from other countries to give to the people who suffered damage. But what he did was to hoard a lot of money in the banks and not give it to the poor. Now he is spending it for his political campaign. Also, he was president of the Consejo de Estado [Council of State] in the time of Ríos Montt. It is thus that we Guatemalans are getting screwed because it's certain that there are three party candidates, Mario Sandoval Alarcón, Jorge Serrano Elías, and Jorge Carpio Nicolle, who they say are independent but are not.

In San José there are five candidates for mayor, five aspirants for the very small salary of Q120. It's true that they aren't doing it because they are thinking of improving the progress of San José. They have very personal interests, or perhaps for being fond of having the luxury of being mayor.

Señor Juan Mendoza Ovalle, blowing his own trumpet, again declared himself a candidate for mayor, saying that he is the one, the best, to run for the tribunal sponsored by the Movimiento de Liberación Nacional and Partido Institucional Democrático. Until now, however, he doesn't have any people backing him. He will get votes only if he pays for them because the people know him and saw how he was as mayor. He was very much a thief. Now he is trying to do the same as before, but it's difficult.

For the Unión del Centro Nacional is Ignacio Arnaldo Bizarro González. This man, who handed over the tribunal to his uncle Andrés during the coup, wants to be mayor again to make some money. He has some pretensions that he had been subordinated. Moreover, this man graduated from the sixth grade, but he doesn't know how to speak Spanish. I don't know why. He's campaigning and saying he's going to win. Sunday, 25 August, he and his supporters went to the *aldeas*. They gave him lunch, and many people talked to him, saying that they would give him their vote.

On Monday, the 26th, it was the candidate of the Partido Democrático de Cooperación Nacional, Benjamín Peña Cholotío, who was offering many kinds of gifts for the people and promising works if elected mayor, without knowing the situation of the money in the treasury. Perhaps the town owes the institutions of the government a lot, or perhaps the government owes money and can't spend it on the promised works. For sure, they do not know how to analyze the budget.

Two persons, the candidate of the Democracia Cristiana and the candidate of the Partido Socialista Democrático, are running a very clean campaign without making offerings. They are appealing to the conscience of the people, asking what they like and dislike. One is the *bachiller* Agustín Méndez Petzey, candidate of the Democracia Cristiana, and the other is the campesino Roberto Mendoza Pérez, candidate of the Partido Socialista Democrático. These two persons allow people to think and make decisions for their votes on 3 November to chose the person for the office of mayor. They are the only candidates who are good democrats. These two have the intelligence to govern the town. The *bachiller* is well educated. Also, the campesino has wisdom. They are the only ones running a clean but poorly financed campaign because they do not have money.

I'm just as an observer of these things. It's certain that a group of people in the town and more in the village have talked to me to see if I would be a candidate for mayor. A lot of people, though not all, are for me. One time I told them I would. Having received news of the activity, many visited me to ask if it was true that I had told them yes. But when I found out that Juanito Mendoza and Ignacio Arnaldo Bizarro González were candidates again, I thought it better not to campaign against these idiots and better to retract what I had said, although it's true my friends were disgusted with me. For sure, I don't have the money to campaign, and I don't want to swindle my own people. I would have been a candidate of the Partido Cooperación Nacional, which directed the cooperatives. When I withdrew, the cooperative member Benjamín Peña Cholotío launched his candidacy.

After retracting my position, I thought many things about the situation that Guatemala is experiencing. One wants to be nothing—neither good nor bad, neither with the right nor the left. To be mayor, one must make many compromises. At times one judges false things, or calumnies. I believe that a mayor is an accomplice of these things if he doesn't investigate them well. The other thing is that I have a lot of work to do for my family. I don't have money for my children to study, and for that reason I am teaching them to work. But if I go to the tribunal, my children will lose time. For me, it isn't worth it. The most annoying part is that a mayor only receives two years of salary and later he must work again in the fields. That is why I decided not to run. I prefer to work, if God will help me.

Teachers Strike for Higher Pay
22 August to 17 September 1985

A problem developed when the *magisterio nacional* [national teaching staff] asked the government for a raise in salary. They say that they can't manage on the salary proposed because almost everything is high in price. The government says that there can be no increase in salary because the country is living in a crisis, that the government has no money and that there are many teachers. Until the end of the month of August, the teachers were always criticizing, but the military government was not paying them any attention. From the 22nd to 31st of August, those who suffered the consequences were the students.

There are days when the teachers give classes and days that the children find the classrooms closed. The *magisterio* stands firm, saying that if there is no raise there will be a stoppage in the whole republic. The government says that if the teachers don't want to work, there are more teachers that don't have work and need it. The two groups are intense.

The situation in Guatemala is very serious. The school teachers, public workers, state workers, and labor unions amassed. They demanded a raise in salary and declared that if their reforms were not accepted there will be an all-out general strike. The strikers are demanding a higher cost of living allowance and travel expenses for urban service. The government refuses. Operators (contractors) want to raise the fares 20 centavos for the urban service. On the other hand, the industrialists and owners of supermarkets are taking advantage of the situation. They are the ones who are becoming millionaires, because each day the situation is more serious. Each of them is raising the prices of their products in general.

On 7 September 1985, the government said in a press communiqué that it will not back down and that the teachers and other organizations will have the same salaries. There isn't money for much. Also, the rise in bus fares is to be 15 centavos.

When the University of San Carlos realized what the government said, it joined the strike supporting the teachers and other organizations. But the government became infuriated with the university personnel. At an opportune time, the representatives of the separate groups asked the *jefe* of state for a dialogue about what is happening in the country. Well, the chief of state conceded. But when the representatives arrived, he told them he didn't want to talk to anyone because the government is capable of resolving the problem. Moreover, he said that he has had good training since his youth, that he is not afraid of anyone, and that he doesn't want to say stupid things to anyone. This was the dialogue and nothing more.

It seems both groups, the government and the *magisterio*, are strong. The students are losing a lot of time, and the teachers are protesting a lot. Then the government took a measure of conceding to them, through the minister of education, to give them a raise in salary, an improvement of Q50. Lamentably, however, the teachers didn't accept the Q50 increase. They told the government they wanted twice more the salary. That is, if a teacher earned Q200, he would get Q600.

I think it isn't justified for the teachers to ask the government for this amount of salary increase. They need to do these things gradually, according to the times, a little now, more later. They want to sink the country into great debt. There are others who need their wages raised, not just the teachers.

This time the government gave in because it had said that there would be no raise and, moreover, that the fares of the urban services (buses) were unauthorized to be increased 15 centavos. But on this 9th of September, the same government said that there will be a raise and that the increase in fares for urban services will be 10 centavos. But this is a lie of the government because it also offered to lower the cost of living; that is to say, to lower the cost of all the products. But they didn't do anything. All was to the contrary. Instead they went up more.

The two groups look out for their own well being. The *magisterio* asked for a triple salary, but those who are fortunate are the military because they raise their salary without making a fuss or going on strike. But lamentably the military government forgets the campesinos who live in the provinces in misery. We live in misery. Already we are unable to eat meat, are unable to dress, nor to wear shoes. There's a lot of sickness in the towns and villages. When a poor person goes to the health clinic to ask for an aspirin, he who is in charge of the clinic only tells the patient what kind of prescription he needs to buy. Because of the government, the ministry of health has no medicine in the health clinics. Thus, the patient must go to the pharmacy to buy medicine, and, most disgracefully, each day at the pharmacies the price of medicine increases. In addition, one has to pay the IVA, *impuesto del valor agregado*. In Guatemala, it's all an injustice for us Indians. I hope to God that one day He will free us from these autocrats.

Well, another problem is also that at times we do not give much importance to what is happening in the country. We only think of our work and family. We know essentially that we are marginal (on the fringe). In the times in which we are living, everything is expensive—a pound of meat has gone up Q2. The pound of soap that cost 25 centavos went up to 50 centavos. Everything that is machine-made went up 50 to 100 percent. Yet, we just earn two to three quetzales a day. If the family is large, one cannot buy anything with Q3. The only thing that helps us Indians is that we plant corn, beans, tomatoes, onions, and other produce. This is what we eat. Also, since childhood, we have been accustomed to eating herbs and tortillas with salt—cereals aren't necessary, nor canned products and milk, because we are unable to buy them. Thus is our life. But the others fight for money. Thus it is. One has to accept it.

On 12 September there was a big problem in the whole republic with the *magisterio* at the beginning of the independence day celebrations. The teachers paralyzed the activities, saying not to celebrate. All of them stayed at home and abandoned the children. In a communiqué the teaching profession said that the classrooms will remain closed during the national celebration until they win. They said that any teacher who celebrates with the government will be punished or dismissed.

What did the teachers say they would do to them?

They said their cars or buses would be burned and that they would be expelled from their jobs.

In San José the problem was mainly with the students in the primary school and also with the students of the *instituto básico*. Earlier it had been decided that the students of the elementary school would go to Huehuetenango to carry the torch, the symbolic fire. Travel expenses had been paid in advance, but because of the teachers' strike, they said that no one was able to leave and that if the students left with the trucks, they would be captured and the trucks would be burned. This was why the students were afraid and didn't want to go to Huehuetenango. They indeed returned the travel money.

The students of the *instituto básico* had prepared to travel to Tapachula, Mexico, to bring the torch. Unfortunately, the parents were not encouraged to give their children permission to go. The students got ready and got into the trucks, but the oppression of the parents did not allow them to leave. I told the children, "Go, nothing will happen. God knows what He's going to do." Also I told the rest of the parents, "Our children are ready for the trip; they should go. Nothing's going to happen. I have faith in God that they will return without incident. Our children have the restlessness to travel. We should let them go even without the help of the teachers. If something happens on the road, it will serve as an experience to them."

But all the parents were oppressors, saying, "No one should leave."

I countered by telling them, "Remember you are bad parents for not helping your children. It's clear that our children have the good intention to go, but it's a pity that we aren't encouraging them. To each student we are giving a mental and moral blow because they already have their suitcases on the truck, and it's demoralizing for them to take their suitcases from it." Some parents wanted to put their children in jail. The parents' not wanting to let their children go to Tapachula was an injustice. Students of San Martín and San Jorge went without the teachers.

When the government realized that the striking teachers had said that participating teachers would be expelled and cars would be burned, the military government put out a communiqué in the press on 13 September, telling all Guatemalans of the country to be calm. The people could celebrate patriotic festivities as they wished, and all the students who were traveling to carry the torch in different parts of the country would have the protection of the army. The teachers wouldn't be able to do anything against the students. Moreover, it said that civilian and military people were standing together to celebrate the national holiday. If the teachers didn't wish to celebrate, well they could rest. Everything was definite.

On this date, all of the national schools were closed. The teachers' union put out a communiqué that no teacher should collaborate to celebrate Independence Day and that if some of the teachers gave in to collaboration they would be punished.

There was no activity. Everything was silent, no fiesta, worst of all in San José.

During the night of the 13th, a group of youngsters came to me and said, "Please, Ignacio, accompany us to carry the torch. If you wish, just go with us to Cocales or Patulul."

"No," I told them, "because I have no money."

But seeing that they had much determination and much desire to travel a little, I then said, "It's fine, but we will only go to San Diego because we have no money to pay for a car."

"Well," they told me, "Let's go then."

They wanted to go to bring the torch, but they were a little afraid because of the situation that was facing the country.

"Yes," I replied, "with much pleasure, let's go. I will accompany you."

I said this because my children wanted to go. Then they told me that they would put me in charge of looking for a car and we would share the expenses.

At 5:00 in the morning on the fourteenth, I went to San Martín to look for a car, where I found one for Q30. When I returned from San Martín, I told the muchachos about it, and they became very, very happy. I told them the departure was at noon, and each one left for his work while we began to make bread. We finished very quickly at noon. Then I began to gather the boys, a little afraid because the mayor told us not to go since the situation was delicate. But we always kept faith in God that nothing would happen.

We left in the car for San Diego la Laguna. Everyone was happy. We arrived there at 4:00 p.m., where they received us. The military and police in San Diego asked us from which town we were, and we told them we were from San José, Sololá. Then they reported to the departmental government to tell the officials that the town of San José was participating in the festivities of the homeland, that in San José there was no violence nor oppression of the teachers, nothing.

That's how it was, by the grace of God, calm. Later some students and I went to my sister's house where very amicably we were served coffee, dinner, sodas, and pastries. After dinner, we went again to the municipality. At 7:00 p.m., we sang the national anthem and listened to the words of the mayor. Later, they asked me to say a few words. Well, I had to make the effort, although I didn't know anything. I had to speak a little like a poet, giving a touch of splendor to the great people as well as the great day:

> Good evening, Señor Municipal *Alcalde*; good evening, Señor *Jefe* of the National Police; good evening, Señor Commander of the Military Post of this pueblo. I am sincerely glad to be here in this pueblo that also is protected by all the services that we see here. Well, for me it's an honor to give a little splendor to this pueblo, San Diego la Laguna, that we are visiting. I'm not a poet; I am nothing. But before everybody, I want to express my feelings to the people of San Diego, San Diego, a pueblo populated by the Cakchiqueles, a pueblo of workers, a pueblo of honored and honest men, a pueblo with the greenery of the coffee plantations protected by the volcano of San Diego and surrounded by all its indigenous people. Thanks to God

and to the grantees of our independence, who previously struggled for independence for us, they did not shed blood to fight for the independence.[25] And like them, we must do these things, fight with intelligence and with peace, not with violence. I want to sincerely thank the great people of San Diego la Laguna for all the participation that it gave me in this moment to take the microphones to talk a little in front of my people. May the celebrations of the fatherland be successful, and on our return to our pueblo, we will ask God to accompany us. Good evening.

It was nice. They set off many *bombas* and firecrackers. Then we left with the torch. The first runner was my son, Ignacito, who received the torch from the hands of the mayor of San Diego.

On the way, everything went well, by the grace of God. We passed San Luis at 10:00 p.m. We passed singing the national anthem in the military detachment at Pijuy, San Luis. We did the same thing in San Martín. At midnight we arrived in San José, where almost the whole town was waiting for us, including the commanders of the detachment. They received us with joy. Out of respect, the torch was delivered to the hands of the second lieutenant, Mendoza, who gave words of thanks, and all was concluded. We paid for the car, and everyone went to his own house. There was no violence as threatened by the teachers. Afterwards, those of the municipality gave us coffee and bread. Twelve of us from San José participated. The whole group of boys are youngsters from 4 to 20 years of age. I was the only veteran (old hand) with them.

On 15 September (Independence Day), only the students paraded, not the teachers. But indeed most of the people marched together with a platoon of soldiers which was encamped on the soccer field. I had an invitation for this fiesta, but I didn't go in order to attend to other friends.

In the afternoon of this same day, there was a big problem on the part of the local authorities: the mayor, the vice-mayor, and the secretary. The municipal secretary called the military commissioner who in turn immediately called the people for a general meeting in front of the old municipality.

The problem began when they saw that the teachers were not collaborating in the celebration of the great day. During this meeting, they drew up an act stating that the teachers committed a crime for interrupting the parade and that the teachers are subversives against the government. It specifically asked for their dismissal, since they were taken as insurgents and collaborators of terrorism. The act was drawn up without the presence of the teachers. The act also stated that copies of the act be sent to the señor commandant of the Military Zone 14, a drastic act of the secretary.

Sincerely, the teachers are not subversives; they are just struggling to raise their salaries. In the act they mentioned that the people of San José want to ask the minister of education for the dismissal of the teachers. Moreover, they said the reason was that only *Martineros* were working in San José as teachers, and they asked for a complete change. But these things are purely because of envy of the *Martineros* on the part of the *Joseños*. On this night, the residents turned into devils. These things they just told me. I did not see them. José did since he was in front of the municipality.

I realized what happened on the 17th when there was a meeting in which the teachers asked the people for an explanation of the more delicate points in the document of 15 September. Unfortunately, the mayor and the secretary didn't wish to present the minute book. Well, some residents gave an explanation of what was in the acts. Not until then did the residents and the teachers fight as if they were great enemies because the latter had not collaborated with the parade of 15 September. Instead, they completely abandoned the children.

At this meeting there was misunderstanding. The teachers said it was not their fault that the strike was national but that the mayor and the secretary continue to involve the people in great problems. Then three of us spoke. We said we weren't friends of the teachers nor enemies of the secretary but that one should do things intelligently. We said:

> The mayor and the secretary had committed a great crime before the law and before God for having raised false testimony against the teachers, saying that they are with the subversion. This is a lie. We are all witnesses that the teachers are from San Martín and all are dedicated to their work. We are witnesses that they are not with the subversion because each day we see them in the school, teaching our children. Moreover, the strike that they are involved in is on the national level, not just in San José. The mayor and the secretary lack wisdom, and they will be responsible for the lives of the teachers if anything bad happens to them; and, moreover, it's known that the teachers have been accused in the military zone of Sololá.

Only then did the teachers calm down, when they saw that we three were in favor of better understanding and not of the bad accusation. When the people realized that it was just the envy of the secretary, they understood everything, and everything was peaceful. Those who should be frowned upon by the people are the secretary and the mayor. Well, neither are we going to say that the teachers are perfect, no. They have faults but that is not reason to have evil intentions for their lives. This was our intervention between these two groups.

The biggest problem related to the teachers' strike in Guatemala was when the military government tried to threaten the University of San Carlos. One night the university was taken by the military. Then they said on the radio and television that the university is a center for crime and that the buildings of the university had subversive papers, arms of different calibers, and, moreover, a firing range where they practice shooting arms. The spokesperson for the national army gave many explanations. Many of the people believed what they saw on the television. But the most concrete information was given by the rector general of the university, Dr. Eduardo Meyer Maldonado, who said in the press and on television that all that the army said against the university was completely false because there were no arms in the university. Moreover, the rector said that the same soldiers had carried in the arms and later said that the arms belonged to the university, but it was a lie. Furthermore, Maldonado said that the military did a lot of damage to the photographs of the graduates.

What kind of damage did they say the military did?

It's not that I saw it, right. Instead, it was on the radio stations and in the newspapers. The university students joined the strike in favor of the teachers. In the university there are photographs of all the graduates with a statement of what they got their degrees in. The military tore up many of them. The students made declarations that the military had done many crimes, but since the military government was in the military's favor, they did nothing to investigate these things. It remained as if nothing had happened.

Problems with the Mayor and Woodcutters
23 September to 8 October 1985

On this date there was a problem in the town. They say that the mayor had sold trees to 17 woodcutters (sawyers) from the villages of Patzilín and Tzarayá. Those that were aware of this illegal business deal were some sawyers who had been told by the villagers. Then the lumberjacks told some carpenters, and the carpenters communicated it to the townspeople. Thus it was that the residents realized that the mayor had sold the trees illegally to the woodcutters.

A group of residents went to the mayor's office to ask for the truth. They say that the mayor told them that he had only given one tree, and then later he said four trees. There were doubts. Thus, they called me to a meeting in the house of one of those who had gone to the mayor's office. They asked me if there should be an investigation of the black market business that the mayor had committed on the communal land in the mountains of Pancoy. We talked until midnight, but we didn't come to an agreement. Everything was negative.

When Tuesday dawned, 24 September, I told the residents it would be better to get other opinions so as not to suffer serious consequences. Thus, we went to San Martín to talk to the priest named José McCall. We told him everything that the mayor had done to the people. He told us we were doing nothing wrong and that we should make a trip to the mountains to see if what the people say against the mayor is true. The priest told us he was going to receive us in the convent of San José so that the directors of Catholic Action will take part in all that is happening in the community.

At 5:00 in the afternoon he indeed received us at the convent. He said that one must take care of the property of the town, especially the trees because with time there will be no trees left to use for construction. Mainly those who will suffer will be the children. Then the priest said to clarify whether the theft of the mayor was a crime and what the people should want is to protect and safeguard the property of the town. Then he said that he would support us in successfully investigating how many trees the mayor had sold to those of the village.

At 8:00 at night the residents consulted a lawyer about the situation. The lawyer told us the same thing—to go to the mountains.

It did not suit the mayor, Andrés Bizarro Mendoza, when the people complained about the illegal sale of the trees on the communal lands of Pancoy. On this date, 24 September, the mayor and the secretary took revenge. The mayor wanted to save himself before the people so he had to sentence unjustly a villager named Pascual Toc, saying that he had cut down the trees without permission from the local authority. This poor man was fined Q20. The mayor did this to demonstrate to the people that he had only sold one tree and to rebuff them.

By the afternoon of this day, a group of citizens went to get a lawyer, Pelayo Eduardo Ixtamer, to examine the sentencing of Pascual. The lawyer told the citizens that Pascual's declaration stated that the mayor had sold the trees, only the mayor did not give them a receipt when they paid for the trees. Therefore, the mayor believed he had the power to sentence the poor woodcutter. The same lawyer told the citizens that the situation with the mayor was delicate. There was confusion in the town; almost everyone was saying things against the mayor. It was thus when we told the lawyer that it would be best to form a commission to go the mountains to determine the truth of whether the mayor had sold the trees; perhaps it was only slander. Thus it was when it was decided to ask permission from the mayor's office to be able to make a trip to the mountains. We were named by the citizens of the town to solicit the permission, and, as things are in the town, Martín Pantzay García, José Severo Gómez, Agustín María Bizarro Toc, Eduardo Flores Xicay, Damián Juárez Xicay, and I had to accept the voice of the people.

On the 26th of September, we went to the mayor's office to solicit permission to go and have municipal guards and policeman accompany us. The vice-mayor agreed to give us permission and authorized the guards and policeman to accompany us to the mountains.

But the mayor did not want the damage in the mountains to be investigated. He looked for a false accusation. The mayor, secretary, and *jefe* of the military commissioners went to Military Zone 14 in Sololá to accuse us six citizens of being subversives, leaving a note and our names in the intelligence section. He said, "Tomorrow the mountains will be investigated by the army and those found in the said mountains will be executed as guerrillas." But we didn't know what the mayor had done against us. Thanks to God, in the afternoon when they returned to Sololá, the military commissioner called the assistants to let them know that tomorrow the army would arrive in the mountains and that if they hear shooting of weapons, they should drop down. Two of the assistants, Arden and Alberto, interrogated the *jefe* as to why he traveled to Sololá with the mayor without informing his assistants. They said that the *jefe* told them that he was pressed by the mayor and therefore went to Sololá. This was when we became aware of the false accusation confronting us. The assistants and reserves of the army met, and together we all went to the military detachment that was meeting in the field in this locality.

The second lieutenant in charge of the military detachment had not realized what the mayor had done, and he first had to know about the problems of the town. When the lieutenant realized that the mayor had unjustly denounced six citizens, the lieutenant was on the side of the people and granted permission to travel to the mountains. The lieutenant knew José Severo as an industrious man who has a store. He also knew me because during the time that they were in this town I was making bread for them. Thus it was that they took the mayor for a liar. The people massively criticized the mayor, saying that if something bad happened in this town, he would be responsible.

On 27 September, in the company of a group of citizens, municipal guards, and policemen, we left at 6:00 in the morning from San José for the communal mountains Chian, Manaca, Patut, and Pancoy to witness the illegal activities. We saw many abandoned cedar and *canoj* trees and a very few pine trees that were cut up. In total, we found 66 felled trees. We met a person who informed us that Juanito Mendoza had sold two trees illegally, the ex-commissioner had sold two trees, and the mayor, Andrés Bizarro Mendoza, had sold 60. We checked part of the communal land. I recorded the day, hour, and minutes that we spent on the mountains and at what distance we found the trees.

We arrived home very late and tired. I was so exhausted I didn't eat dinner. I only drank half an *octavo* of liquor with bitter coffee and lay down. Mayor Andrés turned into an enemy because he had planned to kill us when we discovered his black business deal. Day broke, the 28th, with my being very tired and sick from too much walking. My muscles were so sore it was hard to walk. I didn't work.

At 8:00 in the evening, they called me to a meeting in Benjamín Soto's house to search for a solution to the problem. When we arrived at the house, the question was purely political. We didn't want to accept the ideas of this group. We had to withdraw.

At 7:00 in the evening, 29 September 1985, the group of citizens asked for a meeting with the military commissioners to present the problem that affronts the community and to make them see the damage caused on the mountains. Under oath, the mayor declared he only had given four trees to the sawyers, it wasn't known who sold the trees, and he wanted it to be investigated. For that reason we stated the problem to the military commissioners and told them that it was at their discretion whether it would be investigated or not. We had only gone to see the damage, and we didn't have the authority.

At this meeting, the *jefe* of the military commissioners confessed that he was obligated by the secretary and mayor to go to the military zone to denounce a group of citizens that are against authority and that they gave him only Q10. The assistants of the military commissioner condemned this false accusation of the *jefe*. They drew up a memorandum of agreement noting that if something bad happened in the town, those responsible would be the chief of the commissioners, mayor, and secretary. The chief commissioner cried bitterly, repenting that he had carried out this mission without consulting his assistants. All the town knew that the accused citizens are people of honorable work. How are the violent people? They never want their bad attitudes to be exposed. The first thing they think about is to kill people.

Monday, 30th of September, 8:00 in the morning, at the mayor's office, the corps of military commissioners and the second lieutenant Baudilio were trying to find a solution to the problem. The mayor had said under oath that he was not responsible for the damage caused by the sawyers in the mountains. When he left the second lieutenant, we entered the mayor's office accompanied by the commissioners, but only to read the account of the 27th day, regarding all that was observed on the mountains. Then we left.

At 12:00, with the permission of the second lieutenant, the commissioners went to the villages of Tzarayá and Patzilín for a friendly chat with the sawyers to see who was the liar, the people or the mayor. Not a single citizen went, just the military commissioners. At 7:00 at night the military commissioners arrived once and for all with the 16 pairs of sawyers (who always work in pairs, one above and one below) for a meeting with the mayor. When the poor sawyers from the villages arrived, the lying mayor hid. They went to call him five times, but he did not appear before the people. The villagers said that yes it was true they had cut the trees but they had paid the hands of the mayor, Andrés. Then the people and commissioners realized that he who was guilty of these damages was the mayor. Some of the sawyers said that they had paid him with money, and others said that they had given him timber for construction but without getting a legal receipt. Two of them said that the two trees had been bought by

Juanito Mendoza and two had been bought by the ex-military commissioner, Fernando Timoteo Ramos. The poor men from the villages returned home at midnight. The town and commissioners stated that tomorrow there would be a public meeting in front of the town hall.

In the morning of 1 October, the people, military commissioners, and
sawyers returned again in order to know precisely who was liable for
damages committed. We took charge of making an agenda; also, we were
assisted by a lawyer so as to not fall into the hands of the secretary. There
was so much rain at 8:00 and 9:00 that most people went back to their
houses, and the town meeting wasn't held until 10:00, when the rain had
calmed. But many of the citizens went into hiding and now didn't show
their faces because they feared for their lives, since the whole town knew
that the six citizens, myself and five others, were going to be kidnapped.

To open the meeting, the first speaker was Martín Pantzay G., who
presented to the people all the damages that the mayor had done. All the
town stood at our side. Continuing, a military commissioner spoke to the
people:

> A mayor doesn't have the right to sell anything belonging to the
> town because it is very necessary that the town have wood for con-
> struction. The town's getting bigger each day, and wood will well
> serve the children. In time, a foot of wood will cost a lot of money;
> therefore, it's better to take care of the property of the town. A mayor
> cannot usurp functions. The only institution that has the right to
> license the harvesting of the trees is the National Forestry Institute,
> never a mayor. The whole town already said there would be no more
> cutting trees because the timber that they are getting in the jurisdiction
> of San José, which is going to Totonicapán, Quezaltenango, and
> Mazatenango, is estimated to be only 15 to 20 truckloads. Therefore,
> the town already said that no more wood be taken because it will be
> good to have for the future.

I gave an explanation to the people about the major's denunciation of
six citizens as subversives in Military Zone 14. The whole town condemned
with shouts the bad attitude of the lying mayor, and they said if a *Joseño*
disappeared the mayor and the secretary would be held responsible. We
calmed the citizens a lot so that they would not want to hit the secretary,
and by the grace of God, all turned out well. Using a microphone, villagers
told the people that the mayor had sold them the trees. But the mayor was

insisting to the townspeople that those of the village were responsible and that they will be sentenced according to the law.

We of the town asked the lawyer to record a memorandum to defend the poor sawyers so that they wouldn't be sentenced because they confessed before the people that they had bought the trees. The mayor said that he had received planks of *canoj* as compensation and that these planks were given to the church, Asamblea de Dios, and part of them served for the repair of the pier. These things the mayor had said when he was interrogated in front of the people.

The meeting did not end until 3:00 in the morning on the 2nd day of October. The town was infuriated and resentful. They asked for the resignation of the mayor; but this he refused, saying that he didn't have to resign since he was not elected by the people and was, in fact, named by the chief of state. It is very well that he may continue, but the town already knows that the mayor of these times is corrupt and a thief. Those that spoke in representation of the town are Ignacio Bizarro Toc, Arden Sumoza Sumoza, and Roberto Zacarías Cholotío Sumoza. The last three are military commissioners who condemned the attitude of the mayor and his secretary for accusing six citizens in the military zone only because they uncovered the illegal sale of the trees. I was with them, but I said nothing bad. Yes, I gave the explanation, but I was afraid to speak very strongly because I was aware that they had already accused us in the military zone, although I knew that I had done nothing wrong. I stated reasonable things and with respect. But all of those whom I've mentioned said very strong words, to the point of being immoral. This is because we don't have much education, both those of the mayorship as well as the citizens. The work of the lawyer cost Q50. I don't know for sure that they paid him the money, but I do know that the people were mocked by the secretary.

On Thursday, 3 October, the Catholic and Evangelical churches engaged in prayer because there were rumors that the six citizens accused by the secretary will be kidnapped. My companions and friends felt very much afraid. I told them not to worry that nothing bad will happen and that we are the ones with a clean conscience. The others said that they now are afraid to sleep in their own houses. I never felt this way; I was always peaceful with my family. During the night of this day, the military commissioners called us to a meeting at the headquarters of the *jefe*. In the meeting, they told us that tomorrow we shall make a trip to Sololá to the military zone to investigate the accusation made by the mayor. I didn't want to travel to Sololá because I was short of money, and, moreover, I have done nothing. But in order to not belittle the commissioners, I had to say yes. They already wanted to investigate these things.

On 4 October Damián Juarez Xicay, Martín Pantzay Garcías, José Severo Gómez, Arden Sumoza Sumoza, Ignacio Hernández Toc, Ángel Alberto Mogollón, Roberto Zacarías Cholotío Sumoza, the *jefe* of the commissioners, and I went to Sololá. When we arrived at the military zone, they told us that a commission of the S-2 [intelligence] would go to San José to investigate with respect to the memorandum of the mayor and his secretary. We returned by foot to Sololá, then Panajachel, then in a launch from Tzancuil to San José, arriving at 2:00 in the afternoon.

When we arrived, the commission had already returned to Sololá. The news said that strongly armed men arrived in a civilian dress and entered the mayor's office to interrogate the mayor, questioning if it were true that the six citizens that he mentioned on the note were subversives and stating if what the note said were true, the citizens would be captured and taken to the zone. The mayor and the secretary reflected and told the commission that they had written the note while drunk, that the persons are industrious and honorable, that the only problems are with some trees, and that nothing bad had happened in the town.

The citizens were fearful that something sinister was going to happen. On the 7th of October the commissioners called a meeting with us to let us know that tomorrow they would make a trip to Sololá to settle the situation, which they say is delicate. I didn't go to this meeting. I only sent five quetzales to help with the fares. I felt at ease, with no fear. But the mouths of the people say many things.

On Tuesday, 8 October 1985, the assistants and the chief of commissioners went to Sololá to speak to the chief of the section of intelligence to investigate the situation of the group of *Joseños* accused by the mayor and his secretary. This day I didn't go because I had neither time nor money. Only, they came to me to tell me the reason for the trip. They said that the military didn't want to reveal the contents of the note that they had delivered to the mayor and that it was difficult to investigate the army. The military only would say that there were no problems with the six citizens. But the *jefe* of the commissioners insisted on asking questions, and he was nearly imprisoned because of the heavy repression of the *jefes* in the military zone in Sololá.

For me this was a lesson, or better said, an experience in my life, not knowing what was going to happen. The townspeople just thought it was a warning to the mayor not to finish off all the things belonging to the town, but all was to the contrary. The citizens only planned to tell the mayor not to cut any more trees on the communal land, but since the mayor is corrupt, he went to the military zone to accuse six citizens. Now the people are saying nothing about the trees. What they talk more about is the expected kidnapping. This is an example: it is necessary to be careful with thieves because when one complains to them about something, the first thing they think about is killing people. I swear now that when the people, or better said, the citizens tell me to do something for the betterment of the town, it's best to say no thanks. It's best not to get involved in anything. Now I told my friends "*vale más ser listo observador que ser listo declarador* [it is better to be a clever observer than a clever talker]." If God gives me life, from now on I want to be an observer. This was just another episode about me and my town.

A North American Named Huber Is Accused of Murder
8 October 1985

On this date, 8 October 1985, when my children and I were baking bread in San José, we heard the news that in the neighboring town of San Martín a youth, Chayito Juan Agustín, was hung at 9:30 in the morning after his mother told him to go throw out the trash in the coffee groves. The first time, the child returned as usual, but the second time he lost his life. He had gone with one of his sisters, but she was too little to recognize who did it. The sister said only that when they hung her brother, she ran home to tell her mother that her brother was hung by a man. When the mother arrived, Juan Agustín was still alive, but she was afraid to untie the rope. What she did was to call the justice of the peace. By the time the judge arrived, the child was already dead.

Who knows who did it? They suspected a North American named Huber. This man was dedicated to painting. He was always on drugs, marijuana, and cocaine, playing his radio and dancing in the streets. There was no doubt that this is how he behaved, and therefore they suspected he was the criminal. Truthfully, though, they did not see him. This Huber they grabbed when he was found preparing his breakfast in the house that he had rented from a *Martinero*. Poor Huber, they threw him in jail drugged.

He said that he had killed the boy, but he probably said this because of the drugs. Another version says that it was not Huber, but a man named Roberto because the child was on his land when he died. Others say that he was killed solely because the child was well-educated by the priest of the parish church. Who knows who it was? It's only known that the North American was imprisoned.

About a month later Huber was taken to the scene of the crime by the judge of the first instance of Solola and the national police. Truthfully, we did not see him, but a kinsman did and said that he was very sick. Only God knows who the criminal was, because the mouths of the *Martineros* speak many lies and are very deceptive. In the same place that they killed Juan Agustín, they had killed Bernardo Bolaños Puzul in 1976.

What happened to Huber?

They didn't find him guilty. He returned to San Martín to get his things and left town.

The Political Campaign for Local Offices
Tuesday, 29 October 1985

I'm recording how the day went when the Partido [Democrático] de Cooperación Nacional spoke to me. On this day, we went to the three villages of Pachichaj, Patzilín, and Tzarayá to raise the consciousness of the people so that they would support Benjamín Peña Cholotío, but this Benjamín they hardly knew because he had not participated in anything. We supported him, however, because he is a working man and an onion merchant and because we didn't want more of those whom we already knew. We didn't spend money from the party; we went at our own expense, carrying lunch from our houses. In the three villages, we read the memorandum in public that Juan Mendoza had made in the year 1976. I did this because I have a personal interest in Mendoza not becoming mayor. He, the candidate of the Liberación [MLN], was saying that there is no other person equal to himself in town. He believed himself superior to his four political adversaries. We ran a well-organized campaign. At times I decided not to participate, but at other times I contributed political ideas and did things that the others weren't able to do. More for that reason, my participation sometimes served well. On this day when we went to the three villages, they asked, "Why aren't you the candidate for mayor?" because everyone knows me there.

"Because," I said, "I don't have the money to struggle with the candidacy, because I have a lot of children, and if I am going to be mayor, I will have to neglect my family and I do not want my children to waste time."

The day after we went to the villages (30 October), the candidate of the Liberación went there. He didn't like our criticism of him. He had to search for political dirt, saying to the villagers that the candidate of the national cooperation had obtained Q60,000 from a company for his political campaign and when he wins the elections he will allow the selling of all the communal land into the hands of *finqueros* and then most of the villagers will lose their properties. As the indigenous people are very ignorant, they thought it was true and remained firmly with this man.

It's true that the cooperative had obtained Q27,000 from a company, but it was a payment distributed to all the associates as an advance on the value of the anticipated coffee harvest according to the production of each person. This money is used to buy fertilizer on credit until the coffee is delivered in January, February, and March during the harvest. This money came from the company of Juan Waelti y Sucesores, and it was not a political matter. But Señor Mendoza altered everything, claiming that the candidate of Partido Democrático de Cooperación Nacional [Benjamín Peña Cholotío's party] and the candidate of the party Unión del Centro Nacional [Ignacio Arnaldo Bizarro González's party] had sold the town into the hands of *finqueros* to confuse the people. He said this about the candidate of the union of the center because this person also belonged to the cooperative. This was one of the darker tales about the candidate of the Movimiento de Liberación Nacional party.

Activity in the Catholic Church
30 October 1985

During all of the past 30 days, catechists were ordered in four groups of 15 to 20 persons each to visit the families that do not go to church very often. Every night the families were visited by people carrying an image of the Virgin of Guadalupe. This they concluded on 30 October, and in the afternoon they celebrated a lot with a procession in the streets of the town and afterwards a solemn mass and a fiesta on behalf of the church.

This 30th of October was the birthday of my son José Juan. Before going to mass, my wife prepared tamales, which we ate afterwards. We gave José some tamales to take to my mother, but it's a shame that she wouldn't accept them because she says that she is mad at the kids. But we old folks never should put ourselves on the same level as children. The tamales that she didn't accept were given to other friends. Well, my mother has despised me since I was a baby, and it was an aunt that did me the favor of feeding me from childhood. It's a pity that my aunt died.

More Campaigning for Local Offices
31 October 1985

The 31st day of October was the last day of propagandizing by the parties. There was a lot of ruckus by all the people and a lot of nervousness amongst the candidates. As I already said previously, indeed without exception, I had to go around town accompanying Benjamín Peña Cholotío.

Month of November: The General Election
1 to 3 November 1985

November 1st is the day of the saints [All Saints' Day] that traditionally was celebrated well, but this time there wasn't much enthusiasm. The people only talked about politics. The 2nd is the day of the dead [All Souls' Day]. It wasn't celebrated either. Only in the church is there any activity.

The five mayoral candidates are the dead ones. They aren't doing anything, nor do they know what to say to the people, nor do the people know for whom they are going to the vote. Almost, we don't give any importance to these festivities so sacred. Although my family and I celebrated them, we didn't get much involved with politics, only lending a little support.

On the 3rd of November was the general election. Who won the presidency was less important to us than whether we would win the mayorship. Everything went according to the law, without fraud or coercion. I was a witness because I was a *fiscal* [an official] at a voting table that checked identification and gave citizens their ballots. At the booth where I was *fiscal*, at the hour of the counting of votes, Juan's Liberación party won. It was the booth where those of the *aldeas* voted. But at the tables where those of the town voted, we won with 337 votes in favor of Benjamín Peña and 317 for the Liberación Nacional party. After the count of votes, the mayor and the secretary didn't want to report the results to Sololá. They were committed to Juanito Mendoza's winning, but it was all to the contrary.

What had happened was that the members of the Partido Democrático de Cooperación were all novices in participating in politics; thus, I had to help them a lot. They paid me Q20 for the day because I couldn't afford to lose time. They even invited me to celebrate with a toast, but I had to use a lot of self-control because the losing parties falsely criticized me, saying I fought for Benjamín Peña since I wanted to be the municipal secretary. There was a lot of criticism against my character because they claimed I wanted to be in charge of the office of secretary! But it's all a lie. I can't work as secretary; besides, I haven't considered seeking employment nor have I wanted to be under the hand of those more ignorant than I. I say this because the secretary is a *mozo*. The mayor is the one in command, and if things go bad, the secretary gets the blame. Thus, it's better to be a worker of the fields. At times, I feel screwed, but I'm also a baker, which helps me somewhat. Besides, I have work with Dr. Sexton, which helps me a lot. Therefore, I don't have to look for work in a secretary's office. But so was the criticism; therefore, I'm writing about it. Everyone has to accept what comes in life.[26]

Robberies in Tzarayá
10 to 15 November 1985

From the 10th to the 15th of November, I did a small project planting chili. It was a complete struggle. We worked hard. After sowing, we fertilized and we weeded this plot. I maintained it for more than six months and spent more than Q300 but didn't earn anything from it. They stole it from me. I planted this plot of chili in the village of Tzarayá. Also, I did eight *tareas* [days' work] of firewood, and they robbed all of it from me. Benjamín and Abraham Bizarro, my kin, told me who took the wood. They recognized it when villagers of Tzarayá came to sell it in San José. Since I didn't verify whether it was true that they had my wood, I didn't file a suit in the courthouse. I just entrusted everything to God, praying that He would provide another way for me to do something, or more knowledge for another sowing.

The Tzutuhiles of San Luis Have Been Living and Continue Living Their Lives in Fear and Anguish
25 January to 1 November 1985

One night, armed only with sticks, stones, and machetes, more than a hundred members of the civil defense patrol were guarding the streets of San Luis so that no subversives could enter. The streets were lit. Suddenly, a group of people appeared. The vigilantes went to see who they were. The group took out their weapons and told the patrolmen to go home quick, and if they didn't obey, they would all die. The group was identified as a subversive one that was involved in sabotage. With just sticks, stones, and machetes, the poor patrolmen weren't able to do anything. It was thus when the subversives advanced to the center of the town.

When they arrived in front of the municipality, the *alguaciles* were sleeping in the corridor of the municipality, as is the custom for them to sleep there to guard the office. They were taken out by the guerrillas. They say that before setting fire to the office the guerrillas went to wake up an operator named Vicente Quinto, the richest man in town, who lived very near the municipality. The guerrillas told him to quickly remove his trucks, bus, and cars. Vicente Quinto then went to wake up the drivers and their families, who were able to park the vehicles on the public beach. Then the guerrillas threw gasoline on the doors of the municipality and also on the rural agency of the sub-headquarters of the national police. The police exited through a window to another *sitio*. This is how it was when the terrorists burned the building that held the municipality, secretary's office, civil registry, municipal commissary, rural agency of the Banco Nacional de Desarrollo Agrícola [National Bank of Agricultural Development], and the sub-headquarters of the national police.

During this night of terror, it was the *Sanluiseros* who lost a lot. The big building burned completely, including all the books of birth records, the registry of *cédulas* and other documents of the civil registry, all the books of the secretary, and all of the policemen's uniforms. They were only able to take a little equipment out through a window. Damages were estimated at Q100,000. They also burnt the personal motorcycle of the policeman Enrique Tzal Tuc, a native of San José. He was left with only the clothing he had on. All his other clothing was inside the burning building. They say that the cash box of the rural bank that burned contained a lot of money and documents of people who had taken out loans. After burning the building the terrorists left the town very pleased.

On Wednesday, 31 July of 1985 at 12:30 p.m., everything was quiet. The operator, Vicente Quinto, about 60 years of age and of the Ladino race, was attending his shop and selling things when a man of medium stature very serenely entered the shop dressed in a sky blue shirt, denim pants [blue jeans], and high-top shoes of a commando style as the army uses. First he asked for a soda. He drank it and asked for another. Vicente Quinto went to the refrigerator to get another. He was taking the cap off the bottle when the man took out a 45 caliber revolver and shot three times—two shots in the thorax and one in the forehead. Vicente fell dead inside the *tienda* with the soda in his hand. His body was seen by many people. My brother Gerardo had come from the coast, and he said that he had gone inside the shop to eat bread and drink a soda. He witnessed all these things. He says that the assassin left very quietly with a denim bag, acting as if nothing had happened, and went down a street to the town center. This happened about 40 meters from the sub-headquarters of the national police. At 6:00 in the evening of the same day my brother gave me this information. It is certain that the assassin is of the right because less than a kilometer away there was a military detachment and 40 meters away was the police office and no one made a move to capture the assassin.

The body of Vicente Quinto they carried to the hospital of Sololá. How are people with money? Whereas most of the people have to take a cadaver to Sololá for an autopsy, they just paid a doctor in San Luis who told the doctor in Sololá that he had been assassinated. This crime was not investigated by the authorities. Everything remained peaceful.

Two months later the news came out, only among the *Sanluiseros*, that for sure Vicente Quinto was killed by the right. They say that the deceased Quinto was guilty of contracting the terrorists to set fire to the municipal building. He didn't want the rural agency of the National Bank of Agricultural Development to function because when the bank began to operate, it was a relief to the Tzutuhiles of San Luis since it only charged 8 percent annual interest. And this is what led this man to do something bad. When he lent money to the indigenous people, he charged 10 percent monthly interest. When the person was unable to pay the debt, he took possession of their land and *sitios*. For that reason he was the richest man in town because he earned a lot of money with the interest. More for that reason, he didn't want the bank to operate, but paid with his life.

An Assistant Military Commissioner Is Hacked to Death with a Machete
16 November 1985

Bad news continues to come out of San Luis. On 16 November 1985, a military commissioner was killed. They say that many people saw it. They took the military commissioner out of his house and then to the *corredor* [porch] of the municipality, where they hacked him into pieces with a machete and left him. No one knows for sure why this happened. It could be guerrillas or vengeance from a *Sanluisero*.

They also say an Evangelist was killed. He was going to his house in the direction of the army. It was late. He was returning from an Evangelical board meeting when he met the terrorists, who killed him and left him in the street. They probably thought he was going to tell the army that the guerrillas were in town. What was very strange was that very near the town there was a detachment of the military, but they weren't even aware of this massacre. The bad men were in the town most of the night, and the police did nothing to defend the people.

Sexton Sends Money for Weaving
18 to 24 November 1985

On the 18th of November we left to cut the tops of the corn in Xebitz, working under a strong sun. When one gathers his harvest, one becomes very happy. Besides, it's necessary to sell a little corn to buy flour for making bread. It's true that I already have corn but don't have money for other things.

In the afternoon of this day, after bringing corn home, they delivered a telegram to me signed by Máximo Pinto Motta, the administrator of the post office of Sololá. The text said I needed to go to the departmental post office to collect a remittance. I had doubts about the letters that I had sent to Dr. Sexton on 11 October because I only had certified them in the ordinary way. Perhaps they had been returned.

At 5:00 a.m., 19 November, Ignacito and I left by launch headed to Sololá. Since we weren't carrying any money, we didn't go to a *comedor*. We just brought tortillas and a little food and ate breakfast on the *corredor* of the convent of the Catholic Church. At 8:00 we entered the post office and then saw Don Maximón, who is a friend. He knew me when he was the departmental secretary-general of a political party. He gave me a letter from Dr. Sexton and told me to open it. When we opened it, we found a check for 300 dollars. Don Maximón took down the number and told me that they are doing this to avoid losses because he said that they had lost many checks. This friend asked me why they were sending me checks from a foreign country. I told him the truth that I had asked for help for one of my sons to buy material for weaving.

Then we went down to the Banco Mercantil in Panajachel to cash the check in quetzales. It proved fruitless. The tellers told me that the dollar had already gone down in value and that they didn't have an order from a foreign department to buy dollars for the day. Then I went to the hardware store, the "ANCLA," of Jorge Anleu to sell the check. This man only paid me Q750. He told me that the value of the dollar had fallen greatly, but I don't know for sure. Still I was relieved. We had to go up again to Sololá to buy some things, but we only spent Q25 because I had asked my good friend for this money for the weaving project. In the afternoon when we arrived home, I told my family what we had received. They were very happy and thanked God.

My youngster and I very happily finished harvesting the corn on the 21st of November. Some *mozos* helped us, and we borrowed beasts that transported the corn. I was thankful to God who gave me a good harvest.

The 24th of November my wife and I prepared to travel to Salcajá to buy weaving material. I didn't want to spend the money on other purchases because I didn't want to deceive my good friend Sexton since one day he may come to see the looms and what would I tell him? I'm not going to tell him that I don't have the money to buy material when he himself sent me this amount of money. We spent two days on this trip. It's a pity that I goofed. In the two stores they gave me receipts for the Q150 I spent, but because of carelessness, I lost the receipts.

When the material arrived in the house, the boy began to work very happily but slowly. Since he was new at this work, he was only able to do one *corte* a week, sometimes more.

Little is earned because the price of materials is very high in addition to the taxes. What makes us happy is that the people of the town are visiting a lot because it is a new kind of work here.

Why I'm No Longer in the Cooperative
End of October to end of December 1985

In the last days of October, 1985, the members of the board of administration of the cooperative, La Voz que Clama en el Desierto, Ltd. [The Voice that Cries in the Wilderness, Ltd.], decided to do some coffee business with a company owned by Juan Waelti. Thus, they asked for an advance of Q30,000 from this company for the purchase of fertilizer, the weeding of coffee, and paying for the harvest. When the money arrived, all of the members were called to give their formal data about how many *quintales* of coffee they would produce. Well, everyone provided this information in accordance with the guidelines, and they received the money. They gave me Q575 with the condition that I would have to bring the coffee in *pergamino* [hulled once].

When the harvest was begun in December, the board of administration received the coffee from the associates at a very low price. The board thought they would make a lot of profit. Then I realized what was happening with the associates. I thought about not having problems with the board of administration because the price of coffee was very low. They were only paying Q35 for a *quintal* of ripe coffee, but private houses were paying Q50 to Q52 a *quintal*.

I thought, "I'm not going to be bothered by them about the price." What I did was to present my irrevocable resignation and say that upon their accepting my renunciation, I would return the quantity of Q575 that I had received in advance for the coffee. When I received notification the 19th telling me that they accepted my resignation and return of the money but with the condition that I would have to pay an interest of 15 percent monthly as a fine for not delivering the coffee to the cooperative, I didn't want to talk any more. By the grace of God, I sold my coffee at Q52 a *quintal*. When I received the money, I took the capital that was Q575, along with the cost of the interest and the papers, which in total came to Q270, and I told them, "Very well, I'm going to pay. Moreover, it's my obligation."

Then the secretary and the treasurer told me, "Ignacio, you are paying a lot of interest. It would be better for you to stay in the cooperative with us. If you can bring in a little coffee, the money will serve you well."

I told them, "For me, it's better to pay the interest; I don't want to live any more among hypocrites." And I left the cooperative. I recognized my faults for not having delivered the coffee, but it was due to the very low price that they were offering.

This year the cooperative only had 27 associates. Previously there had been 102 associates. There are 65 who had resigned. The reason is that in the cooperative there are six persons who always want to dominate. There are associates who are very clever, but they do not allow them to participate.

How many quintales *did you sell to the private house?*

I sold 101 *quintales* of coffee in fruit, not hulled [*pergamino*]. But not all of it was at Q50 a *quintal*, some of it was at Q40, the next week, Q50, and so on. I sold 30 *quintales* at Q50. I made about Q1,000 more dealing with the private house than with the cooperative.

Why did they want to offer a lower price than the private house?

They said they were going to do all the work in the name of the members, but their intent was to make a little money for themselves. Rather than destroy the cooperative, I just resigned.

A Curing Secreto *in the Cemetery and I'm a* Brujo *in Another Form*
27 January to 14 February 1986

It happens that my son José suffered a lot to learn to weave and work *jaspes* [making tie-dyed figures or designs in thread or yarn]. When he learned, he began to weave some *cortes* to sell. Without doubt, the traveling merchants from Totonicapán who sold *cortes* realized that in my town there is a new weaver. They made or paid a *brujo* [witch] to bewitch my son.

Then my son was named *alguacil*, and he had to receive the office on the first of January of 1986. He alternated, spending one week in the municipality and the next two weeks working at home.

On 27 January I wasn't home; neither was my wife. Only Susana Julia and Anica Catana were in the house when a man arrived and talked to the two girls, asking for me or José. Well, the children told him that we weren't there. Then they said that the man said, "I'm going to leave a plastic bag, and later I'm coming back to get it."

Susana took the bag and put it in a box where José keeps his notebooks. The man didn't return to get his bag, and the children forgot about it. They didn't tell us these things. In three days, that is to say, on 30 January, José woke up very sick.

We asked him, "What happened? Where do you ache?"

He answered, "I don't know what happened to me. My whole body aches."

Then we called a nurse for an injection. The nurse said that he couldn't cure the illness. I bought medicine in the pharmacy for him, but it didn't help. We could do nothing. Each day he became more ill. We took him to a specialist in Sololá on 10 February. At the examination, he told us that it was a dangerous and very delicate sickness. We spent Q70 on the exam and medicine.

But when José began to take the medicine, he became more serious each day. I began my prayers to God day and night, asking for the health of my son. His mother cried a lot.

On 14 February, we carried him to Sololá again. The doctor told me that he needed more injections and should take more medicine. On this day we spent more than Q100 on medicine and travel.

When I went to Sololá with the patient, Susana remembered that a man had left her in charge of a *bolsa recomendado*[27] fifteen days ago. She told her mother that a man left a bag but he didn't return to get it. My wife asked her for the bag to see what was in it. The girl went to get it, and they examined it. When they opened the bag, it had a lot of pieces of weaving and *cortes* and wool tangled up. All the pieces of *cortes* and wool were stained with blood wrapped in paper and put in the plastic bag. My wife told me that the pieces of *corte* still were very wet with blood. She did not waste anymore time. She made a fire in the *sitio* and burned the bag. She didn't wait to show us; she thought it was witchcraft. Also, she thought that I would whip the girls for taking the *bolsa* so she burned it immediately. That was when we realized that José had been bewitched.

Also, when we went to Sololá on 14 February, the wife of the doctor told me, "It is possible that it was witchcraft because always these things exist. There is a *secreto*."

I told her, "Please tell me what it is to help my son."

She told me that one should trust in the medicine but also always do this *secreto*. The bed of the patient has to be surrounded with *ramas de pino* [pine branches] and the bed has to be covered with pine needles. The pine needles and branches have to be changed every three days.

I told her many thanks for these ideas. The following day I went to Tzarayá to cut pine branches and needles. I did what the señora told me. For the recovery of my son, it was necessary for the power of prayer to God, the power of scientific medicine, and the power of nature, which was a *secreto*. My son got a little better in the last days of March.

What we don't know is who did this witchcraft to us. If I knew who it was, I could ask God for justice since I have not bothered anyone nor have I stolen anything. Why is a witch planning evil against my family? I'm sure that God would hear my prayer to ask him for justice or to ask a favor. I am a *brujo* in another form.

Why do you say you are a brujo *in another form?*

Well, the word *brujo* is very common among us Indians, right. I say *brujo* in another form. It's not that I am something of *brujería* (witchcraft); the only thing that I do is ask God for all those who do me wrong. Because I bother hardly anyone, nor do I offend someone for the fun of it, nor do I steal, I am a *brujo* in another form because I ask God for the grace and also for the justice. If I am to blame for the things, God will have to punish me. And if I am innocent, God will have to liberate me from the things. I say this because I have seen many divine things from God. I remember that in the year 1979, when some *Martineros* slandered me, they said that I was an assassin. I am nothing. I am afraid to hit someone with my fist, and they accused me of killing. Take the case of Don Ignacio Puzul and his nephew, Lucas, who slandered me. They went to bring the judiciary to have me sentenced. But, thanks to God, I had done nothing; I only asked God for mercy and justice. And now, Ignacio Puzul is dead. I'm not going to say, however, that I'm not going to die. We all are going to die, but according to the destiny of each one. I don't like to bother anyone, because I am person who understands that if I bother someone, it is disliked by the person. If they bother me, I also dislike it.

Do you also have a candle that you use when asking for justice?

Yes. When I make my prayers to God, especially. That indeed is a custom of my ancestors. When we kneel or render prayer to God, we light our candle and a little incense. That is a custom of the family and of the house. Now, we always do it, but we are not bewitching anyone. We are only asking God for a favor and justice. If we do a wrong, also, we wait for our punishment.

What's the difference between a brujo *and a* characotel?

It is true that the *characotel* is a *nagual*, but he works differently than the *brujo*. The *characotel* is a *nagual* who during the nights converts into an animal such as a cat, dog, pig, or owl. He goes to the *sitios* of sick people or to a house to bother people when they are sleeping. If the person is frightened, the *characotel* has an influence [hypnotic power], and the person falls sick. If the sickness isn't cured by a *zanjorín* [shaman], the sick person dies.[28]

The *brujo* is very different. He has his *nagual* in person; he has a power of the world. He is able to bewitch a person by doing certain *secretos*. He takes out the bones of the dead in cemeteries and leaves or buries them in the *sitio* of some enemy. Also a *brujo* can be contracted by others to bewitch people.

The *brujo* uses many kinds of *secretos*—bones of dead animals, burning incense in the *cofradía* of Maximón, or a photograph of a person but turned upside down. He draws out blood from dogs, turkeys, and other animals. He carries the clothing of a person to a cemetery. Also, if he wants a person or an enemy to be tortured by alcoholism, the *brujo* buys two *octavos* of *aguardiente* and sprinkles it hot over a brick with a photograph of the person on top of the brick. Then he buries it in the entrance of the *sitio* of the person. This is a very delicate *secreto* that does not have a cure.

In the year 1959, the mayor was Bartolomé Coché, who was said to have misused the funds of the municipality. In 1960, 1 January, he handed over power to Juan Bizarro Gómez, the new mayor, who was a political enemy. As mayor, Juan carried out an investigation of Bartolomé as a means of revenge. In the month of February, Bartolomé went to jail in Sololá. I knew this because in this year I was an *alguacil*. Moreover, I worked some days for Coché before he was mayor. Well, the ex-mayor spent seven months in jail in Sololá. He spent money, even selling a piece of land for his freedom. He got out of jail on 11 August.

In the month of October of the same year of 1960, I worked some more for Bartolomé Coché. The place where I worked is called Chipuac. He told me, "Ignacio, I suffered a lot in jail, seven months. What happened cost me a lot. But it was because of politics. I did not steal money, but the mayor magnified many things against me. Also the syndic signed many false things. I tell you, Ignacio, I suffered a lot with my family. But now I am preparing for revenge."

I asked him, "What are you going to do?"

He said, "I'm going to look for a *brujo* to bewitch the two sons of Juan and the syndic."

I asked him, "Señor Bartolomé, where are you going to look for a *brujo*?"

"The *brujo* that I already have is from San Luis. I'm only going to spend a little."

I insisted asking, "What are you going to do?"

"I'm going to tell you, but please don't tell anyone. I don't want anyone else to know."

"Don't worry," I said, "tell me! I'm not going to tell anyone."

Then he told me, "With a *brujo*, we're going to do a job. I have to buy only two *octavos* of *aguardiente*, two bricks, and obtain two photos. The same I will do for the syndic—one *octavo*, one brick, and obtain one photo. We will heat the *aguardiente* and throw it over the photos on top of the bricks, and then we will bury them in the entrance of their *sitios*. These men will see. But please, Ignacio, don't tell anyone."

What resulted was that they were certainly bewitched. The two children of Juan fell into the trap of alcoholism. Now they live more as drunks. Almost every day they are drinking and asking for handouts for their *tragos*. And they are selling things of their parents. Now the two brothers, Humberto and Antonio, are in the same situation—most of the time of their life they have been losing because of alcoholism.

The syndic in this time was Ignacio Bizarro Ramos, but the same thing happened to him. When he began to drink, he spent 20 to 30 days on a binge. He might, however, go one or two months without drinking. But the two sons of Juan drank day and night. These things I have not told anyone until now, but 27 years already have passed.

Revenge, however, never serves anyone. It's better to tolerate it with patience. There is a saying, "*Con la medida que midieras, sereis medido* [With the measure that you measure, you will be measured]." This is what we call the law of compensation.

Bartolomé Coché has done this witchcraft, and his victims suffer too much. But also he had already lost his two children—María Luisa Coché, who was assassinated by bullets in San José, and Domingo Arturo Coché, who worked for the Aduana Central [Central Customs] and who has disappeared. Who knows where they killed him.

Can you explain more how a zanjorín *cures in the cemetery?*

When a person becomes sick and can't be cured with medicine, the parents take care of it by looking for a shaman to make *costumbres* in the cemetery to bring back the spirit of the sick person. The shaman arrives and examines the sick person. He puts the hand of the sick person on his ear with the sick person's little finger in the shaman's ear. The shaman then says if the spirit of the sick person is with the *dueño* of the dead, or, in other words, the *dueño* of the cemetery. In *lengua* [Tzutuhil] he is called Ixuan Pok'olaj [Ishuan Pokolah].

The shaman goes to the cemetery at midnight, carrying *aguardiente*, cigars, *copal* [incense], and candles. Then he sets up a place in the middle of the cemetery. First he burns the candles and the *copal*, and then he begins to ask for the spirit of the sick person from the *dueño* of death. When the shaman lets the *aguardiente* fall in the *copal*, if it makes a flame, it is a good sign for them—the sick person is going to recover. On the other hand, if the *copal* does not flame up, it's a sign that the *costumbre* is not going to work. The patient's spirit is already among the dead, and the person is going to die. The shaman returns to tell the kin that the *dueño* of the cemetery has the spirit and doesn't want to let it go.

The family makes reverence to the shaman, asking him please to do a special *costumbre* to bring back the spirit of the sick from the cemetery. The shaman makes another trip to the cemetery, carrying the same material as before. He performs the most sacred *secreto* in which he has to carry a shirt, blouse, or skirt, depending on whether the sick person is a man or a woman. This he has to do in the middle of the night. When he arrives in the center of the cemetery, he lights the candles, burns the *copal*, and throws the *aguardiente* where he is burning the *copal*. Then he puts the clothing of the sick person on the left side and he begins to ask the *dueño* of death for the spirit of the sick person, saying the prayers, "Ixuan Pok'olaj, *dueño* of the cemetery, you are the one who guards the spirits of our grandfathers and fathers. You also send the spirits to go fetch the spirit of the sick person (naming the person who is sick). I ask you to give me the spirit of the sick person who is gravely ill. I need you, I love you very much, and I respect you very much. I have brought your candles, your *trago*, and your *copal*. I am a defender, I am an advocate of the world, and for that reason I have the right to ask for the spirit of the sick person. You need to deliver the spirit to me because he isn't very old. He should not go with you yet. You need to give him more luck; you need to give him more life. Give me the spirit so that he can live more and when he is old he will come here to accompany the rest of the spirits."

The shaman finishes this prayer as the candles and *copal* are burning out, and he throws *aguardiente* on the four sides of the cemetery, takes the clothing of the sick person, wraps it up with the spirit inside, puts it inside his shirt, and says good-bye from the center of the cemetery. While continuing to sprinkle *aguardiente*, he walks with his back toward the door of the cemetery [walking backwards]. If he turns around the other spirits can grab the spirit because they want company. They don't want the shaman to take the spirit of the sick person away. At the entrance he finishes sprinkling the *aguardiente*; then he turns around with the shirt in front of him, walking forwards. The *secreto* of sprinkling *aguardiente* at the door of the cemetery is so that the rest of the spirits will not pursue anymore the spirit of the sick person.

When the shaman arrives at the house of the sick person, the shaman puts the clothing that he has brought from the cemetery under the head of the sick person. The shaman waits a half hour and then begins to talk. If the sick person does not respond, he waits another half hour and asks, "Have you come back?"

And the sick persons says, "Yes, I've come back."

"Where did you go?"

"I went to places far away."

Then the shaman offers him a little *fresco* [drink] or coffee. If the sick person drinks the water that he gives him, it is a sign that the patient's spirit has already returned from the cemetery.

To go to the cemetery in the middle of the night is scary, and the shaman who does this kind of *costumbre* is a shaman much better than others. I know that this is true. There are shamans that have power. I am a witness of a shaman who did three *costumbres* of this kind, and he was able to do more. But I only went three times with him to the cemetery. One time was in the cemetery of Santa Ana, another was in the cemetery of San Jorge, and the last time was in the cemetery of San José.

In Santa Ana he went to bring the spirit of a child of Jaime Sicay. In San Jorge he went to bring the spirit of Regino Kan. In my town he went to bring the spirit of Margarita Velasco, a woman who is still living.

I'm not a shaman, but I was reared by and lived with a shaman, my uncle and adoptive father. I didn't want to go with him to the cemetery, but he was *bravo*, so if I didn't go with him, he hit me a lot and treated me badly. His name was Martín, and that was in the year of 1957 and 1958. I was able to observe that the life of a shaman was one of always drinking *aguardiente* and that it was easy for them to get women because they were afraid to resist.

My Family and a New Baby
22 February 1986

I'm going to talk a little about my family. I'm a man with a big family. In all I have eight children, four boys and four girls. At times I suffer a lot to feed them, and I also suffer when they are sick, always asking God for their health. I put up with it. I don't wear fancy clothes or shoes. More than anything else, I am preoccupied with providing food for my children. I can't despise any of them. There are times when I get mad at them, but just for a while. At times I whip them with a belt when they are bad, but if one does not correct his children they will behave poorly, as if they are poorly reared. And more than anything else this is why a father says, "I'm going to correct my son." One kid does one thing and another does something else, sometimes good, sometimes bad. One has to have patience.

Also, children are what make a home happy. I have seen people who have a lot of money, land, and riches, but they don't have children. They enjoy all that they have, but a person who has children spends all his money on them.

But also when there is the need for some kind of errand to fetch firewood or the like, we send a child, and for that reason my wife and I value our children. Although we are poor, we always have this love whether there is or isn't any money, but we always are looking for ways to feed the children.

Three of my children who suffered a lot with us are José, María, and

Ramón. More than the others it was José because when he was smaller I only earned 50 centavos a day, and sincerely with this small amount one isn't able to live and eat well. It was just enough to buy corn.

God, with my wife and I struggling, has allowed us to support our family. After we had seven children, we began thinking of planning the family. An agent of the Asociación Pro-Bienestar de la Familia de Guatemala [APROFAM, Association for the Welfare of the Family of Guatemala][29] always passes through these towns. He is like a contraceptive salesman for the association, and my wife and I agreed that she would begin taking the pills that he recommended. For a time my wife used contraceptives. That's how it happened. Suddenly she told me, "Look, I haven't menstruated this month [of June 1985]."

"Let's wait," I told her, "and see if the menstruation won't fall next month."

"It's two months now," she told me, "I'm no longer menstruating. It seems that I'm pregnant."

Then I talked to the agent of APROFAM who sells the contraceptives, saying, "My wife is taking birth control pills, but she's now two months past her last period."

"Look," he said, "if it's been two months since your wife has had a period, it appears that she's pregnant. But if she's taking the pill and ended up pregnant, it is bad for her health and for the health of the one she is carrying; that is to say, the baby. Be careful, you had better find a way to abort because the medication she has taken is harmful to the baby. A baby boy or girl could be born with physical defects—it could be missing a hand or an eye, and this will be bad for the life of the baby. And if it's not like that, it will be born with mental retardation. Then there will always be problems for you and the baby."

I told my wife what he had told me. We to went to a woman named Virginia, whom we call Doña Carola. We asked her to sell us drugs for an abortion, since we had heard that she always sells medicines for aborting. She sold us eight capsules and told my wife to take two each day for four days. My wife did everything she told her to do, but there was no result. We went to her again and told her nothing had happened.

"Well," she told us, "there's no problem. If the capsules didn't work, I will give you a home remedy that we call *monte* (grass, hay)." She gave us some leaves and told my wife, "Take it two times and you will see whether you are going to abort."

Later my wife cooked and drank the water of that *monte*, but to no benefit—she didn't abort. We were worried because the man from APROFAM had told us that the baby was going to be born with a physical or mental impediment because my wife had conceived while taking birth control pills.

Then I told my señora, "Let's conform. We can't do anything because we tried the things to abort but it was impossible. Now, well, we have to conform to our destiny. Only God for us because we can't do anything else. In Genesis God said grow and multiply, and this is what He wants for us."

For God, everything is possible, and for man, impossible. My señora saw herself pregnant again, but always with uneasiness. She soon was five to six months along.

Then all the days and nights we asked God to forgive us for what we had done because we had wanted to kill the baby in the womb. Many times we try to do things, but God already has His plans. When I worked in the fields, I asked God to give the conception His blessing and that He be able to excuse us.

And that's how it was. Day and night we always entrusted ourselves to God, asking Him for His help, His grace, for what my wife was carrying. My wife and I were both sad because we were being told that a stupid baby was going to be born to us. Well, it was painful for a parent since we were to blame. My señora had taken the pills, and I myself had told her to do so, which means it was both of us.

The most happy day was 22 February 1986. At 1:00 in the morning, a baby girl was born, assisted by the *empírica* [no formal training and laying claim to a profession by experience] midwife, Virginia Ramos Hernández. The first thing she did was to check to see that it had a complete body. We thanked God for the new creature and that she was well; her feet, her hands, her eyes, everything was fine.

In the morning of this day, my real father arrived to see the newborn. He said, "Please give her the name of my mother." We said yes. Thus, for that reason we named the baby Dominga Bizarro Ramos because Dominga was the name of the mother of Jesús Ujpán.

We took Dominga to a doctor of a mother-infant project (mainly for infants) in San Martín. She said that her health was very good. At the same time the doctor included the child on a list. For that reason each month my wife goes to get milk, wheat, oil, and flour of broad beans [in the soybean family] as a gift from the project for all the women who have more than five children.

What do you know about this project?

Just that the money comes from Mexico. It doesn't seem to be a project of the government.

Was the milk powdered milk?

Yes, but it had a label of CARE. All of the items that they were passing out had stamped on it a gift from the people of the United States.

How long can she get this food?

Until the baby is five years old.

Dominga is the one that we love very much; we are a little sad that we wanted to kill her with an abortion. But God didn't allow us to commit this grave sin. We confessed these things in the church. With much reason I say that God and only God is the owner of life and creator of human beings.

Story of My Life
24 March 1984 to 27 March 1986

In this month the Banco Nacional de Desarrollo Agrícola (BANDESA) granted me a loan of Q1,100. This money served to buy some land from a *Martinero* named Roberto Hugo García Tziac. Earlier I had given him Q200 as a down payment, but the agreement was for Q1,200, and I was unable to finish paying for it. Roberto Hugo wasn't able to give me back the Q200. Then we arranged to go to Sololá to the office of the lawyer, Demetrio de Dios, so that Roberto could give me a deed for the sale of the land. In the documents, it said that I had already paid, but this was not true. I arranged with Roberto that when I had the documents, I was going to ask for a loan at the bank. I deposited the deed with the bank, and then they granted me the loan of Q1,100, with the condition that I had to receive Q300 worth (15 *quintales*) of the loan in fertilizer. I answered yes. I received the fertilizer, and they gave me part of the money, Q500, which I gave to Roberto Hugo. On 5 July of the same year, the bank gave me Q300, the rest of the loan, which I in turn gave to Roberto Hugo.

I thought about buying this land for my cultivations. The contract with the bank was for a year, and I was supposed to pay it off in the month of February of 1985. I struggled a lot to get the money. I wanted to pay for it so that I would not be in bad stead with the bank, but it was impossible. I sold a little coffee, but at a very low price. I was a year in arrears of payment. I felt ashamed. They called it to my attention three times. I told the representative of the bank to have more consideration, that I would pay this debt in the month of March of 1986 in two payments. The bank collector is a very good person. He told me that if I wanted another loan he would authorize it for me. I said yes if you authorize it for me. This is the way it was with Sr. Julio Ambrosio Alejandro, the collector and authorizer. With him I had a good friendship. But a lot of my countrymen were eliminated from the bank for not paying in the time of debt. [Ignacio paid this debt on 27 March 1986.]

The Story of Those Who Commit Evil
15 April 1986

Your sons or grandsons are those who suffer the law of *compensación* [compensation, reprisal; "what goes around comes around"] according to what my grandmother Isabel told us. She said that the years of 1914 to 1916 were when the communal lands were distributed to all those who paid the commission to the engineer, Lucas Escobar. The amount of land they got depended on the quantity of money that the residents gave. The poorest only got a few *cuerdas* of land, which was far away in the mountains. They only gave land to the women who were friends of the engineer (friends who gave him sexual favors).

With the repression by the government, all were obliged to fulfill the *mandamiento* [forced labor migrations] in the *fincas* for heavy work so that their families could eat a little. They had to pawn off their land to *Martineros* and a little to their own *Joseños*. Those who pawned their land were on the *fincas* for two to three years. Thus were the times.

In the year of 1914 the mayor, Santiago Puzul, and the syndic, Esteban Godoy, received money from the hands of the *Martineros*. They had the lawyer, Alejandro Galindo, make up the deeds of the *Martineros* in which they falsified the fingerprints of the owners. It was said that the fingerprints were made by Santiago Puzul and signed as a witness of the law by Esteban Godoy. When the poor owners realized what had happened, they could do nothing because their fingerprints appeared already on documents of sellers with the signature of a witness. But they were lies. It was thus when they were swindled out of their lands and could do nothing to recover them. Those who profited were Santiago Puzul and Esteban Godoy.

My grandmother told us that Señor Santiago Puzul was killed with a machete on Easter Saturday (the day after Good Friday) in the year of 1925 about 11:00 a.m. The assassin was a Ladino by the name of Gregorio Martínez, who worked in the village of Patzilín and was contracted by the affected *Joseños*.

Also, when Santiago Puzul died, the whole town was happy. He did not have mourners. He was just buried by his children.

Now I'm going to talk a little about what my grandma and other old folks said. Never should one do bad things to people because, if one behaves poorly and if one steals what is not yours, it will be your sons or grandsons who will suffer a lot and never find solace in their lives. This is quite true. The children of Santiago Puzul were Jaime, Valeriano, Rosa, Caria, and Santiago. Jaime died in 1958. He was not very old. Valeriano? Who knows where he went to die? Rosa died three years ago. Those who are still alive are Caria and Santiago. All of them sold the land that Santiago and Jaime Puzul left them. Now they have nothing, not even their *sitios*.

Now it is the grandsons of Santiago Puzul who suffer a lot. They are only drunks who never are able to do anything. They have no land, so they go around to the houses asking for shelter, but the people don't want them because they say they are thieves. This, then, is the law of *compensación*. Also, the Bible says that the law of compensation goes to the third generation. This is very true.

The same thing happened to the family of Esteban Godoy. When Esteban Godoy realized all of the evil he had committed, he converted to Protestantism, but it was too late to help. When he died he was survived by his children: Isabel, Rosa, Jaime, and Martín. Isabel gave birth to a mentally retarded son. Rosa is deaf and dumb; she never married. Jaime is never going to have a woman. Who knows why he doesn't want one? Martín Godoy and I were in the army together. When he left the army he joined the national police, but he had such bad luck that he fell into the hands of thieves. They took away his weapons and wounded him. Now he has a physical impediment (lost an eye because of thieves, who were policemen). He resides in the capital.

The Church and Father José
11 April 1985 to 14 August 1986

Some important and interesting things are happening in the town of San José. Someday this diary will serve for the future, mainly so that the children will realize how San José was at this time and what changes there were in the future.

Ignorance is a grave illness that we Tzutuhiles carry in our heads. It's difficult to combat ignorance, which is very strong and still reigns in these parts. The intellectuals and the ingenuous suffer a lot when they try to convince or convert the Tzutuhil to a good path. Lately, we have been realizing the suffering of the North American priest named José McCall, who arrived in the parish of San Martín Apóstol of San Martín la Laguna, substituting for the Reverend Father Rutio Estrada from Spain.

Father José arrived to take possession 11 April 1985, Palm Sunday, three days before Holy Thursday. With jubilation those who are the parishioners and loyal Catholics received him. They had a big fiesta. They received him with good carpets of flowers and a lot of *bombas*.

When he made his entrance in the church, he did not want to pass in the middle of the rugs, he just went to the side. Then he said to the people of San José, "Today you receive me with much happiness, even flowers for my feet, but I tell you to adore God, not men, and I tell you today I am seeing these beautiful decorations, but who knows what is in your hearts? Today I'm seeing a Palm Sunday, but how glad I am that no one amongst you is going to spend a Holy Friday with me [that none of you is going to crucify me as Jesucristo was crucified]." The words that the father spoke to the people were very clear.

Thus it was. Then the father began to organize the people in different religious groups with the condition that they had to abolish the *cofradías*.

The *cofrades* of San Juan Bautista from 1984 to 1985 with the image in their house were: *alcalde*, Gerardo Alberto Ujpán Vásquez, and *juez* [vice-head], Santiago López García. They were there doing the *costumbres* without problems. They surrendered their posts in the month of June. In the same month, Lilian Chávez Sicay was named *alcalde* and Juan Fuertes *juez*. By order of the father, these *cofrades* already did not function as before. Before, they did what they wanted. They carried the image of the saint to the house of the *alcalde*, head of the *cofradía*. This 24 June the image was carried to the church.

The house of the *cofradía* was prepared, but just for the meeting of the *cofrades*. Then the father gave the order that the new *cofrades* of San Juan Bautista had the obligation to attend and listen to religious classes an hour each day for 20 days to understand and learn what the life of saints was like and why we respect the saints. Also, he prohibited the drinking of liquor in the *cofradías*. The *cofrades* had to show good deportment in the church and among the people. But as the head of the *cofradía* is the owner of a cantina, he became very angry when they told him no more alcohol. He did not respect the teachers nor go to the classes. He remained an enemy of the priest.

In the month of August of 1985, the fraternal *alcalde*, Agustín María Mario Bizarro Toc, and the *juez*, David Quic, completed their year of service in the *cofradía* of Santo Domingo Guzmán. Still, they had the image in their house. On the 4th of this month, Ignacio Oliva y Oliva was named head and Mario Bizarro Toc vice-head. The father said that they could take the image to the private house of the *cofradía* on the condition that they would attend class. The *cofrades*, however, would not attend the classes, so the father would not let them take the image to the house of the *cofradía*. They attended mass and other acts in the church, but they were not in accord with the orders of the priest.

The same thing happened with the *cofradía* of María Concepción. The last head was Diego Cholotío Méndez, and the last vice-head was David Xicay Pablo. They completed their year of service on 8 December 1985. Then Juan Ixtamer Sumoza was named head and Juan Catalina Ixtamer vice-head. There is a saying that goes: "*Justos payun por pecadores* [The righteous pay for sinners]." The father and Catholic Actionists didn't allow them to carry the image of the Virgin Mary to their house. But these two men don't drink alcohol—they are members of Alcoholics Anonymous, and it had been about five or six years since they had drunk any liquor.

Those of the Church (the father and members of Catholic Action) said that the old *costumbres* are all abolished and that the *cofrades* only were able to participate in mass and rosaries and bury the dead, nothing more. This did not suit the *cofrades*; it made them mad. But I think that the father and the Catholic Actionists want what's good for them so that they will not spend their money. But as the *cofrades* never reflect, they just think of what they have learned from our ancestors, that the old *costumbres* are beneficial for the community.

Can you explain a little more the significance of the images and the dispute of the father and the cofradías?

The father wanted the *cofrades* to listen to 20 days of classes before the *cofrades* could take the images to their houses for their *cofradías*. The *cofrades* didn't want to attend the classes, and the father likewise didn't want to give them the images that were in the church. That was the origin of this problem.

In the month of July of this same year, the father, after the fiesta of San José and San Martín, held a meeting of Catholic Action for the towns that make up the parish of San Martín—San Jorge Laguna, San Benito la Laguna, San José la Laguna, Santa Rosa la Laguna (especially its *aldea* of Tzancuil and *caseríos* [hamlets] of Moján and Chimo), and San Martín la Laguna—saying that it is necessary to help the towns like brothers and work together to improve a little better the social life of each town. He said that there was a need for a building in each town that would serve the medical needs of the indigenous people but that the works would be done collectively. First they were going to build the one in San Martín, which already had a dispensary, but not an office.

Then, "Yes," said the other towns, except San Benito, because the people of that town consider themselves too poor to contribute labor to the projects in the other towns. The priest bore in mind that San Benito was not going to send people to work in the other towns, but that they nevertheless would still receive a benefit on behalf of the priest.

Does the father already have architectural plans?

Yes. The father has traveled to each of these places and asked them what their needs are. He told the people that a town will see changes according to what it wants the most, a church or a dispensary. It seems that in Moján they are going to build a church and a dispensary. In Chimo they are just going to build a church, and in San Benito just a dispensary. This is what the father said in a mass, which I heard, because I was very close to him.

It is not clear what they plan to do in San José. The church leaders say they are going to build a dispensary, but some of the people say they want a new church.

Thus, it was. San José then gave a little adobe and some money, but where they helped a lot was in the labor. All the members of Catholic Action went to work one day each. Also those of San Jorge did the same, and together with the *Martineros* they finished the job and inaugurated the building. But my people of San José didn't work with their hearts. They always showed hypocrisy against the priest by what they said in their loose talk. There is, however, a minority that are true Catholics, respecting the orders of the father.

A little after having completed their works in San Martín, the president of Catholic Action, Ángel Alberto Mogollón, and the ex-military commissioner, José Carlos Pinto, went to ask the father when the construction would begin in San José. The father says that he told them, "Have patience, wait a little, just a little patience until I have a little money to help you." When they heard this response, they began to murmur, saying that the father was a liar. Their rancor was really because the *costumbres* were abolished, which they believed were going to save them in the other life.

Can you explain about these beliefs of the cofrades?

Well, the *cofrades* have their particular beliefs. They believe in the saints because the saints are very good friends of God. If someone serves as *alcalde*, *juez*, or *mayordomo* devoted to the saint of the *cofradía*, they think that in the other life they will be forgiven for their sins because the saint is a very good friend of God and will intercede for them when they die so they will not suffer punishment in the other life.

In these months there have been changes in the marriages and in the baptisms. The priest ordered that the parents and the godparents have to be trained for better care, both in illness and in malnutrition, and how to care for and educate a son or godson. All of these things the parents and godparents have neglected for their little ones. It is because they lack knowledge and the parents and godparents get drunk in front of their children and do nothing to feed and educate their family. It was thus when the father ordered that the parents and godparents attend and listen to good advice for an hour daily for 20 days, and not until the classes are over will the children be baptized.

The same thing happened with the marriages. The woman and man have to be trained because marriage is to take care of the corporal and spiritual life, and in order not to fail in life it is better to attend the religious classes a short time. The father had announced to all the parents of the young that the classes would be for one hour a day for 15 to 20 days.

Previously the other fathers celebrated masses sometimes twice a day and more during the fiestas. Father José said, "One mass each Saturday starting from 4:30 p.m. and no more." Because it was the custom, there were persons who paid to have mass during weekdays. Father José said, "Do not pay for any more masses; one is sufficient. Use the money you pay for mass to feed your children." But since my people had already been accustomed to having more masses, for them the customs had become a law. When they heard these things, they became more loco, to the point of saying that the father is a crazy person. The criticisms began.

In the month of January, 1986, they interchanged the directors of Catholic Action. Then by the order of, or better said, on the approval of the priest, they started the activity of building toilets and showers with hot and cold water. The shower rooms and toilets they built behind the great parochial hall, but the big pit [septic] where the black water [feces and urine] falls they dug in front of the church. This pit was dug by the members of Catholic Action. They were digging the pit one afternoon, when about 2:30, the workers decided to stop working until the next day. They say that Ignacio Có Gordillo, who was next to the pit, gave the child, Bonifacio Sánchez, a big scare. Ignacio yelled, "Oooie, who knows who is coming there!" Bonifacio took off running and fell into the pit—11 meters and 21 centimeters deep. A *Joseño*, Gregorio Gandolfo Peralta, took the child out alive but disfigured.

The authorities [the secretary and the mayor] arrived, but no one said why the child had fallen into the well. It wasn't until later they told me that the child fell inside because of a big scare. But neither the parents nor the authorities knew it. Members of Catholic Action tried to carry him to the hospital, but witnesses said that Bonifacio expired inside the launch halfway across the lake. Bonifacio's parents were Ignacio Sánchez and Isabel Temó, who had gone to Guatemala to sell *trajes*. They came back after he had been taken to the morgue in the hospital of Sololá. When the parents wanted to talk, they were persuaded to say that their son died in the *sitio* of the church. They say that they gave them a recompense of money, and everything remained calm.

In the months of April and May, it was clear that the problem with the church was growing more every day. As has become the custom, Catholic

Action always has the responsibility of taking care of all the things in the church, including the treasury. It is not known who told Father José that the directors of Catholic Action misspent the money to buy *aguardiente* for the fiesta and that all the offerings only serve to get them drunk.

Well, these things are true. I also had realized that after the religious fiestas and after the processions there had been brandies. What I didn't know was whether the money spent belonged to the church. When the father was informed that Catholic Action misused the money, he asked them for a bill. He asked them to hand over the money that they had. Well, they brought Q1,300. He told them that he was going to keep the money and that when there was enough it could be spent for a project or to reconstruct the church. Then he said that all the money that comes in had to be in the possession of the priest in accordance to canonical law and that the priest is the *jefe* of the church. They told him very well. But there were murmurs against the priest because they had been accustomed to using the money as they saw fit.

But later Father José said that he was interested in knowing and seeing the deeds of the *sitio* of the church and of a piece of land planted in coffee. Well, the same directors of Catholic Action handed over the deed of the church and the document for the land. They said that the father said that the papers had to be kept in the parish of San Martín and that Catholic Action did not have the authority to keep the property of the church. The deed then went to the parish in San Martín to be taken care of. This was the poison of the Tzutuhiles. The money and the deeds went to the father. The *cofrades*, *principales*, and a group of catechists got very angry. They spoke badly about the father.

But the priest was always with all of them, celebrating mass, teaching good things to the youngsters and the young girls, and saying to the parents, "Be responsible. No more drunken parties nor adultery. You don't have to steal. If there is life, do not abort. Everyone fight against poverty. No more illiteracy. Struggle to gain knowledge." This is what Father José preached in the church. But as we Indians have become vain and a majority live in adultery, men have children with other women. Moreover, some are in favor of drunken parties and women who just sleep around and abort when they get pregnant. There are groups that just live by stealing. The preaching of Father José did not suit them. Thus it was for some days. They joined together against the father, looking for a falsehood, but they could not find out how to do it.

In regard to the father telling the people not to abort if there is life, can you explain a little more about birth control?

The father doesn't like artificial contraceptives because he says that it damages the health of the woman and the man. According to him, we don't know, the pills that come from the United States are very bad for the health of us indigenous people. They gave a class for avoiding pregnancies, but it was a natural method they taught us. A doctor from Guatemala and a teacher from Xela [Quezaltenango] arrived to give classes in San Martín to impart knowledge to all the women and men that the woman has two stages, or two kinds of menstruation, a month. The time of white menstruation is when the woman is unable to have relations with her spouse, and the husband is not able to enter the woman during this menstruation. But for us this class was very difficult because almost all the women asked the question, "What?" They only knew one kind of menstruation, so it was very strange when the doctor said there were two types of menstruation.

Is was difficult for us to attend, but my wife and I went to this class in the month of May; we attended little. Well, one part was very good. It is a pity that there were people who didn't want to accept these conditions because they say that the artificial contraceptives are able to damage the woman, and also the woman can still get pregnant. And if the woman wants to get pregnant and she already has taken pills, or if she has used some contraceptive, the baby will be born defective—mentally retarded or with physical defects. This is what the father said, and for this reason he did not advise the use of contraceptives. Instead, he gave a class on a natural method, and he said that this is what the Mayas used previously. That is what he said, but I don't know if that is certain because they didn't read some book, just theoretically they told us that the Mayas used natural methods of contraception.

Then the father said that pills are dangerous?

They are dangerous for the women.

And the men don't use condoms?

Well, they say that they cause arthritis or rheumatism. Do you understand?

No.

They say that with the use of rubbers the man is going to come down with a sickness, arthritis or rheumatism, an ache of the bones. This is what they say, but I don't know if it is true.

The father says this is true or the teachers?

The teachers and the doctor. The father didn't actually give a class of this himself. He just called the people to come to the class. He didn't talk about the family; he just invited the doctor and the teachers to go give the classes to the married couples and to the young people who want to participate. It is a free course formed by the parish of San Martín.

When did the classes happen?

The last class took place in the month of May.

This year, 1987?

Yes! My wife and I only went one time. The women didn't understand how there are two kinds of menstruation. They had only noticed one kind, but the teachers and the doctor say that there are two types. Then, who knows which of the women from that point discovered that there are two kinds of menstruation.

What were the names of these teachers?

The male teacher was called Moisés and the woman Ana. The doctor is named Luis, but the surname I don't know, just that he is Doctor Luis.

Were the two teachers also doctors?

No, they weren't doctors, just teachers. But they knew a lot about natural planning. It seems that they were paid by some institution because they say they are going to Sacap, to Chiquimula, to all parts of the country to explain the natural method of family planning.

Do some men in San José use condoms?

It seems so because there is a distribution. In the pharmacies there are plenty. And in San José there are plenty because there is family planning, the national association.

Are they expensive or free?

No, they are neither expensive nor free, but a regular price.

Regular, how much does one cost?

About 50 centavos [Q2.5 equaled $1 in 1987], in the pharmacies.

And in APROFAM?

In APROFAM it costs about 25 centavos, and pills cost 40 centavos for a month.

More or less, they are cheap.

Cheap, exactly. But I don't know; I have doubts about this too. I don't know about this. What do you think about artificial contraception, is it good or bad? Or what do you know about it?

There's a theory that pills are dangerous, but now there are pills that are not very dangerous. And condoms don't cause rheumatism.

They don't cause it?

No.

Yes, they say.

Very well. You told me that you and your wife use the natural method but that it doesn't work well. Why not?

Imagine, we are very confused now because they only gave us the beginning of the course, and we haven't received another class yet. All that we have received instruction on was the natural method, the two kinds of menstruation, but still it isn't known which of the two menstruations. We don't know whether this white menstruation comes first or later, and that's where we are. Then because of the problems of the father with the town, it seems that he has not called back the teachers. My wife and I need to remain in this family planning a lot, because we have a lot of children, eight; we need help. But it's a pity that we are very confused because we have not obtained an additional class because by ourselves we are unable to do so.

Well, I have a book, *Donde No Hay Doctor*, but what this books says is very different than what these teachers say. Then, I am still somewhat confused, and what I need is for them to come again to San Martín, but who knows when they will come because of the problems that have occurred with the father.

What does the book, Donde no Hay Doctor, *say? Isn't this the book that I sent you?*

Yes, it is the book. This book doesn't say that there are two kinds of menstruation. The book only mentions one menstruation a month. And the book says that after 10 days, one is unable to engage in sex. But what the teachers say is another thing. The book says one thing and the teachers another. Then, what is the most difficult for us is to differentiate between two menstruations.[30]

My wife and I sometimes use what it says in the book, but we lost. My wife got pregnant with Samuel, our seventh child, when we were using this method. I don't blame the book, however. It seems that it is our fault for not understanding well the meaning of the words.

The author of this book is a medical doctor.

Yes, a doctor. And there is another method—the operation, to go to a doctor and he operates on a woman, but [Ignacio speaking softly] my wife doesn't want to. She doesn't want to. "It's better to die," she says.

Yes, there's an operation for a man too.

Yes, there is an operation for a man. But the teachers say the operation is bad for the man; I don't know. Who knows? The doctor also said the operation is bad for the man and that the operation for the woman is bad because after ten years or twelve years it causes a cancer. But whether this is true or not, I don't know, perhaps a fear. [Ignacio laughs.]

[I laugh.] I have never heard this. But I'm not a medical doctor.

In the month of May of 1986 they asked the father to return the money of the church because they needed it for the fiesta of the town. But the father did not hand over the money. They told him that if he did not give it to them, they would initiate a judicial proceeding. The priest, to end the *costumbres*, organized a committee to collect money and celebrate, but with the condition that there be no more useless expenses. It seems that they felt another blow of oppression.

In this same month of May, 1986, a group of *principales, cofrades*, catechists, and others held a meeting because they wanted to organize a committee for the construction of a church. But the padre rejected the committee, saying that they could indeed construct a church when the church had a quantity of Q40,000 to Q50,000. For the moment, however, they couldn't do it. If the committee could raise funds for some two or three years, then they could do the work. Then they thought it would be worth asking him for the money so that the committee could take care of it. The priest says that he told them it served for the repair of the car. But without doubt he said this only to see the attitude of the people.

Why do you think he said it for this reason?

Well, I too was a bit bothered because the *principales*, the mayor, and the townspeople were saying a lot about the father, especially that he had spent the money to repair the car. The priest is a person I respect and chat with, and on one opportunity I asked him, "Padre, what happened? Is it true that you spent the money of San José?"

"No, Dear Friend," he told me, "the money has not been spent. What happened is that I didn't want to give the money to the people for them to spend on *aguardiente* and on the marimba. The money is kept with the bishop. We are safekeeping Q3,900. I'm going to contribute another sum of the money for a project that will be done in San José."

That is to say, the money was not spent by Father José. The people thought that Father José had spent the money and criticized him for it. But, in fact, when I talked with him, he told me that the bishop had the money for safekeeping. "This money will serve for the town," he told me. "I'm not doing anything with the money of the people; it's not mine to spend. I don't have a family, so why am I going to spend a lot of money?" I'm very sure that the money is not spent. The people have a misunderstanding. It appears that telling them that the money would be used to repair the car was a mistake. And the people now say that the father is a thief, that he took the town's money. But the truth is that the money is saved.

When they heard these things, they treated the father like a crook and a crazy man. There was a lot more criticism. It was worse for the illiterate people who believed everything they were told. The most mistreatment came from the cantons of Lamak and Jicaro. But the priest is not carrying out reprisals. He always says that everyone changes his own attitude. There's nearly a majority against him, or, more or less, 125 to 150 who are in favor of the good things that he says. Almost all are against what he preaches because he always condemns adultery.

It's incredible but true what the father said in his preaching. On 5 June of this year, the top director and ex-president of Catholic Action, Samuel Luciano Tuc, was found in adultery with his *comadre* [godmother of his child] by the name of Margarita Puzul. This case was very apparent and known by the people. They had given this man much respect and treated him like one of the best, without their knowing what he was hiding. As is the custom, the women assembled to visit the church. On this day they were giving out the food that Cáritas of Guatemala had obtained for San José. After visiting the church, they went to the warehouse to divide the food. After all this, Samuel disappeared momentarily. His wife went to look for him in another *sitio*. His wife said that Samuel Luciano was found in full adultery [in the act] with one of his co-parents by the name of Margarita Puzul, who is better known by the nickname Tala. She says that when she found them, the co-parent was naked with her *corte* to one side. Then Samuel's woman grabbed the *corte* and went to hide it. Thus it was for three days. There was no immediate complaint made to the authorities.

His co-parent, however, was very clever at getting revenge for Samuel's wife having hid her *corte*. She presented a complaint to the justice of peace which stated she had been brutally beaten by Samuel's wife and that she had been pregnant for six months. The adultery remained aside. The arraignment now involved Samuel's wife for having hit her co-parent. Then Samuel's woman had to tell the truth for her defense—that her husband and her co-parent had been found in full adultery. She said that she didn't hit her co-parent, only that she found her naked with her *corte* set aside and the fault, or crime, that she committed was to hide the *corte* among the coffee trees. Not until then did the local authorities go to inspect the place, and at the same time the *corte* was found. Then the woman of Samuel Luciano presented her own legal complaint against her husband and her co-parent. Thus the authorities discovered that they had been adulterous, and the co-parents were investigated. The investigation of this case lasted for 11 days, during which the culprits were in jail in San José. The proceedings ended on the 15th. They were sentenced to be taken to jail in Sololá on the 16th.

I heard of these problems day after day and that they were getting worse. Then one day at the end of the proceedings, I went to talk to Samuel, who was in jail crying, "Now I'm separated; now my family doesn't want me, nor do my friends, nor the religious persons. You, Ignacio," he said, "we are friends. Do me a favor; work a little for my defense. It's true that I am a sinner and guilty of what they say. It's true; it's not a lie. But God forgives, and Ángel [Tata's husband] will forgive me. But now I can't do anything. The papers are signed. Everything is finished. So what I want is for you to work for me. Talk to Ángel because no one in my family wants me. And my woman won't come give me food, and it will be worse when I'm in the jail in Sololá, worse than here. Say something to Ángel. See if you can do something for me, because I'm going to pay you."

"I'm not interested in your paying me," I told him. "We are brothers. I'm going to see if I can do something."

Then Tata's husband, Ángel, did the same to his wife. When her *corte* was found in the *cafetal* [coffee grove], he was the declared accusor of his own wife. It's a pity that Ángel hardly knew that his wife had committed adultery. He had thought that she was faithful, as did Samuel's wife.

They say that the punishment for Samuel's crime would be one to three years in jail and that the woman would have to spend a minimum of six months to a year. But it's a pity that Samuel has 11 children and his co-parent 5. If these two go to jail, who would keep these 16 children? Who would suffer? Samuel's wife is unable to support 11 children, and neither is Tata's husband able to take care of 5. He can't make dinner for five children. The children, however, are innocent. Still the law had seized these two persons.

On the night before they left for the jail in Sololá, I was able to talk with Ángel about his feelings. Then I told Ángel, "You have reason to send your woman to jail, but you will have to take care of the kids. Beforehand, you need to think about what you're going to do. Your wife is going to spend from six months to a year in jail." Then Ángel cried. He had thought that it would be for only 10 to 15 days. "In San José we can fix it," I said, "but once it goes to Sololá, we can do nothing. *La ley es pesada* [The law is heavy]." Then he asked me what he could do to dismiss the case. I suggested some legal procedures, and we went to the secretary. We convinced the secretary that it was of a private act, but he told us we would have to convince the mayor (justice of peace) to drop the proceedings. But when we arrived at the house of the mayor, he was very rude and angry. He told me, "Why do you have to get involved in the business of others?"

"It's for Samuel," I said, "Not the woman. I am asking for this dismissal for the 16 children who will go hungry. The children are innocent! He who asks pardon is the husband of the woman because he cannot take care of five children."

Very angrily the justice of the peace said, "Why didn't this person think about what he was doing when he asked that she be jailed. Now he cries. He deserves his sentence. The proceedings are finished."

As a brother, without any interest in money, with a clean conscience and without receiving a single centavo from the hand of Samuel, I got together with other *principales* and the father-in-law of Samuel, and we all went to talk to the municipal secretary. Together we were able to do something. Then we, there were a lot of us, went to the mayor who received us at 10:00 p.m. We told him to take consideration with Samuel and not send him to jail in Sololá, to let him stay imprisoned here, and to make him pay a fine for all the expenses he had caused, because there were expenses in paperwork and all.

Thus it was that we spoke for the two persons, and the judge accepted our petition. But he was doubtful. He thought that we had made a business deal, but that is not true. What we did was a humanitarian thing. The dismissal of this case ended at midnight on Sunday, 16 June. Only then were Samuel and Tata taken out of jail.

When everything was finished, we realized that about 40 to 50 persons, men and women, were fighting to console these two families. The wife of Samuel was very appreciative. We fought to keep Samuel in San José, but it was expensive. He had to pay a fine of Q60 in addition to Q50 for the paperwork the secretary had done. And the woman it cost Q40.

It is true that not all the people think about others; some still do not want to speak to sinners. But the truth is that in this world, we all have faults. This case had been well spoken of by Father José when he said that there is evil among those who work in the church. It certainly was to be seen.

They say the problems of the church continue. It is premature, but every day it grows. The *principales* and *cofrades* say that they are considered lower and dominated by paternalism, but at times the things that the father says are true. Last year the mass for the *novenario* [funeral service on the first nine days after a person's death] was in the afternoon.[31] The parish priest says that it is better in the morning at 5:00 a.m. because the mind of man is very fresh and is able to concentrate for an hour of God's service. If it is during the afternoons, everyone comes from his work very tired and at times the people only go to mass to sleep. But the old folks say that this is very early, and they are unable to go because of their age. This, however, is a pretext because most of the old folks already weren't going to mass. People of my age [46] and the youngsters can't say it's because of our age. It's more truthful to say it's because of laziness.

Well, one of the things that at times the *costumbres* do is to enliven the fiestas. They attract the attention of the visitors and nearby people. There are good *costumbres* such as the processions of the images, drinking *atol* in the *cofradías*, and the *cofrades* preparing food during the fiestas as gifts. The padre, however, wanted to completely cancel these activities, but this is what provoked problems.

As they had become accustomed to doing in previous years, on the eve of the fiesta, 23 June, the *cofrades* wanted to carry the images of San Juan, Santo Domingo, and María Concepción in procession from the *cofradías* to the church in preparation for a procession through the main streets of the town on the following day, 24 June. The priest, however, had ordered that the images not be in the *cofradías* any more. The directors of the church, catechists, and heads of Catholic Action sent the images out without consulting the priest. On 21 June during the night, each *cofrade* carried his corresponding saint to his *cofradía* so that on 23 June the *cofrades* would be able to carry the images in procession and drink *atol*. When the priest realized this, he gave an order to get them back immediately. The *cofrades* handed over the images during the night of the 22nd, although they had already prepared everything for the following day. The next day they drank *atol*, but with much sadness. In each *cofradía* there was one hour of marimba to call the attention of the people, but the people only arrived to drink *atol*. Each day the problem grew worse.

On the 23rd, the eve of the fiesta, the *cofrades* were only isolated. They didn't go to church. Each group stayed home, preparing for the events of the fiesta. Also on this day, the priest prepared a spiritual retreat in the *salón* of the church in San José for all the *Joseños*, *Jorgeños* [people of San Jorge], *Martineros*, *Beniteños* [people of San Benito], and those of Tzancuil in the form of a get-together to avoid a drunken party during the fiesta. Everyone from San Jorge, San Benito, and Tzancuil came and took part in the retreat, except the *Joseños*. It seemed that they were full of anger, and for that reason did not attend.

Dawn was very beautiful on 24 June. The church committee bought a lot of things with which to celebrate the fiesta, spending hundreds of quetzales. But earlier they had been told not to spend money for pleasure. Always, however, there was a little lying.

The *Joseños* had become accustomed to all the *principales* being invited on behalf of the mayor for eating a succulent lunch, drinking their traditional *tragos*, dancing some hours to the happy, regional sounds of the marimba, and remembering past times. But on this 25 June, the parish priest didn't permit the *principales* to go to the invitation. The same padre took them to the soccer field to watch the game. And they had to say yes, accompanied by the priest. It all seemed very well—the father wanted the best for the *principales* so that they wouldn't get drunk, would avoid injuries, and wouldn't spend money, because their bodies are very delicate due to their advanced age and they are unable to earn money. It is known, however, that the old guys didn't like sports. Many of them just drank their *tragos* secretly and got very drunk. It's difficult for them to change their habits—they are old men, and they have already lived many years with their old, traditional *costumbres*. To change their manners, one must have patience!

All was to the contrary in San Martín where the parish is located. The priest also wanted to abolish the *costumbres*, but he was unable. They celebrated the fiesta of San Martín Apóstol with much jubilation. Much earlier [about 15 years ago] they had dropped the Dance of the Conquest and the Dance of the Mexicans, but this year they presented both of these dances as well as a very cheerful procession. And the *principales* performed their *costumbres* as before. There were hardly any problems with the father.

In the beginning of the month of July of 1986, there was a lot of criticism between the two groups of the church. The majority wanted to continue the old customs with the *cofradías*, and a minority wanted to end these things because they reasoned the well-being was for each individual and not for the priest. This latter group thought a little better, but the majority said to continue as before. Finally, they came to the conclusion that they were going to name people to the *cofradías* but only to bury the dead and to attend mass and other religious acts with the condition that the images of the saints never be allowed to be carried to the house of the head of the *cofradía*. Not until then was there a little peace.

On 17 July 1986 Father José, in a mass celebrated in honor of the Virgen del Carmen, said, "Everyone change your attitude. Give up drunkenness, adultery, and stealing." I was at this mass, and for me all these things were important so that no one would give in to the more serious sins. What Father José said was good for us Indians, but as ignorance reigns in these towns, when a person speaks for others, they say that this person is bad and look for a way to humiliate him.

Father José has good reason and much knowledge and speaks the truth about what is happening in these towns. According to my observations, and at times I have written about these things, in my town there are many drunks, thieves, adulterers, and aborters. It is difficult to investigate and control these things. The religions fight them, but there are a lot of depraved people who don't understand. It was well witnessed this year that from November of 1985 to March of 1986, a lot of people were sentenced because they wanted to steal coffee from the property of some *Martineros*. There were even more who were not captured. It is true that there is a family that, without having a harvest, constructed a good house that is stuccoed and has a cement floor. They even bought a television. Others have bought bulls. Still many others dress well and wear good shoes, but this well-being is from the property of others. One can easily observe the people who struggle and work and those who do not.

In San José, are there families who are thieves, that have television sets?

There are a number of families in the barrio that don't have any coffee lands, but at night they sell coffee to merchants that have cars. The merchants know the coffee is stolen, but they want money too. When I was doing a census for the town this year, the mayor told me once that he didn't have time for me because he was sentencing ten persons from the barrio for stealing coffee from a *Joseño*. But usually they steal from the *Martineros*. There are some families from the town center that subsist on stealing as well. One was sentenced, but he had stolen onions.

At the end of this month of July, Father José left for the United States on a mission for Bishop Benando. José said that he was going to talk to some friends to get money to help the young people who are studying in the seminary. He told us he is interested in the youngsters getting more knowledge for the development of the towns and that he needs to help them.

Father José returned from his country on 14 August. In the morning of the 15th he celebrated a mass in the church in San José. In his preaching he was always orienting the people to quit drinking and stealing, respect marriage, and honor God's commandments. He said that he was witnessing in this town that the church is full and that many say they are Catholics but that they are liars. What he said was true.

My Wife's Birthday
25 August 1986

On 25 August was my wife's 40th birthday. It was the same as it had been on mine (13 August)—there was no rest. I had to go to work in Xebitz, but always giving thanks to God for another day of life. We had a little lunch with the children, but there isn't money to have a party. By the grace of God, we have peace; my wife and I never fight. We always respect the law of matrimony. Many times we have misfortunes, illness, and a lot of poverty. There are always problems, but they also give one experience.

An Abortion
August 1986

In this same month of August a gloomy thing happened. A baby was found dead on the shore of Lake Atitlán in the jurisdiction of San Martín. A woman found the body while she was on her way to visit the padre in the convent. Then the father went to the authorities. Together they went to get the cadaver and send it to the hospital for the legal, medical autopsy. The justice of peace of San Martín opened the investigation. Many of the women of San Martín said that the death of the baby was because of an abortion during the eighth to ninth month, but no one knows who the mother was. The same justice of the peace called all the midwives of his town to go to all the houses of all the pregnant women who are under the care of each midwife, to find out who was responsible for the abortion. The midwives and the rest of the women of San Martín think and say that the abortion was done by a *Joseña* who went to throw the dead one on the beach in San Martín. This surprised the women of San José, but they don't know who committed this crime.

What the *Martineros* say is true because the one who aborted was a *Joseña* named Juana Rodríguez, who works as a domestic servant in the house of *profesor* Máximo Garcías. They were careless, which resulted in Juana becoming pregnant. But since the man already had a wife, who is also a teacher, he was afraid to have another child. Without doubt, he forced her to abort. They say that she went to leave the baby on the shore of the lake when it was still alive. Certain persons witnessed it, but they were afraid to tell the authorities. When the authorities were told that it was a *Joseña*, they renewed their investigation. This woman, however, knew how to defend herself. Where she had been working she left her sister to work in her place. After the abortion she went to hide in San Benito with another sister. She had been considered guilty of a crime. Nothing happened to the teacher because the woman did not identify who gave her the drugs to abort.

When they called her father to the courthouse to present his daughter, he presented his younger daughter. When this girl was examined by the doctor who works in San José on Wednesdays and other days in San Martín, he found her to be a virgin. The truth is, however, that the one who committed the abortion had not been examined. The father said that she was the one who worked in the house of the *profesor* in San Martín and that he didn't have an older daughter. The authorities, in effect, dropped the case. Also, they say that the father bribed the justice of the peace in San Martín. Indeed, the news and her own companions of the Assembly of God Church, where nearly the whole family are members, said that Juana had aborted. Nearly all the people of both towns know this, but the authorities did nothing because they say that they were bribed. The midwives were forced on threat of incarceration to look for the culprit, and when they found her, nothing was done about it. That's the reason the women of San Martín concluded that the authorities had been bribed.

Celebrating the Beheading of Juan Bautista
29 August 1986

This 29 August a mass was celebrated, commemorating the beheading of Juan Bautista. Also, there was a procession around the church. They say that in the afternoon they drank *atol* in the *cofradía* of San Juan, but only among the *cofrades*.

A little earlier rumors were spreading that there were going to be two groups of dances, and today they turned out to be true. They began to do the Dance of the Conquest in the *sitio* of Pablo Bartolo Bizarro González while the Dance of the Mexicans took place in the patio of Julio Flores Ramos. These are persons who want to continue the old customs. For the most part, they say they are modifying the *costumbres*, but this is not the case. Julio Flores is the owner of a cantina, and for that reason he has an interest in the people continuing to drink.

The National Government Gives Money to the Pueblos
2 to 4 September 1986

This was when all the mayors of all the towns of Guatemala asked the President of the Republic to comply with the stipulation of the Constitution of the Republic, which says that the municipalities will receive 8 percent of the national budget. This money serves for public works. Earlier they had organized an association of municipalities, meeting a lot of times in a lot of different departments of the country to direct themselves well.

The two most powerful leaders of the group were the mayor of Chiquimula, a lawyer who knows the laws well, and the mayor of Escuintla.

When the mayors organized their board of directors, they named the mayor of Chiquimula as their president. Don Vinicio had promised earlier in his slogan, *"Por el pueblo y para el pueblo,"* and the mayor of Chiquimula asked him to comply with his words—"for the people and by the people." But what happened? A few weeks later, the mayor of Chiquimula was kidnapped on the road to Guatemala [City]. All the means of communication announced the disappearance of the imminent mayor. The kin and the people of Chiquimula asked the government for an investigation, but it did nothing. Another mayor told me that the mayor of Chiquimula was kidnapped by the government of Cerezo. I'm not able to provide a date, but this is a very certain case.

The date when the 326 municipalities achieved their objective was Tuesday, 2 September 1986. This was a most happy day for the municipalities of the country. On this day the President of the Republic, *licenciado* Vinicio Cerezo Arévalo, had a meeting with all the mayors to come to an agreement and a solution to the problem so that the mayors would be able to work in their communities. Each town would be given Q100,000.

On Thursday, 4 September, the municipal mayor, Benjamín Peña Cholotío, called all the people to inform them that the town of San José had been given Q100,000. So that they would not see any anomaly in managing this money, in a public meeting he asked the people what were the most needed works. They decided to replace the roof of the primary school and elevate its walls because the *lámina* roof was close to the students and hot in the summer time. They also approved cobbling the road to the pier and partitioning the cemetery with a stone and cement wall to avoid epidemics. They claimed that sometimes the *panteones* break and bad odors come out of the cemetery and that the fractures may cause disease. Also, they wanted to keep dogs and *brujos* out of the cemetery so a person would have to ask the municipality for the keys to the gate, although *brujos* could climb over the fence. Three of us asked to buy a *sitio* for the construction of a building for the *instituto básico*, but this didn't receive the approval of the majority. [Presently, the *básico* uses the new primary school.]

How long has this law been in the constitution?

I'm not sure, but they say that the stipulation has always been in the constitution and that it existed earlier. The military presidents had claimed that there wasn't enough money to give the towns their 8 percent of the budget.[32]

The Story of the Midwives
August to 11 September 1986

Previously in San José there were only two *empírica* midwives—Elena Petzey and Micaela Quic. Elena died 36 years ago, leaving only Señora Micaela, but the latter alone could not take care of all of the women because she also went to other places. The *Joseños* discovered that in the village of Pachichaj there was a midwife by the name of Casilda Letona, and it was she who came to help the women. However, to go to get her took six hours by day and seven hours by night, and after the birth she had to be taken back. It was very difficult to negotiate the trip because from San José to Pachichaj it is pure mountains. They would go with a candle and *ocote* [resinous pine].

It was then when the men talked to each other, "My woman is less than a day from giving birth. Come with me to Pachichaj to fetch the midwife, and when your wife is ready, I will go with you." Thus they helped one another. The poor women suffered a lot, though, having to wait for six to seven hours.

Some men went to Santa Ana to get a midwife, but they often had to wait because they found her waiting on or assisting a birth. The same thing had happened with Señora Micaela Quic. One would have to go to San Martín to get her, sometimes to the *finca*, Pacayal. Sometimes the people traveled very far to fetch a midwife.

Thanks to God, however, Don Juan Pantzay came from the coast to live in this town. His wife, Josefina Monroy, was a midwife. Only then did the *Joseños* get some help. But, since life is short and the days of being human are short, she died.. Señora Micaela Quic had more influence in San José, and, since Josefina was not well-known, the *Joseños* were obliged to look for midwives in San Martín. When Micaela died, María Lavarenzo and Juana Quen remained working out of San Martín, but they too went to other places.

Thanks to the shaman, Don Bernardino Ramos Ixtamer, now deceased, there were two other midwives—his two daughters, Virginia and Mabel. They say their destiny from birth was to be midwives. Mabel got married in San Luis. In this town she was famous for being midwife to thousands of births. Virginia, a *Martinera*, worked in San Martín but more in San José. She was the most famous of all! For more than 25 years she worked in San José, attending most of the births of the *Joseñas*.

Since everything has to be learned in life, when Josefina Monroy died, for about seven to eight years San José had no resident midwife, just those who lived in San Martín. In addition to Virginia Ramos, there were Virginia Puzul, Sarafina Cox, and Romelia Pop.

Now there is a midwife named Lucía Sánchez who sometimes assists births during the year. And there is another called Tomasa Urbelina Sumoza, but this woman forcefully named herself a midwife because she is the wife of a *brujo* associated with Maximón. So there are two midwives, but the people, that is to say, the women, have no confidence in them. They are more confident with the *Martinera* midwives.

The two *Joseña* midwives in 1985 attended the courses for *empírica* midwives that the Centro de Bienestar Social de Salud Publica [Public Health Center for Social Welfare] gave for the midwives of San Martín, San José, and the other villages. The course was taught at the center for public health in San José. When it ended, each midwife received the equipment used in childbirth. The *Joseñas*, nevertheless, were valued less. They still didn't have their own women [patients] because no one had confidence in them. They hardly assisted in childbirths. They say that Lucía Sánchez is very old, poorly educated for speaking, and deaf. And they say that Tomasa Urbelina Sumoza, who is a drunk and a prostitute, has no respectability. One can say this is the truth in the case of Tomasa Urbelina. In the first month of the year of 1986, she was assisting a birth in the house of Romeo González, who is first cousin to my wife. After the birth, Tomasa and Romeo gave into drinking for three days. Romeo spent his money and had to sell a horse that had been left him by his deceased father. They spent the value of the horse drinking. For that reason the women don't want her because they are aware of what she did.

They say that in the last days of the month of August, Lucía and Tomasa paid the persons in charge of the *empírica* midwives in San Luis so that only they would remain working in their own town and the *Martineros* only in their own town. But as the saying goes, "*Nadie es profeta en su proprio pueblo* [No one is a prophet in his own country]."

On 11 September 1986 a doctor of maternity from Sololá and the female *jefe* of the midwives arrived, accompanied by the two midwives of San José. They called all the women of San José together to make them see that the only two midwives that had the right to practice in San José were Tomasa and Lucía. At the same time they left a signed memorandum in the municipality stating that only they could work in our town, and they gave a certified copy to the *Martinera* midwives.

The women of San José accepted the meeting and at the same time they looked for a representative to interpret the meaning of what was said in Spanish. Most of the women are illiterate and cannot speak Spanish. The doctor and his companions were oppressors. With the power of oppression, they wanted to oblige the women to sign the act.

It made me very sad, but I was unable to intervene for them. They asked me to do something because I for sure have had experience in intervening in the past, but I didn't want to get involved in such things. Moreover, if I did, they would take me as a leader. For that reason, what I did conformed to the law. I called the representative, Señora Vanessa Pérez, and gave her direction, telling her about two articles of the political constitution of Guatemala. In the middle of the meeting, Señora Vanessa Pérez stood up and asked if everyone had read article 4 and 5 of the constitution of the Republic of Guatemala. This was the solution to the whole conflict. What resulted was that they drew up a memorandum stating that midwives of both San José and San Martín were able to practice in San José. The doctor left upset. No doubt, he certainly thought that we were some wolves, but the truth is that we have a little knowledge.

What do articles 4 and 5 say?

In Guatemala all human beings are free and equal in dignity and rights. Everyone has the right to do what the law does not prohibit.[33]

The law of compensation didn't wait long. Señora Lucía said that the *Martinera* midwives didn't know anything. She thought that she was the only one. But what happened? On 2 October, when Lucía solicited her own service as a midwife in the house of Leo Gerardo Bizarro, the ungrateful woman was incompetent, but she didn't want to be helped by another midwife. All day long the poor señora suffered in labor. Finally she gave birth to the baby, but she was unable to pass the placenta. At 8:00 p.m. Señora Susana died. Since she was kin, there was no investigation. Nothing happened. Nevertheless, there was criticism that Lucía Sánchez didn't know anything and that she only served to kill people. It seems for this event the two midwives lost their reputations.

My Wife and I Buy and Sell Pigs
March to 9 November 1986

In the month of March 1986, my wife and I bought four small pigs. We thought we would sell them in difficult times. We built a pigsty and bought the garbage from other houses to give to the little animals. Little by little they grew big.

All of my school-age children were in school. María is in the third year of *básico*, Ramoncito the sixth grade of primary school, Erasmo Ignacio the fifth grade, Susana Julia the third grade, and Anica Catana the second. My wife and I spent April, May, June, July, and August working at home and in the fields while the older children were in school.

In the first days of September, María told me that she was going to need money because on 12 September she had to make a trip to the city of Tapachula, Mexico, to carry the torch for the celebration of the homeland. On the following day they told me that Ramón and Ignacito needed money for a trip to Chiapas, Mexico, to bring the torch to celebrate 15 September, Independence Day, but my wife and I didn't have the money. Still I did not want our youngsters to be disgusted with us. Moreover, it would serve for their education. To support this, I had to sell two pigs, and with this money we paid the travel expenses for the children. By the grace of God, they left and returned very happily.

Then came the month of October when I had a problem. I had not paid for María's quota of the expenses that I had signed I would pay on 20 October, but I hardly had any money. Herberto Pantzay only gave me Q100 as an advance on the coffee harvest. With this money I paid the Q50 quota in the institute, but they told me that she had to buy new clothing because it is the first promotion of the first class in the institute. Thus we alloted Q100 for María. But also Ramón wanted money for the closure of sixth grade. I told him I was not going to be able to give him any because I didn't have any; if only God would help us with good luck.

On 27 October they called me to the post office and gave me a letter. When I arrived home, I opened it and it had my check from the University of Arizona Press for my percentage [half] of the earnings of *Son of Tecún Umán* and *Campesino*.[34] It seemed like a blessing from God. On the 29th José and I went to Guatemala [City] to cash the check in quetzales. Then we went to a store to buy the clothing for Ramón. We spent Q50. We returned in a car of a friend for Q5 each person, arriving home on the same day.

On this day was the closure and passing out of diplomas to the students of the first promotion of the institute, the first graduating class completing three years of the Instituto Básico por Cooperativa. All of us parents gave our contribution of Q20 for the expense of having some refreshments for the teachers and students. María, my daughter, earned her diploma for the third year of *básico*. The evening was very pleasant. There was a marimba. I didn't go to the invitation for refreshments, however, because we were drinking some *tragos*. I dispensed with all my obligations and contributions.

On 30 October was the closure and handing out the diplomas to the students of the sixth grade. In all, 42 students graduated. My son, Ramón, earned his diploma. We parents contributed Q10 to cover the expenses.

The rest of my money I took to a bank. I don't want to lose it buying things. I want to keep it as a remembrance of our work, which has taken a lot of time. Dr. Sexton is witness because he also suffered a lot with the translation. Translating from one language to another is difficult. As I have an agreement with my sister to buy a small *sitio* adjacent to my own, I'm going to pay her half the price of it with this money.

On the 9th of November, my wife and I went to San Diego la Laguna. We had an agreement pending with my sister for the small *sitio* that she offered me for the price of Q1,000. I told her I was going to see if I was able. When we obtained the money in October, we thought about going to San Diego to give her Q500, and thus we did. The husband of my sister gave us a receipt. We returned very content.

The Problems Grow More Serious with Father José and the Catholic Church
30 October to 31 December 1986

Earlier I have written that a committee was verbally organized to build a new church but without the approval of the parish priest. Well, the committee collected funds in the town. When the priest realized this, he immediately abolished the committee. The committee, however, already had collected Q2,000, which included a little money it had earned in the coffee harvest in the year of 1986. Seeing that the committee could do nothing, the members left the money with the board of directors of Catholic Action. They left it in the hands of the *vocal* [the substitute for various officers] to guard. But as the *vocal* is clever, he profited by using the money in a business deal with coffee. Undoubtedly, he made a big profit because he didn't pay any interest to the church.

Since this board of directors was about to finish its term in office, they were thinking about what to do with the money. They had not told Father José that they had Q2,000. Just as the padre didn't want to construct a building, the Catholic community didn't want to give him the money. They decided to use this money as a donation to buy musical instruments for the four groups of organized singers, but this idea didn't turn out well. The father realized that Catholic Action had a quantity of money hidden. He learned this because one of the incoming members of the new board of directors, who wanted to be president of the board, told him. I don't know for sure, but they say there are three persons who want to be president— Diego José Temó, Eduardo Flores Xicay, and Martín Pantzay García.

On 31 December the father asked for the money, but the board didn't give it to him. He was upset and about 9:00 a.m. took *Santísimo Sacramento* [Blessed Sacrament, or host] from the golden monstrance to San Martín, leaving the church in San José just a simple chapel. In the afternoon he called a meeting of all the townspeople. I thought it would be a sermon, speech, or a sharing of good things. I didn't go to hear a feud or uproar.

When I arrived, the parish priest had already begun the sermon to demand the money. He repeated that he was the only one who could have the money of the church, not the town nor Catholic Action. Formerly, the translator for the priest from Spanish to Tzutuhil was José Carlos Pinto, but on this day the translator was a *Martinero*. When I saw the affair become more serious, I thought it better to leave the church and go home. I noticed that as I was leaving the church there had been more people outside murmuring about the father. When I left, I passed in front of the people who were outside. They saw me and called me saying, "Ignacio, come with us. Help us! We want to get back the things that the priest has taken to San Martín." God forgive me, but I didn't want to talk to anyone. I continued on my way about a *cuadra* [a linear measure of 275 feet] when the lights went out. They say that when the lights went out the father ran from the church to where he had parked his car. But where he had left his car, there were a lot of people. When he left, they nearly hit him. At this point the rebelliousness of the people was seen. No one should hit a another person because everyone should respect human rights. If a person owes, has faults, or commits crimes, there are laws for these things with which to judge them.

The people who comprise the Catholic community are divided into two groups—a majority against the father and a minority in favor of him.

The majority want to get back the papers of the *sitio* of the church and the objects that Father José has taken to San Martín from Catholic Action. They say that they are not going to give the money to the priest and that for the good of the town they are going to build a new church.

It is the custom that all the townspeople go pray at midnight for the end of the old year and the beginning of the new one. But this midnight the church remained closed. It was very strange. The people were upset, but there was nothing they could do. They say that the father has ordered the church closed. Nothing was done for mass or baptisms. The group in favor of Father José went to San Martín for these services, but the majority was against him.

Well, both groups have their own interests, but it was a pity that they could never have a dialogue to find a solution. Instead of rationally exchanging views, they immorally mistreated one another. Each day the situation grew more serious. They were hardly in accordance with God, just thinking of evil. The people on the side of the father said that it was all right to take the things of the church of San José to San Martín and that the father had the right to take care of the money. But the other group said that the priest should return the documents of the church and that the money should not go to San Martín. They also said that in time the padre is going to sell the *sitio* of the church and sell the things of the church of San José into the hands of others. For certain the parish priest made mistakes. To err is human. But since Father José doesn't have a wife or family, I'm unable to believe the he is going to sell the *sitio* of the church because he wants a lot of money. More than anything else what this group is saying is an insult; it is a piece of gossip from lying tongues. This group against the priest has committed a crime by insult and calumny. I think that for this reason the father has ordered the church closed to avoid problems between the two groups. It was a good thing for them.

Political Activity Everywhere: Reflections on National and Local Politicians
5 January 1987

When the presidential candidates of the parties came to San José, all of them said they were in favor of the poor people and in defense of the indigenous people and talked about lowering the cost of living. They said that the past governments were corrupt and a puppet show. Two agents of Jorge Carpio Nicolle visited me to tell me that indeed they needed to win the presidency for him. They said, "If you want some employment we will help you when this man takes power."

I replied, "Thank you, but I don't need a job with the government. I don't have a title, only 'campesino.' I can't occupy positions; I don't have the ability. It's better for you to look for responsible and able persons." Then those men left.

One of them said that the candidate Jorge Carpio Nicolle is helped by the national army. More than anything else, he is of the right wing, and therefore, the people are a little afraid of struggling for Jorge.

On 13 October 1985, the candidate from the socialist party, Mario Solórzano Martínez, came to visit San José. His party has a branch in this town. Thus the members did all the preparations for the reception. But also there is a military detachment in this town. No doubt, when the military men realized that he had come on behalf of the candidate of the socialist party, the first lieutenant of the military detachment assembled the people by means of the military commissioners. Indeed the townspeople gathered to listen to speeches of the lieutenant in front of the town hall where they were waiting for the candidate of the socialist party. The military message was, "Each person has to take more care on election day. There are many candidates, but everyone needs to be careful with the communist parties so that what is happening now-a-days in Nicaragua will not happen in Guatemala. All *San Joseños* are urged to vote, but not for a communist party."

In this meeting he didn't say which party is communist. Soon the soldiers withdrew and Dr. Mario Solórzano Martínez entered. But the people had already begun to withdraw, only so as not to hear about communism. When Solórzano Martínez began to speak, there were very few people because the army instilled fear in them before he could come. This was when I realized that he did not have the support of the army. For me, Mario Solórzano spoke well, telling the truth about everything the Ladino people had done to the indigenous people. But this is the way the candidates are. They say things, but when they gain power they forget about what they earlier have said. Always they favor the millionaires and never the suffering people. On this day I went to hear this group recapitulate, but only to listen and see.

Here there are a lot of politics for a town so small, so illiterate, and ignorant. It is for that reason the politicians are taking advantage of us. There are more Indians than Ladinos, but what we lack is the knowledge and the intelligence, because if we united ourselves—the Mames, Cakchiqueles, Quichés, Pocomames, Kekchíes, Tzutuhiles, and other indigenous races of Guatemala—I'm sure that we would defeat the Ladino people. But what always is happening is that only because they give us a piece of candy, we indigenous people give in to fighting for a Ladino. Then when the Ladinos reach the height of power, they forget the Indian people.

In this town, there is the party of the engineer, Jorge Serrano Elías, the Partido Democrático de Cooperación Nacional. This party is so called because it was founded by the well-known cooperative members, Nery Morales, Félix Gandara Girón, Rolando Baquiax Gómez, and others. They call it the Party of National Cooperation, otherwise known as the party of cooperatives. These things I knew of when I was still secretary of the committee of control of the National Federation of Cooperatives. The formation of a party of the cooperatives was always mentioned, but never the name Jorge Serrano Elías, only that it was a party of cooperatives and indigenous people.

It was when we realized that Serrano Elías was already the pre-candidate that we indigenous people were demoralized. The cooperatives ruined the political plan because [as I have said earlier] it is said that Serrano Elías is corrupt and has airplanes and helicopters, which he acquired when he was the president of national reconstruction after the earthquake in 1976. The people realized that many countries had sent money to Guatemala for the injured people, but part of the money had gone to him.

[Also, as I have said before] after the coup by Efraín Ríos Montt, Serrano was president of the council of state. In addition, he was a private secretary of the department of the special law of General Ríos Montt. During this time a number of poor Guatemalans were sentenced to be shot. Guatemalans remember well that some 10 days before the arrival of Pope Juan Pablo II the prisoners trusted in God and hoped that Juan Pablo would save them from being shot. When Ríos Montt and Serrano Elías received news that the prisoners would be freed for the Pope, they commanded that two Guatemalans be shot before the Pope arrived.

These are the things that the people had noted, and mainly for these reasons Guatemalans didn't express much favor for Serrano Elías. One more thing is that when Ríos Montt became an Evangelical pastor, Serrano Elías also was an Evangelical pastor of the church, El Verbo [The Word]. The people already knew them, and, therefore, Serrano Elías lost the elections. Although in the future he plans on being a candidate, he nevertheless will lose.

Another candidate was the *licenciado* Mario Sandoval Alarcón of the Movimiento de Liberación Nacional [MLN]. The people already knew him because when he was vice-president of the republic in the time of Shell [Kjell] Eugenio Lauguerud, he said in his campaign that the past governments were corrupt and incapable of governing, and for that reason, the country had plunged into crisis. But he also was part of that past government and did nothing for the country.

There was a lot of criticism of the candidates. Many say, "*Son lobos de misma loma* [they are wolves from the same hill]," and that they are puppets for the millionaires. The people of Guatemala came to favor Marco Vinicio Cerezo Arévalo of the Democracia Cristiana party, the best party. He is kin to ex-president Juan José Arévalo Bermejo.[35] He said that when Arévalo was president of Guatemala, there indeed was liberty and democracy in Guatemala; mostly for that reason, the people counted on the candidate of the Democracia Cristiana. But who could predict how it is now?

In the first voting in the month of November, the Democracia Cristiana party was favored [38.59%]; in second place was the Unión del Centro Nacional [20.28%]; in third place, Cooperación Nacional [13.80%], and in fourth and last place, the Movimiento de Liberación Nacional [12.52%]. After the vote in the month of November, the losing parties united to try to defeat Vinicio in the run-off election. Jorge Carpio Nicolle and Jorge Serrano Elías, reputed right wingers, collaborated. Jorge Serrano Elías, representing all the party branches, was saying that all those that had voted for him would have to vote for Jorge Carpio Nicolle in the second election. But those of the national cooperative party did not run. Sandoval Alarcón of the Movimiento Nacional said in the press and on television, "Give freedom to all your sympathizers and friends so that they might emit freely their vote for the candidate of their choice."

From the November elections to 6 December, the day of the final campaigning, there was much criticism of Vinicio and his wife. Jorge Carpio said that Vinicio is a communist and all those that voted for him are the ones that are plunging the country into communism. Also, they accused the wife of Vinicio of being the commander of a group of guerrillas. Day after day there were many false accusations in opposition to Vinicio and his wife on the radio and television, urging the people of Guatemala to save the country and not vote for a communist party. The people, however, didn't pay attention and finally decided on Vinicio Cerezo.

There was much nervousness in the last vote on 8 December. Through the radio we realized the computation of votes, with the Christian Democrats always in the lead. On 10 December the supreme electoral tribunal declared through all the media of communication of the country, radio and television, that the president-elect of Guatemala was *licenciado* Marco Vinicio Cerezo Arévalo, with a total of 1,133,517 for the Democracia Cristiana Guatemalteca party [DCG], while the Unión del Centro Nacional party [UCN] had only 524,306, and 953,816 registered voters abstained. These were official data given by the supreme electoral tribunal. The UCN planned to defeat the DCG, but it was impossible.

The other parties said that the richest party was the UCN. It spent a lot of money. Guatemalan analysts say that it had lost millions of quetzales. This may be true because we observed here in San José the party that handed out a lot of money was the party UCN. But the directors of the municipal branches are all drunks, and UCN didn't know not to give them the use of the money, since the municipal branch claimed that they had struggled in the campaign. These were just lies for they had nothing to do with any political propaganda. They only drank in the bar of one of the directors, who knew how to profit because the money that Jorge Carpio had given him remained in his cantina. He now lives better than before.

Well, the people after the elections were talking everywhere, saying that Guatemala was going to see democracy and a lowering in the prices of products because Vinicio promised the people to end the IVA tax. He also said that he wouldn't be ordered around by the army, promising the nation to be for the people and by the people. This was what moved the people and all the poor sectors, workers and campesinos, to vote for Vinicio. All the month of December was a time for the advent of peace in Guatemala; all of us Guatemalans were hoping for a change in social life and respect of human rights because it is certain that all of us are infuriated about the thousands disappeared and kidnapped. Don Vinicio promised the *Grupo de Apoyo Mutuo* [Mutual Support Group] that he would investigate until the disappeared Guatemalans were found. Therefore, the Mutual Support Group fought a lot to get Don Vinicio elected.

The Mutual Support Group organized in the time of General Oscar Humberto Mejía Víctores. During his governance, they wanted investigations as to the whereabouts of the disappeared Guatemalans, but they made no progress. Then in the beginning, they thought that if Vinicio won the election, their kin would appear, but it was all negative—nothing had been gained!

In the month of January, when Don Vinicio took possession of the presidency, the whole nation celebrated with fiestas to the point of having marimbas in the municipalities and much more festivities in the [victorious] parties. But they were only celebrating one more misfortune in Guatemala. Don Vinicio promised the people of Guatemala to be the president of the poor, but it was a lie. When he took possession in January 1986, we were very happy thinking that he would fulfill his promises to the people. He offered a lot of things but has delivered hardly anything. In February of this year, there was a small change in the prices of the products like fertilizer, metals, and other things. The small vegetable producers were happy because he raised the price of those products, valuing their work.

In March, the president of the republic announced on radio and television a basic project to help the small farmer, stating that from outside the country fertilizer had arrived at the price of fifteen quetzales each *quintal* for the benefit of the small producer. By order of the departmental government, all the municipalities registered all the small producers of corn, beans, potatoes, and other produce of the region.

In San José the list of the persons eligible for fertilizer was made. The first to misuse the list, which in this town was more than one thousand persons, were the secretary and the official in charge of making it. The smallest producers asked for 10 *quintales* of fertilizer. Then they were told to get their money ready to cover the amount of the said offer. Some asked for 50 *quintales*, according to their need. The first deliveries were to be in April.

Without doubt, there were enemies of the government's offering to help the poor. These big operators thought that the fertilizer already had arrived and was in the warehouse of the central customs house in Guatemala City. They set fire to the warehouse, which was devoured by the ferocious fire, consuming many millions of quetzales. Also many important manufactured items were burned. The enemies thought that the fire consumed the fertilizer, but all their efforts were useless—the fertilizer was still at the ports of disembarkation. The government gave a press release for the broadcasting stations of the country, stating that the fire had not burned the fertilizer for which the campesinos were waiting.

Until the month of June, each farmer was given two *quintales* of fertilizer. It is said that in some towns each worker was given only one *quintal* and many received none. This was a deceit or mockery of the people—there was no more fertilizer. They saw that the big operators gave up nothing. They raised the price of fertilizer, and the government did nothing to bring it down. Thus there was more inflation—all prices went up. A *quintal* of sugar went from Q20 to Q30, a *quintal* of flour from Q28 to Q55, a piece of *lámina* went to Q20.

Everything is expensive, but the value of the products of the poor has collapsed. They closed the border so vegetables cannot be exported to the other countries of Central America. We poor are each poorer because we buy at very high prices and sell our own products, such as the onions, tomatoes, and other produce, at very low prices, which hardly cover the price of fertilizer, paying Q35 to 38 for a *quintal* of fertilizer and selling a *quintal* of onions for Q8.

Many say that Don Vinicio is controlled by the rich. Perhaps it is true because one of his cabinet members, Señor Andrade Paiz, is the owner of the chain of stores called Almacenes Paiz [S.A.]. To this point, nothing has changed—the situation in Guatemala continues to be worse.

[As I have said] during the elections, the Mutual Support Group [GAM] of the missing people was very fond of *licenciado* Vinicio because he had promised to investigate the whereabouts of all their disappeared kin. Well that group was feeling very strong because it was counting on the support of the president, but as president, he did nothing for the investigations. GAM, with its motto, "*Vivos se los llevaron y vivos los queremos* [Alive they took them and alive we want them]!"³⁶ organized a demonstration asking the government to fulfill its obligation of clarifying the situation. But who knows if their kin are living? Well, that time they went directly to the presidential palace to question the president about what he was going to do about the disappeared, but unfortunately he supported nothing. The Mutual Support Group was battled by the police with bombs of tear gas, and one of its directors was kidnapped. Many were beaten, and the kidnapped director was not seen until the other day. He said that he was taken away by the police and later freed. That was when GAM demonstrated its discontent and declared to the international press what had happened. A news release of the group says that during the administration of Vinicio, hundreds have been kidnapped and it isn't known who is the cause of this fatal violence. The government has done nothing about the kidnapping of the mayor of Chiquimula; the violence continues the same, no more, no less. In Guatemala there is no respect for human rights.

As far as local politics is concerned, [as I have said] in my town there were five candidates for the mayor: (1) Ignacio Arnaldo Bizarro González for the Unión del Centro Nacional party, (2) Roberto Mendoza Pérez for the Partido Socialista Democrático, (3) Agustín Méndez Petzey for the Democracia Cristiana [Guatemalteca] party, (4) Juan Mendoza Ovalle for the Movimiento de Liberación Nacional party, (5) and Benjamín Peña Cholotío for the Partido Democrático de Cooperación Nacional.

Four of the five candidates were clearly seen as having an interest in the municipal administration, or better said, they had seen something for themselves in the administration. Ignacio Arnaldo, candidate of the Unión del Centro, was the first councilman when the coup took place and is the nephew of the person that was named the de facto mayor by the military. That is, the sitting mayor at the time of the coup was Abraham Có Bizarro, but when the coup took place Abraham Có was terminated from the tribunal. Then Ignacio Arnaldo Bizarro González became interim mayor. Then later Señor Andrés Bizarro Mendoza was named the de facto mayor by the military, and Señor Andrés is the paternal uncle of Ignacio Arnaldo. Ignacio Arnaldo then surrendered the position of mayor to his uncle. Undoubtedly, they saw that it was a very good thing for them, with the salary, bribes, etc.; they could earn something. So at this time Ignacio Arnaldo obtained, by knowing *jefes* of the parties, his candidacy to see if he could receive the mayorship from the hand of his uncle. But it was fruitless.

As far as the Partido Socialista Democrático is concerned, Señor Roberto Mendoza Pérez was also an official of the municipality in those times. When it was about time for the elections, he resigned the position he occupied in the municipality, saying that he was a *Joseño* who didn't want to see his town in the claws of the corruption. But when this man was an official, he was always supporting the bad administration, and, for that reason, the town realized that he had a personal interest in being mayor.

With respect to the Democracia Cristiana party, Señor Agustín Méndez has the title of *bachiller*, but he never has shown he can do a job. He struggles to support his family. To administer a town, the people said "no" because he is too ignorant.[37]

The candidate for the Movimiento de Liberación Nacional party, Señor Juan Mendoza Ovalle, the town already knew. He fought again to win a victory and gain the confidence of a majority of the townspeople, but in the town he accomplished nothing. Later he went to rally the people in the three villages to vote for him, carrying a *libro de actas* [minute book], falsely drawing up acts, writing down all the things he promised to give them if elected—schools, buildings, and other works—and signing them in front of the poor villagers. Many were convinced. Juan spent a lot money, almost paying the residents of the three villages. He sold a piece of his wife's land that had been given to her by her parents as an inheritance, and another piece of his own property. Moreover, the secretary had helped him with Q1,000 because he knew that the people didn't like him. This was a sample of how it would be if Juanito Mendoza became mayor—the secretary would not be removed. On election day, they went in a car to get meat and liquor to provide lunch for all those that voted for the Liberación party. The candidate of this party was very competitive, but it was all fruitless.

Frankly, to tell the truth, the fifth candidate, Señor Benjamín Peña Cholotío, for the Cooperación Nacional party, is not a very intelligent man. He has done nothing bad, but he hardly has participated in community activities. On one occasion, before the elections, he asked me to help with his political campaign. He needed me to propagandize for him.

I told him, "I'm going to think hard about it."

On another occasion, they invited me to the house of the party of the cooperatives. I felt I had to go, but I was accompanied by three more friends. Benjamín was afraid that the candidate of the Liberación party, Mendoza, was going to win. When my friends saw that I favored Benjamín, they asked me to give my technical help in the campaign. Later we got together and went to the three villages to raise the consciousness of the people, stating that together we could vote for a new candidate whose performance we had never seen was either good or bad, but in which case, it was more important to know the character of the person!

However, the people hardly received us happily because almost all were with Juan. One person from the village of Pachichaj told us that Don Juanito Mendoza already had drawn up a document committing himself to public works, which they had signed. Then [as I have said earlier] we told them that's the way it was when Juan Mendoza was previously mayor. He drew up acts and never carried out what he had promised the people.

They questioned us indignantly, as if we had approved these things. Perhaps it was my fault. I was carrying a minute book that went back to when the same Juan Mendoza had drawn up some earlier memorandums when we had been running together for public office—he for mayor and I for syndic. From that time, the book had been in my possession. Juan could not imagine what I was keeping for him. When they saw the other memorandums that Juan previously had drawn up, with their signatures and fingerprints, which had never been fulfilled, [some of] those of the *aldea* realized that they were falling again for false promises.

So it went in Patzilín and in Tzarayá. But Benjamín only won a minority of the people in the three villages. The truth is that Juan Mendoza had done a good job of deceiving the people with money because he had it to give to them.

But we were more united in the municipality. We were fighting a lot so that Benjamín might be mayor. At the moment of the truth, Benjamín won by only 20 more votes because he didn't spend any money. But after the election, Juan didn't agree with the results. He said that we had perpetrated a fraud. The truth is, however, that the law was not played with. The Partido Democrático de Cooperación Nacional is a new party made up by members of the cooperatives. But we didn't join this party for Serrano Elías, rather we joined only because we wanted a new mayor who would make some changes in the municipal administration.

After the elections Juan paid a lawyer to annul the elections that had taken place, claiming they weren't legal. He said that he had won the elections and that he had to be mayor of the town, not Benjamín. Then we just awaited action of the supreme electoral council. By the grace of God, the count of the votes was good, and they came out the same as before. But as our indigenous people are very ignorant, there was much fear that Juanito would be mayor. But this "friend" could do nothing.

Benjamin's taking possession of mayor was enjoyable. Some 60 *Joseños* contributed money for a marimba and lunch. A little community spirit was exhibited on 14 January 1986, but it had cost a lot in time and effort to win for Benjamín.

María and the Teachers' Institute
December 1986 to 19 January 1987

In December, after my daughter had gotten out of the *San Joseño* institute, she asked, "Papá, what are you going to do for me? Please, I don't want my study to go to waste. Please, I want to continue studying because I don't want my education to be wasted. I will lose it. I can't do that."

"I don't know," I answered, "I have problems with you because there are many children. They need food and clothing, and I don't have money to have you studying."

"Look," she implored, "do what is possible for me; I'm your daughter. Make the effort for me."

"Yes, *m'hija* [my daughter], exactly," I told her, "I can't dispose of such things while we are not seeing any money."

In the end, we asked Señorita Melina Bizarro González, the daughter of my uncle who lives in San José, who had obtained her title of teacher of education in the year of 1987, "What's the most important thing to do to get into a national institute?"

"Well," she told us, "the first thing you have to do is have your teeth checked and eyes checked. If your teeth are bad, you must have them fixed. If your eyes are bad, you must get glasses. Also, you have to have your hearing checked. You must be in good health to be received by the institute."

"Also, you have to buy *útiles* [books and school supplies] and food. You must put studying first, because if you don't you will end up losing."

Well, that's the way we did it with my daughter.

But she had a problem with her teeth. I made the effort and struggled to earn some money. That is to say, I sold a little coffee. Then I took her to a dentist. After the exam he told me that the dental work would cost Q200. I paid this amount, which was very expensive for me, for the extraction of three teeth, and their replacements [false teeth] and three fillings.

Seeing that I had to provide for María's teeth, Ramón then said, "Look Papá, I have problems with my teeth. Not only is María your daughter, I'm also your son."

Then I had to do what was possible to cover the expenses for Ramón. The restoration of his teeth only came out to Q71.

In the same month of January, that is, in the beginning of the month, María told me, "Papá, now my teeth are in good shape. The teeth that I have are good. I want to study to be a teacher. I'm going to Quezaltenango; think a little about me, I'm your daughter."

I told her, "I don't have any money; the coffee harvest isn't worth much."

It's true that coffee was not worth as much this year as it was last year. This year, 1987, it was only selling for Q25 to Q31 a *quintal*. I owed Q900 for the value of the fertilizer and Q200 in money, which I had to pay first.

I thought a lot about María and her studies, and finally she was able to convince me. I told her, "Well, we're going to make the effort and the sacrifice. Just for your room and board. Don't ask me for clothing or money. You will have to live the life of a poor person."

She told me that she would accept the poverty. "Look, Papá, I will endure, even though I won't have clothes. I can live. I can spend three years with these same clothes that I have."

"Fine," I said, "We shall see."

"No, look, do what's possible for me." Thus we settled it.

On 12 January we went to enroll her name in the Instituto Normal para Señoritas de Occidente [Teachers' Training Institute for Señoritas of the West]. The registration was on the 13th, and we returned home on the same day.

Señorita Melina had told us that we had to look for a person who runs a boarding house for students, and she gave us the address where she had stayed. Thus when we went to Quezaltenango, we had the address: Calle Javier Salinas 078, Zone 3, Quezaltenango. The owner of the house is called Juan Enríquez. His wife, Juana Castro, will be in charge of my daughter. Also her name is in the institute as the one officially in charge of my daughter. For whatever reason, the institute will notify her, who in turn will notify me.

María left to study on 19 January. We had to buy her a bed, bed clothes, utensils, and other things, spending more than Q300 in one day. Since I am very poor, this is a lot of money for me, a campesino.

María's food costs Q75 monthly, and her dormitory costs Q25. I promised to pay only Q15 for her urban bus fare and small change. But until now I have had some problems. I'm suffering a little bit from the consequences of my daughter's education. I owe four months for the food and lodging. I just sent a letter to the señora telling her not to worry and that I'm going to pay them together. Now I'm thinking about how I can obtain the money. I have faith in God, and I am always working.

Herberto Pantzay, the owner of the *beneficio de café* [coffee processing plant], promised to give me money in effect in the last days of June, but he didn't. He says that the company didn't give him the money until the month of August. It's true that Herberto already has given me Q25 of fertilizer of the formulas 15–15–15 (15% calcium, 15% potassium, 15% nitrogen), 20–20–0, and 16–20–0, worth Q700, that I'm using for the coffee and the milpa. This will have to be paid for during the time of harvesting coffee. Also, I am worried about getting more in debt because the price of coffee can fall.

The Story of José and Carolina
17 November 1986 to 25 January 1987

My wife and I went to Salcajá' to buy a little woolen material for José. I had spent part of the money belonging to José for my work in the fields. This was money that was earned by selling the *cortes* that José had woven with the new foot loom. My wife went with me because she needed to buy thread for her weaving with a back-strap loom. In Salcajá one can find the best prices.

How things are! Always there are problems with children. A father is able to say, "I have educated my son." With children it is difficult. Many times I have said to José, "Please you are a young man and if you want to talk to a woman, that's all right, but do it with respect. If a woman accepts you, come tell me or your mother. We will go to her parents to ask permission for your woman, as is our custom."

"Very well," he said.

I told him these things many times, but they were forgotten. We knew that José had a sweetheart named Carolina, an attractive girl of 23 years of age, and we were waiting for advisement from our son. But he said nothing. Maybe he was thinking that it would cost too much, seeing our situation as very poor people. On the same day that we went on our trip to Salcajá, during the night, José stole a woman for himself.

On 18 November 1986 when we arrived in the morning in San José and left the launch, we were given three notices. The group of Catholic Action gave me the notice of the death of Reverend Padre Samuel, who is well known in these towns of the lake, especially San Martín, San José, and San Jorge, and who is one of those who lived sharing his ideas and experiences in Alcoholics Anonymous. At the same moment, they told us of the death of the paternal grandfather of my wife, Don Remo. Finally, one of my sister-in-laws said that José had stolen a woman.

This last piece of bitter news was *jodido*. My wife and I were very upset. To bring a woman home like that without permission is something delicate because there are parents who are *bravos* and the ones who receive the blows are the parents of the muchacho.

When I got in the house, José and Carolina were very happy. "Why did you come?" I asked Carolina, just like that.

"Yes, it's that I want to live with José."

"And you, why did you bring this woman without permission?"

"Ah, well, she came with me. We love each other very much, and you have to pardon us," he said.

Well, what can you do? He's my son. Then I told him, "That's fine."

"We are going to ask permission of your parents," I told Carolina.

My wife and I had to accept this moral blow. Unfortunately, we didn't have the money to spend for the *costumbres*. We had to sell six *quintales* of corn from our harvest.

On 21 November in the night, we went to the parents of the woman to ask forgiveness of everything that our son had committed. With us went the parents of my wife, my uncle, and two friends. We took bread, chocolate, and some quetzales of money. It's a traditional custom of our town that when a woman is stolen one has to go to her parents and ask forgiveness.

Carolina's parents received us with kind words and much affection. They accepted all the presents that we took them. We talked to them a little, and they said there was no problem. They gave José and Carolina a little orientation about life.

Later we left. There was no problem with my youngster. I won't tell you that he's good, but neither will I tell you that he's bad, because he has been, well, a muchacho. No, he's not *bravo*; he does not anger. He's passive and is patient.

It resulted that Carolina for us was a muchacha. She would work well and take care of all the things of the house. Since our daughter, María, had gone to Quezaltenango, we thought Carolina would stay working with my wife, taking care of our children and hens.

Well, that's how it was until Carolina's mother said, "My daughter does not have cause to go to the Catholic Church, because she has always been Protestant since childhood. My son-in-law and my daughter have to participate in the cult of the [Protestant] Galilea Church because it's our religion."

"I don't know," I said, "I can't send José nor Carolina. They will stipulate, depending on the agreement they had."

"Carolina would never go to live with a Catholic family. She has to be an Evangelist all her life," said her mother.

Well, I said again, "I can't stipulate anything. They're the ones who must decide if they go to the chapel [Protestant Church]. They are the ones. It's different with my wife; I have to say if we do such things or not. But not with them."

In a manner of speaking, Carolina's mother was saying if José did not want to accept the Galilea [church], her daughter couldn't live with him. This was the biggest problem. During the two months that Carolina lived in our house with José, she wanted him to go with her to worship, but the boy didn't want to. Each time Carolina went to worship, she went with her mother.

Then José said, "I'm not going to be Protestant. I have been Catholic, and I will continue to be Catholic."

"I don't know," I told him, "It's not up to me; it's up to you."

When Carolina would tell José, "Let's go to the worship," he said he didn't want to. The girl worked well. It was just because of the religion. The girl saw that she could do nothing to convince the boy and that she had to go by herself.

At 4:00 in the early morning of 25 January, without even saying good-bye, she went back to her mama. She took all her clothes and all that we had given her. Without doubt, she thought the boy would go with her, but José remained. For us it was a bit of a bother because we hadn't realized it was a serious problem, just because the muchacho didn't want to go to the [Protestant] Chapel.

"But *m'hijo* [my son], this, you should have thought of before," I told him.

"Don't worry about it," he told me, "Carolina promised she would go to the [Catholic] Church with me. I never promised her to go to the [Protestant] Chapel, because she promised she would go to the [Catholic] Church with me."

Well, there you are. The thing is that Carolina left without saying good-bye. Neither did we. We didn't go to her house because she came and she left. That's how it was.

Yet we still told José, "You can forgive Carolina. If you want, you can go bring her back because she has no faults. She knows how to work, and she knows what to do in the kitchen. She makes a very fine weave as well."

"No, father, I don't want to bring her again because I don't want to be a Protestant. She said she would be Catholic," he told me.

"*M'hijo*," I told him, "but this you should have thought of before. It's one thing to say something and another to do it."

"No," he told me, "it's that before she came home with me, she told me that she would go with me to the [Catholic] Church and that I would not have to go do anything in the [Protestant] Chapel. 'We are going to be Catholic,' she said. But lamentably her mother was very insistent. Well, God [be] with her and God [be] with me; [it's] better I not speak to her now."

"There you are," I told him. So it goes.

New Year's Day: Image of Jesús Stays in the Church
1 January to 9 February 1987

The first day of the year there was a lot of criticism against Father José by the majority faction in the church. Most of them were drunk. It seems that their criticism against him is not founded.

In previous years the image of the child Jesús was carried by the *cofrades* to visit the homes of the Catholics. But this year there were no directives, and the *cofrades* weren't able to order themselves. For that reason, the visits in the homes were eliminated. They were indeed able to visit the image of Jesús in the church on 4 January. I don't know if they all went to the church. My family and I went. On this affair, I remained neutral.

On 3 January, because of the problems in Catholic Action, it seems that Father José and the group in favor of him sent to call Monseñor Benando Gálvez for a dialogue. In the afternoon of this day, they entered the church for a discussion. Many people spoke against the bad attitude of the father. Monseñor told them to pray constantly to God to give them better understanding. A university student, Gerardo García Cojox, answered the Monseñor, "Singing and praying is not going to achieve peace." Then they labeled this young man as being Marxist. It was very strange! Who knows why they don't understand one another. Among the group against the priest are secondary students, teachers, and university students. The dialogue was not successful. It made things worse. On this day the group in opposition was lead by Juan Mendoza, José Severo Gómez, Ignacio Hernández Toc, and Gerardo García Cojox. From this point it was said that the church would be in purification (a disciplinary action) until further notice.

The two groups leveled a lot of criticism against each other. The minority always stood up in defense of the church. This group was described as believing in the laws of the church. They are not doing anything bad. The other group, which is very large, says that it is thinking better for the welfare of the church. This, however, is not true. The leaders have personal interests. Most of all it is Señor Mendoza, who lost the last elections in his attempt to be mayor again. Now, he is saying that he is a Catholic and in charge of this uproar, claiming that he is the only one in town who can defend the interests of the church. But the church doesn't have problems—they are the ones who are provoking this problem. Juan's motive is to gain the confidence of the more ignorant people so that they will give him money again and see that he gains control over the tribunal again. He's using this trick to pretend to be acting in the interests of others. It is so that they will give them authority to control the church. Moreover, they always have been big shots, not servants.

The minority was always preoccupied. They planned to send a note to Monseñor Gálvez, asking forgiveness for all that the other group had committed so that everything be normalized and that he order the liberty of the *Eucaristía Sacramental* [Sacramental Eucharist, or host] the priest had taken from the golden monstrance of this church that had been in purification. Everyone in favor of the Padre José, including myself, signed it. This letter was signed on Friday, 16 January, 7:00 p.m., in the presence of Sister Francisca Juana Cordón and Deacon Gino Barillas. Two days earlier the directors of the church had given an invitation to come to the church to sign the letter. When the hour arrived to sign the paper, Deacon Barillas read it two times to impart the meaning and to insure than nothing be of coercion so that those who wanted to sign it could and those who didn't wouldn't. Then the group against the priest presented itself to impede the signatures, saying that no one should sign the letter. Thus there were two groups at this time. The big group mistreated Father José while the small group responded in the same manner by mistreating the large group.

The two groups wanted to hit each other. I'm not a religious person. I only went there to see what was happening inside the church, but I saw that the dispute was intense so I intervened. I stood on top of a bench to say to them:

> Please, have patience, don't insult and mistreat one another because we are the same people of San José. Please control yourselves. Don't hit anyone because it's a sin and against the law. Think a little better. We are inside a church, and the church is the house of God. We're not in a cantina. In a cantina you can fight because there are bad people there. But here there are [good] people. Understand a little. The house of God is the house of prayer. Remember the words of God, "The house of my Father is the house of prayer, do not convert it into a den of thieves."

Not until then was there a little calm. When I said these things, the two groups stood up. The large group and small groups separated, and I was in the middle. I didn't know what to do. I would go with neither the big group nor the little group. Instead, I just stood on the bench. I said what I did because I didn't want anything else to happen inside the church since I saw that they had much force and anger. When I spoke very clearly and frankly in a louder voice, the people understood and left the church more tranquilly.

The big group left the church, but also the little group made a mistake because it turned out the light when the people were murmuring. By the grace of God, there were no personal injuries. In such extremes, when two groups are in conflict, no one should ever turn the light off. During these days, the group opposed to Father José tried many ways to threaten him. They went to Panajachel to make up lies against him. They talked with Monseñor Gálvez, but the monseñor did nothing to remove the padre. The two are very good friends.

On 19 January I saw that Juan Mendoza, Gerardo García, José Carlos Pinto, Ignacio García Mendoza, and Diego Castillo Tajay all went to Guatemala [City]. But they say that there were more who went. They went for an audience granted by the metropolitan archbishop. They insisted that they were going to remove Father José and that they needed a priest who pleases them more.

It seems that these men are not thinking about what they are doing. The archbishop sent them again to the bishop of Sololá, who is the only one that can change the priests. But when Monseñor Gálvez came to this town, this group didn't show him any respect and spoke badly against both him and Father José. For that reason, without doubt they were taken as gossipers and deceitful persons against the truth. They said that they were going to take their case to Huehuetenango and then left to consult a lawyer, Guido Mendoza, who really dabbles in politics.

It was Guido Mendoza who wrote a memorandum against Reverend José. When they returned from the trip, they said, "Everyone who wants a new priest, sign it." Because of a false offer of a new padre in San José, the most ignorant people signed it. Two hundred and thirty-five people signed it. They made many copies of this memorandum and sent it to many people. It's a pity that I don't have a copy of it for the diary.

I don't know the exact date, but they say that on 8 or 9 February, they went to Huehuetenango to ask for a new priest. But I'm not sure about this trip. There were nine persons. José Severo Gómez took them from San José to kilometer marker 148 of the Interamerican [Pan-American] Highway. Nothing was gained on this trip, but they say that all they are doing will allow them to little by little get a new father because they are faithful Catholics. Who, however, can believe that faithful Catholics are acting against the church? The truth is that this group has been looking for years for ways to create problems in the church. Now the group has a lot of people, and they have succeeded in involving four wealthy people. They say that Alejandro Morales gave Q400; José Severo Gómez, Q200; Franco Coj Vásquez, Q100; and Ignacio Hernández Toc, Q100. More people only gave a little money, but they say they collected more than Q800 for the expenses of Juanito Mendoza to procure a new priest because for sure they were going to establish a new parish with a permanent, resident priest for the people of San José.

Dreaming About the Conflict in the Church
19 February 1987

At 4:00 in the morning on Thursday, I dreamed about what is happening. I dreamed that Señor Ángel Alberto Mogollón and his father were good and drunk. They left the house of Sr. Manuel Temó and began talking with a microphone and lead-colored loudspeaker, speaking very badly of the mayor and saying false things. In front of them was a burro well loaded down with kitchen garbage and very old, dirty rags. When Ángel Alberto passed through the streets to speak, the burro also neighed and wanted to talk. The two men and the burro walked around the town as if they were in a procession. In my dream I saw Sr. Santos Mendoza answer Ángel, "Shut up you are drunk! You can't say anything bad against the mayor. He's behaving well." This is what I dreamed.

In the morning when I got up, I told my family and Benjamín Coché. During the night, there was a great disturbance through the streets. Juan Mendoza and others were talking with a microphone, saying bad things about the reverend and everyone who is on the side of the church. They assembled the people in front of the parochial *salón* and offered falsehoods. They said, "We want a parish priest of our own for the church of San José. No more gringos!"

There were people with him, but these people were always outside the church. They say that they are faithful Catholics, but this is not true.

The Consecration of Sister Francisca Juana Cordón
21 to 27 February 1987

The whole town received notice that Monseñor Gálvez was coming for the consecration of Sister Francisca Juana Cordón, of Colombian nationality, and that all Catholics were invited for the mass on Sunday at 10:00 a.m. But Juan Mendoza's group, which claims to be faithful Catholics, declared in the evening that no one should go to mass next Sunday in order to demonstrate their protest against Reverend Father José.

On Saturday afternoon, 21 February, the real Catholics went to San Martín to receive Monseñor Gálvez, but the only ones who arrived were

Sister Francisca Juana, Father José, and mothers from other countries. Monseñor Gálvez didn't arrive until 7:00 p.m., when they were celebrating mass. They say that the monseñor was late because he had to be in Santa Elena for the new parish and its new priest.

In this afternoon, some friends invited me, and I indeed went to San Martín for the mass. During the night, after the mass, we met with Monseñor Gálvez to ask that they celebrate mass in San José because it had been suspended since 3 January when the monseñor came to San José for a dialogue with the group in opposition, the group had spoken badly, and the church had been placed in purification. The religious persons talked with the monseñor, and he gave them the liberty to have mass celebrated next Saturday, 28 February, with the *Eucaristía Sacramental* returning to San José. We returned to San José very content at 10:00 at night.

Sunday, 22 February 1987, all the singers went in a truck to sing the early morning mass before sunrise to Sister Francisca Juana. They invited me to go with them, but I didn't because of the early hour. On this day a good number of Catholics went to San Martín to attend mass. People from San Jorge, San Benito, Tzancuil, Chabaj, and Chimo also went.

The mass was very solemn. I attended, and, when everything was finished, the Reverend Father José invited us to lunch. I had to say yes. We didn't return until 2:00 p.m.

On this date Juan Mendoza and others went to San Diego la Laguna to hire a priest for San José. But there was a lot of ignorance because the one who is able to tell the priest in San Diego what to do is the bishop. What happened? The bishop was in San Martín while they were in San Diego. It was very confusing.

On 27 February, a day before the mass, Juan Mendoza, Franco Coj, Ignacio Hernández, and other ignoramuses had taken to the streets of San José to invite everyone to a meeting. In the meeting they said that they were going to bring a priest for San José who is ready to come from San Diego. The padre's name is Alberto. They spoke very badly, as if they were talking to their children or grandchildren, very bad criticism! The meaning of this meeting is not understood. Ángel Alberto was the president of Catholic Action in the year 1986. Now he is against Father José, and he's turned into an enemy. He spoke very badly about Father José with the microphone and grey loudspeaker. What I had dreamed on 19 February came true. It was very bad for the town! I felt much sadness. My race isn't useful, showing a bad side to the world. They are saying to be faithful Catholics, yet asking that no one go to mass. They want a priest for themselves.

On Saturday, 28 February, indeed they celebrated mass with Father Alberto. I didn't go, but my family did. They said there was a good number of people there. On Wednesday, 4 March, the beginning of Lent, they again celebrated mass, which a large number of people attended.

My Daughter Celebrates a Mass of Thanks
7 to 11 March 1987

On this date a mass of thanks was celebrated for my daughter, María, for completing 18 years of age. By God's grace, it turned out well. We attended the mass, and later we had some guests for a dinner of tamales.

Today the news was heard that Father Alberto had died of old age. He had come to San José, contracted by the group in opposition. Everyone mourned.

This group doesn't understand what their pretensions are. They continue insulting Father José and his leaders (sacristans). It is a very delicate conflict. Who knows how it will end?

On the eleventh at 8:00 at night, Juan Mendoza, again like a madman, was calling the people to sign the memorandum asking for a new priest. But who knows why? We know that there is a responsible priest for the church. They say that the day after tomorrow, Friday, they are going to bring the priest that they prefer. Formerly, it had been said that the memorandum had been signed by 235 persons. In this uproar, he said that it needed more signatures.

Discord in the Church Continues
13 to 18 March 1987

Friday the 13th, they say that 55 persons went in a launch to Panajachel to insult the bishop, stating that they need a new priest and that they are not in agreement with the present priest. But it isn't because they are Catholics in action, it's that they are Catholics in fanaticism. They're the ones that go to church once in a while.

Saturday, 14 March, the news was heard that the bishop told the *contras* [those against Father José], "There is no priest for San José—the only one is the one found in San Martín." When they heard this, they insulted the bishop. They are waiting for Monday, the 23rd, to go to talk to him again. They say that the memorandum was signed by 480 persons. Who knows?

In the morning of this same day, rumors were heard that the enemies of the church would not let the reverend in the church at the hour of mass. The real Catholics were nervous. But by the grace of God, the mass was celebrated successfully.

During the night, Juanito Mendoza and his group were telling lies in the street, saying that they are going to have a new priest, solely for San José, and that the bishop is an accomplice of Father José and for that reason he doesn't want to provide a priest for this town. Juanito insulted the leaders of Catholic Action and finally said that Monday, the 23rd, would be the answer, yes or no. It's unfortunate that Juanito's group is so ignorant because among his followers are two teachers and two university students. The rest are illiterate. It's a pity that these señores say that they are intellectuals, but they don't know the rules of the church because if they knew the laws of the church, they wouldn't fall into these problems. More than anything else, they are loco.

By God's grace, Tuesday, 17 March, a mass was celebrated at 6:00 a.m. It was the day of San Patricio who, they say, was kidnapped at the age of 16 years. For three years he was in the hands of his kidnappers. When they freed him, he returned to preach in the same town where he previously had been abducted. A good number of Catholics attended this mass.

On Wednesday, 18 March 1987, I gave Francisca Juana two letters for Monseñor Benando Gálvez, one signed by D. José and the other by me. I have copies. They were not an accusation, just an explanation of the situation.

This Wednesday a letter was given to Juan Mendoza signed by Bishop Benando Gálvez. One of the religious persons told me what was in the letter. Monseñor told them not to return again to his office and to make peace and go back to the church for reconciliation. But they didn't understand these things.

A Mass in Honor of San José Patrono
Thursday, 19 March 1987

Today Father José celebrated mass at 6:00 a.m. in honor of San José Patrono in the church. I didn't go, but my wife and family went. All those who were married were blessed.

Friday I went to Sololá for a notification of the departmental government to authorize the committee for the improvement of the system of potable water. I was paid an honorarium of Q5.75 and money for photocopying (Q.75), sealed paper (Q.75), books (Q3), and travel (Q8). I was a little happy and in good health. In the market Susana, who went with me, bought potatoes and herbs.

Father José Is Nearly Killed
Saturday, 21 March to 6 April 1987

This is the saddest date in the history of the town since it was seen that my fellow inhabitants are full of evil and ignorance. There are people without culture and respect for human rights. They nearly killed a North American priest.

During the morning, Ignacito and I were baking bread when P. Antonio told me that Reverend Father José wanted a meeting of all the organized groups of Catholic Action for the new evangelization at 1:00 p.m. Also, I was notified that the group against him had arrived to attack the father. Well, I told my two sons José and Ramón to finish making the bread while I went to the church to listen to the meeting.

The priest gave a chat to the four choral groups, to Young Catholics, to the Mothers of Families, and to the board of directors of Catholic Action. As I did not belong to a single group, I was there just to listen. And I also had the opportunity to chat with Father José.

At 3:15 p.m. he finished the talk. Then we began to pray a mass, which lasted only a half hour. Then the father listened to confessions. While doing this, about 200 persons arrived covering the entrance of the church and where the car of the father was parked. They did not enter the church. They said that they needed to talk with the padre. The priest said that he could not but tomorrow at 2:30 p.m. he would receive them in his office in San Martín to take care of whatever they wanted. But the people didn't leave. They continued occupying the atrium of the church grumbling and shouting.

Then at 4:35 p.m. he began mass with a regular number of faithful in attendance. The preaching of Father José went well. The real Catholics received Holy Communion, but most of the others were in front of the church contradicting the mass, stating falsehoods and gossiping.

One could not imagine the dark history of the town of San José that was to be. My grandmother, Isabel, had said that 300 years ago the Tzutuhiles of San José beat a priest to death, but I hardly believed this until now, because when my people give into evil, it's easy for them to kill. When the mass was over and we wanted to leave, the people received us with blows and a lot of mistreatment. When Father José tried to leave the church and to go to his car, the first persons to seize him with the intent against his life were Franco Coj Vásquez, José Severo Gómez, and Ignacio Hernández Toc. When the majority saw that they had captured the father, they went to hit him with their hands and fists and stones, or perhaps kill him. Then some interfered to defend him, but since they were fewer in number, it was difficult. I too went to defend him, and we were able to rescue him from the claws of the enemies. We returned to the church. They also hit me hard, but I don't know who it was. A lot of people were shouting, "Kill him once and for all! We don't want to see this man anymore!" When we were able to defend the father, the enemies captured a member of Catholic Action by the name of Martín Pantzay García and nearly killed him. By God's grace, one of his sons-in-law and a son who is a student appeared. It was they who saved him. It's true that one of the leaders of the *contras*, Señor José Severo, a very tall, fat, and wealthy man, was hit by Martín's son, but this was to defend his father. When the majority saw that one of its leaders was hit in the face and knocked down, they retreated. Martín and his son left to go their house. Then we were shut in the church since a lot of people were blocking the door. Father José and we began to pray. Juan Mendoza entered in the church to count how many were inside. A majority inside were able to leave for their houses. We well could have left, but to defend the life of the priest, indeed we stayed with him. Juan Mendoza went to the door to tell his supporters, "I counted these people; there are only 42 persons. They aren't able to do anything. If you want, we can show our strength. We can do what we wish!" The people shouted, "Let's go inside!" There were about 400 of them.

A sister of charity, Juana Avila, told Juan, "Señor everything that happens inside or outside of the church you are responsible for and you will pay the consequences. Once and for all, you are responsible for all the lives trapped inside the church."

Not until then did Juan calm down and say to his companions, "Señores and muchachos, no more. Calm down. Let's let the father leave the church, but with one condition—that he not come back to do mass."

Not until then did the priest leave with us. They say, but I didn't see it, that someone tore a vest of Francisco Có, one of the leaders. They say it was done by the women of the smaller group on the side of Father José.

When the reverend got into his car, a truckload of about 60 *Martineros* arrived to defend him. But as I said, my people were truly rebellious; they didn't allow the *Martineros* to disembark. They were received with stones and were unable to get out of the truck. Many *Joseños* were throwing stones at them, and they fled in the truck. Then the father left for San Martín in his car.

The news says, although we didn't see it, that, without doubt, word reached San Martín as to what was happening in San José. The Evangelists suspended their services and united with the Catholics. More than 2,000 of them came to defend the priest. But thanks to God they met the father at the border of San José and San Martín. If within a half hour they had not allowed the father to leave, for sure there would have been a war between the two towns. But the guilty are those of San José.

The source of the lie is not known, but the *contras* say that they are supported by a priest of North American origin by the name of Mario. There are certain doubts, however, since the priests are supposed to honor the same laws of the church.

Sunday, the 22nd, a regular number of *Joseños* went to mass in San Martín. A number of the group against Father José went to San Diego, and they say that they went to a military detachment. I don't know if the latter is true, only that they went to San Diego because I saw when they returned that night passing near my house.

On Monday, 23 March, a letter was delivered to the leader of the group, Juan Mendoza, sent by Bishop Benando Gálvez, which said that the group could send six persons on Wednesday, 25 March 1987, to the office of the parish in San Martín for a dialogue with the bishop in order to find a solution to the problem and everything will be finished. When the leader realized the content of the letter, he then went to the houses to tell his people. On the same afternoon they prepared a letter protesting accepting dialogue in San Martín.

Wednesday, 25 March of 1987, they sent Juan Coj Mendoza to take the letter to Father José. But what's the nature of ignorance? Juan left the letter for Señor Bishop Benando Gálvez in the office of Father José. But neither of them was there. The bishop was in Panajachel and the padre was on a trip to fulfill a commission. The letter should have been taken to Panajachel, not San Martín.

This would have been a good day for the *contras*, but it's a pity they didn't know how to take advantage of it for lack of respect of the priest of the church, who is the only person who is authorized to find a solution for the problem of the church. Monseñor Benando Gálvez arrived in the parish of San Martín in the afternoon of Wednesday, 25 March 1987. During the visit, he told Father José not to celebrate mass in San José until the group against him repents for what they had done. The monseñor was thinking well because the people are very violent. Mass usually is Saturday, but they said that this Saturday, the 28th, there would be no mass.

What did the group in opposition do? They gathered and lit many firecrackers, saying that they succeeded in removing Father José. Already they had settled it. These are lies. They have not removed Father José. It was the bishop who didn't celebrate mass because the people of San José are very bad. But they had distorted things and told the ignorant people that they had removed Father José.

Monseñor Gálvez waited for the group from San José to come to San Martín to meet and work out a possible solution to what the *contras* were calling a problem. But the truth is nothing more than that they want to disobey the laws of the church; they want to continue with the old *costumbres*. No doubt, Monseñor Benando Gálvez was waiting for these people in the office of San Martín, but they did not come. They set their minds and gathered in front of the patio of the church, waiting to see if Monseñor Gálvez finally would arrive in San José to talk with them. But how can it be possible for a bishop to obey a heap of gossip and falsehoods? With such deeds, they only intended to take the life of a father. This group was in front of the church from 4:00 p.m. to 9:30 p.m. Gradually they left for their houses. There were statements among them that they hadn't gone to San Martín for the dialogue out of fear. They thought the *Martineros* would take revenge for what they had done last week. Perhaps. It isn't certain.

On Saturday, 28 March 1987, the morning began quietly as I was preparing to leave for the coast. Yesterday, a group had gone to San Diego to get the advice of a priest, so they said. Early this morning, I saw Juan

Mendoza, Benjamín Soto, Ignacio Hernández Toc, Jaime Ramos y Ramos, and Ignacio Oliva y Oliva leaving for San Martín. Since I went to the coast, I didn't see what happened, but they say that about 11:00 a.m. the action began. They called all the people to sign an *acta notarial* [notarized document] drawn up by the lawyer, Tomás Ricardo Galindo. They say that the memorandum contained a chain of lies against Father José, and in the same they assigned a new board for themselves without the authorization of any *jefe* of the church. They named two *fiscales*, Ignacio Bizarro Temó and Domingo Asturias Sic; president, Bizarro Toc; vice president, Ignacio Oliva y Oliva; treasurer, Lucas Ujpán García; and secretary, Rolando Cox Sumoza. The *fiscales* were named and sworn in by Juan Pop Mendoza with the service of the lawyer, Tomás Ricardo Galindo, who earned Q300 for his services. Those men are completely ignorant of the laws of the church. They selected themselves to occupy the parochial *salón*, drawing up the notarial act with the lawyer, and they said that they were planning to seize the church. But the sacristans were well aware of things when those in opposition were celebrating the act and they took out the *Eucaristía Sacramental* and left the church closed, as the father ordered. This he had done on the 25th when the group in opposition had disobeyed the bishop's order. Everything is the will of God. The sacristans were able to close the church peacefully, but the *contras* had taken it with violence.

The group against the priest said that, in order to be in good stead with God, they began to pray the *Santo Rosario* [Holy Rosary] in front of the church this Saturday night. This group thinks backwards. The rest of Sunday morning, they prayed on the patio of the church, and they did the same thing during the night. Some of these people never came to mass nor visited the Blessed Sacrament. When they closed the church, they began to pray in front of it in an exaggerated manner to be seen by the people. How is it possible to say they are faithful Catholics and respect the orders of the priests as the law of the church demands? On the 28th, 29th, 30th, and 31st they prayed in front of the church. On 1 April because of the drizzle, they had to pray inside the parochial *salón*.

On 31 March I went to Guatemala [City] to register the committee for the improvement of the system of potable water and buy a book of vouchers for the same. On 1 April, when I returned from Guatemala [City] on the launch, I met with the two groups—that is to say, the board of directors for the church and the group against them. Well, I said, "Buenos días," to the group in opposition, and they answered me with contempt. Then I said, "Buenos días," to the group of the church, and they smiled and answered,

"Buenos días," joking because I had carried a little bread from Guatemala [City]. One of them told me, "It's funny that a baker would bring bread from another place."

"Each region has its own bread." I answered.

One of them told me that they, the representatives of each group, were called to the military zone number 14 in Sololá. They went to the section of intelligence (S-2), and the small group entered first. They were asked, "Is it true that the father is a thief and liar that he stole money from the town and the documents of the church?"

José Martín Fuentes replied, "Father José isn't a thief or liar. He's just the one who keeps the money of the church and its documents because the times are delicate and the subversives could come and burn the things of the church, which has happened in other towns."

The *jefe* responded, "Why are there so many people against the father?" P. Antonio retorted, "It's that the father in his preaching speaks very strongly, condemning the thief, the drinking sprees, abortion, and ignorance. For that reason, the people are against him. They don't want to change their attitude."

"It's true that the truth hurts and bothers bad people," the *jefe* responded. "Well, here's a document, and this is what we're investigating. You can return to your town in total confidence." That is to say, it was not a problem for them.

Then the representatives of the opposition were called, but it's not known how the talk with them went. All that is known is that they didn't take much time.

The opposition does not want Father José to continue doing mass in the church. It is because Father José speaks the truth saying:

> *Joseños*, my dear Indians, be clever, don't be puppets manipulated by the rich and dominated by the vices and the bad *costumbres*. It's for that reason that your parents sold their land into the hands of the *Martineros*. It's because they didn't think of you. The same things are going to happen to your children if you do not change your attitude. This town continues wallowing in ignorance. When are we going to see a *Joseño* who is a congressman, engineer, or doctor? Think of your children. For you, it's difficult to earn money. The firewood weighs a lot and all the other loads that you carry. When you have earned some quetzales, then you go to a cantina and then you don't have anything left of what it took you many days to earn. Take care of yourselves, use

your head. You poor people are fattening the cantina owners. They are waiting for the money that you have earned with a lot of sweat. And for your family there is nothing. For these reasons, your parents were very ignorant and thus so are you and so will be your children.

For that reason, those who are most against Father José are the barmen and those who live the happy life and don't want obedience. They have sworn to the devil that they don't want mass with Father José. What they prefer the most is a priest from another town so that their deportment will not be realized. Of these people, they say most of the leaders live in adultery and what is better known is that all of them are dedicated to alcohol, which affects us Indians a lot.

This Wednesday, 1 April 1987, when the two groups returned, the group of Juanito Mendoza arrived while the group of Catholic Action remained in San Martín to tell the priest what had happened in Sololá. Unfortunately, the opposing group continues to be very rebellious.

After returning from the military zone, they filed a complaint, or, better said, a day before they had filed a complaint against the board of Catholic Action. There were 16 leaders in this majority group. They only wanted to summon the president and the sacristan. But 16 against 2 is not justice. Thanks go to the mayor who permitted the admission of the whole board to his office from 6:00 to 11:00 p.m. because he thought 16 against 2 was not fair. The poor fellows of Catholic Action were sweating under threats and coercion. At first the majority leaders were honey sweet, then bitter. Juan Mendoza, José Tereso Vásquez, Ignacio Hernández Toc and others, especially Ángel Alberto Mogollón, and Enrique Patzay, mistreated the board members a lot, telling them if they didn't hand over the keys to the church, they would be prosecuted. And the board said, "Very well. With much pleasure, we'll be prosecuted along with the priest."

"Hand in your resignation. At present you have no office," the *contras* demanded.

"We have no reason to resign," they replied, "only the father and the bishop can remove us from office. We can't give the mayor our resignation because we know we weren't sworn in by this authority nor are we going to give our resignation to an opposing group. We know they're nothing. Indeed we were named and sworn in, in the name of God, by the priest, and he is the only one who is able to suspend our function."

The *contras* said, "It'll be more convenient for you to get the keys. Things will be calmer."

"We don't have the authority to open the church. We are under the authority of the priest and the bishop. They are the ones who will decide when we are going to open the church, and they are the ones who have the keys."

"We aren't going to continue following in the footsteps of the priest because he is the cause of these serious problems," they said. "No one can prohibit people from looking for the good things of God." They asked the sacristan, Ignacio Arnaldo Bizarro, "How much money did the father get for the value of the coffee that was picked on the *sitio* of the church?" Then the sacristan went to fetch his notebook. But when Ignacio Arnaldo left to get the notebook, he was well guarded by the opposition group. They thought that Ignacio Arnaldo would take flight. But it wasn't true. When the sacristan came back with the notebook, he gave his information. He is in charge of gathering the ripe coffee, and he had to pay the *mozos*. When the account had been settled, he had given the priest Q900.

The opposing group highly reproached him when he said he had handed the money over to the priest. But he said that if there was the necessity, he would get the Q900 tomorrow without fail. The opposition said no. They wanted it right then. Between the men and women, there were some 200 persons shouting without meaning, one person saying one thing and another saying something else.

In the secretary's office, they drafted a memorandum and said that with this act there is a legal proceeding against the priest, sacristan, and the board of directors of Catholic Action. This is a falsehood. The leaders are those who are doing this just for the most ignorant, just so that they can say that they are working a lot for them. There was a lot of discussion and a lot of time lost in talk. He who robbed the most time was Sr. Ángel Roberto Patzay. He believes that he is the only one who can talk. Isn't it true that the more a person talks, the more the meaning of what he is trying to say gets lost?

On 4 April 1987, Saturday those of Catholic Action went to the parish of San Martín to participate in a short religious course given by Father José. It was attended by people from San Jorge, San Benito, Tzancuil, and San José. In the afternoon of this same day, some went to mass in San Martín. On this same day Juan Mendoza, José Vásquez and Juan Mario Méndez went on an errand, but it is not known where they went.

At 5:45 a.m., 6 April 1987, the ex-board of Catholic Action began to talk, calling all the people to meet at 3:00 p.m. in front of the church to wait for Monseñor Bishop Benando Gálvez for a solution to what they called a problem. José Carlos said by means of a loudspeaker that everyone should gather into one group so that when the bishop arrives he will see them praying in one place and authorize a new priest. They definitely did not want Father José.

From 7:00 to 8:00 a.m., the members of Catholic Action gathered in the house of the minister of the Eucharist, Abraham Bizarro Ramos, to think about what they were going to do when the bishop arrived. But they had doubts. Then three men and a woman went to consult with the father to see if it was certain that the bishop was going to come. But when they arrived, the father had gone on an errand to Sololá. They just talked to Señora Juana Avila.

The rest of us who were also in San Martín went into the chapel, a small structure adjacent to the church, praying and asking God for strength because the señor told us that the parish did not know about the arrival of Monseñor Gálvez. After the prayer we went to a *comedor* for refreshments. That is where Juana Avila told us that monseñor is not going to come, that it was just a lie of the group in opposition to anger the people who are Catholics. Señora Juana Avila told us to meet and pray in the house of Abraham at 4:00 p.m., and if the bishop arrives, some religious person would come to tell us what was going to happen. She told us that we would have to exercise more patience and not molest the other group. But she told us with more confidence that the bishop is not coming because when he is coming there is notice three days beforehand.

In the afternoon, the large group began to arrive at 3:30. They were certain that the bishop was coming. Speaking in the microphone, they called everyone, but we just obeyed what sister Juana Avila told us. At 4:00 p.m. we began to pray the rosary and were very content afterwards. The opposing group also prayed in front of the church. At 6:00 p.m. monseñor did not arrive, and we went home. They also left. This was no more than lies of the big group, and the deceit was of their own making. During the night of this day, they said that they were not going to wait any longer. Wednesday or Thursday they are going to tear down the door of the church. We shall see what happens.

There are a lot of lies of the large group. Yesterday they said one thing, today they say another, and tomorrow they will say yet another. It is very confusing. One day they say that they are going to bring a priest from Quezaltenango, another day from Panajachel, then that a priest from Panajachel would be no good, then one from San Luis, and so on.

A Military Patrol Is Attacked in San Luis
7 April 1987

There are two versions. *Prensa Libre* announced that at 2:00 a.m. a military patrol was attacked by the subversives in the lookout southeast of San Luis (about 6 to 8 kilometers from the town). In this engagement, a second lieutenant by the name of Hugo was killed, two other soldiers were wounded and two others died. *El Gráfico* [national newspaper] reported that the army discovered an encampment of guerrillas. Dynamite was planted around the camp in the form of booby traps, and when the lieutenant tripped the wire connected to the dynamite, it exploded. The truth is that no one knows how many were killed because on 12 April one of the *Joseños* went to visit one of his sons in the detachment in San Diego la Laguna and they told him that 65 soldiers left and 6 had not returned. It is not known whether they are alive or dead. It is only known that some arrived to get relief in San Luis.

They say that in the early morning of this day, the 12th, the guerrillas arrived and attacked the detachment, but it was not a major thing. The soldiers just were molested because there were only 25 of them and the number of guerrillas was large.

Which of the two papers do you think is correct?

I believe the *Prensa Libre* was more correct. There are three *Joseños* in the army at this detachment. One of them was wounded by a bullet. Another was not in combat; he was guarding the post. His name is Carlos; the one wounded is named Jaime. Carlos told me that first the patrol detonated the booby trap and then the guerrillas attacked with arms. The army patrol was ready for the attack when the booby trap went off. The patrol returned the fire but they did not find any bodies, just a lot of blood.

José and María
17 to 22 April 1987

For two months and some days José had not spoken to Carolina. We knew that José was visiting a young woman named María, but he was talking to her inside her house, not in the streets. Then I said, "What are you doing? You're talking to a woman in her house!"

"Yes," he told me, "it's that her parents called me, and I have no reason to say no. I want to live there with them."

"Well, it's up to you," I told him; "don't tell me things later. If you want to get together with her, you have to advise me beforehand. I don't want the same thing to happen as before, your bringing a woman home without permission. It's painful for me because there are parents that are *bravos*, and the ones that are *jodidos* are me and your mother. We are the ones scolded for it. The people think that we didn't educate you. What are we going to do with you?"

"Very well, Papá, there's no problem; there's no problem. I will tell you," he told me.

Then comes the 17th of April 1987, Holy Friday, and suddenly José arrives at the house with María. I'm sleeping. My wife goes out to see the procession, and when she returns she sees José and María in the corridor.

My wife came to tell me, "Look, Ignacio, there's your son. He wants to talk to you. He has brought another woman."

The sleep went from me completely. I felt somewhat bad. "What's happening to me," I thought.

"Buenas noches," I said, "What's happening?"

"It's that I came with José," says the woman.

"And I brought her," says the other.

"We came; we love each other," says María.

"But you should have told me. I would have gone to your parents."

"Ah, no."

The next morning I awoke very angry. I told José, "Leave this house. I don't want to see you any more because with all that you are doing you are wounding me morally."

"No, you're not going to forgive us?"

"I think not."

All day Saturday, 18 April, they stayed in the house of my wife's father. I don't know how my father-in-law knew my friend, Roberto.

At 3:00 p.m. Roberto arrived and told me, "Ignacio, have compassion with your son. We are all human. Forgive him for committing a fault before and again now. What are you going to do? He's your son. Forgive him at least this last time, and if he does it again, then you can dispose of him. But for the moment I ask you to forgive him."

When Roberto said that, I began to think of a lot of things. I told him, "It's true that no one in this world is perfect. We all have our faults and make mistakes."

Roberto convinced me, and at this instance I sent Ramón for José and María. They came running and arrived very pleased.

When they came inside the house, I asked them, "Why didn't you advise me beforehand? I felt bad, offended, with what you are doing."

"Yes, Papá," José tells me, "I did this, but I won't do it again."

Then María tells me, "I came to live in your house. I will live with you. I don't know why. Well, it's not because I don't have anything to eat at my house. My parents have plenty, but I, I want to live with you, please."

"It's fine," I told them. "You are forgiven. You can work and eat. Eat." Then I sent my señora to tell María's parents to expect us by the afternoon to ask for forgiveness.

They said, "No, do not come until Tuesday, 21 April at 8:00 p.m., because we still have the fiesta of Holy Week. With much pleasure you can come, but not until Tuesday." We had to respect their request.

At 11:00 p.m., Tuesday, 21 April, my real father, Jesús Ujpán García, died. Certainly there was sadness.

My brothers told me, "Stay with us, Ignacio, you're our oldest brother."

"Yes, brothers," I told them, "but I can't. I have to make bread. But I will send bread to the house where the body of our father is lying so that those who arrive to visit, for those who will be in the wake, there will be bread."

I also told them I had to go to the house of María's parents, which had already been planned. Part of the bread was for Papá's wake and the other part for María's parents.

At 8:00 at night we arrived, and they received us. We were just a few (9), but they were about 20. Then my wife and I asked them forgiveness for all that our son had done. They didn't argue with us. They accepted the bread and other little things that we had brought. They made certain recommendations to José and María to behave well.

María's parents are good people. They received us well. As is the custom, María's father gave drinks of *aguardiente* to all the guests.

Then I told them, "Excuse me, señores, I have to go because I have to go see the cadaver of my father. I can't just stay here happily and forget about my father's body."

They didn't want us to leave, but they understood. We only talked for about two hours. Then María's mother gave María's clothes to my wife, and we took them home.

At noon on 22 April 1987, my father's body was buried. His body had been taken to the Central American Church for people to visit it because his wife belongs to this religion. His señora said that by absolute law Jesús's body had to be taken there even though Jesús was not Protestant. But everything had to be accepted, since when you're dead you can do nothing. There wasn't any understanding among my brothers and sisters because we are of different mothers, and we didn't all grow up with my father—Pedro, Gerardo [Hugo], Josefa, Juana, and I. The ones who were reared with him were Mateo, Juan, and Santos, who died [on the coast], and Gerardo [Jaime],[38] the youngest. We older brothers and sisters, who were not reared with him, went home.

Five days later María's parents sent a big clothes closet. To us this was very strange because we are poor. We hardly have the things that they have, but since it was their pleasure, we didn't reject it.

And María now is living with you?

Yes, she lives with us as if she were a daughter of the house. She's no problem. She's a very patient, attractive, and hardworking muchacha. José is also very patient. It seems that they will live happily, God willing.

What I'm observing is that they aren't persons who talk a lot. With the other children we talk a lot, yell, and joke. But with the two of them, no. It's as if they were babies. They don't converse.

They do, however, live with us, and they are prepared to have a wedding. They haven't done so only because of the problems in the Catholic church. That's why we haven't had the marriage. María is willing to marry José. They will get married when there's a solution to the problems. We have advised María's parents that they will get married, and they are happy that their daughter will have her marriage.

José and His Foot
A Friday in May 1987

In the month of May on a Friday, José went to the institute. As customary, the students received classes in physical education on Fridays. But because of carelessness, he fell during the class and fractured his ankle. He rested a few days and treated his bones with cooked leaves from the mountain.

Well, he's a little better now. But I was the guilty one. I told him to go to work with me in the field because we had much need. José went with me to plant coffee. The work was very difficult, and the place where we were working is sloped. Undoubtedly, it was because of this.

In the afternoon of this same day, José already was unable to walk. He was making his treatments. I too was treating his foot with herbs, but already it was difficult.

We had to call a *curandero* of bones named Juan Quit of San Martín la Laguna. This was the 27th of June of this year. The *curandero* said that the bone had been poorly dressed. The *curandero* was treating it three times— one time daily in the afternoon. Now José walks well, by the grace of God. We only gave the *curandero* Q2, who hardly wanted to take it. Because of the fracture, José did not work on his weaving for part of the month of May and all the month of June.

Now, this Saturday of 17 July, José went to Tzarayá to throw fertilizer on the milpa. For the round trip he walked about 12 kilometers. In the afternoon, I asked him whether he felt any pain, and he told me no.

We Indians, for breaks or fractures, never look for a doctor nor hospital. We have our special *curanderos* of bones who are unafraid because of the gravity of the breakage—they indeed cure it. But if a person with a broken bone goes to a doctor and the break is serious, the first thing the doctors say is that the patient must have his arm or foot amputated, depending on where the fracture is. But the *curanderos* don't know what amputating a bone is. For that reason, it's is better for us to go to a *curandero* when we have fractures. Very well now, we look for a doctor or a hospital for general sickness. We know that the *curandero* is unable to do anything for certain illnesses.

What does the curandero *do?*

Before the *curandero* touches the fracture, he has to do his secret bone prayers. Then he asks the kin of the injured to provide red coals (without smoke) and leaves of green tobacco. When everything is ready, he then takes out his material, or little bone, that he uses to cure. Then he presses the bone over the break, and when the bone is on the place where it's broken, the patient lets out great shouts. If it is a serious break, first he has to drink an *octavo* of *aguardiente* so that he will not feel more pain when the bone is curing.[39] Then the *curandero* heats the broken part with fire and heats the tobacco leaf and ties it around the breakage with a *faja* [band] and piece of pine. He only has to tie and untie, that is to say, that he leaves it tied when he is curing it and unties it another day. If the break is serious, the *curandero* has to be treating it for 20 days to a month, but if the fracture isn't serious, only for some three to five days.

This is what we know, and with this we Indians are cured.

Mission with the Bishop
Saturday, 11 April to 13 June 1987

Between Saturday and Sunday, but I'm more certain that it was Saturday, the 11th, there was a commission with the bishop to tell him to come solve the problem. Monseñor Benando Gálvez had an opportunity to come Wednesday, 15 April, to the parish of San Martín to address the problem with the people. But they misunderstood this communication and said that he was coming on the 13th. The people again got mad.

Sunday, 12 April, Palm Sunday, which the Ladinos call *Domingo de Dolores* [Sunday of Suffering], has the custom of the priests and bishops making a blessing of palm leaves and then handing them out to the faithful. It is a custom that has been done all the years. Now the group of Catholic Action, that is to say, the small group in favor of Father José, went to San Martín for the procession and mass and to receive the palm leaves. With this group there was no problem because they are complying with the orders of the church.

Now the other group saw that Palm Sunday arrived and that another priest had not come from Santa María, as they said he would, just for the people of San José for a mass and the blessing of palms. [He blesses the branches and leaves, but the people only use the leaves.] Out of shame, they took the palm leaves in a car owned by José Tereso Vásquez to Santa Bárbara for a blessing of the leaves by a priest there and then returned. Then their companions went to meet them at Pasara, which is by a river just outside the residential area of town. In the form of a procession, they arrived in front of the church where a *fiscal* passed out their palm leaves. It is a tradition to give a few to each family. When a member of the family dies, the family makes a cross with these palm leaves and puts it in the hands of the deceased.

Holy Monday, 13 April 1987, 5:00 p.m., the group favoring the priest congregated in the house of Señor Abraham Toc Pérez to celebrate Holy Liturgy and Holy Communion. Abraham told me he could only count 103 persons there, not including the children.

This same afternoon the group in opposition received a letter from Monseñor Benando Gálvez. They spoke in the microphone, saying that he is going to arrive in San Martín on Wednesday, 15 April, to see whether it is possible to open the church, if they would agree to obey the laws of the church. But when the people realized what the letter said, they didn't want to respect the bishop. Instead, they went to the mayor to tell him to go with them when they break open the doors of the church. For ignorance and lack of knowledge of duty, the mayor, his secretary, and the councilmen went with the majority to the church. At 6:10 p.m. the majority broke a glass window and Diego Hernández and Benjamín Soto climbed through to release the two safety latches of the door. Then Juan Mendoza and Juan Có Mendoza broke the door lock and opened the big door, and the *alguaciles* turned on the lights. After they had forced open the door, they said that no one should enter until the mayor got an order from the *juzgado de primera instancia* and the government of Sololá. The same mayor promised to find a solution to the problem. Thus they drew up a voluntary act, which they called an *acta notarial*. The mayor was an accomplice of this serious crime. A mayor should not participate in a violent act or be present during a crime so that all will believe in the law more.

Was the major, Benjamín, whom you helped put in office, on the side of the majority?

I don't think so. Since there were so many of them, about 450 including men and women, he felt he had to go with them. Later I asked Father

José what he thought about Benjamín's being there when they broke the door open. He said that he just pitied Benjamín because there were so many of them wanting him to witness what they were doing. This is not to say that Benjamín is on the same side with Juan Mendoza.

When the liturgy was being celebrated in the house of Abraham Toc, the municipal guards arrived very strongly to call some of the sacristans of the board of directors to present themselves immediately in the tribunal. They didn't answer until they finished the service of God, but the guards were very *bravos*. When the service was finished, two sacristans and two members of the board of directors of Catholic Action went. When they arrived, the commissary told them that the mayor of the town had gone to the church. These men then returned to the house of Abraham Toc because the nuns from San Martín and the deacon from Patzún named Barillas were still there. I went with them.

While we were in Abraham's house and the car was waiting to take the deacon and two sisters back to San Martín, news reached us that they wanted to hit the sisters and the deacon. Thanks to God, the car already had arrived. We accompanied them because there had been rumors that on the road they were going to beat the car and the people in it with stones, sticks, and such. It's true that there were seven persons. I recognized Mario Vásquez and Bonifacio Soto, his brother-in-law. We left praying in the car. When we arrived in San Martín, we found two foreign priests, and, finally, other companions. We were twelve in number. The three fathers finished celebrating a mass, and then we chatted a little with Father José. Afterwards we returned to San José.

From this night of Monday until dawn Tuesday, the majority group celebrated their own crime of opening the church. There was a lot of scandal, lighting hundreds of quetzales worth of firecrackers and *bombas*, ringing the bells of the church, music on the loudspeaker, and breaking the silence of the night. During the night, they recorded an act stating that at 8:00 in the morning a new board of directors would enter the church. They themselves authorized their own religious ceremony without ecclesiastical authority. Most of the leaders were drunk.

Holy Tuesday, 14 April 1987, Ignacio Bizarro Toc, Miguel José Argueta, and the secretary of the town, Abraham Có, went to Sololá to look for the authorization of these people to be in the church without problems. They say that the governor took them to consult with the fathers in Sololá, but they told them that only the bishop is the *jefe* of the church because they didn't have the power over these matters and that they too are under orders.

They wanted to talk to Monseñor Benando Gálvez, but he had gone to Chimaltenango and Parramos. They were able, however, to talk to him on the telephone and guarantee that Wednesday, as he had sent them notice, he would meet with them in his office in San Martín. The bishop said the same thing to the governor. Then the governor gave them a letter for the mayor and leaders to read before the group, stating that no one could go into the church until they had talked to the bishop to find a solution to the problem.

After the mayor and the leaders read the letter of the governor, they didn't respect it. Franco Coj said on the loudspeaker that they were not going to respect either the governor or the bishop, that the church was built by their ancestors, not by the governor, much less by the bishop. He invited everyone, including the mayor, councilmen, and military commissioners to enter the church. And many people went inside the church.

Holy Wednesday, 15 April 1987, all those who were in favor of the Catholic church, that is to say, on the side of Father José, marched to San Martín to meet Monseñor Benando. I went with them. Also, the group that had broken into the church went, that is, six of their representatives and the municipal corporation, the latter of whom are accomplices. They were in front of the *contras* when they forced open the doors of the church, yet they did nothing, not even intervene by telling them not to commit this crime. For that reason, this group felt strong because the municipal corporation and the military commissioners were united with them. But they were very mistaken for they did not understand how to do things.

Monseñor Benando Gálvez received the representatives in his office. Those in opposition were Juan Mendoza, Diego Castillo Tajay, José Tereso Vásquez, Ignacio Bizarro Toc, and Gerardo García. Those representatives in favor were named by Father José. I didn't enter. Yes, they would let me enter, but I thought better not to because the group in opposition would think I had some special interest and I didn't want to make anyone angry. I know that they are wicked.

The meeting lasted two hours. It finished at 8:00 at night, and I was informed by one of those who was in favor of the church. He said that the meeting was in disorder. The opposition did not respect the words of the bishop nor of the governor. There were many gibes for the bishop and for Father José. They said they would continue fighting and invading the church. The bishop and priest are nothing to them. They were the ones leading the town, and they can do whatever they wish. They acted immorally. A first councilman of the municipality, who is an elder of the Central American church, got involved with them, speaking vulgarly. This man didn't have reason to be in favor of the opposition; it seemed he was protesting against the Catholic church in general. In this meeting there was a lot of discussion. The bishop said to pray more and ask God Omniscient to help them understand and know the laws and orders of the church because brute force does not help the spirit. But they didn't pay attention when the bishop spoke. The bishop confirmed that 23 April he would . receive six representatives of this group in the presence of the governor for a meeting with the rest of the padres of the diocese [about 20 other priests] and that with their help a decision would be made to settle this problem. After the meeting in San Martín, the governor, the municipal corporation, and the representatives went to San José in a pickup for a meeting in front of the municipality. The bishop told us that whoever wants can stay for mass or go to San José for the meeting with the governor. Almost everyone else stayed for mass, but Gaspar and I went running for my town.

When we arrived the governor was eating dinner. The meeting lasted an hour. A lot of things were discussed. The governor said that in the end that, if the bishop is unable to find a solution to the problem, he himself would go to Guatemala [City] to talk with the *jefes* and he himself would find a solution. The governor said one thing and the translator said other things, to please the people, because the people didn't understand Spanish.

After the meeting, the *contras* bad-mouthed the bishop and the father for not permitting San José to have its own priest. But the truth is that the bishop and the priest, José, have reason. They have observed the bad attitude of the *Joseños*. The latter do not want to correct their faults, and then they get angry and become enemies of the person who speaks the truth. Then they say they are good, nothing more.

On 23 April 1987, six representatives from each group went to Pana-jachel for the meeting with the bishop. Roberto informed me that the bishop didn't admit the group in favor in order to avoid problems with the group in opposition. Just the six *contras* entered along with Father José, two nuns, four priests, and Monseñor Benando. After the meeting, Father José told Roberto that the priests condemned the forcing of the doors of the church and the bad criticism against Father José and Monseñor Benando. The priests and the bishop said that there would be no mass nor father for San José and that the world has seen all the falsehoods that the *Joseño* students announced on the television news. They called this a crime of defamation and insult but said that the church and Father José do not want to actually conform to the law and jail these students. In this dialogue they told the group in opposition to take 15 days for reflection and that the decision that they will be given will have to be made by the episcopal council of the diocese. Then the group left. Not until then did Monseñor Gálvez receive in his office the group that was in favor of José and inform them of these things.

On 30 April 1987 the priests of the diocese met to take care of this problem, but who knows how the group in opposition found out, which sent its representatives to this meeting. They didn't have to go to this meeting because their next meeting had been stipulated for 8 May. But they are full of foolishness and disrespect. The episcopal council [fathers and bishops] made it clear that the bishop had the power to make a decision, and they condemned the bad attitude of the *Joseños*.

What kinds of things did the students say on television?

That Father José was a thief and a bad person.

Was this also in Prensa Libre?

Yes, Father José and the bishop have copies.

On 6 May 1987 Monseñor Benando Gálvez made his decision. He sent in a letter to a representative of the *contras* saying to present the representatives in Panajachel on 11 May at 11:00 a.m. These were: Ignacio Bizarro Tuc, Ignacio Oliva y Oliva, and Lucas Ujpán García.

The group presented itself on the 11th of May to find out the decision of Monseñor Gálvez, but they didn't want to accept the decision. They returned very angry. The bishop had decided that he would give San José a new father by the name of Gino Barillas Tecún, an Indian of Santa Elena, who would earn his title on 23 May, but with the condition that he live in San Martín since there are no adequate provisions or house in San José for a father to live there and with the condition that the *Joseños* follow the laws of the church and that the leaders of the opposition would disband. But the group in opposition did not want this. They insisted on having a priest who would live in San José and who would be ordered by themselves on whatever they wanted him to do. Father José was getting along well with the other towns of the parish, so he would remain in San Martín. Thus, there would be two priests for the parish in San Martín, but the new one would work for San José, not Father José.

Then the opposing group said it didn't want another North American priest. Gino arrived in San Martín on 13 July to work with Padre José and especially with San José, but the group in opposition didn't accept him either. They spent a lot of money making other trips to Sololá, San Diego, San Luis, and Guatemala trying to contract a priest for the masses in San José. The priests never sent one. They have to be authorized by the bishop before they can celebrate mass in a town.

The group of Catholics that are in favor of Father José, more or less 150, including men, women, and children, are fulfilling a mission celebrating the liturgy (small mass) in their homes from Monday to Friday and in San Martín on Saturday afternoons and Sunday mornings. It was approved unanimously by the episcopal council of the church that there will be no more organizations in the church in San José.

Then Monseñor Benando Gálvez sent a letter to Father José McCall and the group in opposition that, in the name of God, starting on 23 May there would be a new priest for the parish of San Martín. This new priest would be working in San Benito, San Jorge, and San José, as deputy of José, while Father José would be the deputy of the bishop.

On 23 May the groups—in favor and opposed—prepared to see the ordination of the new priest, Gino Barillas Tecún, in Sololá. The group in favor of Father José went to San Martín to take the launch. The group in opposition had contracted a large launch, but it didn't arrive. At 8:00 in the morning, they contracted a truck, but only 60 persons went. Because of bad luck, they say that mass had been finished by the time they arrived in Sololá.

Days afterwards, Juan Mendoza and the people went around saying that they won a new priest for San José and that they do not want him to be in San Martín. They didn't understand the letter of the bishop, which said that he would serve San José but live in San Martín.

The 13th of June the group in favor of the bishop was invited, as well as the group in opposition, to receive Father Gino in the parish. The group favoring Father José organized into a group with him to receive the new priest, Father Gino. Also the *Martineros* and the *Jorgeños* organized into groups to receive him. My family and I also went. The reception for the new priest was very joyful.

The large group from San José did not go to the reception. They are very angry because the father didn't go to San José for the reception.

Father Paulo's Spiritual Retreat in San José
15 to 20 June 1987

On this date the small group was celebrating the word of God in Pascual's house when an order of Father José arrived saying that the celebration will end on next Thursday, the 18th. They will have to respect the order of the bishop that all the organizations in San José be terminated and begin anew with just one group in the church, not a group in favor or against Father José. With the new father, there will be a new organization in the church.

Father Gino had to begin his work without any organization. Monseñor Gálvez named only one person who is going to be an assistant to Gino, and that is Señor Abraham Bizarro Ramos who has knowledge because he has been working in the Catholic church for 38 years. The small group has been obeying and respecting the orders, but the large group has been very angry and does not accept them.

On 19 June Father Paulo arrived at 3:00 p.m. to share a spiritual retreat. My family and I went. Father Paulo spoke clearly, saying, "We are all brothers and sisters. We should not offend our brothers and sisters. If we should offend one another, we should reconcile with them. Let's live in one church and with one faith." Father Paulo was talking a lot, but they didn't understand. They were too rebellious.

Father Paulo read Ephesians 4:1 of the New Testament, The Unity of the Body:

> I urge you, then—I who am a prisoner because I serve the Lord—
> live a life that measures up to the standard of God, set when he called
> you. Be humble, gentle and patient always. Show your love by being
> helpful to one another. Do your best to preserve the unity which the
> Spirit gives, by the peace that binds you together. There is one hope to
> which God has called you. There is one Lord, one faith, one baptism;
> there is one God and Father of all men, who is Lord of all, works
> through all, and is in all.

Father Paulo also said:

> In the Quiché region there is a town in which division, for various
> political reasons, caused 600 widows. We're now helping these wid-
> ows. In other towns, like Panajachel, there is division of race. But here
> you are of the same race!

He also read from San Juan in the Bible. Next there were songs. Then he gave the people ideas and then read more from the Bible from San Juan. He also gave exhortations.

On 20 June 1987 Father Paulo arrived with two other priests to tell the group in opposition to respect the order of Monseñor Gálvez and to reconcile with Father José all of the insults and calumnies that they had spoken against him. The large group did not respect him. They didn't want reconciliation.

For these reasons, mass was not celebrated in the church during this fiesta. Instead, the large group made a procession, drinking *atol* and receiving the dancers.

Catholic Action Problems Continue and Ex-Commissioner Caught Stealing
8 April to 2 July 1987

On Wednesday I was sick with a very severe headache. During this day, they injected me two times with antibiotics and twice I went to San Martín for the injections. When I went for the second time, I met the board of directors that had been called by Father José. Then the father told us that he empathizes a lot for the group that has gone astray, but he empathizes more for the group that is in favor of the church. During this day, he authorized that for Friday, 10 April, there would be a liturgical celebration in the house of anyone who wants it, with the presence of Francisca Juana and the minister of the Eucharist for all those who desire Holy Communion. The meeting went very well. [Usually this is done in the church, but because of the problems, they were doing it in the homes.]

The truth is that Friday, 10 April, 5:00 p.m., Holy Liturgy was celebrated in the house of Jorge Méndez Ramos. One hundred and twenty persons arrived to receive the wafer of communion. But there was quite a racket from the *contras*, who say the small group is not worth anything because they are following a father who is a gringo. They say that those who are with Father José are crazy because they are celebrating the liturgy in a private house, but this was due to the church being closed because of the mistreatment by the large group. But they never say what their faults are; they always indicate that it is all Father José's fault.

At 9:00 p.m. on 8 April, the ex-commissioner, Fernando Timoteo

Ramos Castro, and a deserter, José Chavajay, were captured by the auxiliary military commissioners. The two were dedicated to stealing motors used to pump water from the lake for irrigation, of which there are several in San José and San Martín. The poorer people still use cans to carry the water to their plots, but the more wealthy people pump the water out of the lake with motors.

José earlier had deserted two times from the army, once in the military zone of Zacapa and another from the barracks of San Marcos. The second time was in 1986. He was captured by the military commissioners and taken to jail in San Marcos. But as he is very clever, he only stayed in jail for six weeks, and then they set him free.

The first of January they were named as municipal policemen (a free service).

Didn't the tribunal know that they had a bad record?

Yes, but they had to accept the posts. Out of ignorance, they let them be the municipal policemen.

Well, the ex-commissioner always had a bad record because he swindled many people, as many in the pueblo as in the *aldea*. They gave the two men possession of the office of municipal policeman. They were two in the same group, but without their companions knowing what they were up to. Without doubt, they left to do these things knowing when there wouldn't be many people about. The two went to break into the storage house of Jesús Fernández on the beach where he keeps all his equipment for irrigation. Jesús Fernández did not ask for an investigation. He just bought another motor to water his onions. As the thieves are very clever, they realized when Jesús had replaced the motor. So they went to break into the storage house again to steal the other motor.

Jesús was very sad and told me: "Ignacio, they stole another motor from me."

I answered, "Why don't you investigate who the thieves are?"

"I can't," he told me. Perhaps he was aware that the thieves were connected with the commissioners. This is the way it was for some weeks.

On 9 April 1987, José and Fernando Timoteo arrived at the house of Humberto to offer him an irrigating motor to buy. Humberto asked what it cost, and they told him Q250. Humberto told them to bring the motor tomorrow, and he would have the money to buy it from them. But as Humberto knew very well that two motors had been stolen from Jesús, he went to Jesús's house to tell him, "Tomorrow José Chavajay and Fernando Timoteo are bringing a motor to sell me. If you like, you can come to see if it is one of the motors that was stolen from you." Jesús went to the *jefe* of the military commissioners to denounce these two men.

On 10 April, the military commissioners covered the entrance of the *sitio* of Humberto Rafael. There is where the two thieves were captured with a motor, but the motor that they had didn't belong to Jesús. It was a more recent robbery. They had stolen a motor from Benjamín Peña Cholotío, the actual mayor of the town. When the commissioners captured them, they discharged their arms and nearly killed José; a bullet just missed his head. At the same time, the two were taken to jail in San José. There was a disturbance throughout the town because of what had happened.

When these two persons were in jail, Jesús Fernández arrived to tell them, "If you stole my two motors, tell me so. I myself will spend a little money to set you free."

The two thieves confided in him, "Yes, we are the ones who robbed your motors. One we sold on the coast in San Pedro Cutzán and the other we sold to Guido Vallejo Salazar in San Martín la Laguna. You can send word to have the motors brought back. We only received Q150 for the two motors."

Everything that the two thieves told him, Jesús repeated to the justice of peace. By order of the justice, a car was paid to go to San Pedro Cutzán to get the motor. Then the other was gotten in San Martín. When the motors belonging to Jesús were taken to the courthouse in San José, they asked him whether he would pardon the two thieves as he had said earlier. But instead, Jesús asked that they be taken to jail. Thus it ended.

The 13th of April, they went to Sololá with the three motors. Twenty days later the three motors were returned to their owners.

The 2nd of July, 1987, these two men were sentenced by the *juzgado de primera instancia* of Sololá to four years in jail. This information comes from a brother of José Chavajay.

Dream of Principales
7 July 1987

I had this dream at 5:30 a.m. when I was in Panajachel working with Jaime D. Sexton. It was a strange dream! I dreamed that I was in my town united with the *principales* and *cofrades*. That is to say, with the large group that is opposed to Father José.

In the dream I saw when the *mayordomos* came in carrying *atol* in their hands to give to the *principales* and *cofrades* and when they began to drink the *atol*. The *jícaras* (gourd jars) became glasses of *aguardiente*. The *mayordomos* collected the *jícaras*—one group got *jícaras* and the other glasses where they were serving the *aguardiente*. I didn't enter the house, I only watched what was happening.

Then a *principal* by the name of Roberto Chavajay got up and told one of those by the name of Martín, who was in favor of Father José, "Forgive me for having offended you a lot and talking bad against you—to the point of thinking about killing you. I have thought evil against your life, even about denouncing you as a subversive, but I ask that you pardon me. I won't do these things again." This is what the *principal* told the other person, but I saw that the *principal* was drinking.

Martín began to answer when my dream stopped.

Possibly the meaning of this dream is that the *cofrades* and *principales* are going to be conquered; that is to say, that the *costumbres* that they want so much will be cancelled because the *atol* and the *aguardiente* indicate sadness for them. But we are going to see whether this happens or whether it is just the madness of my dream.

Dream in Panajachel of Bull Colored like a Jaguar
8 July 1987

I dreamed that I was in San José. I was in front of the church. In the door of the church were two men, one by the name of Diego Sánchez Batz and the other I didn't know very well. I greeted Don Diego, but I didn't enter into the church; I only went to the door.

I passed in front of the church on the way to my house when I saw in the *sitio* of Abraham Bizarro Ramos that they were untying a bull the color of a jaguar. I saw a lot of people, tying and untying the animal.

I don't know if it's the madness of my dream or if someone is going to die in Abraham's family or in the group of *contras*, but indeed this is going to happen—there is going to be a death by accident or killing.

Coffee a Much Appreciated Product in My Town
10 July 1987

I chatted with my Uncle Bonifacio about coffee. He told me that the first cultivation of coffee in San José was in Chimax, planted by Humberto Bizarro García in the year 1935. He just planted two *cuerdas*, but no one knows where he got the seed. Before dying, Don Humberto divided his coffee grove among his children, who were Ignacio Gerardo, Francisco, Marcos, Alejandra, María, and Ruben.

It is certain that when my grandfather, Ignacio, died in 1950, he left us 20 *matas* [tree] plants of coffee that his father, Humberto Bizarro, had left him. These *matas* of coffee still exist. Because they are very old, they do not provide much coffee. [Ignacio owns them, but without papers. They are not even a half-*cuerda* because Humberto divided his property into smaller parcels for his children.]

Coffee is a much appreciated product in my town. The only *Martineros* who had cultivated coffee in 1955 were Malco Leonel Cojbx, and Teodoro Par Navichoc, who had their cultivations of coffee in San José.

In 1965 *Martineros* and *Joseños* began to plant coffee, but very few of them. In these last few years, most of the land has been cultivated in coffee. The whole town is half-hidden among the coffee groves, more so in the last five years. Very few people plant corn and beans. There are two varieties of coffee seeds—"Bourbon [Coffee *arabica*, variety *Bourbon*]" and "Caturro Pacho."

Coffee is what gives life to the *Joseños*. It's true that we don't have a lot because we *Joseños* lack land. This year, 1987, there are four *beneficios* of *Martineros* in San José and there are four belonging to four of the richer *Joseños*. Also, there is a small group that processes its coffee. This group is made up of seven persons who are members of the cooperative.

The harvest of coffee is from December to March. The processing of coffee begins with the picking of ripe coffee beans, and then carrying them to sell to the *beneficios* by the *quintal* to process.

First, they put the coffee into water tanks. Then the water carries it to the pulping machine. The pulper has two outlets. In front it takes out the grain [or "bean"]; in back it takes out the pulp. The grain is carried to another tank without water in it to ferment naturally 24 to 30 hours, depending on the weather at the time of processing. Then the fermented grain is washed with sufficient water. When the grain doesn't have any more *miel* (honey), or isn't *meloso* (sugary) and is white, it is taken out of the tank and spread out in the sun for 5 to 6 days, depending on the weather. When it is good and dry, it is known for the color of the grain. If the *grano oro* [the seed inside the silvery, nearly transparent skin, or parchment] has turned the color of olive green, then it is has dried enough. It is then put into bags and carried to the export company to sell. This kind of coffee is called *pergamino* [pulped but unshelled, or with the parchment still intact]. In the company there are special machines to take off the cap [husk, or parchment] that covers the grain and converts it into *café [en] oro* [shelled but unroasted coffee]. This is what they export to the foreigner. It costs more.[40]

Dream of Grandmother
14 July 1987

By the grace of God, I slept the whole night peacefully. I dreamed I was in the market of Santa Ana buying bananas, and I saw my grandmother, Isabel, selling herbs. But when I went to her, she hid from me.

A Little Bit About My Family
14 July 1987

I have eight children, seven of whom I'm going to say something about their character.[41] José is a boy taller than I am. His vice is soccer. He is a famous goalkeeper in *Joseño* sports. His face is always smiling; he is very calm. Almost all the time he is happy. He is a boy who is able to work in the field, as a baker, and as a weaver with the footloom, making *labores de jaspe*. He isn't a flashy person. He dresses very poorly, wearing second-hand clothing. He's a God-fearing boy, and he always goes to church. He's very friendly with everyone. He neither smokes nor drinks.

María works to help her mother, but she is very short-tempered. She says that she doesn't like to work in the kitchen. She would prefer more to be a merchant or a student. When she was studying in primary school, her grades were good. In the first year of *básico*, she flunked two courses. But in the final days, that is to say, in the second and third year of *básico*, she did well. María also plays a lot of basketball, participating in local and departmental games. She has a diploma from the national confederation of sports of the capital city. She actually now is studying at the Instituto Nacional para Señoritas de Occidente in Quezaltenango.

Ramón Antonio is very robust in stature like me. He is a little lighter than his brothers and sisters. He works in bread-making and is learning how to weave on a footloom, but he works mostly in the fields. He doesn't have a love for soccer, nor does he like to go to fiestas. He doesn't talk much. He's an observer—he likes to listen, not talk. He has a strong character. When he says yes, he means yes, not later, no. He will say don't bother me, and then don't bother him. In tidiness, he is very fastidious. When he was a child, he didn't like to go to school. Now, he's in the first year of secondary school (*básico*). He speaks Spanish a little better. He says that he wants to study in a military academy, but I told him it is very difficult because we don't have money. His desire is to become an officer in the army. His sport is very different, he practices *lucha libre* [free style wrestling, Roman wrestling, not karate, similar to self-defense taught in the army]. What is apparent is that he wants to make money.

Ignacito is very entertaining. He talks a lot and gets along well with everyone. His mind is a tape recorder. His Spanish is very much appreciated by the teachers. It is apparent that he will be able to become a reporter or painter. He makes perfect drawings. He assures me that it is easier to study than to work in the fields. When there are no classes, I take him to help me a little, but his body is very delicate and, upon being bitten by an insect, he becomes infected. For that reason, he says that it is better to study and not work in the fields. He likes soccer. All the time he is happy. At times when I'm thinking of my work or what I'm going to do for them, Ignacito begins to act up like a clown until I feel like smiling with him. He can mimic exactly what someone has said, like a tape recorder, and makes people laugh. He's funny to his family. And he makes me forget my worries.

Susana Julia hardly likes school. I don't know if it is because of her age (10 years). This year she is in the fourth grade. What's notable about her is that she likes to work in the house. She also likes to be a merchant, selling bread and fruit in the street and in the houses, without shame. In her free hours, she buys oranges by the hundred, also mangos and *jocotes* [yellow or red, plumlike fruit], and then she sells 10 to 20 in the houses at a higher price. She has luck. She is able to sell them and earn her money. It is true that she doesn't earn more than centavos, but indeed one can see that she has luck selling. She gets annoyed with her brothers and sisters and even fights with the boys.

Anica Catana is in the second grade. School for her is a sacrifice. There are days when she goes and days when she doesn't. She says that it's better to work at home and not study. She says that her teachers are *bravos*, but the teachers aren't bossy. What's happening is that she is not learning what they are trying to teach her. Her mother says, "If you don't go to school, I'm not going to give you your food."

She says, "Very well." It doesn't worry her. But then later she says, "Give me something to eat, Mamá. Tomorrow I'm going to school." And that's the way it is. Sometimes she goes and sometimes she doesn't. Right now she is attending school, but it is a struggle on the part of her mother. I appreciate Anica Catana a lot, and I feel very sad when her brothers and sisters hit her.

At home we call Samuel Jesús "Morenito [little brown one]" because he is brown like me. This baby is most appreciated by his mother. When he was two and a half years old, he was sick a lot. My wife suffered a lot with him. We spent a lot of money. I recognize my serious faults, and sometimes I said that he should die.

What kind of faults?

We didn't have money for medicine and doctors when he was sick, so I said it would be better that he die. When I didn't have any more money, I said "What can I do? I don't have anymore money; it would be better if he dies." But God is great, and finally He helped.

Now he plays a lot and is very fussy. He doesn't like dirty clothes, and he doesn't eat herbs (wild greens). He talks a lot and is very friendly. He has been speaking Spanish and Tzutuhil equally for three years. His brothers and sisters call him the bilingual. Jesús is very much loved by Ramón. When Ramón goes to school, Jesús cries for Ramón. When Jesús is not home, Ramón says, "Where's my little brother?" It's apparent that Jesús is very clever. Already he knows people and their names. He's only three years old as of last April, 1987.

The baby Dominga Marta is very tiny. She is light complected like Ramón.

My wife, Josefa, can't speak Spanish, just the Tzutuhil language. She understands Spanish, but she is unable to answer. Now, she blames her parents for not having gone to school. She says that when she was a girl the teachers went to the houses to list the number and names of new students. But her parents hid her from the teachers because they were bad people. When she was in the streets looking at a Ladino, she cried a lot and hid. Her parents were to blame. She was taking care of her two sisters, María and Dominga, but when they were big they attended school. María was in the fourth grade, and Dominga in the sixth. For that reason, many times my wife cries over the sorrow that her parents caused her.

Almost every day she tells the children, "Children, go to school, learn to speak, read, and write. It's true that we are poor, but your Papá and I are going to struggle for your food. Look at my situation. I would like to be able to speak, to greet a person in Spanish, and I can't. But the fault is my parents." These are the words of my wife.

At times she gets very angry at the kids. I tell the youngsters, "Don't talk back to your Mamá. Work! Obey her! She has reason, and my children, don't sass her."

My wife and I have had a lot of poverty, sickness, and suffering. For our children, we work a lot—I in the fields and she at home, washing clothes and preparing meals for all of us and during the night weaving. She works very hard.

My wife is an enemy of the cigarette. She doesn't like me to smoke. I have to respect her. I don't smoke any more. She doesn't drink *aguardiente*. During the fiestas, I ask her, "Why don't you have a beer or a *trago*?"

She tells me, "No, thanks." Those are her words, "No, thanks."

We also dress very poorly, but we never have problems over clothing.

She has a lot of luck raising chickens. When the birds are attacked by pestilence, the neighbors' chickens die, but not hers. They always live, and she has her chickens. She just continuously cleans where the chickens sleep.

On 5 November of this year, 1987, we are going to complete 25 years of marriage. It's true that it is an impoverished marriage, but by the grace of God, we respect our marriage a lot. With money or without it, we are the same. Never do I think I am superior to her, nor she to me. We understand each other very well. I keep respect and esteem for her, and she does for me.

When I have money, I say to my wife that we have a little money. She has to know how we are going to use the money. And when I want to take out a loan or an advance, she has to know how we are going to spend this money.

When she sells a weaving, she tells me, I have Q10 to Q15 we can spend. I say, "Very well."

Always there are problems, but not for hitting my woman when she calls my attention to something. When I have faults, she tells me calmly, and I do the same with her because we are just human. There are always faults; no one is perfect.

God willing and the Virgen María and our patron saint, San Juan Bautista, if we are living, we plan to celebrate a Holy Mass in the month of November to give thanks to God for the 25 years of marriage, one time in life, as an example for our children.

What has helped to carry out life in my home is my reading a lot in the New Testament, Ephesians, Chapter 5, verses 21 to 32:

> Wives and Husbands, submit yourselves to one another, because of your reverence for Christ.
>
> Wives, submit yourselves to your husbands, as to the Lord.
>
> For a husband has authority over his wife in the same way that Christ has authority over the Church; and Christ is Himself the Savior of the Church, His body.
>
> And so wives must submit themselves completely to their husbands, in the same way that the Church submits itself to Christ.
>
> Husbands, love your wives in the same way that Christ loved the Church and gave His life for it.
>
> He did this to dedicate the Church to God, by his word, after making it clean by the washing in water, in order to present the Church to Himself, in all its beauty, pure and faultless, without spot or wrinkle, or any other imperfection.
>
> Men ought to love their wives just as they love their own bodies. A man who loves his wife loves himself. (No one ever hates his own body. Instead, he feeds it and takes care of it, just as Christ does the Church; for we are members of his body.) As the scripture says, "For this reason, a man will leave his father and mother, and unite with his wife, and the two will become one."
>
> There is a great truth revealed in this scripture, and I understand it applies to Christ and the Church.
>
> But it also applies to you: every husband must love his wife as himself, and every wife must respect her husband.

Also, [I read] The First Letter from Pedro, Chapter 3, Verses 1 to 7:

> In the same way you wives must submit yourselves to your husbands, so that if some of them do not believe God's word, they will be won over to believe by your conduct. It will not be necessary for you to

say a word, because they will see how pure and reverent your conduct is.

You should not use outward aids to make yourselves beautiful, such as the way you fix your hair, or the jewelry you put on, or the dresses you wear. Instead, your beauty should consist of your true inner self, the ageless beauty of a gentle and quiet spirit, which is of the greatest value in God's sight. For the devout women of the past, who hoped in God, used to make themselves beautiful in this way, by submitting themselves to their husbands. Sarah was like that; she obeyed Abraham and called him "My master." You are now her daughters if you do good and are not afraid of anything.

You husbands, also, in living with your wives must recognize that they are the weaker sex. So you must treat them with respect, because they also will receive, together with you, God's gift of life. Do this so that nothing will interfere with your prayers.[42]

Whenever I have time, I read these verses and I tell my wife in Tzutuhil. This has been medicine for our home.

Problems That Don't End, They Just Change Their Names: Socialists in San Martín
17 July 1987

In San Martín la Laguna, there is a mayor named Bartolomé Yac García, who was a candidate of the Partido Socialista Democrático. In the 326 municipalities of Guatemala, San Martín la Laguna is the only town where a socialist won the position of mayor.

Bartolomé is a Tzutuhil who can't speak Spanish well. He wears his typical shirt and pants, and he doesn't wear shoes. He walks around barefoot and once in a while wears *caites*. His behavior is Indian. He's a very simple man. That's why many Mexican journalists came to congratulate him when he won the election.

During the electoral campaigns of 1985, there were two other candidates. For the Unión del Centro [Nacional] party, there was a man of business and a lot of money named Guido Vallejo Salazar. For the Democracia Cristiana party, there was a teacher of secondary education, Roberto Lionel Cojbx.

Bartolomé of the PSD took possession in January of 1986. The two losing powers looked upon Bartolomé with envy when he arrived at the tribunal. They murmured a lot, but there was nothing they could do.

In February of this year of 1987, three companions of the mayor resigned—the syndic, first councilman, and second councilman all left. Bartolomé remained in his office alone. Bartolomé says that he advised them to resign because they were only drunks. They were drunk every day, and he said it was better for them to resign. "The people elected them to work, not to come drinking," said the mayor. [The syndic and first councilman were socialists too, but the second councilman was of the Unión del Centro Nacional party.]

The political enemies of the mayor saw that Bartolomé didn't have councilmen, and they asked for a new election. But they weren't able to get one. Now, in order to end the tribunal of Bartolomé Yac, they raised a false accusation. Those who caused this false denunciation are the politicians involved with the ex-commissioners and their kin. They go around saying that Bartolomé Yac is receiving money from the Sandinistas of Nicaragua, saying that he is a communist and that he wants to deliver the people of San Martín into the hands of the communists of Daniel Ortega.

Now, every day this problem is becoming more serious. On Thursday, 16 July 1987, the commander of the military zone in Sololá arrived to investigate to see whether it is true that the mayor maintains communication with the Sandinistas.

Friday, 17 July 1987, the governor of Sololá arrived to see whether the mayor had a lot of money. Well, they say that in the pocket of his jacket, they found Q300, which they took to Sololá for an investigation of where he had gotten it. But this amount of money anyone can have. Bartolomé is an industrious man; he has a lot of corn and property. Now they are making their investigations. The town is divided into two groups—one is for the mayor, and the other (the losing politicians, ex-commissioners and their kin) is against him.

But the point is very clear—the politicians are resentful of Bartolomé because they lost the election. The ex-commissioners are very angry with Bartolomé because he himself is the one who went to talk in the office of General Efraín Ríos Montt to denounce all the assassinations committed by these men. They were responsible for the violence, and they went to jail. For that reason, they are not in agreement with Bartolomé. Now for revenge they are looking for falsehoods to put him in prison or kill him.

We are going to continue this episode to see how it comes out.

Story of the Patrolmen of the Autodefensa Civil
20 July 1987

I'm not going to say that civil defense patrols are cancelled because I know that the Congress of the Republic approved a law which says that it is an obligation to organize a civil defense committee in the towns. But right now it is quiet in the towns of San José, San Martín, San Jorge, San Benito, and San Luis. It's hardly functioning. But indeed in the other towns, the functions of the patrolmen continue. For example, in Santa Ana, Santa Bárbara, Santa Elena, and all the parts of El Quiché the patrols go on. The people of Santa Ana say that they always take turns from 6:00 in the afternoon to 6:00 in the morning every 10 days, depending on the number of men in the town.

Well, what happened in San José is that there has been a number of more than 400 persons from 18 to 60 years of age taking turns. They took turns by night and by day. A little later the *jefes* of the military zone of Sololá said that only those from 18 to 50 years of age could be pressed into service. Thus, the number of patrolmen went down to 378 persons. Eighteen shifts were composed of 20 patrolmen and one *jefe* per turn. That is to say, each person took a turn each 18 days.

I was in Group 16. The *jefe* of this shift was José Pantzay Cumes. We were pretty good in this group. When we went to keep watch on the town, two companions remained behind making coffee. Each patrolman gave 25 centavos to buy firewood, coffee, and bread. The group was divided into two parts, half for a turn from 6:00 p.m. to 12:00 midnight and the other half from midnight to 6:00 a.m. When one group entered to assume the shift of the other, the two groups would drink coffee and eat bread. Then one group would sleep and the other group would go out to guard the streets. They all had to sleep in the house of the military commissioners next to the municipality. The *jefe* would not get to sleep; he pulled a 12-hour shift.

I have to speak frankly. In my town, we hardly paid attention to looking for subversives. It is certain that 10 men guarded the town at a time. How can ten individuals confront a group of subversives, as if there were any, with sticks and machetes? So when the patrolmen were in the streets it was no more than fear for them, looking for a place to hide to pass the hours away. By the grace of God, not one group was attacked by the subversives.

There were problems between the groups, but these were very personal, or because of the drunks.

In the case of Group 16, many times I didn't take a turn because I had to work at night making bread and didn't go. I just sent bread to my companions. I get very hot baking bread and if I went out into the night, I would get very sick. It was a collaboration because they would not have to spend money on bread.

One night my companions didn't eat bread. More clearly, on this night I was not with them. Before drinking coffee, Clemente, Ignacio Amado, and Santiago got drunk. They say that when the *jefe* of this shift saw that these three patrolmen were drunk, he sent to call the *jefe* of the military commissioners. When this *jefe* arrived, these three patrolmen were taken to jail. They weren't let out until the night of the next day. The ex-commissioner asked them to give him money not to put them in jail, but they didn't. Then the ex-commissioner advised the military zone in Sololá that the three patrolmen had threatened him with death. These three patrolmen were under investigation.

I didn't realize this until my next shift. That night when we were taking a turn, these three companions were called again to the military zone in Sololá. Clemente, Ignacio Amado, and Santiago now had a lot of worries. Jorge and I went to the house of the man who was the then commissioner, Fernando Timoteo Ramos Castro, to tell him to go to Sololá to withdraw his accusation and take care of this problem.

He told us, "I don't have money for travel."

I told him, "I'm giving you Q10 to drop the matter. Have some consideration. It's another matter in the military zone. You are a commissioner, and they hardly speak Spanish. It's a question of their being drunk."

"Very well," he told me, and he went to Sololá. We had no further problems with the three patrolmen.

Until now, there are nine 97.62 mauser rifles, four 12-gauge shotguns, and two .22 rifles used by the commissioners and their assistants during patrols. The first two kinds of weapons are those of the military. One of the .22 rifles belonged to Homero Coché and the other to Hugo Zamora Tuc, both from the village of Pachichaj. The rifles were taken from their houses by the ex-commissioners during the regime of Lucas García and Ríos Montt when there was an order to collect all the arms. These weapons are now in the houses of the commissioners and their assistants (with all the other arms, not just the two .22 rifles). In the month of November of 1985, some days before the elections, the assistant commissioner, Samuel Hernández Flores, had a turn with a mauser. One night he went to visit his sister, wife of Juanito Mendoza, after hiding the rifle under the mattress of his bed. He was afraid that if he left it in plain view someone might steal it. He and his wife left, but they left a candle lit in the house. The candle fell down and caused a fire, burning all the bedding, street clothing, furniture, the mattress, and the rifle. All that was wood was consumed by the fire; all that was left was the steel. The next day, Samuel was taken to Sololá for an investigation of how this fire occurred in this house. A launch of military personnel arrived to investigate, and this same group took Samuel to Sololá. But it was all negative. Samuel wasn't guilty of anything, and he returned the same day.

In my town, the civil defense patrol served no purpose. We weren't in agreement with it, but we weren't able to say no because we were living under repression. Many of us poor people support our families with daily work. When we took our turns, our day-wages were lost as day laborers. It's true that in my town only 10 persons took turns guarding the exit to Santa Ana, to San Martín, and to San Jorge, but this shift never had merit. It only made us lose time and become poorer, causing more malnutrition for our children and more hardships for our wives. At times there wasn't any firewood and the women had to go to look for it to help their husbands, because if their husbands did not fulfill their turns they were thrown in jail.

When my town took turns of 10 persons during the day, it was a time when a man earned Q2.50. In a day, Q25 was lost, in a month Q750, and in a year Q9,000. This impaired us a lot and caused more suffering of poverty in a town so small. Well, in the big towns like San Luis, Samayac, Ixtahuacán, Santa Elena, they had 100 patrolmen daily. Thus, what they were calling us for was to have more poverty in all the towns. In these big towns mentioned above, they were taking turns during the day for more than a year. Thus, a lot of money was lost because of the lost days of work. The truth is that in my town, all of the above mentioned amount wasn't lost because we only took turns during the day for six or seven months.

The *jefes* did not realize how we live in our pueblos—the poverty, the ignorance, and the illnesses that afflict us so much. Going out on patrol was a loss of time and money. In the case of guard duty at night, sometimes the man comes too tired for the work because we work very hard in the fields, up to 12, sometimes 14 hours daily. Sometimes fulfilling the duty very tired and suffering was not worth the pain. One day the *jefes* of the military zone Sololá arrived, and we stated our problem to them. I wasn't the one who talked; I only helped to coordinate the muchachos so that they could talk in front of the *jefes*. The ones who spoke were Arden and Alberto. They told the *jefes* that they should have more consideration for us Indian people because in our town there are no subversives and because we are losing a lot of time and money, that Q9,000 a year was being lost, and that this is missed much by the poor. Then thanks to God, the *jefes* came to understand and ended the duty by day, leaving us the liberty to do our own work during the day.

When our brothers [fellow *patrulleros*, or patrolmen] of the other pueblo of San Martín saw that we were not standing duty by day, they did the same thing that we did. They stated their case to the *jefes*. They also were given the consideration, and they no longer did the duty by day. Like that, when the other pueblo of San Luis saw that San Martín and San José no longer stood guard, they also stated the same conditions and their day shifts were eliminated. No doubt, San Luis lost hundreds of quetzales daily because they would have shifts of more that 100 *patrulleros* in one day. So there was a big loss in the larger pueblos.

Well, in other pueblos, it still continued for a long time, more than one year. Undoubtedly, they now are standing guard by day around Chichicastenango, around all those parts where the violence is strongest. Without doubt, there are two reasons for this state of affairs: they don't have courage to state the problem to the *jefes*, but also some *jefes* are not interested in knowing the conditions of the poor, whether a person is eating or is hungry. They only order since they have a good salary, they have no cause to suffer the things of the poor. And the poor have to put up with it. But also we indigenous people are to blame in one respect because we don't have the courage to express to the *jefes* our feelings, our pain. Sometimes we only say, "Sí, sí, sí," and the *jefes* are very content when we say sí. But in my way of thinking, well, I always plan a little to express my feelings and to say what I feel. I'm not saying that we will fully achieve an objective but that, more or less, we have the discontent of telling the *jefes* what we feel.

Didn't you tell me that in Samayac, Santa Elena, and Ixtahuacán there still is daytime service?

Now?

Now.

Now there is none by day, only by night. Principally, where there is still guard duty by day is in the area of El Quiché.

When did the duty by day and by night begin?

Well, by night, they started first. Later they saw that the situation [unrest] in other places was more resistant, and they then obligated us to take turns by day. But, first it was started with duty by night in February of '83. Later they said that we would have to take shifts also by day. But, as I said, we only took shifts by day for about seven months, unlike in other pueblos where day shifts were prolonged for a long time. We took turns by day and night more in '83 and only in parts of '84.

The patrolmen of my town presented themselves for the night shift at 6:00 in the evening. At 8:00 or 9:00 p.m., the first shift left to watch the streets with 10 men. The other ten men slept in the headquarters of the commissioners. The *jefe* of the shift did not sleep, it was a little hard for him. All the nights when I was taking a turn, I wasn't able to sleep at all in this house because of the racket and fleas.[43]

The house where the *patrulleros* would gather is a house that the commissioners occupy. There were some *petates* (palm-mats) of *tul* [lake plant], where the ones taking a rest would sleep. During the times that I was taking turns, not one night could I sleep there because of the noise of the people that pass very close to the house. And also, in that house there are many fleas; one can't sleep at all. During the nights that I would do my turn, I would sit outside in the hallway, covering myself with a poncho. Like that I would stay all night. During all the time that I was doing my turn, I could not sleep a single night where my companions slept. It made me feel strange and sad that my people could sleep in these conditions. Although I'm very poor, I couldn't sleep. No, my body couldn't bear to be sleeping among those insects. We asked the *alcalde* to buy us a gallon of insecticide to kill the fleas. He didn't. We asked the commissioners, and they didn't either. They would do nothing to take a little care of our health.

We took turns patrolling at night for three years, until '86 when the new government (Democracia Cristiana) of Vinicio Cerezo Arévalo took possession. The first town to end the night patrols was San Martín, then San Luis, and then San José. Since the socialist party won in San Martín, the *Martineros* had a strong connection with Mario Solórzano Martínez,[44] the political leader of the socialist party in Guatemala City. And Solórzano had promised in a visit that he would end the duty if the socialist party won in San Martín, and that's what he did. The people were very happy. There were no longer problems in any of the patrols. Well, they cancelled everything.

Is there a patrol in San Luis?

Look, in San Luis, there is none. Now, there are no civil defense patrols, but what is there is a military detachment that is one kilometer from the town. Well, in one sense, it's good that they are called in these cases because they have a little bit of salary and have good weapons. Then, they can do something for us. But previously, it was the contrary. We were placed in front of the difficult things when we didn't have good arms, right, only a stick or a machete. But how can one battle with sticks? In no way.

In the big pueblos, for example in Quezaltenango and Guatemala, are there patrols?

In some parts. In the large cities, there are no patrols. Well, in the exact center of Quezaltenango, there are no patrols. In Guatemala [City], the capital city, there are no patrols. Otherwise, in the townships of Quezaltenango, in the areas, in the provinces, there are patrols.

In the countryside?

Yes, there are. Well, in the history of Guatemala, there is one department, Totonicapán, that didn't accept the patrols at all. Its representatives made many trips to Guatemala to talk with General Ríos Mont and to the ministers of state.

Have there been any shifts in San José this year, 1987?

After the patrols had been abolished in 1986 in my town, the *jefes* of the shifts said, "It's okay for whoever wants to take a turn. There isn't much obligation." In the month of February of 1986, there were times when three or four patrolmen arrived, and nights when none did. In July of 1986, the military arrived to say it was essential to reorganize the committee of self-defense and continue with the turns.

"Yes," said the patrolmen, and they complied two or three nights. When it was time for Group 16 to takes its turn, only three of us arrived. And the three people left too.

Only when the agents get here, the commissioners gather the people to take a little more care there to guard the town. But it is useless to take care, we don't have good arms, only single-shell shotguns. One can do nothing with the enemies. In addition, by the grace of God, into San José they haven't come. It's been years since they came here, but since then they haven't come again.[45] They say that where many guerrillas go is to the *aldea*, Pachichaj. Now, in San José in the very core of the municipality, they haven't come recently.

Are there still turns in Pachichaj?

Yes, there still are turns in parts of the municipal district of San José.

Dream of Crystal Clear Water
22 July 1987

I dreamed I was in my town. The place I saw had been the source of a small river. From the river came water very crystal clear. I felt very content in my dream, and I told my wife, "Let's bathe in this very clean water."

She told me, "We need to keep the water in a cask [or keg]."

"Yes," I said, "run to get a cask."

Then the water we kept in the cask, but I dreamed that the cask was full, and we spilled water in the place. But what was more strange was that the water that was coming out of the spring was very crystal clear and clean. I realized this when I left my clothing in the house and bathed with this water.

There is a belief that when a person dreams that he or she bathes with rainwater or crystal water, there will be good luck. I expect God will have something good for me in the future.

This dream was in Panajachel at 4:30 a.m. When I woke up, I looked at my watch.

Another Episode of San Luis
1 August 1987

Each day the violence continues in San Luis. What no ones knows is exactly which of the two forces (left or right) is the cause of the death of the Tzutuhiles. One version says that the death of a lot of people is caused by the right, the other says that it is the subversion that is killing. But more say that it is the right.

On 1 August, Saturday, I was chatting with Juanito Quit, the *curandero*. Earlier I had news of the death of the military commissioner of San Luis, and moreover, the death of an old man of 80 years. But I had no concrete piece of news. Not until this Saturday did I have the opportunity to speak with the *curandero* who arrived in the house to treat José's foot. He told me that it was true that Friday, 17 July, the military commissioner of San Luis was assassinated. They gave him death when he was spreading insecticide on his cultivation in a place called Cerro de Tamalaj, an *aldea* of San Luis. Very near where they killed the commissioner, they also killed an old man, whom they found cleaning beans. The people say that the old man recognized those who had killed the commissioner and so that he would not tell who they were, they killed the old hombre. This is what they thought because they found the two bodies close together. Juanito told me that this event was certain because on this day he passed through San Luis, coming from the coast where he had been curing bones, and he heard everything the people were saying but that already the bodies could not be seen, just the commentary of the people who were saying that the commissioner and the old man were killed by the subversives.

There was also violence on the night of the 25th to the dawn of the 26th of July. But no one knows who it was. There was hardly an investigation. It seems that the people are accustomed to it and now don't feel sadness at looking at bodies.

The news says that during the night of this day an Indian man about 33 years old was hacked to death with a machete. The cadaver of this man was found at the airfield in the place called, "La Bahía de San Luis," about three kilometers from the military detachment. Some say that drunk soldiers did it, but others say it was subversives who did it as a *burla* [taunt, gibe] because it was pretty close to the detachment. In any case, it is known that a particular group caused the death; it attacked three persons who were walking, but two of the victims escaped. The escapees said it was a group of men and that the attackers had only killed one of them.

Money Problems
1 August 1987

My daughter, María, came home yesterday to tell me that she needed money for other expenses, but it was a pity that I didn't have the money that she needed. After working in the afternoon on this Saturday, I had to go to San Martín to talk to Herberto Pantzay. Since June this man had promised to give me money as the anticipated price of coffee. So I went to Herberto's to see if he would give Q200. But Herberto told me that he had a problem with his trucks, and for that reason, he didn't have money to give to coffee sellers.

I went to Jaime Cojox to offer him 500 sprigs from the nursery. Jaime told me he had the same problem. He needed the coffee seed, but he didn't have money to buy it because he also had a student in the institute (INVO) [Instituto Normal para Varones de Occidente, Teachers' Training Institute for Young Men of the West] of Quezaltenango.

I went to the house of Pascual Soto Ixtamer to offer him some avocado orchards, that is, to sell him the harvest, but Pascual told me that all his money was invested in the avocado business, but, thanks to God, this friend helped me with Q50. I arrived home at 9:00 at night. I suffered a lot to obtain the money.

Marino Cintora Is Ambushed in San Luis
Sunday, 2 August 1987

Sunday, 2 August, all day I was making bread for the Central American Church. The members gave me the material; we only charged for the work. At 4:00 in the afternoon of this day, Radio Fabulosa of the capital of Guatemala announced the violence perpetrated in San Luis at 9:00 in the morning of this same day when the pickup of Marino Cintora was ambushed and he was killed. The news says that Marino left his house at 7:00 a.m. to go to the summit of Jiote to get some avocadoes belonging to some

Sanluiseros. When he returned from the trip, he passed through the Pepinal *finca*, taking some women to the market and three other men, two of whom were going to take classes in the military reserve at the detachment. They say the two reservists were accompanying their father. They were almost to Bahía de San Luis when a group of armed men appeared. Radio Fabulosa announced this event at 4:00 in the afternoon. It only announced the name of the father of the two boys, Jaime Ixtamer, but not the names of the two boys. The announcer also said the driver's name was Marino Cintora. The armed men indicated for him to stop, and he did. Then the men bent over the car to the two reservists and told them, "Get out the car, we have something pending with you."

They got out, but the father asked the men, "If my sons owe something, I'm able to pay it for them. Don't kill them!"

Then the men said, "If they are your sons, come with us." Then they took the father and his two sons below the coffee grove very near the road where they machine-gunned them.

Then the driver, who was the owner of the car, asked the men, "Why did you kill these men? I can testify that these three men you have just killed are honorable men. But, yes, I know you are always the ones that commit this kind of crime in the town of San Luis, not the subversion."

The men said. "Well, one of you we are going to kill."

Marino answered, "Kill me! God and the people know that you are the assassins." Thus it was when Señor Marino Cintora was machine-gunned.

This information the radio did not give in total. The women who witnessed this bloody deed said it. The one who gave this information to me was Desiderio, a *Joseño* who works in a marimba group that had left its car at the house of Marino Cintora, who was in charge of watching the car. For that reason, this boy knew what had happened, and he says that he saw the bodies of the four murdered men.

They also say that not until this Sunday did they kill the two men who had escaped when a group was slashing their companion with a machete on the night of 25 July. The only crime of these two men who also were killed was that they had criticized the killers who had intended to kill them too, had they not run a lot to get away.

Desiderio told me that there were no investigations of any of these killings. The people didn't feel tranquil because during the 45 hours that they were playing marimba music the people disappeared. That is, everyone had gone home by 8:00 at night. Only the members of the *cofradía* remained because they stayed sleeping in the house of the *alcalde*. They didn't go home until the next day.

A Separate Episode of San Martín
31 July to 9 August 1987

Bartolomé Yac,[46] mayor of San Martín, continues to be slandered, his enemies saying that he is a thief and communist because he has taken a lot of money from the municipality. His enemies didn't want him to be in the mayor's office anymore.

On 31 July, Friday, the members of an Evangelical church named Esmirna, members of the Unión del Centro Nacional party, some of the ex-commissioners that were previously jailed, two councilors, and the syndic united into one force to eliminate the office of Bartolomé Yac. They did this for personal revenge and politics. If they had been able to do it well, Bartolomé would have been relieved of his position.

His enemies in the tribunal drew up an act allowing the first councilor to be proprietary mayor of the office. It's true that also there was a majority that was in favor of the mentioned Bartolomé, but they were unable to help him because his enemies are more brusque. And Bartolomé said that everyone should have patience and not to use brute force, so Bartolomé's supporters were calm.

Bartolomé went to the supreme electoral court to fight for his innocence. He was not in agreement with the dismissal that they gave him. But his enemies did not realize that the ex-mayor went to Guatemala [City], declaring all the injustice, his record, and the previous record of the councilors. The court took steps according to the law.

On Wednesday, 5 August, came the order of the court that Bartolomé was to be reincorporated immediately to the mayorship of San Martín. The supreme electoral court sent the order to the mayor's office of San José la Laguna for the mayor of San José to give the oath so that Bartolomé would be the mayor and no one else. Bartolomé was sworn in again at 7:00 p.m., Wednesday. His enemies did not go, but those in favor of him arrived to witness the dismissal of the first councilor, who had only been in power for six days. When Bartolomé was reincorporated in his office, there was a fiesta with a lot of firecrackers and *bombas*. I was in San Martín on this afternoon, and I saw what happened.

On Thursday, 6 August, the enemies of the mayor organized a general meeting for the whole town to ask again for his dismissal, but they could do nothing. His enemies announced the general meeting, but in the afternoon there was protection of the mayor by the national army. With the help of the army, the enemies of the mayor were unable to arrive in front of the municipality. All was calm. José Horacio, José Manuel, and I went to San Martín to see what was going to happen, but when we arrived, the army had already left on the boat, and all the people were happy. We thought that when the soldiers had left the town, there would be a new meeting for the manifestation. But now nothing happened. We left San Martín at 9:00 p.m.

Constantly the enemies of Bartolomé go around saying that he is a thief and communist, claiming he has stolen a lot of money from the municipality and has misused the funds. Then it was decided to check the accounts to clarify the situation with regard to the state of the treasury, although previously they already had been checked and audited by the national comptroller's office, concluding that the mayor and the treasurer are functioning well in their office. They did it because of the misunderstanding of the people who go around saying false things.

On 9 August, the mayor, Bartolomé Yac García, asked all the people to come to the front of the municipality to clarify the situation. Moreover he sent a note to each Catholic and Evangelical church. Well, when all the people were united, the mayor and the treasurer took out all the books, documents, and receipts as well as the quantity of money that existed. Then the mayor ordered everyone to approach and check for faults, promising them that if they found some embezzlement of funds or a false document or a quantity of money lacking, then he would agree to hand over the office and be consigned before the courts of justice to be sentenced by the law. But in all the examination conducted by his enemies, nothing false was found. Everything was in order. The members of the church, Esmirna, the members of the Unión del Centro Nacional party, and the ex-commissioners were ridiculed and embarrassed in front of the rest of the citizens who witnessed these things. The councilmen and the syndic were unable to speak because they had criticized Bartolomé for being a thief and communist. But the truth is that Bartolomé came out triumphant, and the people congratulated the mayor and said that they didn't want more lies and that no one can tell more lies against the mayor.

To this point, that was this problem of the *Martineros*, but who knows if the enemies will be silent or continue with another new falsehood.

Epilogue

Ignacio's Family

I closed Ignacio's diary with the episode about how Bartolomé Yac, the socialist mayor of San Martín, was being treated by his townspeople, because it was the last in a series of pages that I edited during my six week field period in Guatemala while working with Ignacio in the summer of 1987, and it made a natural ending for the present volume. But there is no real closure to his life history. As of the writing of this epilogue in January 1991, Ignacio was alive and recording what he considers to be significant events of his life, but with a new concern. Teachers in Sololá have learned about a Maya author in one of the towns of Lake Atitlán, perhaps from seeing Son of Tecún Umán *and* Campesino *for sale in Antigua or by reading Mike Salovesh's positive review in the journal* Mesoamérica, *which is published in Spanish and distributed in Guatemala. The teachers are trying to discover who the author is.*

On the negative side, the violence, although more sporadic, has continued around Lake Atitlán, especially in San Luis, where there is a nearby military detachment. A famous artist was assassinated, and there are periodic skirmishes between the army and guerrillas. San José and San Martín continued to fight over water rights, a problem exacerbated by the growing numbers of inhabitants in both towns. The factionalism over Father José's reforms continued to sharply divide the community. A national strike in 1989 created new problems with the teachers in San José.

On the positive side, Ignacio's investing in two footlooms and hiring an instructor to teach his son José Juan to weave has paid off. In fact, his entire family has benefited from the introduction of a new weaving project that exports Mayan textiles to international markets, especially to the United States.

As Ignacio's children become adults, some of his problems have become more complicated. He and his wife, Anica, became grandparents, but it was a mixed blessing. In her last year of school to become a teacher, María got pregnant and dropped out to marry José Mario, who, according to María, promised her a better life. They ended up living in Ignacio's sitio, but José Mario deserted María and took up with Ignacio's sister, who is much older than he is. With some reluctance due to the demands of rearing her own young children, Anica agreed to take care of María's baby while María returned to the teachers' institute in Quezalte-nango to finish her degree.

Unlike José Juan's first common-law marriage to Carolina, which failed because he refused to convert to Protestantism, his second common-law marriage to María succeeded. Living in Ignacio's sitio, however, has created some friction, although José Juan and María set up their own kitchen and are not a financial burden to Ignacio. María also had a baby.

In July of 1989 a doctoral candidate in anthropology from Texas arrived in San José and asked Ignacio if he were the author of Campesino. Ignacio suspected that the student revealed his identity to a local teacher who also queried him. The doctoral candidate began using his ex-son-in-law, José Mario, as a research assistant. Later, José Mario was bragging in the streets that he would have a book with the anthropology student, but Ignacio was skeptical, stating that a book takes a lot of work and help from God and that "the dog that barks never dies."

National Political Violence and Turmoil

Since the CIA sponsored the 1954 coup that overthrew the freely elected reformist government of Colonel Jacobo Arbenz Gúzman, Guatemala has been ruled primarily by the military, even during the regimes of the civilian presidents Julio César Méndez Montenegro (1966–1970) and Vinicio Cerezo Arévalo (1986–1990). During these 36 years, it is estimated that more than 100,000 people have been killed and 50,000 have disappeared. According to most observers, including Am-nesty International and the American Embassy, most of the killing has been at the hands of the army and the extreme right. Moreover, the army stated it had destroyed 440 towns and villages.

In 1985, in addition to permitting popular elections of municipal tribunals and replacing military appointees, General Oscar Humberto Mejía Víctores, who had become chief of state in a coup ousting Ríos Montt in 1983, permitted the return to presidential elections. Cerezo Arévalo, a 43-year-old lawyer, cam-paigned for president on a platform to reduce the power of the military and curb the abuse of human rights.

"On the night of Cerezo's inauguration, at least 50,000 people jammed the main square of Guatemala City, dancing, singing, and cheering in an emotional display of hope and confidence in their youthful new leader" (Bebusmann 1986:15). When he won, hopes were raised in Guatemala and abroad that the military

would be reined in and progress would be made toward alleviating glaring poverty and social injustice.

Cerezo did disband the despised Department of Technical Investigations linked to the death squads, although no one in the agency was charged with any crime and all the angency's files have disappeared. His strong position that the civil defense patrols should be voluntary enabled many towns to disband the despised patrols. He returned 8 percent of the national budget to the municipalities for much needed improvements. Although opposed by big business organizations such as the Comité Coordinador de Asociaciones Agrícolas, Comerciales, Industriales y Financieras (CACIF, Coordinating Committee of Agricultural, Commercial, Industrial and Financial Associations), he made progress toward direct taxation. Unlike the existing system that emphasized sales taxes, the new system would put more of the burden on the rich than on the middle class and poor, a recommendation by the International Monetary Fund that Mejía shelved (Volman 1985:15; Latin American Regional Reports, Mexico & Central America 1989a).

Some of Cerezo's economic measures, however, did more harm than good to the poor. The release of price controls on basic commodities, the continuation of the value-added tax, and the devaluation of the quetzal all adversely affected the lower classes. Inflation and unemployment grew. Cerezo was unable to persuade the private sector to raise salaries to offset the increase in prices.

Although there was a significant decline in the number of kidnappings and murders after Cerezo took office, he was unable to halt such abuses completely nor did he investigate the status of the "disappeared" as the Grupo de Apoyo Mutuo para Familiares de Desaparecidos (GAM, Mutual Support Group for Relatives of the Disappeared) had hoped. Moreover, not a single military officer was prosecuted for human rights offenses.

During Cerezo's four-year tenure in office, the U.S. provided almost $1 billion in economic and military aid (Hackel 1990:8). *At first Cerezo resisted the Reagan administration's trying to give military aid to Guatemala's security forces, stating that the real challenge for Guatemala was not to have the best army in Central America but the best democracy* (Latin American Regional Reports, Mexico & Central America 1986:8). *By 1989, however, Cerezo was requesting lethal military equipment. The U.S. House Subcommittee on the Western Hemisphere Affairs had prohibited the sale of lethal arms to the Cerezo government, an 11-year-old policy since the Carter administration had cut off military aid completely. The Bush administration argued that lethal weapons were needed by the Guatemalan Army to fight Guatemala's Marxist insurgency. The full Committee on Foreign Affairs took up the issue in the middle of June.*

With the help of Democratic Representative Stephen Solarz, the Bush admin-
istration won a compromise allowing sales of M16 rifles and ammunition begin-
ning 1 October 1989. It was rumored that Solarz, an influential committee
member, received a personal phone call from Cerezo assuring Solarz that military
aid would not endanger his civilian government and that he needed the aid to
appease the military. Permission for this sale passed the full House on 29 June
(Latin American Regional Reports, Mexico & Central America *1989b:7*).

In 1986 the government was unable to stop human rights abuses. Depending
on the source, there were between 79 and 160 political murders and 131 to 463
kidnappings (Ford 1987:12; Latin American Regional Reports, Mexico &
Central America *1987c:6*). *Compared to previous years, massive repression clearly*
had given way to selective repression. Still, toward the end of the year, there was an
upsurge of abductions and killings with 137 disappearances between November
1986 and February 1987. Also several persons received death threats by the Ejército
Secreto Anticomunista (ESA), an extrajudicial organization linked to death
squads (Latin American Regional Reports, Mexico & Central America
1987b:8). *The government claimed that criminals might have been responsible for*
the increase. Nevertheless, the number of "disappearances" continued, including
those of four Catholic activists. Their abductions could hardly be attributable to
criminals. As Bowen (1987) points out, since the army by this time had the upper
hand in the civil war, ignoring such abuses by soldiers could no longer be justified
by reference to the exigencies of war.

Cerezo admitted publicly that 1,706 Guatemalans disappeared during 1988.
He claimed, however, that 90 percent of the cases had been solved and that 60
percent were of domestic, not political origin (Latin American Regional Reports, Mexico & Central America *1989b:4*).

GAM and the Oficina de Información del Sector Empresarial (OFISEM,
Office of Information of the Management Sector), the information office of big
business, reported that from January to July of 1989, 1,598 people were murdered,
2,517 injured, and 906 "disappeared." Defense Minister Héctor Gramajo identi-
fied death squad members as army dissidents linked to big business and the
extreme right who he claimed turned to terrorism after they failed to pull off a
military coup in May of 1989 (Latin American Regional Reports, Mexico &
Central America *1989d:3*).

Amnesty International reported that there had been a resurgence of kidnap-
pings and extrajudicial killings in 1988 and 1989. Moreover, there were more than
200 unresolved cases of "disappearances" between January 1986 and January 1989
in which the evidence points to complicity on the part of the government. The
victims crosscut society, including campesinos, members of peasant organizations,

journalists, clergy, academics, and especially students. Eyewitnesses reported kidnappings by armed men in civilian clothes, using white vans, known as death vans. In March 1988 members of the guardia de hacienda *[treasury police] were arrested. The national police collected overwhelming evidence implicating them, but the judge in charge of the case was kidnapped for 52 hours by* desconocidos *and afterwards the accused were released for lack of evidence.*

Several agencies reported the increase in human rights violations in 1990. The associate procurator for human rights, César Alvarez Guadamuz, said 163 persons were murdered in the first six months of 1990 and 103 were abducted or disappeared (Latin American Regional Reports, Mexico & Central America *1990a:3). Article 19, a London based human rights group, reported that 585 people were killed by the security forces and paramilitary squads in the first 8 months of 1990* (Latin American Regional Reports, Mexico & Central America *1990d: 4). For the entire year more than 1,000 people were murdered* (U.S. News and World Report *1990:17), including, on 8 June, the beheading of Michael DeVine, an expatriate North American who had run a tourist ranch near Poptún, Petén, for the last 19 years. Witnesses identified a pickup known as a "death truck" that belonged to the army. State department officials warned that they would cut military aid, which totaled $3.3 million in 1988, if the murder was not fully investigated. Although Guatemalan authorities took credit for identifying the suspects, the evidence was collected by an independent investigator hired by DeVine's widow, Carole. Nevertheless, the rapid progress in solving the case drew resentment in Guatemala. Opposition congressman Skinner Klee stated, "They kill one gringo and whole world moves, but they kill Guatemalans every day and nothing happens"* (New York Times *1990b; 1989c).*

The New York Times *(1990a), however, reported that the case of two other gringos who had disappeared was moving much slower than the DeVine case. An aspiring young journalist, Nicolas Blake, and a Maya merchant and amateur photographer, Griffen Davis, disappeared while hiking through an area of the Guatemalan highlands thought to be occupied by the Organización del Pueblo en Armas [ORPA, Organization of the People in Arms]. They were last seen near the* aldea *of El Llano. Blake, who sympathized with the poor and oppressed in Guatemala, had just completed a novel about a young North American journalist who was killed while traveling with guerrillas.*

At first Blake's prosperous Philadelphia family thought the guerrillas were responsible, but they changed their minds. From summer vacations in Maine, they knew Vice-President Bush's daughter Dorothy, who appealed to her father. Bush telephoned General Oscar Mejía Víctores, then chief of state, but to no avail. In 1987 a Guatemalan teacher familiar with the people of El Llano told U.S.

Embassy officials that villagers had told her that five civil patrolmen had escorted the two North Americans out of their village and shot them. For two years, U.S. officials requested the army to locate the patrolmen and question them. When Bush appointed Thomas Strook, a former classmate at Yale, ambassador to Guatemala in 1989, he instructed him to pursue the case.

On 27 March 1990, two of the patrolmen were questioned, but they denied any knowledge of the two missing gringos. The family continued trying to get Guatemalan officials to question the other three patrolmen. General Héctor Alejandro Gramajo Morales, who was then defense minister,[47] denied a cover-up to prevent the exposure of those responsible for the North Americans as well as the disappearance of some 50,000 Guatemalans.

The killings in 1990 also included Myrna Elizabeth Mack Chang, a Guatemalan anthropologist. She was stabbed repeatedly in Guatemala City presumably because she was investigating the situation of refugees and people displaced because of the political violence (Manz 1990).

On 2 December 1990, the army opened fire on Tzutuhil Indians of Santiago Atitlán who were protesting abuses of the military stationed just outside their town. Newspaper reports varied on the number of killed and wounded. An army news release said 10 civilians were killed and 17 wounded. However, a reporter for the independent television channel Noti-7 said 25 were killed and 71 injured—all of them Indians and most of them children. The townspeople collected more than 15,000 signatures and thumbprints protesting the massacre, and bus drivers and restaurant owners in Guatemala City flew black flags in honor of the slain. Under such pressure, the army relocated their detachment (Associated Press 1990:15; Reuters 1990:A7; Hackel 1990:8).

Later in the same month, the U.S. State Department froze $2.8 million in U.S. military assistance to the Guatemalan government because of the army's role in human rights violations. However, about $100 million was still earmarked for economic aid in 1991 (Hackel 1990:8). If the bulk of such aid actually reaches the poor, it certainly is needed. Guatemala has suffered 41 percent unemployment, 42 percent inflation, and 70 percent still live in dire poverty (U.S. News and World Report *1990:17*).

The crisis in the Persian Gulf has exacerbated the economic problems. Even though Guatemala is the only Central American country currently producing oil, exporting 4,000 barrels a day to the U.S., Raúl Castañeda, minister of energy and mines, announced a 42 percent increase in the price of oil, claiming that the government could not bear the huge increase in the price of imported oil and subsidized oil consumption (Latin American Regional Reports, Mexico & Central America *1990b:6*).

In January of 1991, the body of Oscar Agusto Miranda, a leader of GAM, was found mutilated. Government officials have accused members of GAM as having links with leftists (Latin American Regional Reports, Mexico & Central America *Jan 1991:3*).

Local and National Elections

On the local level, Ignacio's political rival, Juan Mendoza Ovalle, was elected alcalde *again in 1988. His attempt to jail the outgoing mayor for misuse of municipal funds created ill will in the town.*

On the national level, when Cerezo assumed the office of president in 1986, he never expected to hold more than 30 percent of the power during his first two years in office and no more than 70 percent at the end (Bazzy 1986:23; Perera 1986:25). It was painfully clear that Cerezo never realized even 51 percent of the power. By the end of his administration, he seemed paralyzed from fear that the military would replace him.

Throughout Central America, both the Reagan and Bush administrations have equated elections with democracy. The electronic and printed media seemed to be reinforcing this belief in their reporting on the significance of the 1989 presidential election in Guatemala. An open and fair vote is a step in the right direction, but countries where free speech is repressed and where the politicians and the populace are under the thumb of the military hardly warrant the label of democracy (Hess 1990:20; U.S. News and World Report *1990).*

In the Guatemalan election, there were a dozen candidates, most of them rightist. The ex dictator, General Ríos Montt, launched a write-in ballot even though the constitution expressly forbade candidates who had been president by coup from running. In October the Guatemalan Supreme Court ruled that Ríos Montt's attempt at the presidency was unconstitutional. This left two contenders, Jorge Carpio Nicolle and Jorge Serrano Elías, for a run-off election on 7 January 1991. Both had run for the presidency in 1985.

Carpio, running for the Unión del Centro Nacional (UCN) party, is a conservative newspaper magnate (proprietor of El Gráfico *and* La Razón*). Serrano, running for the Movimiento de Acción Solidaria (MAS, Movement of Solidarity Action), is a conservative Protestant businessman who headed the council of state under General Efraín Ríos Montt. When Ríos Montt was declared ineligible, his backers switched to Serrano, who won, like Cerezo before him, with 68 percent of the vote (*Time *1985:40; Ostling 1991:86).*

Only 56.3 percent of the registered voters participated in the 11 November

*elections. The high rate of abstention in the departments of El Quiché, El Petén,
and Izabel may be accounted for in part by the Unidad Revolucionaria Nacional
Guatemalteca (URNG) guerrillas telling voters to stay home and by the general
lack of transportation in rural areas. Also, unlike in 1985, voting was not
mandatory in 1989. People didn't have to be afraid of being accused of communism
if they didn't vote* (Latin American Regional Reports, Mexico & Central
America 1990c). *The most import explanation for not voting, however, appears to
be apathy. Many have lost faith in democracy and equate it with anarchy. Hackel
(1991:8) cited a 19-year-old scavenger named Germán who said, "We don't have
much faith in our country's political leaders here. They talk and talk and talk and
the words fly in the wind."*

   *Critics worry that the shift to the right in Guatemalan politics may lead not
only to more repression modeled after the brutal tactics of Ríos Montt but also to
increased tension between Roman Catholics and Protestants. Hackel (1991:8)
quoted Jorge Skinner Klee, "The danger is if Serrano gets to be president and
looks upon it as a gift from God, then we've all had it. Then Serrano will really get
us into bloody confrontation."*

Appendix

Summary of Ignacio's Life to the Beginning of the Present Volume

Born on 13 August 1941, Ignacio was abandoned by his real father, Jesús Ujpán García, and mother, Elena Bizarro Soto. He was reared by his mother's sister, María Bizarro, and her husband, Martín Coj, a heavy-drinking shaman. For that reason, Ignacio took the first surname, Bizarro, of his aunt rather than the first surname, Ujpán, of his real father, which is the custom in Guatemala. He retained Ujpán as his second surname. Altogether, Ignacio has eleven half but no whole brothers and sisters by his real father and mother, who went separate ways after Ignacio was born.

Although an excellent student, Ignacio only completed the third grade because in 1953 that was the highest grade available in his town. He was too poor to leave San José to continue his education elsewhere.

In 1957, when Ignacio was 16 years of age, he fell in love with a 14-year old girl, Lucía Mendez, and tried to get married in the neighboring town, San Martín. The priest, however, refused to marry them because they were too young. Feeling hurt and depressed, for the first time in his life, Ignacio got drunk.

A year later, Ignacio fell in love again. This time it was with a señorita named Julia Méndez. They married in a traditional wedding ceremony consisting of the groom giving gifts of food and clothing to the bride's family and the exchanging of vows. Unfortunately, within six months, irreconcilable differences caused the union to fail and they separated.

Later in the same year, Ignacio fell in love with a pretty señorita named Josefa Ramos. They did not perform the traditional marriage ceremony but nevertheless began living together. In less than a year they too separated. Drinking heavily, Ignacio decided to join the Guatemalan Army in 1960 along with his cousin Ignacio Mendoza, who had already separated from his woman. Ignacio stated, "We were in the same situation. Two Ignacios in the same disgrace."

In the military, Ignacio became more exposed to Ladino culture and improved his Spanish, although Tzutuhil Maya was his mother tongue. While assigned to protect the paymaster of the Agricultural Company in Tiquisate, he learned of the huge banana fincas that paid what seemed to Ignacio large amounts of money to its employees. After his tour of duty in the army ended, Ignacio returned to the fincas first as a regular laborer and then as a labor contractor.

In 1961, while still serving in the army, Ignacio was placed on alert because students from the University of San Carlos were demonstrating against Guatemala's government allowing the CIA to train Cuba expatriates for the Bay of Pigs fiasco. Ignacio did not know the reason that the students were demonstrating. Nevertheless, his general intelligence enabled him to rise to the rank of sergeant.

After returning to civilian life, Ignacio reunited with Josefa (Anica) Ramos. On 2 November 1962, they were married by the justice of peace and the following day in the Catholic Church. They began an impoverished married life, Ignacio working as a jornalero *(day-laborer) and campesino and Anica taking care of the home and helping in the campo when possible. Their first two children died of the measles. To escape the haunting memories of deceased loved ones in their house, they migrated to the southern coast as farm laborers, working on the cotton fincas.*

In 1967 Ignacio and Anica celebrated the birth of their next child, José Juan Bizarro Ramos. He too caught the measles but survived.

In 1968 four of Ignacio's family, including his foster mother and aunt María, went to work in a cuadrilla *on the Caoba Farm on the coast. When they returned, María celebrated their homecoming by drinking liquor. She fell, hit her head on a chest, and died. His adoptive father, Martín, accused Ignacio of killing María while drunk; but his maternal grandmother, living in her* sitio *adjacent to Ignacio's, vouched that Ignacio had not touched a drop of alcohol.*

In 1969 a labor contractor, Andrían Sánchez García, of San Martín, asked him to be his assistant, organizing cuadrillas *from San José to work on the southern fincas. Because of a promise of regular pay, Ignacio agreed.*

I met Ignacio in 1970 during my first field season in San José. He became my research assistant, helping me interview a random sample of household heads as a part of a larger field project studying cultural change and stability in the Lake Atitlán region. Ignacio worked with me again in 1971 and 1972. At the end of my third field season in 1972, I asked him to write his autobiography and keep a diary of the significant events as they unfolded in his family and town. My main motive was to keep in touch with what was happening in San José while I was in Santa Monica, California, finishing my dissertation, and to establish a research project for which I could pay him. To my delight he agreed.

Ignacio vividly recorded the devastation and terror of the earthquake of 4 February 1976. Later in the same year he told of his successful campaign for the office of syndic in the municipal government only to resign before completing his term because of corruption by his former friend, the mayor, Juan Mendoza. To this day, Mendoza is Ignacio's most significant political rival in San José.

Realizing that he had a severe drinking problem, Ignacio joined Alcoholics Anonymous in October of 1976. He managed to stay sober until 20 February 1979, when, during an upsurge of political violence throughout Guatemala, a young man in the neighboring rival town of San Martín was found hanging by his belt from a tree. Ignacio again was falsely accused of murder and a band of desconocidos *was sent to capture him. The persecution that Ignacio suffered seems to have been instigated by an envious businessman of San Martín who was upset over Ignacio's role in establishing an agricultural cooperative in San José that took business away from San Martín. In any case, the pressure of dodging the death squad and clearing his name drove him back to alcohol.*

On 27 July 1979, Ignacio's wife Anica, who was 32 years old, gave birth to a baby girl named Anica Cantana. This was her their sixth surviving child. At this time their eldest son, José, would be 12 in October; their eldest daughter, María, was 11; their next son, Ramón Antonio, was 7; their youngest son, Erasmo Ignacio, was 5; and their next youngest daughter, Susana Julia, would be 3 in October. With a steadily growing family, Ignacio has played a leading role in improving education in his home town. He also has struggled to teach himself and his children trades such as baking.

Perhaps the most dramatic psychological impact on Ignacio's family, which occurred from 1980 to 10 May 1983, was the political violence due to insurgency and counterinsurgency. Ignacio recorded numerous incidents, including the following ones. He and a schoolteacher, Julia Isabel, were detained by guerrillas from Organization of People in Arms (ORPA) on a road between San Martín and San José. Julia was terrified, but less than 8 months later, while three months pregnant, she was raped and murdered by army personnel, not the guerrillas. Guerrillas, however, burned buses and cremated alive a driver's assistant outside of Panajachel. On the same day, to make a point, the army killed 16 humble Indians dressed in the traje of Sololá, *claiming that there had been a confrontation with the guerrillas.*

In San José, the army kidnapped two masons and assassinated a young woman suspected of being a communist. When Ignacio tried to resign from the official political party, Partido Institucional Democrático (PID), he was told that a person who leaves the party is taken as a subversive and executed. To guard against guerrilla intrusion into San José, Ignacio and his fellow townsmen were forced to participate in the unpopular civil defense patrols. In San Luis, a North American priest was murdered by the right, and the army ambushed a shaman accused of performing ceremonies for the guerrillas.

In San Martín, military commissioners extorted, kidnapped, and killed scores of citizens. Finally, in Santa Bárbara guerrillas killed a military commissioner, cutting off his fingers, cutting out his tongue, cutting off his testicles and hanging them around his neck, and crucifying him to a tree.

Meanwhile Ignacio and the people of San José attempted to maintain as much normalcy in their lives as possible during the reign of terror. Ignacio participated in the Christmas celebration of Las Posadas. He became alcalde *of the* cofradía *of the Virgin Mary and patron of the Dance of the Mexicans. Earlier, he had just been a dancer and did not have opportunity to learn to learn the folklore behind the dance. In fact, by the time of the writing of this appendix in January of 1991, Ignacio had managed to serve in enough key civil and religious offices in his community to become a* principal, *or town elder.*

Notes

1. Norman Schwartz (1990) published an excellent account of the history of the Petén region and current developments there, including civil instability and the destruction of the rain forests. For a revealing account of the impact of the most recent cycle of violence, which depended in part on the Guatemalan army's reaction to a perceived threat in a given zone, see Carmack (1988). For a holistic cultural introduction to Ignacio's life story see Sexton (1981), and for a thematic analysis of the first volume of Ignacio's story see Sexton (1982). An historical summary of cultural and political developments in Guatemala is in the appendices of Sexton (1985). Research results of an earlier project examining modernization, development, and demography, from which Ignacio's life history emerged, appears in Sexton (1972, 1978, 1979a, 1979b), Woods (1975), and Sexton and Woods (1977, 1982).

2. As in *Son of Tecún Umán* and *Campesino*, I have tried to stay as close as possible to Ignacio's own words, but once more I have used a free translation where needed for stylistic and grammatical reasons. In translating I have relied mainly on García-Pelayo Y Gross and Durand (1976), Armas (1971), Robb (1980), Arriola (1973), Cárdenas (1987), and Rubio (1982). If a Spanish or Indian word appears in *Webster's Ninth New Collegiate Dictionary* with the same English definition as my usage, I did not italicize it. The first time I used an italicized word I defined it in brackets. If the reader forgets the meaning of an italicized word, he or she will find it in the glossary at the end of the book.

To aid in organizing the document and avoid unnecessary repetitions, I have contributed most of the subtitles of episodes, except the following which were named by Ignacio: "The Life of a *Principal*"; "The Case of my Granny"; "A Little About Religions: Charismatics"; "The Tzutuhiles of San Luis Have Been Living and Continue Living Their Lives in Fear and Anguish"; "Political Activity Everywhere in Guatemala"; "Coffee, a Much Appreciated Product in My Town; Problems that Don't End, They Just Change Their Names"; "The Insects Also Do Justice"; and "A Separate Episode of San Luis".

3. The Guatemalan navy is an integral part of the army, under control of the Army General Staff (Dombrowski et al. 1970). There is a detachment outside of San Luis, which is on the shore of Lake Atitlán.

The last episode of Ignacio's diary in *Campesino* was on 10 May 1983. While the first three episodes of *Ignacio* occur from 7 to 8 March 1983 and on 3 May 1983, before the end of the chronological sequence of *Campesino*, these episodes cover new information and warrant inclusion in the current volume.

4. Maximón is supposed to be able to invoke negative forces. He is usually appealed to when someone wishes to bewitch someone else. Maximón sometimes is

referred to as Don Pedro de Alvarado, Saint Simón, and Judas of Iscariot, all considered to be powerful but sinister spirits.

5. An *alcalde* can either be the head (or mayor) of a municipality or the head of a *cofradía*.

6. The value of the quetzal once was equal to the dollar, but by the summer of 1987 the ratio was $1 to Q2.5 and by fall of 1988 it was $1 to Q2.7.

7. I received this information after *Campesino* went to press, but I am including it here in *Ignacio*.

8. According to McBryde (1945:154), when the quetzal was introduced in 1924, 60 pesos were worth one U.S. dollar and as late as 1933 pesos still were circulating almost as much as the quetzal in some rural communities. As late as 1945 the peso and real were "verbal" units of currency in Indian markets. A *tostón* was one-half of a peso; a real was one-eighth of a peso; and a *cuartillo* was one-quarter of a real.

9. *El Baile de la Conquista* (Dance of the Conquest) reenacts the conquest of Guatemala by Pedro de Alvarado in 1524. The dance drama is similar to a play, or opera, since the actors, both Indians and Spaniards, have prescribed speeches or songs and acts. Tecún Umán, the Quiché warrior prince who led the Quichés into battle against the invading Spaniards, engaged Alvarado in hand-to-hand combat. Tecún Umán killed Alvarado's horse with his obsidian-edged sword, but he was no match for Alvarado's steel sword and armor. According to legend, Tecún Umán was wearing a headdress of iridescent green plumes of the quetzal bird. Also a beautiful quetzal bird, Tecún Umán's *nagual*, accompanied him into battle. When Pedro de Alvarado killed Tecún Umán, it is said that the quetzal bird, which symbolized the beloved liberty of the kingdom, died too (Gordillo Barrios 1982:110; Stuart and Stuart 1977:120, 131). The Mexican Indians who had accompanied the Spaniards gave the area where Tecún Umán died a Nahuatl name—Quezaltenango, or the territory where there are quetzales. Not far from where the battle took place is the present-day City of Quezaltenango. Tecún Umán is now a national hero, especially among the Indians of Guatemala.

10. Ignacio is indicating that in the towns with more people, a person doesn't have to pull a shift as often as a person does in the smaller towns. He isn't suggesting that those who have to take turns like doing them, only that they don't have to do them as often.

11. Instead of *estado de alarma*, Ignacio used *voz de alarma*, voice of alarm. When I asked him what this was he explained that Ríos Montt ordered the radio stations to announce the state of alarm, and when they did so they stated, "Attention this is the *voz de alarma*." Then, after thus attempting to get the attention of the listener, the announcers stated the country was in a state of alarm.

12. There are two kinds of carpets used on the streets, sawdust and wild flowers. They may also be mixed. According to Ignacio, sawdust is cheap, but the paint isn't.

13. A latrine, or cement platform with a toilet seat, may have a structure, plastic, or nothing over it.

14. The name has nothing to do with the agricultural cooperative. The similarity is that the parents cooperated to establish the *instituto* and to pay the salaries of the teachers, contributing Q5 a month for ten months, January through October.

15. Scorpions have a tendency to get inside the houses and into clothing. One morning in 1970 a scorpion gave me a scare. When I was putting on my trousers, just before putting my leg into the top I discovered a scorpion inside the crotch area. Either it had climbed up a chair where I had left my trousers lying, or it had dropped from the roof, which was not sealed with a ceiling.

16. Although this episode took place in 1984, I asked him additional information about it in 1987 with my questions that appear in italics in the text.

17. This is the same *aldea* in which Ignacio and his friends earlier, as recorded in Sexton (1985:199–204), sold alcohol and felt remorseful over doing so.

18. These are left in a corner of the cemetery, not buried. Adults have big *trastes*, children small ones.

19. Ignacio believes Agustín had cancer or something like AIDS. He went back to San Luis with his wife, who is still alive, but she had the same disease. He died 26 November 1986 in a hospital in Guatemala City. Twenty-seven November he was buried in San Luis.

20. The Xocomil (also spelled Chocomil) is a strong wind that blows over the lake when the cold currents that descend from the highlands collide with the warm ones that ascend from the hot lowlands. The meaning of the word expresses the idea that the wind will cause the death of the sinners of the towns and drown them in the waters of the lake. Indians generally believe the wind is sacred and that it is the breath of San Lorenzo. When strong hurricanes blow, they invoke the protection of this saint so that he will moderate his breathing and save human life.

21. There is also a training project for working with iron, such as learning how to make iron gates and grilles for windows, and for working with leather.

22. Ignacio Puzul Robles, a pseudonym, is the *Martinero* who earlier had tried to have Ignacio killed when his sister, Olga Puzul, accused Ignacio of killing her son, Julio Padilla Puzul. See Sexton (1985:70–94).

23. Ignacio's version is nearly identical to a version taken by Benjamin Paul. They vary only in two details. According to Paul's sources, the man who discovered the body was going after a load of firewood, not taking a load of coffee. Also Paul was told that there were 15 people arrested in the killing of Ignacio and Mario Puzul instead of 17. In a later version of this episode, Ignacio said some of the original ex-commissioners were released in August but he first said 25 June, as did Paul.

24. These are symbolic meshes, or nets, made of *tul*, a plant from Lake Atitlán that is also used to make mats and *tejidos* (weavings), that protect Guatemala at its borders from any enemies. According to Ignacio, the *mallas de tul* may be thought of as something like a protective, symbolic fence of plants because they are perceived as alive and growing.

The flag of Guatemala has three wide vertical stripes, the middle one is white, the other two are blue. The blue color represents the sky over Guatemala and stands for justice and loyalty. White symbolizes purity and integrity. The coat of arms is in the center of the white stripe. The coat of arms has two crossed 1871 Remington rifles with fixed bayonets. Below the rifles are two crossed swords. A laurel wreath surrounds and entwines the weapons. The wreath symbolizes victory. A scroll that has the words "Libertad 15 de Septiembre de 1821" (the national day of independence) is in the center where the two rifles cross. A quetzal bird is located on the upper right part of the scroll. If the coat of arms is used elsewhere than on the flag, it must be on a clear light blue (*celeste*) background (Dombrowski 1970:178).

25. Ignacio is referring to 15 September 1821, when Guatemala broke its bonds with Spain with a group of leading citizens signing the Declaration of Independence without revolution or bloodshed.

26. Ignacio didn't write about the results of the presidential election, held on the same day as the mayoral elections, until 5 January 1987, when he reflected about politics in Guatemala in general and in San José in particular. Thus this information appears below, under the heading, "Politics Everywhere in Guatemala: Reflections of the Recent Elections." In the election of 3 November, Vinicio Cerezo won the most votes and Jorge Carpio Nicolle came in second. Since there were 8 presidential candidates running, neither Cerezo nor Carpio won a majority of the votes, and there was a run-off election on 8 December, in which Cerezo won. He took office on 14 January 1986, as did the mayoral winners of the municipalities.

27. It is common to leave someone in charge of an item or to send an item such as a bag (*bolsa*) of food for a friend or relative by a second party. Such items are referred to as *recomendaciones*.

28. According to Tax and Hinshaw (1969:93–94), *characoteles* are evil spirits that may take the form of humans or animals. Every person is considered to have a dual essence, a *nagual*, or soul, that is separable from the body.

29. On 3 July 1987 the Seminario Nacional de la Mujer inaugurated a seminar, "Problems of Health." It was for 50 women leaders involved with the health of various communities of the Republic of Guatemala. It was organized by the ministry of Trabajo y Previsión Social, the Oficina Nacional de la Mujer, and the Asociación Pro-Bienestar de la Familia de Guatemala (APROFAM). The themes discussed in this seminar included: (1) the situation of the health of the Guatemalan woman on a national level, (2) the effects of multi-parity, (3) prevention of cancer of the neck of the uterus, (4) intestinal parasitism, (5) oral rehydration, (6) importance of maternal lactation, (7) importance of immunization for mother and infant health, (8) health, nutrition, growth and development of women, and (9) alternatives for the development of the women of Guatemala (*El Gráfico* 1987a:18).

30. It's possible that the teachers were trying to explain both the rhythm method and the mucus method and called the latter "white menstruation," thereby confusing Ignacio and his wife and other women who attended the lecture. However, Werner (1980:283–294) clearly discusses both methods with illustrations, along with other kinds of more effective birth control methods such as pills, condoms, and diaphragms. Also, Werner states that 1 in 20 women will get pregnant despite using the pill, 7 in 20 using the rhythm method or mucus method alone, and 5 in 20 using the rhythm method and mucus method together.

31. There are two kinds of *novenarios*. The novena of a saint begins nine days before the date of his or her death and concludes the morning of the actual day. For example, the *novenario* of San Juan Bautista begins on 16 June and ends the morning of 24 June. The other kind of *novenario* is for the deceased. This begins on the first day of the death of the person, and when they finish all nine days, in the morning they go to the cemetery to say good-bye. Thus, for a person a *novenario* is the first nine days of mourning or a funeral celebrated on the ninth day after a person's death.

32. *Prensa Libre*, 15 July 1987:2, reported in an article that the government was giving another Q40 million to the towns. President Cerezo made the announcement during a meeting with 16 mayors of Chimaltenango. This money is equivalent to 8 percent of the general budget of the nation. The majors petitioned the money for various public works, such as constructing local roads and paving sections of highways with asphalt.

33. The following is a complete translation of Articles 4 and 5 of the Guatemalan Constitution (1985:11) that Ignacio had the woman quote:

Article 4. Liberty and Equality. In Guatemala all human beings are free and equal in dignity and rights. Men and women, whatever their civil status may be, have equal opportunities and responsibilities. No person may be subjected to servitude nor other condition that lessens his/her dignity. Human beings must maintain brotherly conduct amongst themselves.

Article 5. Freedom of action. Everyone has the right to do what the law does not prohibit; no one is obliged to observe orders that are not based in law and issued in accordance with it. Neither can one be persecuted nor molested for his/her opinions or for acts that don't involve infractions of the same.

34. Ignacio receives one-half the royalties directly from the Press, which I had written into each publishing contract. Of course, this leads to the questions as to whether Ignacio is just collaborating for money. I don't think he is, and as others have pointed out, informants who work primarily for money give sterile accounts.

35. José Arévalo Bermejo was a liberal president from 1945–1951. In 1954 his liberal successor Jacobo Arbenz Guzmán was overthrown with the aid of the CIA.

36. As Fauriol and Loser (1988:108) point out, Cerezo's electoral commitment to establish a commission to investigate past human rights abuses has continued to be a uncomfortable problem for him. He has maneuvered around GAM by first suggesting that the Supreme Court rather than the planned commission would investigate GAM's list of disappeared. Cerezo agreed to create an investigatory commission, but he also excluded the military's record from consideration. According to *El Gráfico* (1987b: 3,21), GAM, led by Ninth de García, occupied Congress, trying to get action on an accounting for the thousands of persons "disappeared" and/or kidnapped. They were not able to get an agreement. In short, delegates of the Executive told them there was nothing they could do. Ninth de García was clear in expressing before De León Escribano and González Roche that "GAM did not believe anymore in the government and that moveover it didn't have any interest in carrying on a dialogue with those who are able to do nothing for them." At the time this manuscript went to press, GAM has been unable to get either the army, congress, or President Cerezo to cooperate in an accounting for their kidnapped and disappeared loved ones.

37. It is interesting to note that early in the campaign, Ignacio personally thought that since Agustín had graduated from secondary school, he had the intelligence to govern the town.

38. There are two brothers with one first name Gerardo: Gerardo Jaime and Gerardo Hugo.

39. According to Frazer in Lessa (1963:301–315), this is a case of sympathetic magic in which a like substance is used to have an effect—bone curing bone.

40. The coffee plant is usually referred to as a tree and its fruit as cherries, but it's actually a tropical evergreen shrub with berries, which left unpruned can grow to a height of 14 to 30 feet (Struning 1990). The shrub may be propagated from cuttings or shoots, but most new "trees" are started from seeds. Although seeds may be planted directly into a plot of land, called a *cafetal*, in San José they are usually planted into nursery beds and then after one or two years transplanted as seedlings into a *cafetal*, or permanent coffee grove. Usually they are planted under larger shade trees, although its uncertain whether shading them makes them more productive.

Inside the thin, glutinous, succulent, sweet pulp, are two grains, or "beans," each with one flat surface. The *beneficio* in San José that Ignacio and I visited is called a *beneficio humedo*, or wet processing plant. Elsewhere there is also a *beneficio seco*, or dry processing plant, that does not use water. In this latter process, the beans are placed directly into sunlight or hot-air blowers. In both of these processes, the *pergamino* is removed by friction machinery (Munoz and Ward 1940:38–40; Rubio 1982:23–24; Goetz and Coste 1990).

Unpulped coffee is sometimes referred to as *café en cereza* (cherries), pulped but unhusked coffee called *café en pergamino*, and husked but unroasted coffee called *café en oro*. *Café en oro* also is referred to as green coffee. Roasting it turns it tan or dark brown (McBryde 1945:34; Rubio 1982:23). Guatemalans also refer to their coffee harvest as the *lluvia de oro* (rain of gold), and it is the leading source of commercial revenue (De la Haba 1974:677).

Sol Tax (1972:56) reported how Indian families removed the pulp with grinding stones or hand pulping machines. Then they place the "beans" into clay pots and bury them in the ground for a day for the natural fermentation. Next they wash the beans and sun them on mats for three days. They may sell the resultant coffee as *café en pergamino*, or they may sell it at a higher price by removing the outer parchment by grinding the *café en pergamino* on the grinding stone or by grinding it in a mortar hollowed out of a tree stump.

Some experts think that wild coffee plants are originally from Kefa, Ethiopia, and that travelers carried them to southern Arabia in the 1400s. Others are not certain whether Arabia had its own wild plants. In any case, a popular legend is that an Ethiopian goatherd observed his goats acting in an unusually agitated manner after munching on the berries. When the herder tried the berries, he too was pleasantly stimulated (Starbird 1981; Struning 1990).

Before coffee became a beverage, it was a food and medicine. Rhazes, an Arab physician, was the first to mention it in the literature about 900 A.D. The coffee berries were dried and crushed and mixed with fat to form a ball that was eaten. It apparently was first made as a beverage in Yemen, Arabia, about 1000 A.D. Muslims, who don't drink alcohol, were kept awake with coffee during their nightlong rituals.

Coffee spread with the spread of Islam. Coffee was first grown as cash crop in the 1400s in the Arabian colony of Harar in Abyssinia (Starbird 1981; Struning 1990). Coffee didn't reach Guatemala until the 1700s. It was first grown experimentally as an ornamental plant. In the early 1800s it was sold in pharmacies and on the street as a remedy for intoxication (Cambranes 1985:25).

Today, Brazil, Colombia, Indonesia, and the Ivory Coast are the major exporters of coffee. In Brazil there is now a coffee-picking machine. But in other parts of Latin America, including Guatemala, the mountainous terrain isn't suited for picking coffee with these machines, and such automation would put scores of people out of work (Starbird 1981).

Much of the coffee produced in the exporting countries is consumed at home. Finland is the highest per capita consuming country, ingesting on average five cups per day for each man, woman, and child. While the United States only consumes about half the amount on a per capita basis, it nevertheless imports more coffee than any other country in the world, 1.2 million tons in 1979 (Starbird 1981). Starbird (1981:405) traces U.S. addiction back to the Boston Tea Party, when the colonists refused to drink British tea and coffee preempted it as a household staple.

The Javanese believe their best coffee is processed by a *luak*, a small catlike animal that gorges itself after dark on coffee fruit. It digests the pulp and expels the beans which Javanese farmers collect, wash, and roast. The people of Java call the coffee *Kopi luak* (Starbird 1981:395).

41. This section was prompted by my asking Ignacio to write about his family since several students had commented that they would like to know more about the members of his family than he had written in the first two volumes.

42. Ignacio has this last paragraph marked on pages 813–814 of his bilingual (Spanish and English) Bible, *El Neuvo Testamento, Versión Popular* (*The New Testament, Today's English Version*), which I copied directly from the English version rather than from the Spanish.

43. The shifts began at first as just night shifts in 1983. In the same year, they became shifts for day and night. Within six to seven months in San José, upon petition to the *jefes*, the shifts during the day were stopped on the basis that they were costing too much in money in lost wages and that there were no subversives in the town. Whether the patrols remained in a given lakeside town seemed to depend on the willingness of the townspeople to negotiate with the *jefes* and the level of guerrilla activity in the towns. The night shifts for San José lasted until 1986, when Cerezo took over. Most *Joseños* didn't want to do the shifts, and they protested to the minister of defense. San José was the first to stop the day shifts, San Martín followed, and then San Luis. But San Martín was the first to stop them altogether with the help of their socialist mayor and two socialist congressmen on the national level.

44. Solórzano was one of the presidential candidates in the 1985 elections running under the auspices of the Partido Socialista Democrático (PSD). His was the only party that represented the left. According to Fauriol and Loser (1988:70), his party's participation was overpublicized in an attempt to show the significance of the political opening. During the 1985 elections, two socialists of the PSD won seats in the Guatemalan congress.

45. For a report on guerrillas arriving in San José, see Sexton (1985:169–72, 230–35).

46. Bartolomé Yac is the one who initially led the opposition to have the ex-commissioners removed. See Sexton (1985: 336–46).

47. By 3 December of 1990, Gramajo had retired from the military and was studying at the John F. Kennedy School of Government with help from a fellowship for mid-career officials from developing countries, but not without controversy (Golden 1990). Also, Guatemalans protested U.S. Funds for a two-year old army think tank, Centro ESTNA, that Gramajo founded. It is widely believed in Guatemala that the English-speaking general has presidential ambitions for the 1995 elections and that he is a U.S. favorite (Scott 1990).

Glossary

Acronyms

APROFAM: Asociación Pro-Bienestar de la Familia de Guatemala (Association for the Welfare of the Family of Guatemala)

BANDESA: Banco Nacional de Desarrollo Agrícola (National Bank of Agricultural Development)

CACIF: Comité Coordinador de Asociaciones Agrícolas, Comerciales, Industriales y Financieras (Coordinating Committee of Agricultural, Commercial, Industrial and Financial Associations)

CAN: Central Auténtico Nacionalista (Authentic Nationalist Central party)

DCG: Democracia Cristiana Guatemalteca (Guatemalan Christian Democratic party)

ESA: Ejército Secreto Anticomunista (Secret Anticommunist Army, death squad)

FECOMERQ: Federación de Cooperativas Agrícolas y Mercadeo "Quetzal" (Federation of Agricultural and Trade Cooperatives "Quetzal")

FEDECCON: Federación Guatemalteca de Cooperativas de Consumo (Guatemalan Federation of Cooperatives of Consumption)

FUN: Frente de Unidad Nacional (Front of National Unity party)

GAM: Grupo de Apoyo Mutuo para Familiares de Desaparecidos (Mutual Support Group for Relatives of the Disappeared)

INACOP: Instituto Nacional de Cooperativas (National Institute of Cooperatives)

INSO: Instituto Normal para Señoritas de Occidente (Teachers' Training Institute for Señoritas of the West)

IVA: impuesto del valor agredado, (value-added tax).

INVO: Instituto Normal para Varones de Occidente (Teachers' Training Institute for Young Men of the West)

MAS: Movimiento de Acción Solidaria (Movement of Solidarity Action party)

MEC: Movimiento Emergente de Concordia (Emergent Movement of Concordance party)

MLN: Movimiento de Liberación Nacional (Movement of National Liberation party)

OFISEM: Oficina de Información del Sector Empresarial (Office of Information of the Management Sector)

ORPA: Organización del Pueblo en Armas (Organization of the People in Arms, revolutionary group)

PDCN: Partido Democrático de Cooperación Nacional (Democratic Party of National Cooperation)

PNR: Partido Nacionalista Renovador (National Renovator Party)

PSC: Partido Social Cristiano (Social Christian Party)

PSD: Partido Socialista Democrático (Social Democratic Party)
PID: Partido Institucional Democrático (Institutional Democratic Party)
PIN: Partido de Integración Nacional (Party of National Integration)
PRG: Partido Revolucionario Guatemalteca (Guatemalan Revolutionary Party)
PAC: Patrulla(s) de autodefensa civil [Civil defense patrol(s)], organized against guerrilla intrusion into towns
PUA: Partido de Unificación Anticomunista (Party of Anticommunist Unification)
UCN: Unión del Centro Nacional (Union of the National Center, Centrist party)
URNG: Unidad Revolucionaria Nacional Guatemalteca (Guatemalan National Revolutionary Unit)

Spanish and Indian Words (The plural of the word is in parentheses in Spanish and English. In Spanish the adjective agrees in number and gender with the noun.)

Acta: memorandum of action, official document.
Acta notarial: notarized document.
Aguardiente: firewater, sugar cane rum.
Ajau: God.
Alcalde: head of a town, mayor, or head of a *cofradía*.
Aldea: village.
Alguacil(es): municipal police, aide(s), and runner(s).
Arroba(s): 25 pound measure(s).
Atol: a ritual drink of corn meal or of rice, wheat, or corn flour, boiled and served hot.

Bachiller: high school (secondary school) graduate.
Beneficio de café: coffee processing plant.
Beniteño(s): person (people) of San Benito.
Bolsa: bag, purse.
Bolsa recomendado: a bag, or bundle, intended for a friend or relative but sent or left in charge of by a second party.
Bomba(s): bomb(s), firework(s) shot from mortars.
Bourbon: variety of coffee seed; coffee *arabica*, variety *bourbon*.
Bravo(s): irritable, bossy, rude
Brujería: witchcraft.
Brujo: witch.
Burla: taunt, gibe.

Cafetal: coffee grove.
Café en oro: shelled but unroasted coffee.
Café en pergamino: See *pergamino*.
Caite(s): typical (Indian-style) sandal(s).
Caja: box, coffin.
Cargos: offices, burdens.
Caserio(s): hamlet(s).

Caturro Pacho: variety of coffee seed.

Cédula(s): national identification card(s).

Centro de formación de desarrollo de la comunidad: training center of community development.

Cerveza(s): beer(s).

Cofrade(s): member(s) of a *cofradía*.

Cofradía(s): religious brotherhood(s).

Comadre: ritual co-parent; woman friend; godmother.

Comandante(s): commander(s).

Comedor: small restaurant.

Comisión de vigilancia: committee of control.

Compadre: ritual co-parent; man friend; godfather.

Compañero: companion.

Compensación: compensation, reprisal; "what goes around comes around."

Confidencial(es): spy (spies) of the military.

Contras: people in opposition; those against Father José.

Copal: incense.

Corte: skirt.

Corredor: porch.

Costumbre(s): custom(s), ritual(s).

Cuadra: a linear measure of 275 feet.

Cuadrilla: crew.

Cuartel: barracks.

Cuartillo: coin valued at one quarter of a real.

Cuerda(s): areal measure(s) equal to .178 acre.

Curandero: curer.

Chamarra: heavy wool blanket.

Champa: little hut with a roof.

Characotel: a *nagual*, or spirit, that converts into an animal form at night to bother people. The *characotel* has hypnotic power to make someone ill.

Chirimía: Flute.

Chirmol: sauce or appetizer, mixture of chili and ground corn flavored with tomatoes, onions, parsley or coriander, and salt.

Desconocido(s): unknown man or woman, person (men or women, people).

Día de Reyes: Epiphany.

Domingo de Dolores: Sunday of Suffering (Palm Sunday).

Dueña, dueño: owner, master, goddess, god.

El Gráfico: national newspaper.

El Mundo: God of the World (Earth).

El poder: the power, or ability.

El Radio Periódico el Independiente: The Independent Newspaper Radio.

empírica: no formal training and laying claim to a profession by experience.

En suspenso de garantías: suspended constitutional rights.

Escrito: a writ.

Eucaristía Sacramental: Sacramental Eucharist, or the host or wafer kept in the golden monstrance.

Faja(s): sash(es); belt(s); band(s).
Federación de cooperativas: federation of cooperatives.
Finca: farm.
Finquero(s): farm owner(s) and administrator(s).
Fiscal: the person in charge of the local Catholic church where there is no resident priest; an official.
Fresco: drink.
Fuero especial: special law court.

Ganadero: cattle dealer.
Granja: prison farm.
Grano oro: the seed inside the nearly silvery, nearly transparent skin, or parchment of a coffee grain, or "bean."
Guardia de hacienda: treasury police.
Guarda espalda seguridad: security bodyguard.

Impuesto tributario: tributary, an obligatory sales tax.
Instituto básico: secondary school similar to junior high.
Intendente: political chief of a municipality beginning in 1935, replacing the term *alcalde*, which in turn was replaced by the term *alcalde* in 1948.

Jaspe(s): tie-dyed figure(s) or design(s) in thread or yarn.
Jefe: chief, head, boss.
Jícara(s): gourd jar(s).
Jocote(s): yellow or red, plumlike fruit. There are many varieties, of which "*de corona*" is in greatest demand because of its delicious flavor.
Jodido: screwed up, screwed.
Jorgeña(s), *Jorgeño(s)*: woman (women), man (men), person (people) of San Jorge.
Jornalero: day laborer.
Joseña(s), *Joseño(s)*: woman (women), man (men), person (people) of San José.
Juez: vice-head; judge.
Juzgado de primera instancia: court of first instance.

Labores de jaspe: works or adornment of tie-dyed thread or yarn.
Lámina(s): piece(s) of sheet metal for roofing.
Lengua: Tzutuhil; tongue.
Libro de actas: minute book.
Libro de conocimiento: book of acknowledgment.
Licenciado: lawyer, licensed, or graduate.
linterna: bottle of kerosene with a wick, homemade lantern, lantern.
Lucha libre: free style wrestling, Roman wrestling, not karate, similar to self-defense taught in the army.
Llevadero(s): "going along with whatever comes along," tolerant.

Madejador: hank or skein maker.
Magisterio nacional: national teaching staff.
Malla(s) de tul: meshe(s), or net(s), of a plant.
Mandamiento: forced labor migrations.
Mantel: cloth, tablecloth.
Martinera(s), Martinero(s): woman (women), man (men), person (people) of San Martín.
Mata(s): tree(s); plant(s).
Mayordomo: low ranking officer of a *cofradía*.
Mecapal: porter's strap.
Meloso: sugary.
M'hija: My daughter.
M'hijo: My son.
Miel: honey.
milpero: small-scale farmer.
Misa del cuerpo presente: funeral mass when the body is present.
Misa del réquiem: funeral mass without the body present.
Misterio: the rosary.
Monte: grass, hay.
Mozo(s): helper(s).

Nagual: spirit and animal forms of humans, especially of witches; soul.
Novenario: Nine-day religious observance. For a person the first nine days of mourning or a funeral celebration on the ninth day after a person's death. For a saint the novena begins nine days before the date of his or her death and concludes the morning of the actual day.

Ocote: resinous pine.
Octavo: one-eighth, one-eighth liter bottle of liquor.
Oficialismo: bureaucracy.
Oratorio: small church.

Panteón: above-ground tomb.
Patojo: youngster, child.
Patrulla(s) de autodefensa civil: See PAC.
Patrullero(s): patrolman (patrolmen), member(s) of a *patrulla*.
Pergamino: second-class coffee; hulled once; pulped but unshelled, or with the parchment still intact.
Petate: palm-mat of *tul*, or lake plant.
Pita: agave string.
Policía judicial: judicial police.
Prensa Libre: national newspaper.
Principal: town elder.
Profesor, profesora : male, female teacher.
Promotor social: social promoter.

Quintal(es): measure of weight, one hundred pounds, hundred-pound units

Ramas de pino: pine branches.
Rancho(s): rustic house(s).
Ruk'ak Tiox: sacred fever of the saints, cholera morbus.

Salón: ante-room, lounge, sitting room, assembly hall.
San Beniteña(s), San Beniteño(s): woman (women), man (men), person (people) of San Benito.
Sanluisera(s), Sanlusiero(s): woman (women), man (men), person (people) of San Luis.
Santa Misa: Holy Mass.
Santísimo Sacramento: Blessed Sacrament.
Santo Mundo: Sacred World.
Santo Rosario: Holy Rosary.
Secreto: sacred or magical act.
Sitio: homesite.
Soldados Kaibiles: special forces similar to US Green Berets.
Suerte: luck; fortune.
Sut/sute: cotton headcloth.

Tamalito(s): little tamale(s).
Tamalón(es): large tamale(s) that may last 8 to 12 days.
Tarea: job; day's work.
Tarjeta(s): quota card(s).
Tejido(s): weaving(s).
Teleprensa: television news.
Tienda: small store; shop.
Tostón: coin valued at one-half peso.
Trago(s): drink(s).
Traje(s): suit, typical clothing.
Trajes antiguos: old clothing.
Traste: plastic tub.
Tribunal comunal: common court, ordinary court.
Tul: lake plant.

Urdidora: warper.
Útiles: books, school supplies.

Vara(s): linear measure(s), 32 to 33 inches.
Vocal: the substitute for various religious officers.

Zacate(s): grass(es), herb(s).
Zanjorín: shaman.

References Cited

Aguirre, P. Gerardo G.
    1972   *La Cruz de Nimajujú: Historia de la Parroquia de San Pedro la Laguna.*
            Guatemala City: Litoguat, Ltda.

Armas, Daniel
    1971   *Diccionario de la Expresión Popular Guatemalteco.* Tipografía Nacional
            de Guatemala, Centro América.

Arriola, Jorge Luis
    1973   *El libro de las Geonimias de Guatemala: Diccionario Etimologico.* Guate-
            mala City: Seminario de Integración Social Guatemalteca.

Associated Press
    1990   "Guatemalan Villagers Slain." *Arizona Daily Sun,* 3 December, p. 15.

Bazzy, Derrill
    1986   "Nowhere to Go." *Christian Science Monitor,* 10 December, pp. 22–23.

Bebusmann, Bernd
    1986   "Guatemala Celebrates Return to Democracy but Country Still Is
            Polarized." *Los Angeles Times,* 9 February, Part I, p. 15.

Bowen, Gordon L.
    1987   "Four Candles in the Wind; Once More the Disappeared." *Common-
            weal* 114, 18 December, p. 726.

Burgos-Debray, Elisabeth, editor (Ann Wright, translator)
    1984   *I Rigoberta Menchú: An Indian Woman of Guatemala.* London: Verso.

Cambranes, J.C.
    1985   *Coffee and Peasants in Guatemala.* South Woodstock, Vermont:
            CIRMA/Plumsock Mesoamerican Studies. Original title: *Café y Cam-
            pesinos en Guatemala: 1853–1897.* Universidad de San Carlos de Guate-
            mala, 1985.

Cárdenas, Eduardo
    1987   *Diccionario Comprehensivo de la lengua Española..* Panamá: Editorial
            América S.A.

Carmack, Robert, editor
    1988   *Harvest of Violence: The Maya Indians and the Guatemalan Crises.*
            Norman: University of Oklahoma Press.

Choice
    1982   Review of *Son of Tecún Umán,* February.

Constitución Política de la Republica de Guatemala
    1985   Titulo II, Derechos Humanes, Capitula I, Derechos Individuales,
            Decretado por la Asamblea Nacional Constituyente, 31 Mayo de 1985,
            Guatemala, CA 1985.

Crist, Raymond E.
    1985   Review of *Campesino*. *Latin America in Books*, July.
De la Haba, Louis
    1974   "Guatemala, Maya and Modern." *National Geographic*, November, pp. 661–89.
Dombrowski, John et al.
    1970   *Area Handbook for Latin America*. Washington, D.C.: U.S. Government Printing Office.
Fauriol, Georges A. and Eva Loser
    1988   *Guatemala's Political Puzzle*. New Brunswick, N.J.: Transaction Books.
Ford, Peter
    1987   "After Year of Civilian Rule, Guatemalan Death Squads Still Active But the Number of Deaths Has Dropped Since Army Left Office." *Christian Science Monitor*, 23 March, p. 12.
Frazer, James G.
    1963   "Sympathetic Magic." In *Reader in Comparative Religion: An Anthropological Approach, Second Edition*, edited by William A. Lessa and Evon Z. Vogt, pp. 301–15. New York: Harper and Row.
García-Pelayo Y Gross, Ramoón, and Micheline Durand, directors
    1976   *Diccionario Moderno: Epañol-inglés, English-Spanish*. New York: Larousse.
Goetz, Philip W. and René Coste
    1990   "Coffee." In "Beverage Production." *The New Encyclopaedia Britannica*, vol. 14. Chicago: Encyclopedia Britannica, Inc., pp. 737–41.
Golden, Tim
    1990   "Controversy Pursues Guatemalan General Studying in U.S." *New York Times*, 3 December, p. A6.
Gordillo Barrios, Gerardo
    1982   *Guatemala: Historia Gráfica*. Guatemala City: Editorial Piedra Santa.
El Gráfico
    1987a   "Seminario Nacional de la Mujer." 17 July, p. 18.
    1987b   "Congreso-GAM sin llegar a un acuerdo." 17 July, pp. 3, 21.
Hackel, Joyce
    1990   "Guatemala Army Killings Raise National Debate." *Christian Science Monitor*, 11 December, p. 8.
    1991   "Guatemala Shifts Right with Choice of President." *Christian Science Monitor*, 8 January, p. 8.
Hess, Karl W.
    1990   "Despite Election of Civilian Government, Guatemalan Army Still in Control." *Christian Science Monitor*, Letter to editor, 7 December 1990:20.
Latin America Regional Reports, Mexico & Central America
    1986   "Guatemala/ Military Aid Delay." 10 January, p. 8.
    1987a   "Guatemala: Army Denies Blame for Massacre." 23 March, p. 7.
    1987b   "Guatemala/ Political Violence." 26 March, p. 8.

1987c   "Guatemala: A Time Bomb." 7 May, p. 6.

1989a   "Calif Critical of Cerezo's Polices." 16 February, p. 3.

1989b   "Upsurge in Rights Abuses in Guatemala: Amnesty Questions Cerezo's Commitment to Rule of Law." 17 August, p. 7.

1989c   "Guatemala/US Military Assistance." 21 September, p. 8.

1989d   "Guatemala: Army Dismisses Coup Rumors, Cerezo Says Terrorism Seeks to Halt Democratic Process." 26 October, p. 3.

1990a   "Guatemala/Conservative Politician Murdered, Cerezo Says Terrorism Seeks to Halt Democratic Process." 23 August, p. 3.

1990b   "Oil & The Gulf: Price Increase Hits Fragile Economies." 27 September, p. 6.

1990c   "Guatemala: Serrano and Carpio in January Run-off." 6 December, p. 2.

1990d   "Violence 'A Way of Life' in Guatemala." 6 December, p. 4.

1991   "GAM Leader Murdered." 17 January, p. 3.

Lewis, Oscar

1959   *Five Families: Mexican Case Studies in the Culture of Poverty.* New York: Basic Books.

1961   *The Children of Sánchez.* New York: Random House.

1964   *Pedro Martínez.* New York: Random House.

Logan, Michael

1987   Review of *Campesino. American Anthropologist* 89:155–156.

Manz, Beatrice

1990   "In Guatemala, No One Is Safe." 27 October, p. 15.

McBryde, Felix Webster

1945   *Cultural and Historical Geography of Southwest Guatemala.* Washington, D.C.: U.S. Government Printing Office.

Munoz, Joaquin and Anna Bell Ward

1940   *Guatemala: Ancient and Modern.* New York: Pyramid Press.

New York Times

1990a   "U.S. Kin Press Case of 2 Killed in Guatemala in 1985." 3 April, p. A3.

1990b   "3 in Guatemala Sought in Killing of American." 21 September, p. A6.

1990c   "Guatemala Arrests Five in Killing of an American." 10 October, p. A9.

Ostling, Richard N.

1991   "The Battle for Latin America's Soul." *Time* 137(3), pp. 68–69.

Perera, Victor

1986   "Can Guatemala Change?" *New York Review of Books* 33(23), pp. 39–43.

Prensa Libre

1987   "Dinero a las municipalidades." 15 July 1987, p. 2.

Preuss, Mary H.

1986   Review of *Son of Tecún Umán* and *Campesino. Latin American Indian Literatures Journal* 2(1):50–51.

Recinos, Adrián and Delia Goetz

1953   *The Annals of the Cakchiquels.* Norman: University of Oklahoma Press.

Reuters

    1990   "Guatemala Troops Said to Kill 11 Protesting Raid." *New York Times*, 3 December, p. A7.

Robb, Louis A.

    1980   *Diccionario de Términos*. México: Editorial Limusa.

Rubio, J. Francisco

    1982   *Diccionario de voces usado en Guatemala*. Guatemala City: Editorial Piedra Santa.

Salovesh, Michael

    1986   Essay review of *Son of Tecún Umán* and *Campesino. Mesoamérica* 12: 465–72.

Schwartz, Norman

    1977   *A Milpero of Peten, Guatemala: Autobiography and Cultural Analysis.* University of Delaware Latin American Studies Program Occasional Papers and Monographs No. 2, Kenneth Ackerman, general editor.

    1984   Pre-publication review of *Campesino*. University of Arizona Press.

    1990   *Forest Society: A Social History of Petén, Guatemala*. Philadelphia: University of Pennsylvania Press.

Scott, Clark

    1990   "Guatemalans Protest US Funds for Army Think Tank." *Christian Science Monitor*, 3 December, p. 4.

Sexton, James D.

    1972   *Education and Innovation in a Guatemalan Community: San Juan la Laguna*. Los Angeles: Latin American Studies Series, Vol. 19.

    1978   "Protestantism and Modernization in Two Guatemalan Towns." *American Ethnologist* 5:280–302.

    1979a   "Modernization Among Cakchiquel Maya: An Analysis of Responses to Line Drawings." *Journal of Cross-Cultural Psychology* 10:173–90.

    1979b   "Education and Acculturation in Highland Guatemala." *Anthropology and Education Quarterly* 10:80–95.

    1982   "Ignacio Bizarro Ujpán: Thematic Analysis of a Tzutuhil Maya's Life Story." Paper presented at the Annual Meeting of the American Folklore Society, Minneapolis, Minnesota.

Sexton, James D., translator and editor

    1981   *Son of Tecún Umán: A Maya Indian Tells His Life Story*. Tucson: University of Arizona Press. Third Paperback printing Prospect Heights, Ill.: Waveland Press.

    1985   *Campesino: The Diary of a Guatemalan Indian*. Tucson: University of Arizona Press.

Sexton, James D. and Clyde M. Woods

    1977   "Development and Modernization among Highland Maya: A Comparative Analysis of Ten Guatemalan Towns." *Human Organization* 36:156–77.

    1982   "Demography, Development and Modernization in Fourteen Highland Guatemalan Towns." In *The Historical Demography of Highland Guatemala*, Robert M. Carmack, John Early, and Christopher Lutz, editors, pp. 184–202. Institute for Mesoamerican Studies, State University of New York at Albany, Pub. No. 6. Austin: University of Texas Press, distributor.

Smith, Carol and Jeff Boyer
    1987   "Central America Since 1979: Part I." *Annual Review of Anthropology* 16:197–221. Palo Alto, Ca.: Annual Reviews Inc.

Starbird, Ethel A.
    1981   "The Bonanza Bean—Coffee." *National Geographic*, March, pp. 388–405.

Struning, William C.
    1990   "Coffee." In *The Encyclopedia Americana, International Edition*. Danbury, Conn.: Crolier Incorporated.

Stuart, George E. and Gene S. Stuart
    1977   *The Mysterious Maya*. Washington, D.C.: National Geographic Society.

Tax, Sol
    1972   *Penny Capitalism*. New York: Octagon Books. First printed as Smithsonian Institution Institute of Social Anthropology, Publication No. 16.

Tax, Sol and Robert Hinshaw
    1969   "The Maya of the Midwestern Highlands." In *Handbook of Middle American Indians*, vol. 7, *Ethnology*, Robert Wauchope, general editor, Evon Z. Vogt, volume editor. Austin: University of Texas Press.

Time
    1985   "Guatemala: Reaffirmation, Cerezo Is Elected President." 126(25), 23 December, p. 40.

U.S. News and World Report
    1990   "Democracy, Guatemala Style." 19 November, p. 17.

Volman, Dennis
    1985   "Cerezo Raises Hopes in Guatemala." *Christian Science Monitor*, 6 December, pp. 15, 20.

Werner, David
    1980   *Donde No Hay Doctor*. Palo Alto, Ca: La Fundación Hesperian.

Will, Marvin W. and Edward M. Dew
    1985   "New Currents in the Caribbean Basin." *Choice*, April, pp.1099–1130.

Woods, Clyde M.
    1975   *Culture Change*. Dubuque, Io.: Wm. C. Brown Company.

Index

This book has been set in Linotron Galliard. Galliard was designed for Mergenthaler in 1978 by Matthew Carter. Galliard retains many of the features of a sixteenth century typeface cut by Robert Granjon but has some modifications that give it a more contemporary look.

Printed on acid-free paper.